SAVING STUYVESANT TOWN

SAVING STUYVESANT TOWN

How One Community Defeated the Worst Real Estate Deal in History

DANIEL R. GARODNICK

THREE HILLS
AN IMPRINT OF
CORNELL UNIVERSITY PRESS
ITHACA AND LONDON

First published 2021 by Cornell University Press

Printed in the United States of America

Library of Congress Cataloging-in-Publication Data
Names: Garodnick, Daniel R., 1972– author.
Title: Saving Stuyvesant Town : how one community defeated
    the worst real estate deal in history / Daniel R. Garodnick.
Description: Ithaca [New York] : Cornell University Press, 2021. |
    Includes bibliographical references and index.
Identifiers: LCCN 2020039625 (print) | LCCN 2020039626 (ebook) |
    ISBN 9781501754371 (hardcover) | ISBN 9781501754388 (pdf) |
    ISBN 9781501754395 (epub)
Subjects: LCSH: Rental housing—New York (State)—New York. |
    Housing development—New York (State) —New York. | Real estate
    development—Corrupt practices—New York (State) —New York. |
    Middle class—New York (State) —New York.
Classification: LCC HD7304.N5 G54 2021 (print) | LCC HD7304.N5
    (ebook) | DDC 333.33/8097471090512—dc23
LC record available at https://lccn.loc.gov/2020039625
LC ebook record available at https://lccn.loc.gov/2020039626

To the tenants of Stuyvesant Town and
Peter Cooper Village for never giving up

and to my most favorite neighbors,
Mom, Dad, Zoe, Asher and Devin

CONTENTS

Character List

Bill Ackman is an activist hedge fund manager and CEO of Pershing Square Capital Management, which along with Winthrop Capital sought to partner with the Stuyvesant Town tenants.

Justine Almada was one of the first members of my city council staff, who served as my liaison to Stuyvesant Town and later became my chief of staff.

Michael Ashner is the chairman and CEO of Winthrop Realty Trust, which along with Bill Ackman's Pershing Square Capital sought to partner with the Stuyvesant Town tenants.

Charles Bagli is a *New York Times* reporter who closely covered the Stuyvesant Town story.

Barry Blattman is vice-chair of Brookfield Asset Management, which partnered with the Stuyvesant Town Peter Cooper Village Tenants Association in making a bid to CWCapital in 2012.

Rafael Cestero served as commissioner of the New York City Department of Housing Preservation and Development (HPD) from 2009 to 2011 under Mayor Michael Bloomberg.

John Crotty is a resident, housing expert, and key behind-the-scenes player in the tenants' effort to control their destiny in Stuyvesant Town.

Al Doyle is a lifelong resident of Stuyvesant Town and was the longest-serving president of the Stuyvesant Town Peter Cooper Village Tenants Association, from 1989 to 2012.

Soni Fink was the outspoken board member who was the communications director of the Tenants Association for over a decade.

Alicia Glen served as deputy mayor for economic development in the de Blasio administration from 2014 to 2019.

Jon Gray is president and chief operating officer of the Blackstone Group and was a critical force behind the acquisition of Stuyvesant Town and Peter Cooper Village in 2015.

Leonard Grunstein was a partner at Troutman Sanders who represented the Stuyvesant Town Peter Cooper Village Tenants Association in its bid to buy the property in 2006.

Gerald Guterman is a real estate developer and investor. He is one of the largest multifamily apartment owner/operators and condominium converters in the United States.

Doug Harmon is a leading real estate broker who helped to negotiate the sale of Stuyvesant Town from CWCapital to Blackstone in 2015.

David Iannarone is chief executive officer of CWCapital, the special servicer for Stuyvesant Town from 2010 to 2015.

Meredith Kane is a partner at the New York law firm of Paul Weiss Rifkind Wharton & Garrison LLP and represented the Stuyvesant Town Peter Cooper Village Tenants Association.

Maura Keaney served as deputy chief of staff to city council speaker Christine Quinn.

David Kimball-Stanley served as my district office chief of staff.

Ilona Kramer served as my chief of staff.

Andrew MacArthur served as a managing director of CWCapital Asset Management and was a prime antagonist of, and ultimately partner to, the Stuyvesant Town Peter Cooper Village Tenants Association.

John Marsh is a lifelong resident of Peter Cooper Village, one of the community's best organizers, and served as president of the Stuyvesant Town Peter Cooper Village Tenants Association from 2012 to 2015.

Nadeem Meghji is a senior managing director of the Blackstone Group and a chief negotiator of the 2015 deal with the tenants and the city.

Genevieve Michel served as my chief of staff.

James Patchett served as chief of staff to New York City deputy mayor for economic development Alicia Glen.

Adam Rose is copresident of Rose Associates, a property management firm, which managed Stuyvesant Town and Peter Cooper Village on and off for nearly a decade.

Jim Roth served as a board member of the Stuyvesant Town Peter Cooper Village Tenants Association.

Alex Rubin is a managing director of Moelis & Company, who represented the Stuyvesant Town Peter Cooper Village Tenants Association.

Steven Sanders grew up in Stuyvesant Town, worked for the local assemblyman Andrew Stein, and then succeeded him in the State Assembly. Sanders served as the assemblyman for Stuyvesant Town from 1978 to 2006.

Alex Schmidt was a partner at Wolf Haldenstein, a law firm that represented the tenants in the *Roberts* case, a class action against both MetLife and Tishman Speyer for illegally taking apartments out of rent stabilization.

Zoe Segal-Reichlin is my wife.

John Sheehy is a longtime resident of Peter Cooper Village and joined the board of the Stuyvesant Town Peter Cooper Village Tenants Association in 2010.

Jen Shykula is an organizer at the public strategy firm Berlin Rosen.

Charles Spetka is chief executive officer of CW Financial Services, which was the special servicer for Stuyvesant Town from 2010 to 2015.

Andrew Sullivan served as the campaign manager of my 2005 city council campaign and became my first chief of staff.

Rob Speyer is president and chief executive officer of Tishman Speyer, which bought Stuyvesant Town in 2006 and defaulted on its loans in 2010.

Susan Steinberg joined the board of the Stuyvesant Town Peter Cooper Village Tenants Association in 1998 and became its president in 2015.

Marianna Vaidman Stone served as my senior policy adviser.

SAVING STUYVESANT TOWN

Prologue

MIDDLE CLASS ON THE BRINK

Six and a half months into my first term as a New York City councilman, about 20 percent of my district went up for sale. Needless to say, this doesn't usually happen.

Built by the Metropolitan Life Insurance Company as housing for veterans returning from World War II, Stuyvesant Town and Peter Cooper Village is the largest rental community in the United States and home to about thirty thousand mostly middle-class people on the East Side of Manhattan.[1] A stone's throw from the East Village, the Flatiron Building, and Gramercy Park, for nearly sixty years Stuyvesant Town and Peter Cooper Village had stood as a beacon for middle-income New Yorkers, a place to enjoy a stable and affordable life in the heart of Manhattan. The redbrick buildings are uniform and pedestrian—to many outsiders, they resemble public housing. But under the care of "Mother Met," as Metropolitan Life, or MetLife, was known to tenants, and protected by rent-stabilization laws that provided for stable and affordable rents, it was designed to resemble suburban living, where people could raise their kids, build a community, and grow old in peace. Residents tended to stay for decades.

Then, in July 2006, at the height of the real estate boom, MetLife announced that it would put it all up for sale. Its marketing materials emphasized the opportunity for a new owner to transform the drab and nondescript buildings into a luxury product, and the opportunity to own eighty acres in Manhattan caused the real estate world to go crazy. In October 2006, bidders from across the globe participated in a white-hot auction that bid the property over $5 billion—*billions* more than what experts had been predicting. To the real estate developers, Stuy Town and Peter Cooper had the potential to be the biggest residential deal ever consummated and a source of enormous profit for years to come. To the people who lived there—many for decades—the message was clear: their stable, middle-class community was on the brink.

When the dust settled on the bidding in October 2006, Tishman Speyer Properties and BlackRock emerged as the winners, paying a record-shattering $5.4 billion in a deal that in fact went down in the books as the largest residential real estate transaction in US history. Despite public pressure to do so, the new owners had no interest in making a commitment to the long-term preservation of affordable housing in Stuyvesant Town beyond what the law already required. To many in the real estate community, and even to Mayor Michael Bloomberg, that was more than enough. Unfortunately, it was clear to many of us that a sale of this magnitude could only be justified with a business plan that would seek to drive up rents and drive out existing tenants.

Almost immediately, our fears were confirmed. Tishman Speyer wasted no time in attempting to usher in a new era of luxury to this largely middle-class community. The new owners hung "luxury rentals" banners on the sides of the redbrick buildings. They closed the local supermarket and replaced it with a gym. They offered new amenities—for a fee— that could attract younger tenants, and hosted rock concerts in the middle of Stuyvesant Oval. But most significantly, Tishman Speyer tried to push out existing tenants in order to increase rents on new tenants who moved in. They had borrowed $4.4 billion to buy Stuy Town and had to find a way to generate more revenue from the property to pay back their enormous debts.

Most of the units in Stuy Town were protected by rent stabilization, which is a state law that limits the amount of rent increases the landlord could apply to the units. But the law allowed for the owner of rent-stabilized units to make upgrades to a *vacant* unit, and to apply a portion of the cost of those improvements to the legal rent. Once the monthly rent was over $2,000, an owner was allowed to take the unit out of rent stabilization and charge any amount for it. That meant that in Stuy Town the remaining lower-rent, rent-stabilized tenants were the prime obstacle to Tishman Speyer getting rental income up and allowing the firm to repay its debts. Tishman Speyer and BlackRock's deal would fail unless they got these people out of their units, and fast. Legal notices, many with flimsy allegations, rained down on longtime, perfectly legitimate tenants, putting them on notice that they were going to be evicted and creating an atmosphere of fear among the tenant community. The tenants were suddenly in a battle that they did not want to fight.

For me, this was personal. I was not only the new city councilman for the area, but the people affected by this were my neighbors. I grew up in the neighborhood, an only child of a public school teacher and portfolio manager, and my formative years were spent in a two-bedroom apartment in Peter Cooper. My mother had moved into the community in the late 1960s, and once she got married to my dad, they never seriously considered leaving because it afforded them a reasonable and stabilized rent, beautiful grounds, and more space than they otherwise could afford in Manhattan. Over the years, I had developed a personal relationship with many of the people who now had a target on their backs. When I had run for public office the year before, questions about Stuyvesant Town were mundane and focused on the routine conflicts between landlords and tenants in a city housing development—like brown water, or rent increases. Now, the entire property was up for sale, and tenants' futures were hanging in the balance.

Like me, the people of this community were invested in its stability as an affordable, middle-class neighborhood. The people who lived there— some had been there for the entire life of the community—were being treated as an afterthought by corporate titans, and, as the sale and its aftermath unfurled, they banded together to fight back. Over the course of a decade, the newly energized Stuyvesant Town Peter Cooper Village Tenants Association and I used every ounce of leverage that we could find.

We assembled our own competitive bid to buy the property on behalf of the tenants themselves—and did it twice. We defended the interests of residents who found themselves subject to baseless legal claims, we litigated and won the biggest tenant victory in the New York Court of Appeals in a generation, and we were courted by nearly all the major real estate players across the globe. Ultimately we put ourselves in a position to strike a deal that would preserve thousands of units as affordable housing for the next generation of residents.

Our fight to save Stuyvesant Town faced significant obstacles, however, and not just from the real estate world. Mayor Bloomberg viewed the transaction as purely private in nature, and despite the city's history of direct involvement in the creation of the community, he didn't believe there was a continued role for the public to play in the sale. We were constantly challenged by Tishman Speyer and, when they defaulted, by a special servicer called CWCapital. We worked to navigate the shark-filled waters of New York real estate, with many viewing the Tenants Association as an active foe. Some residents also objected to the plans that the Tenants Association itself was advancing, either because they focused too much, or too little, on the long-term affordability of the community.

Moreover, public sentiment was not always on our side. Though MetLife historically had imposed a *minimum* income requirement for new tenants, there was no income cap for any resident. Accordingly, though most of the members of the community were middle class, some had more means, and all were paying below market rate for their units. If you are paying less than a third of your income in rent, the housing is, by formal definition, affordable to you. By 2000, the median household income in Stuy Town was $68,422, and the median monthly rent was $1,000. Those households were paying only about 18 percent of their income for rent, well below a third of the median income, making Stuy Town "one of the few bargains left in Manhattan." To many, this appeared to be a relatively well-off community enjoying affordable housing while many others throughout the city struggled to make ends meet.[2]

However, others wisely saw the value of preserving a middle class in a city where the divide between the very rich and the very poor was growing. New York City in 2006 had the lowest percentage of middle-class residents of any of the hundred largest metropolitan areas in the United States. That posed risks for New Yorkers of all income levels. A Brookings study revealed that the absence of middle-income neighborhoods limits opportunities for upward mobility, making it tougher for lower-income people "to move up the property ladder, to buy into safer neighborhoods, send their children to better schools, and even make the kinds of personal contacts that can be a route to better jobs."[3]

While many middle-class people who started their lives in New York City were ultimately priced out, the people who lived in Stuy Town generally were able to stay. Thanks to affordable prices and a stable, quiet community, they were able to work and raise their families in the heart of New York City, contributing to its vibrant nature. Were there some very wealthy people living in their midst, taking advantage of the system? Admittedly, in the context of rent stabilization, there are always some who will benefit from a program that is not intended for them. But people of great means ordinarily did not gravitate toward nondescript buildings without a doorman, and next to a major highway, just for a bargain. My own building when I was growing up included multiple public school teachers, a furrier, a literary agent, an accountant, a truant officer, and a former NYPD detective. Like my own parents, these were people who likely would have left the city but for the housing in Stuy Town and Peter Cooper that was affordable to them.

It also is important to recognize that part of our success in pushing back against real estate excesses was based on the very advantages that these middle-class people—and because of the community's horribly racist origins, *predominantly white* middle-class people—had in contrast to more marginalized groups. We had an active, vocal, and well-connected constituency vested with an inherent privilege. Among us were top mayoral aides, prominent tenant advocates, and elected officials, past and present. While in the community's very earliest days, residents challenged MetLife and won one of the most important civil rights victories in New York's history to put an end to MetLife's official whites-only policy, Stuy Town continues to be an overwhelmingly white neighborhood to this day. And while the vast majority of the community is still middle class, we have some more affluent neighbors among us as well. These were people who had moved in when they were just starting their careers but who had stayed—and some even later fought side by side with us to protect middle-class housing because they saw the importance of offering this opportunity to the next generation.

Against this backdrop, one might be tempted to have little sympathy for today's Stuy Town residents. It is undeniably true that there are far needier communities in New York City. And yet it is also true that it is in the interest of all New Yorkers for the middle class to survive. Having a healthy middle class is critical to the economic growth and success of any city. This group relies on public services—like infrastructure and schools—and has an interest in demanding results that improve outcomes for all residents. Indeed, this group of residents used its power and energy to fight back against landlord excesses, to strengthen rent laws, and as a result created benefits for tens of thousands of New Yorkers. The tenants of Stuy Town represent New York's middle class; their future is linked to the future of the city.[4]

The book is mostly told from my own perspective, informed by a decade of work on behalf of Stuyvesant Town and Peter Cooper Village tenants. I had the fortune of being the local city councilman during the period of time central to this story. I was present at nearly every meeting to plot the tenants' strategy to respond to MetLife's sale, to push back against Tishman Speyer's aggressive behavior toward tenants, and to develop a solution that would ensure the long-term stability of this, my childhood home. I supplemented my own memory with interviews with many of the main players and also framed some of the details through press accounts. And a note for the reader: I often call Stuyvesant Town and Peter Cooper Village together just "Stuyvesant Town" or "Stuy Town," to simplify matters.

This story starts with the development of Stuy Town by MetLife, with the strong support of Mayor Fiorello La Guardia and Robert Moses. To build on the eighty-acre site, the city used its power of eminent domain and gave MetLife a blank canvas, a tax abatement, and a guaranteed return on its investment that would last for twenty-five years. The city also blessed MetLife's racist rental policies, which prohibited Black residents from getting an apartment. The story then shows how the tenants of Stuy Town used their organizing mettle to successfully push back against MetLife's racism and to integrate the community. Twenty-five years later, the tenants again organized, this time to resist the impacts of an immediate rent hike when MetLife's tax abatement was set to end. They banded together to form the modern Tenants Association and again won a critical victory by getting their rent protections extended. With MetLife's sale in 2006, tenants faced another challenge: a new owner and an unknown future. The book focuses primarily on the period from the 2006 sale to the uncertain years following Tishman Speyer's default in 2010 and the negotiated sale to the Blackstone Group in 2015. It tells the story of the Herculean efforts by leaders of this community to ensure that tenants' interests would be protected.

It will answer the question of how the tenants of Stuy Town got from a place where they were being ignored by local government and threatened with eviction, to a place where the largest real estate entities in the world were not only fighting to join forces with us—but a new mayor would help us to deliver a once-in-a-generation win for tenants. This is the story of a community with a history of activism banding together to fight back against corporate greed and excess, and who forced the real estate community to ultimately conclude that working with the tenants would yield a better outcome than fighting them. The negotiations played out both in public and in private over many years, and the process was often choppy and sometimes bitterly contentious. The result was an extraordinary outcome for middle-class New Yorkers.

Figure 1.1. Stuyvesant Town and Peter Cooper Village sit between 14th and 23rd Streets east of First Avenue in Manhattan. The Empire State Building and Chrysler Building are in the background. Photo credit: Beam Living, Stuyvesant Town / Peter Cooper Village Archives.

1

Activism from the Start

You can't miss the wall of redbrick buildings that emerges out of the East Village on Manhattan's East Side. The plain and unenticing facades of Stuyvesant Town and Peter Cooper Village carefully disguise the unique slice of city life that takes place within. Just inside, flower beds bursting with tulips line the paths connecting the buildings, sunbathers sprawl on lush grassy areas, and children play in fifteen well-maintained playgrounds. Young families come together for picnics on the lawn, teenagers fill the basketball courts, and elderly New Yorkers sit on benches, passing the day.

Its idyllic quality belies the tumultuous history that produced this middle-class enclave tucked in the midst of Manhattan. In reality, the history of Stuyvesant Town is anything but idyllic. Born of government-backed, and subsidized, racist policies and the displacement of poor New Yorkers, Stuyvesant Town's roots are planted in bitter soil. But the history of Stuyvesant Town is punctuated by something else, too, which is deeply woven into the fabric of the community. From its earliest days, the story of Stuyvesant Town is also one of activism, where elected officials, civil rights leaders, and tenants joined together to fight—and in most cases ultimately win—against corporate greed and unjust policies, and for the rights of New Yorkers.

Stuyvesant Town emerged from a housing crisis in New York City that began during World War I. The war had placed a significant demand on manpower and materials, sending the cost of construction of new buildings through the roof; in the city, housing construction basically came to a halt. Between 1915 and 1919, the number of new apartments built in New York City dropped by 94 percent, at the same time that wartime prosperity was bringing many new families to the five boroughs. That combination of factors drove vacancy levels in the city to a staggeringly low .36 percent in April 1920. By contrast, the 2018 vacancy rate in New York City was ten times higher, at 3.63 percent, which is still considered a housing emergency. The result was that apartment units in the 1920s tended to be severely overcrowded, and the conditions were poor. Occupants of these units had no protection from sudden rent hikes, and eviction cases clogged the courts. With the support of the Socialist Party and its allied labor unions, tenants began to organize to demand reforms. Sometimes their advocacy took the form of rent strikes, and in other cases tenants directly challenged their landlords in court.[1]

In an effort to stem the crisis, the New York State Legislature decided to offer incentives for the construction of new housing. Among those incentives was a program for insurance companies to build new housing for people of low and moderate means. The program—formalized in a 1922 law—allowed a municipality like New York City to offer insurance companies a ten-year tax exemption on new residential construction so long as rents for tenants did not exceed $9 per month per room. The Metropolitan Life Insurance Company, under the leadership of Frederick Ecker, decided to take advantage of this program. MetLife, as it came to be known, built 2,125 apartments in western Queens. Opened in 1924, the apartments proved to be popular, not only because of the reasonable rents, but also because they afforded certain comforts, like steam heat and hot water, which were not common for housing developments at the time.[2]

Things got harder for both tenants and landlords in the Great Depression years of the early 1930s, as many tenants could not pay their rents, landlords could not afford their mortgage obligations, and courts received a flood of eviction and foreclosure cases they did not even have the ability to enforce. In 1938, the state renewed its incentive program for new housing construction. This time, Ecker and MetLife took advantage of the incentives to build the Parkchester community in the East Bronx. Parkchester's 171 buildings and 12,271 apartments were designed to be a parklike suburb, which opened in 1941. As MetLife expanded its housing portfolio, it was enjoying a high level of success, even earning a higher return on its Parkchester investment than on its own bonds and other core investments.[3]

Robert Moses, New York State's powerful parks commissioner and city planning commissioner, working in concert with Mayor Fiorello La Guardia, had even bigger development plans in mind to address the crisis. He was determined to clear so-called slums for urban renewal and had his eye on building a large housing development on the East Side of Manhattan. Major projects like these were much more difficult in Manhattan than other places because a prospective developer not only needed to build the buildings but also usually had to first demolish existing ones—and that meant evicting the people who lived in them. In pursuit of his large-scale Manhattan project, Moses reached out to two of the biggest insurance companies already doing business in New York to gauge their interest in doing a development on the East Side. New York Life Insurance Company demurred, but MetLife, emboldened by its recent successes in Parkchester and in Queens, was ready to engage.

Moses initially offered MetLife a twenty-year property tax abatement for the new buildings—which was more generous than the ten years that had been guaranteed in the 1922 law—but would require MetLife to find new housing for the people who would be displaced. This was not good enough for MetLife, and Ecker pushed Moses for more benefits and fewer obligations. Eager to lock them in, Moses went to Albany to argue for a sweeter deal for MetLife. Moses emerged with a new package of incentives that included extending the tax exemption to twenty-five years and dropping any requirement that MetLife find replacement housing for the eleven thousand existing residents in the area from 14th to 20th Streets who were going to be forced to move. The law also set minimum income requirements for the future residents of the new development, "in order to attract a higher social class of tenants." The resulting Hampton-Mitchell Redevelopment Companies Law of 1943 was tailored specifically to suit MetLife's requirements.[4]

Green-lighted in Albany, the 1943 law also gave the city the right to confiscate the private homes of the people who lived at the site, for the benefit of MetLife's development. City officials condemned eighteen blocks of this allegedly blighted land and sold it at cost to the Stuyvesant Town Corporation, a new branch of MetLife, named for Peter Stuyvesant, the Dutch governor of colonial New Amsterdam. (In the seventeenth century, Stuyvesant's farm had occupied the site of the future development.) The city negotiated a contract that froze MetLife's tax bill for twenty-five years at the low rate in effect for the area when the property was considered "blighted," and gave MetLife the right to apply to the New York City Board of Estimate—which at the time was the city's primary legislative body, operating alongside a less-powerful city council—to raise rents as necessary to guarantee MetLife a consistent 6 percent return on its capital investment.[5]

Mayor La Guardia made the announcement of his important plan for Stuyvesant Town in his regular radio broadcast on WNYC on April 18, 1943. It was front page news in the *New York Times*—above the fold—with the headline "East Side Suburb in City to House 30,000 after War." This suburb was going to be designed to be separate and apart from the hustle of the city; Ecker described it as having a parklike atmosphere and a special emphasis on the recreational needs of children. To La Guardia the deal was "not only vision, it is prudence and good business." Stuyvesant Town was unique in that it would create homes for thirty thousand people but would be built on only 30 percent of the entire lot. The rest would remain for landscaping, roadways, and open courts, in order to maximize light and air for residents. La Guardia also promised that people already living in the area did not need to worry about being forcibly dispossessed, at least not until after the war.[6]

The news surprised the eleven thousand low-income New Yorkers who lived in modest tenements in those blocks east of First Avenue and who had been given no prior warning or been consulted by La Guardia, Moses, or any local elected officials about this plan. A debate erupted about the seemingly private nature of the proposed development and the fact that it would displace people from their homes. One critic wrote, "It will be a company-walled town with eight entrances, each marked private; at the company's will any non-resident of the town could be barred from walking through the project. The streets within will obviously not be dedicated to the city but will be company owned and maintained." Robert Moses responded, saying that New Yorkers should support MetLife because it was "the only company which has been willing to run the risk of undertaking a large rehabilitation project in wartime as a matter of public service."[7]

MetLife responded to the controversy over its plans by establishing a Tenant Relocation Bureau, with the stated purpose to help these soon-to-be displaced residents find new housing. Unfortunately for most of them, their prospects of moving into the future Stuyvesant Town were remote. The Community Service Society in 1945 interviewed 836 families in the neighborhood and concluded that only 3 percent of them had "a reasonable hope" of being rehoused in the future Stuyvesant Town. Twenty-two percent were looking to public housing as their next best option, and the remaining 75 percent "must find shelter in other slum areas." To these disadvantaged New Yorkers, many of whom were recent immigrants, Stuy Town, despite its expected contribution to the public good of housing, added nothing but pain as it forced them to uproot their homes without any promise of improvement to their quality of life.[8]

MetLife's physical plan was approved by the City Planning Commission, on which Moses sat as a member, on May 20, 1943, by a vote of 5 to 1. The lone dissenter, Lawrence M. Orton, cited the fact that the city was going to demolish an existing public school (and not replace it within the boundaries of Stuy Town) as the reason for his negative vote. Orton found it incredible that the children growing up in this new city in the city, which was to be the size of Jacksonville, Florida, would not have a school in its midst. Having secured approval of the physical design from the Department of City Planning, MetLife had to then persuade the powerful Board of Estimate to approve the terms of its proposed contract with the city. (At that time, all administrative actions like this, as well as laws passed by the city council, needed to be approved by the Board of Estimate.) The June 3, 1943, Board of Estimate hearing was a hotbed of dissent, as people learned that MetLife, while enjoying the benefits of tax incentives and condemnation, actually intended to deny Black people the opportunity to live in the future Stuyvesant Town. Assemblyman William Andrews read into the record a written exchange he had with George Gove, MetLife's director of housing, who had said cryptically that "no provision has been made for Negro families" in Stuy Town. When Andrews asked MetLife administrators for clarification about what exactly that meant, he got a terse second letter, which said the original MetLife communication had been "direct and explicit and requires no further clarification."[9]

At the Board of Estimate hearing in City Hall, Councilman Stanley Isaacs read aloud a quote that MetLife's chairman, Frederick Ecker, had given to the *New York Post*: "Negroes and whites don't mix. Perhaps they will in a hundred years but they don't now." Isaacs then turned directly to Ecker, who was sitting in the front row of the hearing at City Hall, and asked if he had been misquoted. As everyone watched uncomfortably, Ecker sat stone-faced and did not answer. Hearing the exchange between the elected officials and Ecker, Moses was infuriated by the politicians' grandstanding and complicating his development plan with civil rights concerns. "If you don't want this contract," he huffed at the hearing, "I can assure you that it will be the last opportunity we'll have to attract private capital. It will mark the death knell of slum clearance by private enterprise." Moses continued: "Those who insist on making projects of this kind a battleground for the vindication of social objectives, however desirable, and who persist in claiming that a private project is in fact a public project, obviously are looking for a political issue and not for results in the form of actual slum clearance."[10]

One member of the Board of Estimate, Borough President Edgar Nathan, attempted to table the project, but Moses and La Guardia pushed it through. The Board of Estimate approved the Stuyvesant Town contract on June 3, 1943, by a vote of 11 to 5. About a week after the vote, at a "Negro freedom rally" at Madison Garden, before a packed house, Adam Clayton Powell Jr.—a member of the New York City Council— demanded the impeachment of Mayor La Guardia because he allowed the city's contract with MetLife to proceed. Clearly sensing that they were on the wrong side of a losing issue, the Board of Estimate soon thereafter passed a local law under which *future* projects receiving real estate tax relief would be barred from discriminating against applicants because of their race, color, or creed. But they declined to make this law applicable to Stuyvesant Town. It was official: MetLife had secured the government approvals it needed to proceed.[11]

Almost immediately, advocates opposing segregation challenged the city's approval of the Stuy Town contract in court on procedural grounds, but their suit was later dismissed. By February 1945, MetLife had formally filed its building plans and took to the task of vacating and demolishing the hundreds of four- and five-story tenements in what had become known as the Gas House District, because of the giant, circular gas storage tanks or "gashouses" that once existed there. It also took to removing several laundries, three churches, three schools, two theaters, and many small factory buildings that were relics of the Civil War. Hundreds of tenants were notified that they needed to vacate their buildings by March 31, 1945, to make way for this massive new development. Sidewalks in the community became cluttered with household goods as people prepared to move, and tenants, many with limited English proficiency, crowded MetLife's relocation bureau seeking help. MetLife's bureau had translators who spoke Polish, Russian, and Italian, who transported soon-to-be displaced residents across the city in a station wagon looking for new housing. The *New York Times* called it "the greatest and most significant mass movement of families in New York's history."[12]

But not all of the tenants were willing to go without a fight. The one hundred residents of one rent-protected building—called Stuyvesant House—held an emergency meeting in March 1945 at Stuyvesant High School, and objected to being evicted. They urgently called on Mayor La Guardia and Governor Dewey to keep MetLife from tearing down their building until after the war, as La Guardia had promised, or until 1946.[13] La Guardia's promises were meaningless now that the city had given MetLife the green light to proceed. In fact, this project, hailed by La Guardia and Moses as the pinnacle of public-spiritedness and the best way to achieve the city's social objectives, suddenly had the feeling of a private real estate development project where the public was just in the way.

By May 1946, the Gashouse District was a "vista of wrecked buildings and hills of debris."[14] As the number of residents dwindled, those who remained watched as bulldozers demolished their neighbors' former homes. In a little over a year, MetLife had successfully removed the residents and razed all the buildings. The last tenants, Mr. and Mrs. Harry Delman, and their ten-year-old son Gerald, moved out on May 5, 1946 (twenty-six years to the day before my own parents welcomed me into the world and brought me home to our Stuy Town apartment). The Delmans lived at 441 East 15th Street, an address that, because Stuy Town was designed as a single immense superblock, disappeared off the city grid forever.[15]

Meanwhile, thousands of people were lining up for a chance to occupy one of the future Stuy Town apartments. One day after MetLife announced that applications were open, it was flooded with seven thousand letters and telegrams for the 8,759 units that wouldn't even be finished for another two years. MetLife had declared that veterans were going to have preference in the application process, and many of them in their letters described how they were struggling to find housing now that the war was over. Many were newlyweds and desperate to get out of their in-laws' homes; others described how they wanted to get married but couldn't

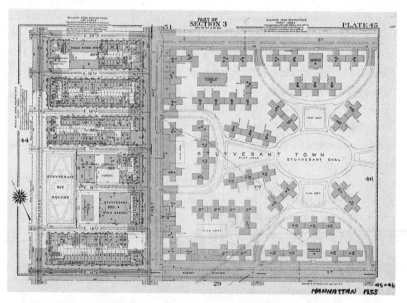

Figure 1.2. Early maps of Stuyvesant Town show the tower-in-a-park design, with buildings interspersed through ample green space, including an oval gathering area in the middle. This map shows the western two-thirds of Stuyvesant Town, between 14th and 23rd Streets, in contrast with the more densely situated buildings across First Avenue. The layout added to the feeling that this community was insulated from the rest of Manhattan. Photo credit: New York Public Library.

because they had no place to live. By the time the first building was ready to be occupied on August 1, 1947, MetLife had received one hundred thousand applications.[16]

Even as demand for Stuy Town apartments crested, MetLife was already making its first appeal to the city to raise rents on future tenants. Citing a 50 percent increase in construction costs—from $60 million to $90 million—MetLife asked the Board of Estimate to approve a $3 increase in the amount it could charge per month per room. In exchange for the bump, Ecker promised to keep the new rents at $17.00 for at least four years. After that, he said that he would regularly seek increases to ensure MetLife's guaranteed 6 percent return. At a public hearing at City Hall, civic groups asked the Board of Estimate to deny the rent increase unless MetLife agreed to a nondiscrimination clause in its contract. Their efforts were unsuccessful, and the increase went through.[17]

Despite the high demand for future Stuyvesant Town apartments, the project's racist rental policies were giving MetLife lots of bad publicity. Discrimination in housing was not illegal at the time, and the right of an owner to screen prospective tenants for so-called appropriateness was well established. However, this development was unusual because of its size and scale and most importantly because the city was so integrally linked to its creation. There would have been no Stuy Town without New York City condemning the land and offering generous tax incentives and profit guarantees to MetLife. Moses and Mayor La Guardia had moved mountains to get MetLife to redevelop the property, and by approving a deal that so clearly was going to exclude renting apartments to Black people, the city's Board of Estimate had sanctioned the racial discrimination. "At a time when Negro and white Americans are dying on the battlefields to preserve our Nation, it seems shocking that such a project could even be proposed," said a representative of the Permanent Committee for Better Schools in Harlem.[18]

MetLife responded to the controversy—but not by changing its policies in Stuy Town. Instead, the company announced a new, much smaller housing project geared toward African Americans. Called Riverton, it was to be located in Harlem. MetLife executives clearly hoped that this new "separate but equal" development would mitigate racial and political tensions.

Anger over the Stuy Town project, however, continued to grow. Armed with the support of the American Civil Liberties Union, the American Jewish Congress, and the National Association for the Advancement of Colored People, three Black veterans sued MetLife in 1947, arguing that housing discrimination based on race was barred by the Constitution of the United States and the State of New York. MetLife countered that because it was a private corporation, it had the right to decide the policies—like keeping Black people out—to protect the safety of its investment. Ignoring the $50 million tax abatement that had been given to MetLife by city taxpayers over twenty-five years, MetLife asserted in its legal briefs that Stuy Town had been built entirely with private funds, and "not one dollar" of public money was used. MetLife also urged the court to consider as a matter of mitigation that it had also recently built the Riverton Houses in Harlem, now occupied principally by Black people. The Black veterans argued that MetLife still could not discriminate in Stuy Town because the entire development was made possible by state action.[19]

On July 19, 1949, the New York Court of Appeals—the state's highest court—decided the question in favor of MetLife, saying that the legislative intent of the Redevelopment Companies Law, which enabled the creation of Stuy Town, was "clear to leave private enterprise free to select tenants of its own choice."[20] The United States Supreme Court declined to review the case on appeal in June 1950, and MetLife's racist policies were allowed to stand by the highest court in the land.

Outraged that MetLife was being allowed by the city, and now the courts, to exclude Black residents, some of the earliest tenants of Stuy Town decided to fight back themselves. In a first act of community organizing in Stuy Town, twelve white residents formed a group called the Town and Village Tenants Committee to End Discrimination in Stuyvesant Town. They started to gather petition signatures from their neighbors, objecting to the policy and demanding that the city take action. On April 5, 1949, they asked for a meeting with Mayor William O'Dwyer (who had succeeded La Guardia in 1946 and was then in the middle of a reelection campaign), to deliver the petition signed by thirty-one hundred people. O'Dwyer received representatives of the group and politely told them that while the contract between MetLife and the city was "unwise," all parties to the agreement were equally at fault. He promised that his administration had done everything in its power to end discrimination in all housing developments but that there was, practically speaking, nothing he could do in this case.[21]

Jesse Kessler, an organizer for Local 65, the Wholesale and Warehouse Workers Union, was one of the early members of the Committee to End Discrimination in Stuy Town and decided that he would take matters into his own hands. If MetLife wouldn't integrate the community, Kessler decided that he would do it himself. He and his family were scheduled to take a trip out of New York City in August 1949, so he invited a Black couple named Hardine and Raphael Hendrix to live in his apartment during that time. On August 11, 1949, Hardine, a twenty-eight-year-old war veteran and art student, along with his wife, became the first Black people to ever live in Stuy Town. The action was cheered by Kessler's fellow committee members, and some of them started to follow his lead.[22]

Within two months, a half dozen other Stuy Town families were also hosting Black people as "houseguests," and the action was gathering momentum. The committee announced that even more tenants were expected to participate in this act of civil disobedience. One of those participants, Lee Lorch, a World War II vet, had seen Black soldiers forced to do some of the military's most difficult work on the battlefield, and was appalled that they were now being shut out of Stuy Town. "The courage and sharpshooting of a Negro machine gunner saved my life with a dozen other white G.I.'s," said a pamphlet issued by Lorch and the committee. "Can any one of us say he can't be my neighbor? I can't." Surveys of residents conducted by the committee showed that two-thirds of Stuyvesant Town's twenty-five thousand tenants opposed MetLife's exclusionary policy.[23]

The leader of the committee was a man named Paul Ross, who decided to launch a campaign for city comptroller on the American Labor Party line in 1949, and the integration of Stuyvesant Town was central to his platform. At a Saturday night party on October 29, 1949, in support of his candidacy, Ross invited all the Stuy Town tenants who were hosting Black families and encouraged them to bring along their houseguests. He used the occasion to showcase the advocacy of his neighbors and to take aim at Mayor O'Dwyer and MetLife. "The tenants are proving that the legal curtain behind which the Metropolitan is hiding with the assistance of Mayor O'Dwyer is not strong enough to keep out democracy," Ross said.[24]

On June 20, 1950, two members of the New York City Council, Early Brown and Stanley Isaacs, introduced a bill that would force MetLife to reverse course. The proposed bill prohibited discrimination or segregation in private housing projects that had a total or partial tax exemption, or which received any financial aid from the city. And, most importantly, it would apply retroactively to MetLife. Concerned about losing control of this emotional issue, Mayor O'Dwyer asked the council members to table their bill while he appointed a committee to work with MetLife to privately negotiate an amicable solution. After some halfhearted behind-the-scenes work by O'Dwyer, on August 25 MetLife said that it would lease "some" apartments to "qualified Negro families." When reached by phone to ask if this meant a change was imminent, Ecker would not confirm or deny the report, saying only "Deponent sayeth not." MetLife was unwilling to deviate from its official position that it maintained the right to select the residents of Stuy Town, even as it opened the door to a few Black families. Council member Isaacs said, "Nobody has ever questioned the company's right to select its tenants. What was questioned was the company's right to discriminate on the basis of race, creed or color." O'Dwyer tried to avoid the growing controversy around MetLife's apparent decision to keep its racist rental policies. "Well," he shrugged dismissively, "a landlord leases to some tenants."[25]

Five days later, on August 31, Mayor O'Dwyer was forced to resign as a result of a growing police corruption scandal, and the city council president, Vincent Impellitteri, stepped into the role of acting mayor. With O'Dwyer out of the way, council members Isaacs and Brown reintroduced their antidiscrimination bill in September, and by February 16, 1951, it flew unanimously through the council, and then the Board of Estimate by a 12–1 vote. Mayor Impellitteri signed the bill into law on March 14, 1951. The bill made discrimination in Stuy Town punishable by a $500 fine, and, much more importantly, gave those who were discriminated against a right to go to court to end such discrimination. Council member Isaacs called the action a step toward "elimination of a blot on this great American city, which will now be able to hold up its head again." And yet, a year after the bill passed, MetLife was still resisting its legal obligation to integrate the community. It cited its extensive waiting list of white residents and said that it would be "unfair" to let Black applicants jump the line.[26]

MetLife was so outraged by the infringement on its authority that its representatives attacked the supporters of the new law as communists and simultaneously moved to evict the thirty-five families most closely identified with the effort to desegregate Stuy Town. The targeted residents printed a flyer, "A landlord vs. the people." "For the first time in American history," the flyer said, "a landlord has tried to evict citizens from their homes for their social beliefs." The city marshal who was helping to enforce the evictions ordered the targeted tenants to vacate their apartments by nine o'clock on the morning of January 17, 1952, and hired a moving company to drag their furniture onto the street. In response, the families barricaded themselves in their units, and their neighbors, many of whom were former servicemen, stood guard outside the targeted apartments, ready if necessary to defend themselves against the landlord. They sent their children to stay with relatives and passed baskets of food from window to window with ropes.[27]

As news got out about MetLife's coldhearted plan to evict these sympathetic activists, a city and statewide movement grew to protect them. State legislators introduced a bill to prevent their eviction, while protesters surrounded Ecker's apartment building at 660 Park Avenue and raised a large red balloon outside his window with a streamer that said "Stop the Evictions." Hundreds of New Yorkers picketed at Stuy Town, at City Hall, and at MetLife's headquarters at 1 Madison Avenue, where protesters held a round-the-clock vigil that lasted for three days.[28]

Mayor Impellitteri declined to intervene in the fracas on the flimsy basis that it would be improper for him to ask for "favors" of MetLife since he would ultimately have to decide on their proposed rent increases. The city council president, Rudolph Halley, seeing an issue that he believed to be "charged with a public interest"—and clearly a political opportunity for him—offered himself as a mediator. Halley sat with Churchill Ridgers, MetLife's general counsel, and Irving Kalish, another lawyer representing the insurance company, along with Paul Ross, the chairman of the committee. They reached an agreement whereby MetLife would allow most of the families to stay, while some of the leaders of the movement would voluntarily vacate the property. As part of the settlement, Mr. and Mrs. Hendrix—the first Black family to move in to Stuy Town as guests—were offered their own lease to an apartment. Ross called it a vindication of his committee's activities over the years. *Town & Village*, the community's local newspaper, concluded that MetLife was likely relieved to be off the hook from all the controversy, "in the face of the violent public reaction."[29]

By fighting for integration in Stuy Town, tenants had started a tradition of the community's residents creatively attacking an issue and affecting public policy far beyond their eighty-acre footprint. But change came slowly. By 1960, only 47 of 22,405 residents in Stuy Town were Black. The New York City Human Rights Commission in 1968 filed a complaint against MetLife because of the jarringly low number of Black residents in Stuy Town, and also in its other properties like Parkchester in the Bronx. Throughout the 1960s, civil rights advocates more actively joined together and advanced the larger cause of racial justice in housing. Committees to combat discrimination in housing were formed to influence the New York State Legislature and the US Congress. New York State passed its own law barring discrimination in private housing in 1963, and Congress did the same with the federal Fair Housing Act in 1968. And while the structural impact of Stuy Town's racist origins continues to impact the community's racial composition to this day, the advocacy of the Stuy Town tenants showed that these civil rights battles could be won, and gave rise to broader reforms in housing at both the state and federal levels.[30]

Most of the children born to white veterans in Stuy Town were unaware of this painful recent history. As white kids, they had the privilege of not having to think about these difficult questions of race, and to them Stuy Town was just home, where they played with their friends, went to school, and enjoyed a quiet, peaceful existence. That's how it was for Alvin Doyle Jr. and Steven Sanders—one Irish, one Jewish—who represented the extent of the diversity in Stuy Town at the time. As children, they stood steps apart from each other in late October 1960 as they waited to catch a glimpse of Senator John F. Kennedy as he spoke into a microphone on a flatbed truck on East 20th Street. Both boys were sons of veterans, and their families had moved into Stuy Town right after it opened in 1947. Now, just twelve days before the presidential election of 1960, they were among thousands of neighbors who filled the street to hear from the vibrant young senator from Massachusetts. New York's forty-five electoral votes were up for grabs that year, and Kennedy was barnstorming through the city. Eight-year-old Al Doyle, a Roman Catholic like Kennedy, fought with his two brothers for a turn to be lifted up by their dad, Alvin Sr., to peer over the crowd next to Plymouth's Department Store. As it was, he could only see shoes, coats, and a sliver of sky. Steven Sanders, who was one year older than Al Jr., didn't fare any better. He knew he was in the presence of an exciting candidate and saw lots of "Kennedy for the 60s" buttons on the coats of the adults around him. Even though he was only twenty-five yards away from Kennedy, as he remembers it, he couldn't make sense of what was going on.[31]

Kennedy's youth and optimism resonated with the Doyle and Sanders families and many others in this growing community of young— overwhelmingly white—middle-class World War II veterans and their families. Patriots who had returned from battle fifteen years earlier, they had faith in God, in family, and in their country. They were in Stuy Town

Figure 1.3. As the election campaign of 1960 wrapped up, New York's electoral votes were still up for grabs. Thousands of new residents—mostly veterans and their families—turned out when Senator John F. Kennedy made a campaign stop on 20th Street and First Avenue, right in front of Stuy Town. Photo credit: *Town & Village* newspaper.

to put down roots and enjoy some peace in this fresh, new community that had just been created for their benefit. With its crisp, manicured lawns, ample play spaces for kids, and saplings planted in harmony with the winding pathways, Stuy Town felt more like suburban America than the middle of New York City. And there were kids everywhere. Part of the baby boom, this community became known as "Rabbit Town" because children were popping up everywhere, and nearly every apartment was occupied by a growing family.

Like many other residents, Al Doyle Sr. was a veteran—a proud, religious marine who had served in the Pacific theater, as a combat correspondent for the Third Marine Division. Before joining the marines on February 15, 1942, he was a copy boy, and later the City Hall reporter for the *New York Daily Mirror*. In 1946, when his service was complete, he met a woman named Therese O'Connor, who worked for a typewriter company near Grand Central. They got married and, starting in 1950, had three boys together. Alvin Sr.'s brother, Frank, helped him complete an application for an apartment at 18 Stuyvesant Oval in the heart of the development.[32]

To get into Stuy Town, you needed to prove that you earned a minimum level of income and that you would be a positive addition to the community. The Doyles met the income requirements and, like all prospective tenants in those days, had a visit from MetLife's inspectors, who evaluated their current living conditions. This check was ostensibly to ensure that they were clean and neat and knew how to care for their home. The visit also gave MetLife administrators an opportunity to quietly weed out tenants that the company did not want. The Doyles passed that second test and were invited to be the very first tenants in their unit at 18 Stuyvesant Oval. With three boys in a two-bedroom apartment in Stuy Town, Alvin Sr., among his other duties, wrote captions for photos of the finishers at the Roosevelt and Yonkers Raceways during harness racing season, which were released to the news wires. Therese worked at home until all her boys were in grammar school and did volunteer secretarial work at the Epiphany School and Church. She later went to work for a company that manufactured fencing equipment.[33]

Next door in 20 Stuyvesant Oval, the Sanders family occupied apartment 3H. Steven Sanders was born in Stuy Town and was the son of two original tenants. Like Doyle Sr., Sanders's dad, Murray, had been in the military, but stationed in Saint Louis, where he wrote training manuals. "My dad was a war hero," Sanders jokingly recalled. "You can tell because not a single German bomb or Japanese soldier ever made it to Saint Louis." Murray, who was Jewish, met a girl named Helen at a synagogue event in Saint Louis in 1945, and they got married the next year. After he was discharged, they moved in with his parents on Fordham Road in the Bronx. They heard about a new housing project in Manhattan for veterans and put their names in the lottery. When their number came up, Murray and Helen moved to Stuy Town in 1949 with their daughter Doreen. Steven was born just two years later, and his younger sister, Arlene, was born in 1963.[34]

Stuy Town was unusual as a community in the heart of New York City. It was as vast as it was new. The tenants there were largely the first to ever live in their units, and there was a high level of pride and appreciation for the community. With 110 buildings, spread out over eighty acres, this was suddenly home to about thirty thousand people who were building a life for themselves, meeting their neighbors, and raising a family.

Because of its isolation, kids pretty much had free rein of the entire neighborhood. It was perceived as one of the safest communities in the city, and parents tended to know each other's children. In the early years, people generally did not even bother to lock their doors, and moms did not hesitate to leave sleeping children in their strollers outside the 20th Street supermarket when they went in to shop. Kids were allowed to go to the playgrounds next to their buildings, with parents—usually moms—keeping a casual eye from the buildings up above. Steven Sanders ran around the community with his friends, playing in its playgrounds, feeling totally safe. "There was almost never a break-in," he said. "Violent crime in Peter Cooper and Stuyvesant Town is virtually nonexistent. This was unique in New York City."[35] Most of its residents were happy to be separated from the more dangerous city around them.

Race was rarely something they thought about; it was a luxury they had because nearly everyone was white. But they were keenly aware of ethnicity. In fact, because there were so many Irish and Jews living together, the white residents actually believed the community was diverse. The unofficial kid rules were that the Irish played in playgrounds 1, 7, and 9, and the Jews were in playgrounds 10 and 11. There were some mythical "Murphy Boys" who hung out at playground 1, who would beat you up if you looked at them the wrong way. "The Irish kids were always tougher than the Jewish kids," Sanders said. "I'm not sure they were ever afraid of us." One Stuy Town resident recalled that when Kennedy was elected, his mother told him that he was the first Catholic president. He asked his mom, "Haven't they all been Catholic?" No, she said, "why would you think that?" He responded: "Mom, you told me there had never been a Jewish president, so what else is there?"[36]

2

TIME FOR A TENANTS ASSOCIATION

When I was born on May 5, 1972, my parents brought me home from NYU Medical Center to our Stuy Town apartment at 410 East 20th Street. My mom, Barbara Riotto, was a public school teacher who had lived in Stuy Town since 1968. She grew up in Sheepshead Bay, Brooklyn, with two siblings, Aileen and Anthony. Her mother, Josephine, was a seamstress, and her father, Randolph—born in Sicily—was a handyman. After being robbed at gunpoint at her Union Square apartment, my mom sought out a much safer neighborhood and discovered Stuytown. She went through the application process and was offered a typical one-bedroom apartment at 440 East 20th Street. Her new unit had plenty of light and a reasonable rent at around $150 a month. She met my dad, David Garodnick, at a Fire Island party. My dad grew up in Newark, New Jersey, with a younger brother named Roger. Their father, Louis, founded a trucking business, and their mother, Bess, served as his bookkeeper. He had moved into New York City after law school, and when he met my mom he was the New York counsel at the National Association of Securities Dealers (now called FINRA). They were married in June 1971.

Settling the real estate question was first on their list. While my dad had a bachelor pad on the Upper East Side, my mom was more comfortable with the safety and much lower rent of her Stuy Town apartment. They decided my dad would move to my mom's place, and just before I was born, they moved to a Stuy Town two-bedroom apartment at 410 East 20th Street. When I was four years old, we all moved across the street to Peter Cooper Village, at 431 East 20th Street.

MetLife had developed Peter Cooper Village at the same time as Stuyvesant Town, and it covered the area from 20th to 23rd Streets. The two communities operated as a united whole, with the same security and maintenance staff serving them. But there were some differences. There was more open space between the Peter Cooper buildings, and the apartments were a little bigger than those in Stuy Town. Two-bedroom units like ours had a second bathroom (a feature lacking in the Stuy Town apartments). Rents tended to be a little higher, in part because Peter Cooper was built without tax incentives and for many years had not been subject to any rent regulation. Stuy Town tenants always felt that management seemed to pay more attention to Peter Cooper. They would talk enviously about their neighbors in the "fancy" and higher-rent part of the community. Gabe Pressman, the legendary reporter for WNBC-TV, was an early resident of Stuyvesant Town after he left the navy. According to Pressman, they called Stuy Town the "enlisted men's quarters" and Peter Cooper Village the "officers' quarters."[1] The names MetLife chose for the communities possibly reinforced this divide. While Stuyvesant Town was named after the Dutch director of the colony who owned a farm on the site in the seventeenth century, Peter Cooper Village was named after the nineteenth-century industrialist, inventor, and philanthropist Peter Cooper, who founded Cooper Union.

We were a typical middle-class family that had enough resources to take on a slightly higher rent in exchange for a better quality of life. Our new apartment in Peter Cooper was only across the street, but it was going to mean real change for us. The new apartment was bigger, quieter, and (unlike Stuy Town at the time) had air conditioning. The building also came with a new set of neighbors. Next door were Ruth and Seymour Altman. Seymour was a furrier who showed me proudly that he advertised his business in *Penthouse* magazine, and he and Ruth worked in his factory in Manhattan's Garment District. Upstairs were two celebrities, *Daily News* sportswriter Peter Vecsey, and Bob Stovall, a financial analyst who was a regular panelist on Louis Rukeyser's *Wall $treet Week.* Down the hall were Al and Elizabeth Chappel. Al was a grizzled, raspy-voiced retired captain in the NYPD, and his wife, Elizabeth, was a flinty New Englander. Every holiday, I would find a greeting card from Al and Elizabeth under our door—and on Halloween it came from "the goblins in 13F." Peter Lampack upstairs was a literary agent; Abdelkader Ab-badi worked at the United Nations; Herb Langerman was a truant officer; Steven Sanders, a lawyer (who frequently got mail intended for our assemblyman of the same name); Sam Boorstein, an accountant, and his wife, Esther Boorstein, a teacher. Barbara and Paul Ringel in 4F were both teachers; I was about six years older than their two boys, Jonathan and Peter, for whom I babysat from time to time. The vertical neighborhood in our building reflected the nature of Stuyvesant Town's Jewish, Italian, and Irish middle class. "If our fathers weren't doctors or dentists, lawyers or school principals, they worked in offices and on hot days still wore their jackets home from work, with their ties just loosened. If our mothers worked at all, they were teachers," wrote Corinne Dumas in her memoir about growing up in Stuyvesant Town.[2]

Our neighbors tended to have a strong affinity for their landlord. The insurance company was delivering what it had promised: a leafy enclave, safe and isolated from the rest of the city, with rents that went up only by small increments. Known as "Mother Met," MetLife could be counted on to reliably repair things that needed to be fixed and to keep the property in pristine condition. And yet, by the early 1970s, when I was born, some residents started to take note that MetLife's twenty-five-year tax abatement was nearing its expiration date, and that change loomed on the horizon. MetLife had stepped in to develop Stuy Town with a flourish of public interest and mayoral support in the 1940s but had no plan to cap its returns at 6 percent forever. By 1974, without further governmental intervention, MetLife would start paying full taxes and be free to raise all rents to the market rate.[3]

In the second burst of real activism by Stuy Town tenants, a group led by Charles Lyman decided to get together to explore ways to protect themselves and their community after 1974. A dozen or so residents started to meet regularly in the office of their New York State assembly-man, Andrew Stein, across the street from Stuy Town on First Avenue and 18th Street. Over coffee and doughnuts, they would sit on folding chairs and strategize with Stein's staff about their options. One of the members of Assemblyman Stein's team was a young intern named Steven Sanders, whose first exposure to politics was Kennedy's 1960 speech, but now was volunteering for the office in his final year of City College. Sanders sat in on all the meetings of this group, which was calling itself the Stuyvesant Town Tenants Association, and listened to the passion and concern in their voices. "With the expiration of the tax breaks, they saw a light at the end of the tunnel. And that light was from a train coming right at them," Sanders recalled.[4]

Lyman and his group began to print flyers, to make phone calls to neighbors, and to educate them about what was about to happen. While they hoped to organize the tens of thousands of Stuyvesant Town residents in support of new rent protections for their neighbors, the Republican-controlled state political establishment in Albany was slowly working to chip away at such protections across New York State. At the time, there were two types of legislatively imposed rent protections for New Yorkers: rent control and rent stabilization. Established during the post–World War I housing shortage, rent control applied to apartments in buildings with three or more units that were either constructed or converted to residential use prior to February 1, 1947. Under rent control, a landlord was allowed to raise a tenant's rent by 7.5 percent every year until a cap, or a "maximum base rent," was reached. Rent stabilization was created in 1969 and applied to some 325,000 apartments that had been built after February 1, 1947, and another 75,000 that had come out of rent control for a variety of reasons. For rent-stabilized apartments, rents were set by a Rent Guidelines Board, appointed by the mayor, which evaluated landlord costs, vacancy rates, and financing to make its determinations. In 1971, Peter Cooper was already subject to rent stabilization, but Stuy Town was not, because it was governed by the terms of MetLife's contract with the city.[5]

New York's Republican governor Nelson Rockefeller was philosophically opposed to all these tenant protections. Rent control, he argued, had "worked to the detriment of the very groups it was designed to help"

Figure 2.1. When Stuy Town opened, MetLife rented apartments only to white residents, and its chairman, Frederick Ecker, famously pronounced "Negroes and whites don't mix." This set the stage for an early civil rights battle, with Stuy Town tenants pushing back against their landlord's racist policies. Photo credit: Beam Living, Stuyvesant Town / Peter Cooper Village Archives.

and had led to building abandonment by landlords and the reluctance of investors to build new housing.[6] In 1971, with Rockefeller's support, the Republican-controlled State Legislature passed a landlord-friendly law referred to colloquially as vacancy decontrol. Just as Stuy Town tenants were looking to gain protections against rent hikes, vacancy decontrol allowed landlords to weaken existing rent-stabilization laws by giving them the right to deregulate individual units when a tenant moved out or died.

Tenant rights advocates had been opposing such a measure for over twenty years, and they had the backing of New York City officials. When the bill passed the state legislature, Mayor John Lindsay urged Governor Rockefeller to veto it, saying that it would force middle-class residents out of the city and provide "irresistible incentives" to landlords to harass tenants in rent-protected apartments. While the law provided for stiff penalties for landlords who harassed tenants, landlords had many tools at their disposal to make a tenant's life difficult, like failing to make repairs, or even initiating small construction annoyances—which by themselves were not considered harassment under the law. "A landlord could delay making toilet repairs or calling in a plumber," said Benjamin Altman, the New York City housing commissioner at the time. "Why, I know one landlord who ran water on his roof so that it came through the ceiling of an apartment just to get rid of a tenant." Commissioner Altman called an emergency meeting of tenant advocates and predicted immediate and regular harassment of tenants if the law went into effect.[7] Speaking at the meeting, his colleague Albert Walsh, the housing and development administrator, anticipated "increased polarization of the segments of society as the middle-ground meeting place—the middle class—leaves town."[8]

Despite the warnings, on July 1, 1971, in one of the darkest days for tenants in New York State, vacancy decontrol of rent-stabilized apartments went into effect. In anticipation of the new law, some landlords had begun to hold back, or "warehouse" rent-protected apartments in order to rent them to a friend or family member after July 1, who would voluntarily vacate it after a month. By doing that, a landlord could take it out of rent stabilization completely. Other landlords were trying to take advantage of the decontrol law by moving some tenants, such as recipients of government assistance, from one apartment to another, or more aggressively suing people who were late paying their rents. They hoped to create the vacancy they needed to allow them to remove the apartment from rent stabilization, to jack up the rents, and to find new tenants who were willing and able to pay the higher rates. Vacancy decontrol created a direct financial incentive for building owners to push rent-protected tenants out of their apartments.[9]

Not surprisingly, over the next two years, 144,000 apartments lost their rent protections. The city commissioner of rent and housing maintenance, Nathan Leventhal, said that harassment complaints to his office had doubled since the state law on vacancy decontrol had taken effect.[10] Trying to slow the tide, in 1973 Leventhal announced a new policy of regularly publishing the names of landlords who were fined for harassing tenants. "If public exposure will cow those who would deliberately make others suffer," said Leventhal, "then we will spotlight these names continually."

Vacancy decontrol had served some of its purposes, but at the same time, Governor Rockefeller was starting to feel pressure from the bad press it was creating for him. In October 1973, the governor asked Assemblyman Andrew Stein—coincidentally the representative of Stuy Town, and a Democrat—to study the impacts of the 1971 initiative as part of a Governor's Commission on Living Costs and the Economy. Some, like Mayor Lindsay, saw this as an admission by the governor of how bad this policy truly had been for New York City tenants.[11]

Stein's commission studied the effects of the law and, not surprisingly, declared vacancy decontrol to have been a total disaster. The policy, Stein asserted, had led not only to significant rent increases but also produced few of the benefits that landlords had predicted. "Vacancy decontrol has neither stimulated new building construction, stopped abandonment, spurred renovation nor has it brought substantial new money into the city's housing stock," he found. The Stein Commission recommended that full-scale rent regulation be reimposed. The real estate lobby challenged the report, saying that Stein had overlooked all of the positive impacts, such as the significant increase in new construction in 1972.[12]

Lyman and the newly formed Tenants Association (TA) watched closely as the rent protection debate proceeded in Albany and as their local assemblyman Andrew Stein took on the real estate industry. Having seen what he could accomplish in Albany, tenants knew that Stein and his staff, which now formally included their neighbor Steven Sanders, would play a pivotal role in negotiations when the Stuy Town contract expired in 1974.

MetLife was less worried about the upcoming contract expiration. Under the terms of its agreement, the city had given MetLife a property tax abatement that froze the real estate taxes in Stuy Town at the assessed value of the property from 1949, a mere $13.5 million, much less than its $89.3 million value in 1974—an 85 percent tax abatement. While losing the abatement was going to affect MetLife's tax status in Stuy Town, ultimately MetLife likely planned to pass along the bill to tenants by raising the rents to the market rate.[13]

But for the nineteen thousand tenants in eighty-eight hundred rental units in Stuy Town, the future was suddenly very uncertain. Rents that averaged $190 to $230—about $1,000 in 2020 dollars—could have more than doubled overnight.[14] On the cusp of the expiration of the 1943 agreement, there hadn't been a more urgent moment for the community to organize since Stuy Town tenants had successfully moved the needle on the cause of racial justice in 1951. This was an existential crisis for the middle-class tenants in Stuy Town—many of whom had moved there right after the war and could not afford such an increase. With the support of Assemblyman Stein, the Tenants Association decided to argue for a change in state law that would put Stuy Town under rent stabilization, and more slowly phase in MetLife's taxes.

To accomplish this, the Tenants Association had to approach the New York State Legislature, and the governor, for relief. In 1974, that meant that Republicans, already hostile to rent regulations, needed to be on board with the outcome. Ordinarily, this would have been impossible, but on December 18, 1973, Rockefeller resigned as governor to focus on a presidential bid, and he was replaced by Malcolm Wilson, his lieutenant governor. Wilson, along with other local Republicans, was trying to find ways to distinguish himself from the national party, which was reeling from President Nixon's Watergate scandal. Wilson had to figure out how to handle not only Rockefeller's vacancy decontrol policies generally, but also the Stuy Town situation. Tenant advocates that year saw an opportunity and made a lot of noise for reforms. The growing Stuyvesant Town Tenants Association was threatening mass demonstrations at MetLife's corporate headquarters and had called on elected officials for support, flooding their mailboxes with letters and tying up their phones.[15]

Republican Roy Goodman was the state senator for Stuy Town and an unusual breed among Republicans, because he represented tens of thousands of left-leaning New York City tenants. Goodman called Stuyvesant Town and Peter Cooper Village the "Anchor of Manhattan."[16] In the middle of the 1974 debate over the rent laws, Senator Goodman crossed party lines to join Assemblyman Stein in advocating for the relief the Stuy Town Tenants Association sought for when the contract expired. They formally proposed exactly what the tenants wanted: a ten-year phase-in of the mammoth increase in property taxes, and inclusion of Stuyvesant Town apartments under the rules of rent stabilization, along with the already covered Peter Cooper Village units.

The Tenants Association joined the cause of tenant advocates around the city to endorse broader reforms, like ending vacancy decontrol altogether. Seeing his electoral fortunes hanging in the balance, Governor Wilson agreed to bipartisan legislation called the Emergency Tenant Protection Act (ETPA), which extended the rent stabilization law to all previously decontrolled apartments. It also gave tenants a legal right to a lease renewal and totally eliminated vacancy decontrol. After the ETPA, when an apartment became vacant, it could only be rented to the next tenant for precisely the same rent, eliminating all incentives to harass an existing resident. Also included in the session's reforms was subjecting Stuy Town to rent stabilization. It was the second time in the community's young history that Stuyvesant Town tenants had vocally fought for and won a public policy battle, and they were beginning to understand their own power. "We waged an active campaign to arouse public and political support and to crack 'Met Life,'" Lyman crowed. "We hit them where it hurt, in their public image," he said.[17]

While the tenants cheered the inclusion of Stuyvesant Town in the rent-stabilization system and the elimination of vacancy decontrol, these were just the first of the modern organizing challenges for the newly formed Tenants Association. Because the rent-stabilization laws themselves expired every few years, these tenants almost immediately had the sense that their protections could disappear at any moment. Moreover, the tenants now had to contend yearly with the city's Rent Guidelines Board, which had the power to decide how much a landlord could increase their rents. When Andrew Stein was elected Manhattan borough president in 1977,

Steven Sanders succeeded him as the local assemblyman and focused on these questions full time.

Sanders had quickly risen through the ranks of the young Tenants Association even while he was an aide to Stein, serving as the organization's vice president and later as its president. It was in that context that Assemblyman Sanders met a thirty-year-old construction worker named Al Doyle—the man who, as a boy, had unknowingly stood in the same crowd with Sanders to welcome John F. Kennedy to Stuyvesant Town. Doyle and his wife, Pat Sallin, had joined the Tenants Association because they were angry that Mayor Ed Koch's Rent Guidelines Board was approving double-digit percentage increases on rent-stabilized tenants.[18] The couple enjoyed being advocates for their neighbors and showed up personally at the Rent Guidelines Board hearings to protest the increases, and went to Albany to lobby for the renewal of rent stabilization every few years. Sanders watched them quickly become two of the hardest-working members of the Tenants Association. "Doyle was a man of quality and humility," Sanders said. "He was unassuming and was not looking to be involved for personal credit or aggrandizement. He brought a certain kind of calm to the association. He was a steadying force." Doyle and Sanders, longtime neighbors who had never met before, struck up an easy friendship.[19]

Doyle became president of the Tenants Association in 1989, and his first big test came in 1993, when rent stabilization was again set to expire. Much like the dynamic in 1974, every time these laws came up for renewal was a crisis moment for Stuy Town and Peter Cooper tenants. The loss of rent stabilization would mean that rents would shoot up basically overnight. Doyle, Sallin, TA member Jo-Ann Polise, and other Stuy Town residents went to Albany to make the case for renewal. They stayed in dingy motels and spent their July Fourth holiday weekend approaching every legislator they could find. While they succeeded in getting the rent-stabilization laws renewed that year, vacancy decontrol—like a zombie resistant to all deadly force—was reintroduced into the conversation. In exchange for renewing rent stabilization, Senate Republicans insisted on bringing back vacancy decontrol for apartments that had already reached a legal rent of $2,000 per month. There were very few apartments in the city that rented for that amount at the time, and it passed as a temporary measure that lasted three months, from July to October 1993.[20]

Figure 2.2. Al Doyle, the longest-serving president of the Tenants Association, testifying at City Hall before Mayor Michael Bloomberg in support of the renewal of rent stabilization. Doyle, who is both gentle and cautious in nature, was yet one of the loudest and most respected tenant voices in New York. Copyright © 2015 by Anne Greenberg.

While a weak law itself, the state vacancy decontrol law had a powerful subcomponent, which allowed local municipalities like New York City to expand the law's effect. With a Republican mayor, Rudolph Giuliani, and rising numbers of foreclosures in New York City, the real estate industry saw an opportunity to expand on its gains. Joe Strasburg, who had served as chief of staff to the city council speaker, Peter Vallone Sr., had just moved over to become president of the Rent Stabilization Association, the somewhat ironically named advocacy group for landlords. Coincidentally, Strasburg had lived for many years in a Stuy Town rent-stabilized apartment and was active in the Tenants Association. Strasburg and Speaker Vallone put together a coalition in the New York City Council (which became New York City's exclusive legislative branch in 1989 after the US Supreme Court called the composition of the Board of Estimate unconstitutional) to make vacancy decontrol permanent in New York City. The bill they pushed and ultimately passed in 1994 allowed an automatic 20 percent increase to base rents whenever there was a vacancy and provided for vacancy decontrol when any apartments in the city rented for over $2,000. Strasburg framed the issue as an egalitarian reform, a way to force rich renters to cough up their fair share. For many city council members in Brooklyn, Queens, and the Bronx, rents over $2,000 felt wildly remote. After all, in 1994, the median rent in New York City was under $600, and very few tenants outside Manhattan's fanciest neighborhoods were paying $2,000 a month or more. Strasburg argued that vacancy decontrol was a way for small building owners to maintain their buildings and to survive, lifting the city's depressed housing values. The city council passed the measure by a vote of 28 to 18, and it was signed by Mayor Giuliani. Suddenly, there was again a strong incentive for an owner to get a moderately priced apartment vacant. Three years later, the State Legislature expanded the benefits to landlords and allowed them to make physical improvements to individual vacant apartments, and to apply one-fortieth (2.5 percent) of the cost of the improvements to the base rent. The improvements allowed landlords to get rents over the critical $2,000 mark, pull them out of rent stabilization, and rent the units to the next tenants at much higher market rates.[21]

Consider a two-bedroom apartment renting for $1,000 a month, well below the $2,000 threshold that would allow for deregulation. When the occupant died or moved out, the owner was entitled to a 20 percent vacancy bonus—bringing the unit up to $1,200. An investment of $32,000 in apartment renovations—like a dishwasher, granite countertops, cabinets, a wine fridge, and a stainless-steel refrigerator, for example—would allow an owner to add one-fortieth of that cost, or $800, to the base rent. The rent of the vacant apartment was now $2,000, and the owner was allowed to deregulate it as a matter of law. That $2,000 apartment could now be rented for nearly $3,000 (which was the average for Manhattan apartments south of 96th Street in 2000), and by 2019, for over $5,000 a month.[22]

Of course, not every building in the city had a landlord who could invest $32,000 in improvements into a single unit just to raise the base rent, but deep-pocketed MetLife could certainly do it in Stuy Town. And with these new state laws in place, MetLife was well positioned to take advantage of them. MetLife's corporate status also was changing in a way that even required it. By April 6, 2000, Robert Benmosche, the chairman of the MetLife's board, had taken MetLife through the process of becoming a public company.[23] With the company subject to regulatory filings and greater public disclosures, shareholders were now in a position to demand greater performance from MetLife's real estate assets. MetLife added two new law firms—Greenberg Traurig and Borah Goldstein—to its complement of legal counsel, and these firms slowly and steadily worked in concert to use vacancy decontrol, plus individual apartment improvements and major capital improvements (which could be added to the rent of existing tenants), in order to break the units out of rent stabilization. Al Doyle and his compatriots objected to these additional charges almost immediately, and the table was set for conflict between MetLife and its increasingly agitated tenant group with their neighbor and assemblyman at their side.

Sona Holman, known to her friends as Soni, met Peter Cooper resident Karl Fink at a party in the Berkshires in July 1961. Karl was a widower who had two kids, and in the early days of their relationship the couple spent most of their time at Soni's apartment on East 16th Street. Karl was an industrial designer who lived with his children in a two-bedroom Peter Cooper apartment with spectacular views of the East River. One weekend, when Karl's kids were out of town, he invited Soni over to his place for dinner. When she got there, Karl was still getting ready, and Soni had a few minutes to make herself at home. She came in, looked around, and was stunned by the magnificent view of the river from his living room window. In the early stages of her relationship, considering the prospect of becoming a stepmom to Karl's kids, Soni thought to herself, "I don't care if those children have two heads. I'll take him, and I'll take that view!" Soni and Karl got married in October 1961, and she moved into his Peter Cooper apartment at 601 East 20th Street.[24]

Soni Fink was employed as a feature writer for *Women's Wear Daily*. She authored a book titled *How to Lie about Your Age* and penned a lighthearted column called "Constant Consumer," which paid her an extra fifty dollars a week. She had gotten adjusted to her life in Peter Cooper and over the years got to know many of her neighbors. One afternoon in 1980, Fink was riding down the elevator of her building on her way to work, and a fifteen-year-old boy, looking forlorn, got on at the sixth floor. That boy shyly said hello to her, and she looked him up and down. "What's a fine young man like you doing in an elevator like this?" she asked him, with a mischievous smile. His name was John Marsh. His

Figure 2.3. A normal day in Peter Cooper Village in a photo that was taken in the 1950s, facing south toward 20th Street. It looks very much like this today. Photo credit: Beam Living, Stuyvesant Town / Peter Cooper Village Archives.

parents were recently divorced, and he was having a very hard time coping with the changes. Fink could sense that he was feeling down and invited him up to her apartment for a visit. Marsh agreed, and went upstairs when his school day was over, admiring Fink's tidy but warm apartment, decorated with beautiful art on the walls and unique Nakashima wooden furniture. He also took note of this older woman's red hair and eyes—one bigger than the other—which he thought were brimming with intelligence. Despite the age difference, Fink and Marsh became friends and started to have more regular visits after school. She had no kids of her own and enjoyed looking after this skinny boy in her building.[25]

Marsh's divorced parents—a former World War II reconnaissance pilot named Jack, and a public school teacher named Frances—lived at opposite ends of Peter Cooper Village. They had moved into Peter Cooper in 1964, one year before Marsh was born, and later sent Marsh to P.S. 40, the local public school. Marsh was only eighteen years old when his father moved out of the city, leaving him alone in his Peter Cooper apartment. By age twenty-five, he was working for American Express as a data security expert and paying his own bills. Marsh took note of MetLife's capital improvement charges that were now regularly appearing on his rent bill, which were causing his rent to slowly creep up. One afternoon in 1999, Marsh pulled out a Tenants Association flyer from the mailbox in his building's lobby and read that MetLife was planning to charge tenants for yet another capital improvement that Marsh felt they didn't need, and which he couldn't afford. He went online for more information and was surprised that he couldn't find a website for the Tenants Association. It was the early days of the internet, but Marsh was dismayed that his own community's tenants group did not have any presence online. Marsh asked Fink whether she thought he should offer to help them out, and she encouraged him to get involved. He called the telephone number on the flyer and introduced himself as a longtime resident who wanted to help them expand the community's presence on the web. A volunteer named Virginia Rosario returned his call and suggested that he come to a meeting in Al Doyle's Stuy Town apartment with the all-volunteer board of the Tenants Association.[26]

Two weeks later, in Doyle's apartment, Marsh met a small group that included Doyle and his wife, Pat Sallin, Virginia Rosario, and Susan Steinberg (the vice president). Steinberg shook Marsh's hand with a smile and welcomed him. Steinberg was happy to see a new face in the mix. A resident of the community for sixteen years, she was a relative newcomer in the group. She had moved into 5 Stuyvesant Oval, with her pet iguana, from an apartment on the Upper East Side in 1980 to be closer to her parents, who already lived in the neighborhood. A marketing professional for the Gruzen Partnership, an architecture firm, Steinberg decided to join the Tenants Association after attending a community meeting where she watched Al Doyle and Jo-Ann Polise, another active member, parry questions from frazzled neighbors about brown water. The more animated of the two, Polise was giving a pitch to the audience to be active and engaged in defense of their rights. As the meeting closed, Doyle invited people to submit their names for a seat on the Tenants Association board if they wanted to serve. Steinberg went home after the meeting and thought, "OK, I pay my taxes, vote at all elections, and serve on juries—but what else do I do as a citizen? How do I contribute to my community?" She joined Doyle and Polise on the Tenants Association board in 1996. She had already served a few years in the role when Marsh walked into the meeting.[27] With Doyle, Steinberg, and Marsh all in the same room, the modern Tenants Association was born.

When Doyle called the group to order, the top item of business was one of MetLife's newest major capital improvements (or MCIs), for a new electrical system in Peter Cooper. Doyle explained that rents had been creeping up because MetLife was in the middle of a spending spree—ultimately totaling $120 million in capital improvements—which meant permanent rent increases for people in the community. Not all of them were universally considered improvements by residents, either. In 1991, for example, MetLife had initiated a $30 million project to replace all 147,000 windows in Stuy Town and Peter Cooper. After 58,416 twin-pane, gas-filled windows had been installed to improve insulation, 2,000 of them exploded into people's apartments because of pressure irregularities, leaving glass everywhere. But MetLife still tried to pass along the costs to tenants in the form of MCIs. In the now firmly established tradition of Stuyvesant Town tenants, they decided to fight back. With the support of Assemblyman Sanders, the tenants sued MetLife to block the $30 million charge. After three years of litigation, in 1997, MetLife had settled with the tenants for a $4 million rent rebate, which was the largest rent rebate ever awarded in a single case involving capital improvements to rent-stabilized tenants.[28]

Now, the tenants in Doyle and Sallin's apartment were discussing irregularities with the new electrical system that MetLife was implementing. These irregularities had been reported to Doyle, coincidentally, by none other than Marsh's neighbor, Soni Fink. Fink was not yet formally part of the Tenants Association, but like Marsh, she was getting increasingly annoyed by the charges on her rent bill, too. One MCI application after the next had hit her and her neighbors, and the bills were adding up. One afternoon in 2000, Fink came off the elevator in her building and saw that the electrical closet was open. She had heard that MetLife was in the process of upgrading the electrical system in Peter Cooper and struck up a conversation with the contractor who had unlocked the closet. He wiped his brow and politely responded to this diminutive woman asking him questions, explaining that he was just changing the wires in the building. As she chatted with him, she peered around his back and had a closer look at what he was doing. She was surprised to see cables labeled "RCN"—a private cable company—being installed by the contractor, and asked him if he wanted to come into her apartment for a soda. He agreed, and she probed more. "Why do you have RCN cables in there?" she asked him. "It's cheaper to do it this way," said the electrician as he downed his Coca-Cola, not realizing he was sharing information that would eventually form the basis of a legal claim. Fink made a mental note and immediately called Al Doyle to ask him if he knew that MetLife was installing wiring for a private cable company at the same time it was upgrading Peter Cooper's electrical systems. After some investigating, Doyle learned that MetLife had a side deal with RCN to install its cable television and phone infrastructure at the same time that MetLife was opening the walls.[29]

At the meeting in his apartment that night, Doyle explained to Marsh and the rest of the assembled tenant activists that MetLife intended to pass all $30 million of the improvements for the electrical system on to Peter Cooper residents, with no reduction based on any economic benefit to MetLife from the RCN agreement. The increases were going to amount to $135 a month for a one-bedroom apartment and $170 for a two-bedroom apartment. The average two-bedroom apartment was renting for about $1,000 at the time.[30]

Calm in demeanor, Marsh had a friendly boy-next-door appeal, but his voice rose as he asked the group how MetLife could possibly be allowed to do this. Steinberg smiled at the eagerness of their new member, as Doyle gently asked Marsh if he would be interested in helping to fight back against this MCI. Marsh agreed and, when the meeting was over, sat down with the TA's lawyer, Jack Lester, to learn how to file a challenge to a landlord's application for an MCI like this one. Lester told Marsh that the most effective way to challenge it was to get the affected tenants—as many of them as possible—to file a formal objection to the New York State housing agency. That meant that Marsh needed to find a way to get the five thousand residents of the twenty-one affected Peter Cooper buildings to sign papers in support of the challenge. He had been around the community long enough to know that it was going to be very difficult to explain the minutiae of this regulatory filing to his neighbors, many of whom were original tenants and now in their eighties.[31]

Marsh went up to Fink's apartment to ask for help. As she sipped on a drink, Fink cheekily reminded Marsh that she was the one who had discovered MetLife's apparent scam. Marsh explained that the Tenants Association was now trying to challenge the MCI, and he needed someone to explain to Peter Cooper's residents the complicated rules in plain language. Who better to do that than a writer for *Women's Wear Daily*, Fink thought to herself. She polished off her drink and agreed to be Marsh's communications director. Marsh called upon a few other neighbors who could help him go door to door in Peter Cooper Village and explain how unjust it was that MetLife was passing the entire cost of its rewiring program along to tenants at the same time that it was getting paid by RCN.[32]

When word of this controversial MCI spread in the community, Marsh's network grew. People called the TA to volunteer, and Marsh deftly gave them a specific role, either as a building leader or a floor captain. When Marsh did not have a representative in a particular building, he scoured the TA's existing lists for names he recognized, and made calls to find someone to support the Tenants Association. With Fink's carefully drafted but catchy explanations, Marsh and his team started to knock on doors, asking people to sign on to the application. Doyle and Assemblyman Sanders encouraged Marsh to push as hard as he could for participants, so if someone was not home, he would make a note and go back for a second visit. To Marsh's surprise, despite their own economic interest to challenge this MCI, many neighbors responded in disgust. "How dare you go up against Mother Met," they said. "You should be grateful. We have such a good landlord. They love us." For many of the senior citizens with roots in the military and a more conservative approach, signing a government document to challenge their landlord was a line they would not cross.[33]

On the other hand, all tenants were facing the increasing economic burdens of the MCIs, and many were getting less patient with their supposedly benevolent landlord. Marsh made visit after visit and asked his neighbors why, if MetLife was so benevolent, was it constantly passing along these questionable charges?

Assemblyman Sanders reinforced these themes at the broader community meetings of the Tenants Association. While many specific MCIs did not affect every resident, the community meetings had become a productive place for the TA to talk to large groups of tenants, to explain these matters more generally, and to give people a chance to ask questions. They were ordinarily held at Junior High School 104, on 20th Street, just west of First Avenue. JHS 104 had an auditorium that could accommodate nearly four hundred tenants. As MetLife got more aggressive with its MCI program in the 2000s, there was rarely an empty seat in the house. Doyle tapped the personable Steinberg to stand onstage in front of hundreds of tenants at these community meetings, a task that the shyer Doyle did not enjoy. Steinberg had a relaxed demeanor and naturally spoke slowly and deliberately, which was appealing to many senior citizens in the community. While Marsh would run around at the back of the auditorium signing up volunteers, Steinberg would calmly invite Sanders and other elected officials to speak and give people a chance to have their questions answered.

In August 2000, Assemblyman Sanders took to the stage of the junior high school to rail at MetLife for its outrageous "double dipping" on its RCN agreement. He argued that MetLife's alleged $30 million cost for the electrical rewiring was surely offset by income they were getting from RCN. Sanders held up a marketing agreement between MetLife and RCN and said that RCN had compensated MetLife for the access to the buildings and gave them a percentage of every new subscriber. In front of the crowd, Sanders accused MetLife of outright fraud for omitting significant revenue as a result of that agreement and passing the full $30 million in expenses on to Peter Cooper residents.[34]

Behind the scenes, Sanders and Lester continued to push Marsh to get more Peter Cooper residents to sign on to the tenants' petition. Sanders felt that the Republican-controlled Division of Housing and Community Renewal in Albany could be bent to the prevailing political will if enough tenants were on the record as upset. Marsh took that as a challenge and, through his own tenacity and sheer determination, got residents of 70 percent of the apartments of Peter Cooper Village to individually sign on to the petition. This impressive result required many months of labor and gave Marsh a chance to build up a large network of hundreds of volunteers, many of whom had never done any work for the Tenants Association before. "Marsh was an organizing force," said Doyle. While the DHCR ultimately approved the MCI for the electrical work—with no reduction for the RCN deal—nobody could ignore that the Stuy Town tenants' power was at a peak, much as it had been in 1951, when residents were fighting for civil rights, and in 1974, in support of key rent protections.[35]

After the RCN conflict in 2000, Sanders, Doyle, and the Tenants Association found themselves more regularly at war with MetLife. Tenants felt that MetLife was slowly abandoning its mission to protect middle-class residents. In 2002, MetLife quietly and without any comment whatsoever removed a plaque that had been dedicated to Frederick Ecker on August 30, 1947. Ecker, the MetLife chairman who had initiated the property's development, had been honored with the plaque on the occasion of his eightieth birthday. It celebrated his creating and delivering Stuy Town and other projects "so that families of moderate means might live in health, comfort and dignity in parklike communities" and expressed hope that Stuy Town would set a pattern of "private enterprise devoted to public service." Ordinarily, progressive minded-residents might have enthusiastically cheered the removal of a monument to this known racist, who, when Stuy Town first opened, had insisted on the whites-only rental policy. But many tenants were outraged by the monument's sudden removal, because to them, the words on the plaque were so important. If Stuy Town was no longer for people of moderate means, then whom exactly was it for? Between the MCI charges and this, it felt to many tenants like MetLife was turning its back on its commitment to public service. At around the same time, MetLife increased the height of the fences around the property in a way that made it feel more like a gated community, and gave a reward to its building porters to report residents who, against Stuy Town policy, were harboring a pet in their apartments. "Met Life had always been a company that you could work with. They didn't seem to only care about the bottom line. They cared about the welfare of their tenants. That started to change. It was almost palpable," said Assemblyman Sanders.[36]

The final battle between MetLife and the Tenants Association came in 2004, when MetLife decided to implement an electronic key card system for entry to the front door of its buildings. Since there have never been doormen in Stuy Town or Peter Cooper buildings, residents always had a common metal key to enter their building's front door, and individual metal keys for their own apartments. MetLife's property manager Adam Rose, copresident of Rose Associates, planned for the new electronic key cards to replace the common metal keys for the front doors.

Electronic key cards, which could be issued and discontinued with a single computer keystroke, would give much more control over who was gaining entry to the buildings, and importantly, allow Met Life to build a case against a tenant who was not using his apartment as a primary residence, which was required under rent stabilization. To many of the aging World War II veterans, this move smacked of totalitarianism and an opportunity for an oppressive landlord to watch, and even to control, their movements. Questions of surveillance had been hotly debated after the World Trade Center attacks of September 11, 2001, when Congress passed the Patriot Act, making it easier for the government to monitor phone and email communications, to collect bank records, and to follow people's activities on the internet.[37] In that context, MetLife was insisting that tenants not only get cards, which expired periodically, but also to include their names and photographs on them.

The fears by tenants about how the data were going to be used were not fantastical. Rose Associates, on behalf of MetLife, had already started to take legal action against tenants they believed were not using their apartments as their primary residence. Because vacancy decontrol gave MetLife the opportunity to raise rents by creating vacancies, the concern was that MetLife only wanted the electronic key card data in order to prove that some tenants were not living in their rent-stabilized unit for more than 180 days (the legal minimum) and to provide grounds for eviction. Tenants worried that MetLife could use this data improperly, by manufacturing a legal claim, for example, out of an extended vacation, or an absence to care for a sick relative in another state. While nobody, including the Tenants Association, supported tenants abusing the law, they rightly feared that vacancy decontrol was a strong incentive for a landlord to evict people, and the TA did not want to give MetLife yet another weapon. "This is not security, it is surveillance," Sanders hollered to another packed Tenants Association meeting at Junior High School 104. "It smacks of totalitarian police state tactics." Sanders urged the crowd, made up of mostly senior citizens, to stand up and shout together "Don't Get Met! Don't Get Met!" The footage of hundreds of senior citizens standing up—slowly—and hollering at MetLife was replayed on the evening news.[38]

Much as it had done with the RCN claim, the Tenants Association decided to challenge MetLife's key card program at the state DHCR, arguing that it invaded tenants' privacy and illegally reduced their service under the rent-stabilization law. The association threatened a rent strike in opposition, and with Assemblyman Sanders joining as a plaintiff, the TA sued MetLife in court over the key cards. MetLife responded by taking the unusual step of cutting off all formal contact with the community's local state assemblyman. The days of a docile group of tenants viewing MetLife as "Mother Met" were over. The role that the increasingly aggressive Tenants Association was playing on behalf of its thirty thousand neighbors was becoming more visible to the tenant body, and it was coming at exactly the right time.

3

An Unexpected Challenge

Harry Giannoulis, one of MetLife's lobbyists, called me in my city council office on July 18, 2006. I wasn't expecting to hear from him. Giannoulis was a partner at the Parkside Group, a political consultancy and lobbying shop best known for its work with the Queens County Democratic Party and the New York State Senate Democrats. I was first introduced to Parkside through Giannoulis's partner, Evan Stavisky, whom I had met a year earlier when I first ran for office. Over iced coffees at Starbucks on 29th Street and Park Avenue South, we talked about the work the firm did for candidates, as well as its lobbying efforts. In that conversation, Stavisky disclosed to me that his firm represented MetLife, and paused for effect. As a Peter Cooper resident and first-time council candidate at the time, I knew, as did Stavisky, that MetLife was going to play some role in my political life—I just didn't know what it was.

Now my phone was ringing, and Stavisky's partner Giannoulis was on the line. I was in the middle of a staff meeting around a small conference table in the middle of my twentieth-floor office near Grand Central

Terminal, and I stepped into the corner to take the call. Giannoulis told me that MetLife was exploring the possibility of putting Stuyvesant Town and Peter Cooper Village up for sale, and that he just wanted me to know before it became a public matter. Nothing was definite; the company was just considering its options, he said. He promised to follow up with more detail. The call lasted less than a minute.

I returned to my meeting, where I shared this tidbit with the group. My office liaison to Stuy Town, Justine Almada, a smart, young Wesleyan graduate, looked at me nervously and then peppered me with questions: "He only said that they were 'exploring' it?" "What does this mean, exactly?" I didn't have any answers for her and held out hope that this was just idle speculation, merely a remote possibility. MetLife was far from the perfect landlord, but in my whole life as a resident I had never considered that there could be anyone else. Still quite green, I did not yet appreciate that lobbyists don't make phone calls to council members in the early stages of their clients' exploratory process. They make the call when they absolutely have to, as a courtesy, just before news breaks. And that moment was now.

When Giannoulis made his portentous call, I had been in office for only six months as representative of the New York City Council's Fourth District. When I ran for the council one year earlier, I made the case that I would be an ideal advocate for the community, as someone who had been born and raised in Peter Cooper Village. Stuy Town and Peter Cooper had an outsize concentration of Democratic voters in the Fourth Council District. While the district ran from 14th to 97th Streets, including Turtle Bay and Tudor City, Central Park South, and much of the Upper East Side, fully 30 percent of the voting Democrats came from Stuy Town and Peter Cooper. That was where the election was going to be won.

As a political matter, because MetLife had used vacancy decontrol to take about a quarter of the units in Stuy Town out of rent stabilization, for the first time in the community's history there were now two classes of renters—the traditional rent-stabilized residents, and newer tenants living in nonregulated apartments, paying market rates. After leaving for college and law school, I had returned to Peter Cooper Village and rented one of the market-rate units. Even though I had grown up in a rent-stabilized apartment, and my parents still lived in it, I more resembled the newer residents, who were mostly young professionals and families who tended to be transient and not too focused on local affairs.

As I started building a campaign for the city council in 2004, I was working as a litigation associate at Paul, Weiss, Rifkind, Wharton & Garrison LLP, a big New York law firm. I was also thinking about how I might get more active in local affairs, including with my local tenants association. I had met both Doyle and Sanders when I was a sophomore in high school in 1988, volunteering on my first campaign being run out of the Jefferson Democratic Club on East 21st Street. I was working for a Democratic district leader candidate named Andrew Kulak, who sent me all throughout the Stuy Town and Peter Cooper buildings slipping materials under my neighbors' doors. I perfected methods to sneak into the doormen-free buildings, and I would regularly time myself on how fast I could stuff a hundred apartments with flyers. I was hooked by the excitement of the campaign.

At the time, Doyle was the newly elected president of the TA, and Sanders had just finished a decade of service as the local assemblyman. Kulak won his election, and I became a regular at the Jefferson Club, right next to Ess-a-Bagel. The club was a gathering place for active tenants and local Democratic leaders. On Monday and Thursday nights, the club would open its doors, and local elected officials like Assemblyman Sanders would be there to offer an update and to answer questions. Al Doyle made a point of being there too. He felt it was important for Stuy Town tenants to have not only organizing, but also political strength. The meeting space was small and narrow, filled with folding chairs and paraphernalia of past elections. I loved the energy, the excitement, and even the aroma of the Jefferson Club, which was a mix of cigar smoke and bagels. Doyle and I saw each other regularly, and he was always kind to me, even though I was a high school student with no obvious reason to be there. He certainly did not fit the stereotype of a firebrand tenant leader, and while others would walk right by me, he always remembered my name. Doyle and I volunteered together on other local campaigns, like that of Carolyn Maloney when she was redistricted and had to run for the city council in 1990 in our area, in the district that I later came to represent.

By the time I became a candidate for public office in 2004, Al Doyle— who still lived in Stuy Town—was the longest-serving president of the

Stuyvesant Town Peter Cooper Village Tenants Association. He worked for a firm that managed construction projects but spent most of his free time thinking about how to protect the interests of his neighbors. Over many years of battling MetLife, Doyle, along with Assemblyman Sanders, became the most identifiable name in the community. The Tenants Association under Doyle's leadership, and with the regular support of John Marsh and Susan Steinberg, had gotten bigger and more influential. As a novice political candidate, I reached out to Doyle to see how I could help out and to be more visibly active in the Tenants Association. I was perfectly willing to do the grunt work of slipping flyers under doors in support of their work—after all, I was an expert—but as a candidate for public office, I also hoped for a high-profile assignment.

I called Doyle in his office and told him that I was looking to volunteer for the Tenants Association. Even though my political motives were transparent, Doyle was open and agreeable, and he said that they would love to have me helping out. I suggested to him that I could organize the newer market-rate tenants, who were a small but growing group within the community. While they represented only 25 percent of the tenant body at the time, they were entirely absent from the Tenants Association board. I chose my words carefully, because I did not want Doyle to feel I was creating a competing tenants association. Doyle, in his very understated way, said that he thought it would be a good idea to do something like what I was proposing. He said that he wanted to introduce me to John Marsh, who could help me get it going.

Marsh had, only four years earlier, come off the RCN battle and had deftly organized the community. Only a handful of years my senior, he acted like a seasoned tenant activist, and he clearly valued my desire to work. In his direct and sincere way, Marsh agreed that the Tenants Association needed something to capture the interest of this newer group of tenants, and he was ready to help me get something off the ground. In an early phone call, we had discussed what we should call this group. "You can't just call this a 'market-rate group.' No. Younger people have *networks*," he told me. Together, we landed on a name: the Market Rate Residents Network.

In 2004, while the Tenants Association was having a fit about MetLife's electronic key card plan, the newer tenants didn't seem to mind it much.

Most of them were already using the cards in their offices, and many saw it as a convenience rather than a burden. They also were not eager to join up with their local tenants association, because with higher rents and roommates, most did not intend to stay for more than a year or two. For those who wanted to remain longer, they were most worried about the prospect of rent increases when lease renewal time came along. We cobbled together a handful of interested market-rate-paying tenants to talk about ways we could support this growing group. "Protect me from getting priced out of here," one of them said pointedly. "Yes—how do I become rent stabilized?" asked another. Unlike the rent-stabilized units, the market-rate units had rents that were far less predictable and could go up by any amount once the lease term was over. Over the course of two meetings, the members of the incipient network decided that the best and only practical course to help market-rate tenants was to establish a way for them to share information about what MetLife was charging other market-rate residents when their leases came up for renewal. We figured that more information would help tenants' bargaining position, and we hoped that people would share their experiences.

Marsh spent a couple of weeks setting up a market-rate message board on the Tenants Association's website, and we invited people to post, and to use it as a resource. Almost immediately, tenants started to share information about rents and to ask questions of their neighbors. "Which leasing agent cut you a break?" "What percentage increase did you see for a 2BR in Stuy Town?" Over a few months, the message board became quite popular, and, in 2004—a time before social media—it was a unique place for people to communicate online.

My official new role in the Tenants Association (as founder of the Market Rate Residents Network) gave me a chance to meet some more neighbors and also to get to know the Stuy Town property management team—including Adam Rose, the sharp-tongued copresident of Rose Associates. Rose Associates had been brought in by MetLife in 2002 to replace the Douglas Elliman firm (just purchased by archrival Prudential) as the manager of Stuy Town. Stuy Town was now the biggest assignment for Rose Associates, and Adam Rose prided himself on knowing every inch of the property. Rose had set April 1, 2005, as the date for key card implementation, when the metal keys would no longer open front doors of buildings. In protest, many tenants simply refused to get the new key cards. This meant that some people—by their own doing—were about to be locked out of their own homes. Once again, Marsh organized the resistance, getting volunteers throughout the buildings to unlock doors for neighbors who refused to get key cards, and even set up shifts of volunteers to act as doormen who would open lobby doors to key card resisters. "Tenants were crazed that we would ruin their lives; everyone was crazed," Rose later remembered. Because of the controversy, Rose had organized the key card launch like a "meticulously coordinated military operation." On the day they planned to flip the switch, they brought out their security force, and Adam Rose was personally in Peter Cooper for twenty-four hours to ensure a smooth roll-out.[1]

The first building to go "live" was 2 Peter Cooper Road, and I decided to go watch to see if there were any fireworks, like senior citizens lying in protest on the sidewalk. Rose introduced himself warmly but could not help but needle me. "How can you care so much about these key cards?" he asked. "Give me a break! The only people worried about these cards are people who are illegally in their apartments!" I laughed at his rather forward approach and told him that I was there to just check out the scene. Moments later, Rose's cell phone rang, and he picked it up. He looked around and then said to me, "C'mon, let's take a walk." I walked with him out to 20th Street, and we got into a deeper conversation, which was mostly Rose playfully challenging me about the Tenants Association's (and my own) advocacy against these cards. What I didn't know at the time was that, typical of MetLife's new approach, executives had connected the Peter Cooper security cameras onto their laptops in a conference room at 200 Park Avenue and saw Rose chatting with me outside of 2 Peter Cooper Road. "You shouldn't be talking to that guy. He's a troublemaker," one of them had told Rose on the call.[2]

While Doyle appreciated my efforts to organize the newer tenants, he was already committed to another candidate running for the city council. Jack Lester, who at that point had served for fifteen years as the lawyer for the Tenants Association, was one of my three opponents in the Democratic primary. Lester and Doyle were joined at the hip, having fought (often with the help of Assemblyman Steven Sanders) against nearly every one of MetLife's MCI applications. In fact, in 2005, the year of the city council election, Assemblyman Sanders, Doyle, and Lester together held town hall meetings in every Peter Cooper building lobby, explaining why the electronic key cards were so problematic. Lester was best known by most tenants for his MCI work, and while the Tenants Association did not win too many of its challenges, Lester managed to induce some delay. Lester did have an Achilles heel, though. John Marsh—who controlled Stuy Town's community's organizing apparatus—had resolved never to support him for anything because he was unhappy with Lester's handling of the RCN case.[3]

The issues in the campaign between me and Lester centered on our experience, as well as improved transportation options for East Siders, stronger public schools, and of course, the need for more affordable housing and stronger rent protections. One issue markedly not on the agenda during the 2005 campaign: the future ownership of Stuy Town. At that point, only one year before the property was to go up for sale, we had no idea that it was even a possibility.

Even though I had lived in the community for most of my life, and my parents were still there, I did not know many of my neighbors. I knew people in the building where I grew up, a handful of people from the Jefferson Democratic Club, and a few more from my recent work with the TA, but I did not go to P.S. 40, the local public school, and while my parents had friends in their own building, they were not otherwise very social in the neighborhood. Despite those disadvantages, I was determined to make the most of my status as a lifelong resident of the community. While Lester distributed campaign flyers around the community signed by Doyle and most of the active members of the Tenants Association, reminding voters that he had served as the community's lawyer for fifteen years, I was successfully picking up endorsements from elected officials and prominent Democrats throughout the rest of the East Side. But for me to beat Lester in Stuy Town and Peter Cooper, I needed to overcome my lack of name recognition and build support for my campaign one neighbor at a time. My campaign consultant, Micah Lasher, described it as our "chicken in every pot, yenta in every building" strategy. One way to have impact with individual residents was to embark on an effort to knock on the doors of every Democrat in Stuyvesant Town and Peter Cooper Village's 110 buildings. With my campaign intern Lindsey Allison at my side, on March 29, 2005, I knocked on my first door.

I soon learned two things about the community. First, nobody had knocked on doors in Stuy Town since Andrew Stein ran for borough president of Manhattan in 1977. Second, I found that Stuy Town residents appreciated the fact that a neighbor might serve them in the city council. "It's your neighbor, Dan Garodnick," I would cheerily say when people asked who it was on the other side of the door. My status as a fellow resident was an instant connection, and I made the most of it. Nearly every night for six months, I knocked on doors, with my parents' door as the very last. My mom had been diagnosed with multiple myeloma, a blood cancer, two years earlier, and even though she had lost most of her hair and had flagging energy, she smiled for the photo op that I generated for *Town & Village* newspaper. She also made phone calls to all her friends and neighbors, asking them to support me. My dad got a baseball cap that said "Dan's Dad" and went out onto every corner of Stuy Town and Peter Cooper to ask people to "Vote for my son."

The Tenants Association did not make formal endorsements, but individuals were free to do so on their own. I begged Marsh and Susan Steinberg to support my council run. I knew it was a long shot, because they were now both vice presidents of the Tenants Association, and Lester was the organization's lawyer. Still, I had gotten a sense that they were not entirely satisfied with Lester, and were open to my candidacy. To my surprise, they both broke with Al Doyle and agreed to endorse me.[4] I hyped the split within the Tenants Association, putting "endorsed by Tenants Association Vice Presidents Susan Steinberg and John Marsh" all over my literature, and held a campaign rally on the steps of Marsh's Peter Cooper building at 601 East 20th Street as we celebrated their joint endorsement. Assemblyman Sanders decided to stay neutral in the race, which was extremely helpful to me, because most residents assumed he would have stuck with Lester, his longtime ally.

I won the Democratic primary on September 13, 2005, with 58 percent of the vote to Lester's second-best 17 percent in a four-candidate race. I won every election district in Stuy Town and Peter Cooper—except for one in Peter Cooper, in which Lester and I wound up tied. I ran up the score in Turtle Bay, Tudor City, and the Upper East Side, the areas where I had secured most of the key endorsements, and where Lester had far less visibility. I ran into Doyle outside his poll site campaigning for Lester

Figure 3.1. As a city council candidate, I knocked on thousands of doors in Peter Cooper and Stuyvesant Town to introduce myself to neighbors. Here I am in a photo op, knocking on the door of my parents, Barbara and David Garodnick, in the rent-stabilized unit where I grew up. Photo credit: Garodnick for New York Campaign.

on the night of the primary, and I invited him to my victory party. Lester, bitter from the loss, had never called to concede—but his campaign manager, Keith Powers, who went on to succeed me in the city council twelve years later—called me on his behalf. I went on to beat Patrick Murphy, a Republican who was endorsed by Mayor Michael Bloomberg, in the general election on November 8, 2005. Doyle and the entire TA leadership became united in support of my candidacy, and I saw Doyle frequently in my campaign office making calls to our neighbors, encouraging them to vote for me.

Six and a half months into my first term, MetLife's lobbyist had just told me that my childhood home, and home to 20 percent of my new constituents, was possibly up for sale. My formal role as a member of the city council was to propose legislation, to conduct oversight of mayoral agencies, and to pass a budget. I also had a responsibility to help address constituent concerns, but dealing with something like this was far from anything that I might have found listed in the City Charter as part of my role.

I had barely hung up the phone with Giannoulis when the news broke that MetLife was "evaluating options" with respect to Peter Cooper and Stuyvesant Town, "including the possibility of marketing the assets for sale." The head of real estate investments for MetLife, Robert Merck, commented, "We believe current market conditions are very favorable, and we have decided to test the market to gauge buyer interest in these properties." He observed that "there is a lot of capital seeking high-quality real estate of this caliber and [MetLife] anticipates that it will see excellent market pricing for these properties." The possible sale Harry Giannoulis had described minutes earlier on the phone call was now a public matter.[5]

Testing the market? Gauging buyer interest? It all sounded pretty speculative and probably won't happen, I thought. After all, I had lived in the community my whole life, and a change in ownership had never even been rumored; this was completely out of left field. My painfully naive public statement revealed as much: "It remains to be seen whether MetLife is truly interested in selling this property, or if anyone is actually inclined to buy it from them." Either way, I said, "I will be vigilant to ensure that the rights of tenants—both rent stabilized and market rate—are protected in the event of any transition."

As I tried to figure out how to handle this ambiguous news, I got a call from my Stuy Town neighbor John Crotty, who urgently wanted to pay me a visit. Crotty is a big personality: crass and funny, he talks fast and always with a high degree of confidence. He had served as Mayor Bloomberg's director of intergovernmental affairs and in 2006 was a senior official at the Housing Development Corporation (HDC). I had met him during my campaign, at the suggestion of his mother Jane Crotty, who had lost a race for my council seat in 1993 to Republican Andrew Eristoff by only fifty-seven votes. During my campaign, John Crotty had dozens of suggestions for me about what I could do to build support. (To Crotty, no idea was too big or out of reach. In 1999, he had developed a practical, if failed, plan for the fans of the New York Jets football team to buy the team and to become owners.)

Crotty had been thinking a lot about Stuy Town in his professional capacity at the New York City Housing Development Corporation (HDC), a mayoral agency that had the ability to finance housing development. As leaders of the Bloomberg administration's housing policy team, he and his colleagues Emily Youssef and Rich Froehlich had gotten wind earlier in the spring of the fact that MetLife was thinking about selling Stuy Town. Concerned about what such a sale would mean for this massive number of units, they started to brainstorm ways to ensure its long-term affordability to middle-class New Yorkers. Among these experts, one idea emerged as promising: converting the units from rentals into a cooperative where they could be sold to people who qualified as middle income. The HDC team believed that such an option would not only be feasible but that it would also allow for a reasonable sale price for MetLife. They quietly worked up a plan to give Stuy Town and Peter Cooper residents a chance to become homeowners, but with a catch. After an initial sale to residents, in order to protect the long-term affordability of the community, the apartments could only be sold to people—and at prices—that qualified as "middle income." This was called a "limited equity" cooperative; profits would be limited, and any future buyers actually were obligated to disclose their income and prove that they were part of the middle class, which meant that their income could not be more than 165 percent of the area's median income. There are numerous examples of such cooperatives in New York City, like Penn South, West Village Houses, and Hillman Houses, all in Lower Manhattan. The HDC plan anticipated that the city would have to waive at least one tax due at the sale—the transfer tax—in order to help keep the purchase prices low enough for current residents to want to buy their apartments.[6]

The HDC team was quite enthusiastic about this opportunity and felt that the potential of a Stuy Town sale—with the property's unique history, and enabled by significant public support—created a very strong argument for public intervention. The alternative of just letting a new owner use vacancy decontrol to take units out of rent stabilization with increasing urgency was totally unappealing; Stuy Town was, they felt, intended to be a middle-class community and deserved the protection of local government. In May 2006, they made a pitch directly to Bloomberg's deputy mayor for economic development, Dan Doctoroff.[7]

Doctoroff was deeply skeptical. He had questions about the proposal and raised a number of objections. The HDC team felt that for every issue they solved, Doctoroff would come up with a new area of concern. He strongly objected to waiving the transfer tax and worried about the overall cost and about the tradeoffs it would create for the city. The city did not have an unlimited pool of resources, and to step in with a plan for Stuy Town meant that an even needier community might be left without help. Beyond the substantive concerns expressed about cost, Crotty felt from his tone that Doctoroff was not interested in getting involved in this transaction. And he and his colleagues knew that without the influential deputy mayor's support, the Bloomberg administration would never take the lead in proposing a way forward—homeownership or otherwise—to save Stuy Town.[8]

When Crotty and Youssef read the public announcement two months later that MetLife was "exploring a sale," they felt like they needed a new strategy. Crotty turned to Youssef and said, "City Hall may not want the city to propose a buyout on these terms, but there is nothing keeping the tenants from doing it, right?" Youssef thought for a moment and agreed. "I know Dan Garodnick, the new councilman over there," Crotty said. "He might be into it. Let me get in to talk to him." She told Crotty to go for it.[9]

Crotty came to my district office on July 20 for a meeting. He started calmly but got increasingly animated as he described to me how unacceptable it was for MetLife to take advantage of the booming housing market, turn its back on the community's history, and screw the tenants of Stuy Town. I offered the possibility that this was just hypothetical and that—as MetLife had put it—they were just "exploring" a sale. "Dan, don't believe it for one fucking second," he said. "That's bullshit, just watch." Crotty said that the situation demanded immediate action by me, and from the tenants. He started making a most extraordinary pitch about how the tenants of Stuy Town themselves should try to buy the property from MetLife—and give people a chance to own their apartments.

"What, what? Slow down, Crotty," I said. "You want the tenants to buy Stuy Town? How is that even possible?" He put it as simply as he could: we could make an attractive bid to MetLife premised on the idea that we would sell apartments to individual tenants and use the proceeds to pay down part of the purchase price. As he explained the mechanics, he also warned me that, without our intervention, when MetLife sold the property, it would be to the highest bidder, who wouldn't care at all about the importance of middle-class housing in New York. "And when that happens, Dan, the tenants are fucked. Seriously fucked," he said.

Crotty has an infectious personality: passionate and persuasive—part salesman, part professor. This idea was interesting, but I had no idea of how it could be accomplished. After all, the Tenants Association had only about $30,000 to its name, and this was expected to be a multibillion-dollar deal. I told him that I pictured myself standing on the corner of 20th Street and First Avenue, or going door to door, asking people to donate to this cause. He brushed that off. The tenants would need to find a partner, someone with deep pockets and a mission to preserve middle-class housing in Stuy Town. By converting the rental units to co-ops with limits on profit, we had a chance to preserve affordability for the next generation of residents, while also raising enough money to allow us to make a credible bid to MetLife. "Dan, don't worry so much. The money will be there," he told me near the end of our forty-five-minute talk. I couldn't even conceive of what he meant when he said that.

When I was first elected to the city council, outgoing speaker Gifford Miller had told me, "If someone says 'don't worry'—then it's time to worry." I believed that Crotty had good motives, but I did not understand the mechanics of why anyone would help the tenants to buy Stuy Town. I also was a brand-new councilman and did not have any reliable assessment of what my constituents would even want. Approximately 75 percent of residents in the community were still covered by rent stabilization, where rents were protected, and lease renewals were guaranteed. While this was an exciting opportunity, it was not obvious to me that I could persuade this group that forgoing a low-rent, rent-stabilized unit in favor of homeownership could be to their advantage. What Crotty was proposing was also politically dangerous for me. What if I announced publicly that the tenants were going to put together a bid to buy Stuy Town, and Crotty was wrong, and the money wasn't actually there? This could be a spectacular failure, and not a propitious start for a brand-new city councilman.

However, with each day that went by after MetLife's announcement, I realized that I had no real options other than simply protesting the sale. I also knew that if MetLife actually proceeded with an auction, people would be panicked, and would look to me for leadership. And Crotty kept at it. "Dan, trust me, have some faith," Crotty said on his second and third meetings with me in my district office, each within a few days.

I was a few years younger than Crotty, and we didn't know each other growing up in Stuy Town. Because of our own middle-class roots in the neighborhood, though, we had lots of shared experiences. We knew the same people and had grown up with the same community of teachers, nurses, firefighters, other government employees, and recent immigrants. We also had watched our neighbors struggle to make ends meet and saw MetLife turn from acting like what people had perceived to be a genteel insurance company to a more aggressive real estate owner. I understood that what he was proposing to me wasn't just a political ploy. If it worked, it was an opportunity to do something bold to protect the neighborhood, and could be precedent setting in New York. But it still seemed crazy to me.

I called Al Doyle and did my best to explain the idea. Even as I was saying it, I had to acknowledge how wild it sounded for the Tenants Association to lead a bid to buy Stuy Town, and how little I understood about the details of how we would do it. Regardless of our chances of success, Doyle and I agreed that we would need a plan to respond to this momentous change. When I was finished with my summary description, I asked Doyle what he thought. He paused, and I heard nothing on the other end of the phone for a full ten seconds. The cautious and reserved TA president spoke hesitantly and agreed that it was creative, before pausing again. He then said it might be best if we also patched in Marsh and Steinberg to the call. Once we had them on the line, I again explained Crotty's idea for the tenants to propose a bid, and to champion a limited-equity co-op conversion to allow people to own their own apartments. The law provided that if 15 percent of the community committed to a conversion plan like this, then it could proceed. Feeling far less confident than I sounded, I channeled Crotty and argued that passively watching MetLife sell Stuy Town was not an option for us. "When they sell it for billions of dollars," I concluded, "it is not going to turn out well. There will be zero effort to preserve Stuy Town's origins as a middle-class community."

There was silence, followed by some nervous laughter. "Dan, are you serious?" Steinberg asked. We all knew that homeownership had always been a dream of some Stuyvesant Town and Peter Cooper residents, because it offered a way out of spending money every month on rent. But while the tenants of Stuy Town had regularly fought back against landlord abuses, from civil rights to MCIs, embarking on an effort like this was on a different plane from anything else in our history. "It was a concept that was so foreign to me," Steinberg recalled. "I couldn't imagine how it could be pulled together. It was as if an alien had just landed on the planet and proposed a future for humanity that didn't seem possible."[10] Doyle, Marsh, and Steinberg peppered me with questions that I couldn't answer; I frantically started writing them down. They wanted to know why anyone would want to partner with the tenants rather than simply buying the property without us, and how a conversion plan from rentals to homeownership would work. Marsh asked whether there would be resistance from tenant advocates about speeding up the loss of rent-stabilized apartments from the system (even in the context of advancing an affordable homeownership plan). I resolved to get them answers to all these questions. Personally, I was concerned about whether city ethics laws even allowed me to propose a real estate transaction as an elected official that would affect me as a tenant. On a much larger scale, I was worried that the Tenants Association and a local councilman might put into motion something that we might not be able to control. With more questions than answers, Doyle, Marsh, and Steinberg agreed to start discussing the idea with their colleagues on the board.

On July 26, Al Doyle sent off an email to the entire Tenants Association board with an update and a number of questions about what would happen if MetLife sold Stuy Town. The first and most serious concern was how MetLife's potential sale would affect the existing rent-stabilization laws. He also teased out the idea for the first time: "Can the tenants play a part in this sale? Could the tenants put together the resources to buy ST-PCV?" I shared with Justine Almada all the questions that had been thrown at me. If we were going to make a case with our neighbors for a tenant bid with a homeownership option, that meant that we had to be prepared to answer all conceivable questions posed by the TA board and then the entire community.[11]

Over the next two weeks, Crotty sent me some background material about other conversion plans, like West Village Houses, which had been completed the year before. He also introduced me to Kevin Gallagher of the AFL-CIO Housing Investment Fund. An energetic deal-maker, with short, well-combed blond hair, Gallagher echoed Crotty's enthusiasm and told me that he was prepared to use his perch in the labor community to advocate for a tenant bid. Crotty also invited me and Gallagher to HDC's boardroom to meet with his colleagues Rich Froehlich and Emily Youssef, who along with Crotty had been the quiet architects of the conversion plan.

As I continued to push for clarity on who might be our partner, and our chances of success, Crotty explained that while I couldn't know the answers to all the questions up front, they would surely come in time. He compared our predicament to a general contractor of any sizable project. If you knew how to do everything, you would do it yourself, but since you can't, you put together a team of subcontractors who can help. "That's what our search for money is going to be like," he said. "They will help us figure this all out." Days later, Gallagher gave me the first tangible news in support of our effort, that the AFL-CIO Housing Investment Trust would likely support a tenant bid with an investment of $200 million. With this first sign of real support behind an effort like this, I began to think that we might be onto something. Crotty pushed: "As time went on, as we were thinking through the options, we realized there wasn't a better plan. There was no better option."[12]

Only eight months into my new role as the city councilman for the East Side of Manhattan, I knew that I had no exclusive right to speak for Stuy Town tenants, and certainly could not propose something like this without the support of the Tenants Association. The Tenants Association board's own ability to do so was also questionable. The Tenants Association itself did not include as a member every resident—far from it—and the board was not a representative group. For example, in the summer of 2006, approximately 27 percent of the community was in apartments that were renting at the market rate, but 100 percent of the board of the Tenants Association lived in rent-stabilized units. The TA also had not had a community-wide election in a number of years, and Doyle had earned the nickname "Fidel" for the length of his continuous and unchallenged service.

However, over years of standing with and up for the community—from advocating the passage of the Emergency Tenant Protection Act in 1974, to the battles over exploding windows and electrical MCIs in the 1990s and early 2000s and, most recently, over electronic key cards—the Stuyvesant Town Peter Cooper Village Tenants Association had become the only trusted voice for tenants in our neighborhood. An all-volunteer group, they communicated regularly to the community by mail and hosted periodic community meetings to update neighbors about their progress. Their effectiveness was periodically challenged by a discontented neighbor in a letter to the editor of the local *Town & Village* newspaper, but as a group they worked hard, strove to be good representatives, and most importantly, they were the only game in town. It was with that context that, as I scrambled to fill in the details, I asked Doyle in mid-August to prepare to bring this issue to the TA board to seek its formal endorsement of a tenant bid.

Meanwhile, speculation about MetLife's true intentions had started to pick up publicly. MetLife had, the prior year, sold the MetLife Building at 200 Park Avenue to Tishman Speyer for $1.72 billion—which was the highest recorded price for an office building in America. Now, the press was reporting about MetLife's plans to monetize other real estate assets. MetLife hadn't yet officially announced that Stuy Town was up for sale, but that likelihood certainly didn't feel far off. We needed professional help. On August 15, I was frantically dialing for lawyers, hoping to present a few good options to the Tenants Association. And I was striking out, big time, because everyone had either a conflict of interest or was unwilling to take us on without a significant retainer. I called Meredith Kane, who headed the real estate practice at Paul Weiss, the firm where I had worked before running for office, to see if she would consider providing some expertise on how to pull together a bid. Kane heard me out and wished me well but demurred, saying that the firm was likely conflicted. She gave me a few other names, which I jotted down in my notebook and called.

I then reached out to Christine Quinn, who recently had been elected as speaker of the city council, to ask for her help. Quinn represented Chelsea and the West Village and was well aware of the importance of Stuyvesant Town to me both personally and politically. She had spent many hours helping me in my 2005 election, even taking the time to accompany me on my door knocking in Stuy Town buildings. Of course, Quinn had reason

to get behind my candidacy, beyond any altruistic motives. She was looking for votes in her race to become the council speaker, an election among
the fifty-one members of the city council, and if I won, I would be a voter
in the speaker election. Over the course of the campaign, Quinn and I had
grown close, and after I won my election, I decided to back her campaign
to be council speaker (over then Brooklyn council member Bill de Blasio).
Now leading New York City's legislative branch, Speaker Quinn, who had
been a tenant organizer, was happy to support me, her newest colleague.
Quinn directed one of her senior staff members, Maura Keaney, a former
labor organizer for UNITE HERE with sharp political instincts, to help
me. I told Quinn and Keaney that should the TA board decide to move
forward with this plan, the tenants would most urgently need professional
support, presumably a lawyer or a banker.

Doyle had been working the phones with TA board members individually,
calming their nerves and letting them know I was working on a concept
that I would pitch to them before long. Many told Doyle that they were
relieved that we had direction, but most were skeptical that a tenant-led
bid to buy Stuy Town initiated by their brand-new councilman was anything more than a political statement.

As Doyle answered questions from his board, uptown, the partners of
Troutman Sanders, a New York law firm based in the Chrysler Building,
were chatting over drinks and appetizers in a conference room as they
hosted a fund-raiser for Andrew Cuomo's bid to be the state attorney
general. Quinn and Cuomo were both on hand to give remarks and to
work the crowd. Now that the speeches were over, they found themselves
chatting with Leonard Grunstein, a real estate partner at the firm, and
someone whom they both knew from a recent real estate deal in the West
Village that had involved the city and the state. Quinn introduced Stuyvesant Town into the conversation and asked Grunstein if he would be willing to help out the new councilman from Stuy Town.[13]

Four months earlier, Grunstein had successfully represented the tenants
of the West Village Houses in Quinn's West Side district, in their effort
to become homeowners. The West Village Houses consisted of forty-two
walk-up buildings that had 420 apartments. They were built as part of the
state's Mitchell-Lama Housing Program, which, like the 1943 Stuyvesant

Town deal, allowed private developers to enjoy a tax abatement and low-interest mortgages—as well as a guaranteed 6 percent return on their investment—in exchange for creating housing for low- and middle-income tenants and keeping it that way for twenty years. In 2002, the owner, Andrew Farkas, announced a plan to take the units out of Mitchell-Lama. Katie Bordonaro, a Latin teacher at the Village Community School who was president of the tenants association, took the initiative in leading a push to convert the rental units to co-ops. She and other tenant leaders spent years organizing, raising money, and advocating for their cause, in anticipation of developing a plan for when their rent protections would end. "We figured we should be prepared and know who the politicians are," Bordonaro told the *Times*. "We had $50,000 in the bank from dues and contributions for legal fees."[14]

At Cuomo's suggestion, Grunstein had stepped in to support the West Village Houses residents who faced the possibility of 300 percent rent increases when the owners left the Mitchell-Lama subsidy program. He worked with them to develop a plan that allowed for existing tenants to be able to either buy into the co-op or continue to rent their units at far below market rates. That meant outright ownership for as little as $165,000 for a typical two-bedroom apartment, and $330,000 for three-bedroom duplex apartments with private gardens or cathedral ceilings. If sold at market prices, the apartments would have sold for $800 to $1,200 a square foot, or about $1.5 million for a three-bedroom. New owners also had the right to resell at gradually higher prices. After twelve years, they could sell to anyone, at full market prices. A large flip tax, between 15 and 25 percent of the gain, would help pay off a city mortgage.[15]

Working directly with the tenants association, Grunstein helped to create and finance the Article 11 co-op structure, which was key to the tenants' proposal. From a matter of public policy, the deal was far from perfect, because it gave tenants an opportunity to sell their units without any restriction whatsoever after only twelve years. "If there's no long-term resale restriction, what we're essentially doing is giving a big benefit to a handful of folks," said Brad Lander, an affordable-housing expert at the Pratt Institute, and later a Brooklyn city councilman. Cuomo defended the deal. "You bought twelve years of affordability," he said. "You can buy more affordability, but it costs more. It's a pure economic calculus."[16]

Grunstein had grown up in Laurelton and then Forest Hills, Queens, an Orthodox Jew and son of two Holocaust survivors. His father, Morris Grunstein, was a businessman, who had bought, sold, and operated a number of supermarkets. Morris had a knack for watching foot traffic, understanding neighborhoods, and buying a business at the right time. For Morris, having a good instinct and the confidence to take a chance were the key ingredients to success in business, and Len watched him closely. When Len was seventeen years old, the family moved to Forest Hills and sold their supermarket in Laurelton. Len knew that they would need to start up a new business. While his parents were away on a vacation to Israel, Len noticed a supermarket near Queens College, where he went to school. Employing the skills he had learned from his father, Len walked into the store and told the owner that he wanted to buy it. The owner looked at this seventeen-year-old and smiled. "Kid, c'mon, how are you going to buy the store?" he asked. "Never mind how," Len responded. "My parents are away, and they are going to be back soon enough." The owner shrugged, invited him to the back of the store, where Len made him an offer. Right there, they agreed to the terms of the deal, which Morris promptly ratified when he came home from his vacation.[17]

In 2006, at age fifty-six, Grunstein was a graduate of Brooklyn Law School and a veteran of the real estate bar, and he was looking in the eyes of the soon-to-be attorney general and the speaker of the city council in his conference room in the heart of Manhattan. They were asking for his help.

Grunstein came to my district office on August 17 for a meeting with me and my senior policy adviser Marianna Vaidman Stone, a friend of mine who had previously practiced law at Debevoise & Plimpton. He entered our small office, which did not have a formal reception area, cutting a small and dapper figure, dressed in a three-piece suit with a tie with an enormous knot. He sported professorial glasses and a meticulously trimmed gray beard. Vaidman Stone saw him wander in and pause, with his arms behind his back, appearing with a friendly and slightly awkward smile. Grunstein presented as a cross between a banker and a lawyer. A jovial and clearly religious man, if you asked him how he was doing, his response was inevitably to look up to the sky, put his hands in the air, and say "Thank God!" without further elaboration. We welcomed him to the small circular conference table in my office, and Vaidman Stone and I presented the possibility of tenants making a bid to buy Stuyvesant Town. Grunstein listened carefully, paused, and then said confidently, "Yes. We can do it."

Grunstein explained what he had done at the West Village Houses and how we could structure an Article 11 cooperative in Stuyvesant Town, with significant resale restrictions to ensure that it would stay affordable for future middle-class owners. Vaidman Stone and I grilled him for two hours about what a plan might look like and how we could get there, and he answered every one of our questions. He was in no rush to get to his next client. It was clear that he was intrigued by this assignment and that he was up for the challenge. After he left, Vaidman Stone and I looked at each other, smiled, and shrugged. This could work. Grunstein clearly knew his stuff, and we did not have a lot of time, or choices.

I made arrangements for the tenant leaders like Marsh, Doyle, Steinberg, and another board member, Jim Roth (a lawyer and former FBI agent), to meet Grunstein at the Troutman Sanders offices in the Chrysler Building. They, too, asked him questions about our viability and how we could possibly execute a bid. Grunstein walked them through how we could get a partner and convert units to a cooperative; he was patient and knowledgeable in responding to a myriad of follow-up questions. "He had a twinkle in his eye," Marsh recalled. "He was seducing. You felt like he had your back, and that he was going to save us." The Tenants Association voted to hire Grunstein for an all-inclusive retainer of $10,000, a pittance for his law firm but a good portion of the money in the TA's bank account. Grunstein clearly was struck by this group and what they were trying to do. "These were really good people," he told me. "And there were very few ideologues. It was more about how we could get this done in a way that made sense. Based on my experience in negotiating a lot of tenant-sponsored plans, I thought this was a great group. They were interested in doing something that made sense as opposed to fighting for fighting's sake."[18]

Concern was picking up around the community beyond the TA board. News broke that the real estate brokerage firm CBRE (Coldwell Banker Richard Ellis) had landed the "massive Met Life Residential Listing" and was going to serve as the broker for the Stuy Town sale. Real estate giants

Related and Apollo publicly expressed interest in buying Stuy Town, and people were no longer speculating that the property could be sold for $3.3 billion; instead, they were predicting that it would be closer to $5 billion. I also learned for the first time that there were hundreds of thousands of square feet of unused development rights both vertically and for infill development in Stuy Town, something that could prompt a new owner to rip down and build bigger buildings, or even to build on playgrounds. Once his firm got to work, CB Richard Ellis's Bill Stranahan was reportedly telling bidders that maybe there could be a way to add some new affordable units on some of the "unused" space. Residents like me didn't regard any of our open spaces as unused, and all Stuy Town tenants had reason to be concerned about this possibility.[19]

One constituent emailed me out of the blue on August 21: "A friend of mine works at one of the firms handling the purchase offers for Peter Cooper / Stuy Town. This will come as no surprise to you, I'm sure, but the potential purchaser's stated plans are to get rid of the rent stabilized tenants and bring everything to market rate rentals. These are powerful people and if the deal goes through it will probably be because they think the city will rezone Peter Cooper for them. . . . I'm sure you know all this, but they seem pretty confident." While I knew that I could stop any proposal for zoning changes in the city council, this email confirmed my deepest fear: that a new owner would work actively to push people out of their apartments. Tenant advocates like Mike McKee of Tenants PAC were also getting increasingly nervous, and Doyle had looped him into our conversations about the potential tenant bid. McKee knew that because of vacancy decontrol, the status quo—even with MetLife—would result in Stuyvesant Town and Peter Cooper losing all of its rent-stabilized units over time. With a bad owner, that could happen much faster. McKee had fought vacancy decontrol in 1993, 1994, and every year since, and watched as MetLife had deregulated 27 percent of all the units in Stuy Town. McKee's group had estimated that as many as half a million affordable units in New York City had been lost to decontrol since 1993 (the equivalent of nearly twenty entire Stuy Town communities). It was "a freight train moving one hundred miles an hour," Grunstein observed, and we felt enormous pressure to act fast.[20]

We didn't have much time or money, but the Tenants Association and I had one thing that other bidders did not have: political clout. We had the potential to be a trusted voice to educate and organize the tenant community behind a plan, and a thorn in the side of competitors. If we could persuade the tenants of the community to line up behind a single tenant-led bid, we could change the calculus of potential buyers, and even of MetLife. We wanted everyone to fear the political consequences of crossing us, and to preclude any other entity from proposing a homeownership plan without the support of the Tenants Association. Grunstein suggested that we organize our neighbors by asking them to sign a pledge that they would only buy their units in a transaction that had the Tenants Association's support. Because a basic market-rate conversion plan needed a minimum 15 percent of the tenants to buy their units to be effective, to be airtight we needed more than 85 percent of our neighbors to join in with our plan to stop any other conversion plan from proceeding.

Telling John Marsh that we needed to organize 85 percent of the community was like waving red in front of a charging bull. "I was like, I can do that," Marsh recalled, eager to get to work.[21] Meanwhile, Crotty, Gallagher, and I, guided by Grunstein, started to work on the details of a plan for the TA board to consider. We all understood that any concept that we proposed had to guarantee absolute protection to rent-stabilized tenants, who still represented 73 percent of the units in the community. How to handle the market-rate tenants—far less organized, more transient, but more affluent—was a little more complicated. They had fewer protections under the law, and as a result we feared that if we offered them the opportunity to own their apartment, they might actively oppose any limitations on their upside potential.

On August 23, I invited the entire fifteen-member board of the Tenants Association to my apartment at 3 Peter Cooper Road. There was one item on the agenda: I wanted to ask them for permission to announce that we were going to pursue a tenant-led plan to buy Stuy Town. Doyle had prepared his colleagues for what was coming. Once we all had helped ourselves to store-bought cookies and soft drinks on my dining room table, we settled in to discuss the impending sale. I barely had enough chairs for the group, and board members squeezed uncomfortably onto my couch. Everyone knew that there were active bidders who could drive the sale price over $5 billion. And we were increasingly aware of the fact that at the prices in question, an owner would have economic pressures to use vacancy decontrol to evict rent-stabilized tenants.

Figure 3.2. John Crotty, another lifelong Stuy Town resident, was a housing expert and my secret adviser as the tenants put together our 2006 bid to buy Stuy Town. Brash, funny, and smart, Crotty helped me to strategize how to move the tenants' agenda forward. Photo credit: Tom Cranker.

Having conferred with Grunstein and me in detail, Doyle, Marsh, Steinberg, and Roth had already come to the conclusion that we needed to proceed. This August 23 meeting was my moment to present some details to the group about how we could make it happen. I began by proposing that we state publicly that we were looking to assemble an investor group, with an eye toward buying Stuy Town and Peter Cooper from MetLife. By making that one public statement, we could create an enormous amount of attention and give ourselves the chance to attract a partner who could help us put the billions of dollars necessary onto the table. Soni Fink—now with years under her belt as the TA's communications director—had already been working arm in arm with Justine Almada of my office, drafting documents that would explain to the community in plain language what we were doing. While we were far from nailing down all the details of a plan, as a framework, I proposed that we give all residents an *opportunity* to own their units, but make it clear to everyone that it was not an *obligation*. Our plan also should, I argued, create limits on how much our neighbors could make on any future sale of their unit, so as to avoid the pressures that come with the opportunity to make massive profits. And owners could sell units only to future residents who could prove that they were in a moderate- or middle income bracket, which usually meant that their income was, at most, 165 percent of the area's median income. It was roughly the plan that the HDC team of Crotty, Youssef, and Froehlich had cooked up months earlier and pitched unsuccessfully to Doctoroff.

I had spent the summer getting comfortable with it, but for a few members of the board, this was the first time they had heard any of the details. Their expressions showed that they were suddenly burdened with a responsibility that they hadn't asked for. Much like what Crotty had said to me a month earlier, my argument came down to "Sitting on the sidelines is not an option. We have nothing to lose." Steinberg then spoke up and urged the group to proceed. But she cautioned that we think carefully about how we were going to talk to the community. Doyle quietly explained how he felt this was the best move and that we needed to take this important step. Roth had some choice words for MetLife and urged that we proceed, immediately. Marsh was already past the should-we-or-shouldn't-we discussion and was telling his colleagues how we would get 85 percent of the community to sign a "no buy" agreement, which would symbolically commit our neighbors to our bid. After about an hour of discussion, the TA unanimously voted to move forward with an announcement on the terms I had proposed. The prevailing view was that we had few credible alternatives, and a tenant-led plan with a homeownership option would create more opportunities for their neighbors.

Not everyone agreed with my approach of rolling the dice with this plan. Steven Sanders had recently retired from the State Assembly but was still one of the most trusted voices in the community, and certainly in the Tenants Association. Sanders had been my local assemblyman since

I was in first grade, and his views carried a lot of weight with me. Sanders warned me, and the board, that by proposing a homeownership plan—and succeeding—we would expose stark divisions among the tenant body. He argued that such a plan could breed resentment between owners and renters; there would be people who had their incomes tested before they moved in and those who didn't; there would surely be objections to apartment prices, to the quality of maintenance, and to everything that people ordinarily complained to a landlord about. "If somehow you think that you can put together a genuine counter offer that Met will take seriously, consummate a deal, manage Stuyvesant Town and Peter Cooper Village to the satisfaction of most of the tenants, and offer them a conversion plan that will somehow save them money and not cause deep divisions in our community, then I say go for it." He added: "Believe me when I say that if you are seen having let this genie out of the bottle that it will not be to your benefit." As a first term councilman, the political risks were clear. This would either show me to be a shrewd actor who could deftly navigate the treacherous waters of New York real estate and politics, or a fool.[22]

My law school friend David Leibowitz, who was at the time an assistant United States Attorney in Manhattan, raised similar concerns at one of our weekly Saturday morning breakfasts at the Coopertown Diner on 20th Street. I had been keeping him posted in real time through the summer and shared with him Sanders's concerns. "It sounds like you're biting off a ton, and I think it heightens the stakes and the expectations for you, unnecessarily," Leibowitz said. "To over-deliver on this issue, I think you need to under-promise and make it clear that we may not win if we do this, but there is no downside to taking this step." I wondered if this were even possible. The challenges Sanders had outlined were real, and no venture on this scale could be without risk.

4

MAKING A BID

A story about the tenant bid was expected to pop up on the *New York Times* website on Monday night, September 4, 2006. I was eager to see how it came out, but I had an issue. I was on a blind date, and this was before smartphones, so I couldn't just excuse myself to the restroom and sneak a look. My date was a recent Harvard Law School graduate named Zoe Segal-Reichlin, who was in town to work on a congressional campaign for her former boss, City Councilman David Yassky. I desperately wanted to see how the *Times* portrayed our effort, but the date was going well, and I didn't want to rush our dinner. The Tenants Association and I had scheduled a press conference for the next morning, and I shared most of the details with Zoe, including my nerves about the fact that the article had probably been posted during our dinner.

Zoe, who is now my wife, mercifully agreed to come up to my Peter Cooper apartment "for reading purposes only," and we pulled it up online together. The headline read "Official Sees Way to Buy 2 Developments" and went on to say, "Daniel R. Garodnick, who grew up in Stuyvesant

Town and Peter Cooper Village and now represents their 25,000 residents on the City Council, intends to announce today that he is organizing a group of investors who, with the backing of tenants and the Council speaker, will try to buy the two complexes and keep them affordable to the middle class." It quoted Christine Quinn and the AFL-CIO's Kevin Gallagher, as well as John Marsh and Jim Roth from the Tenants Association, and told our story exactly the way we wanted. Tenants were taking control of their destiny and fighting back against big real estate. Zoe—who was not as impressed by my efforts as I hoped she would be—acknowledged that the article had turned out well. I had promised a quick visit, so I walked her down to East 23rd Street and put her in a cab before I began a late night of emailing with the TA board members.

The month of August had been a whirlwind of activity in getting us to that point. Doyle and I had prepared ourselves to answer the many questions that the community would have when the news became public. We hoped that our plan, publicly disclosed the right way, would—as Crotty promised—bring potential partners out of the woodwork and give us momentum. In our minds, showing up on MetLife's doorstep as a partner with the Tenants Association could be extremely desirable for a bidder. It was therefore important that we announce our plan in a way that got maximum public exposure. In the final days of August, Justine Almada, Marianna Vaidman Stone, and my chief of staff, Andrew Sullivan, worked with Grunstein, Crotty, and Quinn's staff to refine a formal letter from me to MetLife advising them that the tenants were planning to assemble an investor group to make our own bid. Almada and Soni Fink prepared answers to what we believed would be the most common questions; we drafted letters to the community from me and from Doyle; and we generated briefing documents for the press and elected officials. Drafts of everything went to Doyle and Fink, and also to Grunstein, for review and approval. And we were moving as fast as we could because we did not know exactly when MetLife was going to announce that the property was officially up for sale, and we certainly didn't want our plan to leak out before we were ready to explain it. MetLife had only teased that it was "exploring" a sale in July, and we knew that whenever MetLife made its announcement, as we were expecting it to, our neighbors were rightly going to be worried.

With careful coaching from Sandra Mullin of the city council press office, on August 29 I pitched my first story to a reporter. Our dream scenario was for a *New York Times* article about the tenants' bid to come out on the day after Labor Day, which would be the same day we would hold a press conference right outside Stuyvesant Town. Our hope was that a *Times* story would break the news, but that because it was of such significant public interest, television cameras—and everyone else—would still come to the press conference and give us a second day of coverage. Mullin recommended that I call Janny Scott of the *Times*, a reporter with significant experience covering real estate. I learned that pitching a story amounts to sharing a few details of your proposed "news" off the record and offering an exclusive opportunity to write the entire story. For our strategy to work, we would also need to ask Scott to embargo the story until the day after Labor Day. With butterflies in my stomach, I called her and explained to her, off the record, what the tenants were planning to do. Scott agreed not only to write it but to hold it until September 5.

We started planning our public press conference for September 5. Soon after I spoke to Scott, Grunstein got a call from another reporter at the *Times* named Charles Bagli, to talk about Stuy Town. We had no idea what Bagli wanted, and we did not know if he was going to try to break our news early. We had scripted our announcement very carefully and were already talking to a *Times* reporter, so his call alarmed us. Even if the *Times* was about to print a bigger story about MetLife's sale of Stuy Town, we did not want the tenants' plan to be buried in the eleventh paragraph. Nobody on our team spoke to Bagli, and we prayed that his story wouldn't mention what we were about to do.

We didn't have to wait long. The lead story of the national edition of the *New York Times* on August 30, 2006, proclaimed, "110-Building Site in N.Y. Is Put Up for Sale." Our quiet community was suddenly the focus of the world's attention, and MetLife's plans were now known to all. My phone rang at 5:45 a.m. It was Doyle. "Um, Dan, I just wanted to make sure you saw the front page of the *New York Times* today." Doyle was famous for his extremely early morning calls, and it was not the first time he had woken me up. I bolted out of bed to have a look online. Doyle also noted, while I scanned the story, that there already were TV news trucks surrounding Stuy Town and Peter Cooper, with reporters giving a live update for the early morning news. The *Times* reported that the asking price was expected to be nearly $5 billion, "the biggest deal for a single American property in modern times." The real estate world was practically salivating over the opportunity—the article revealed that everyone from New York's top real estate families, like Rudin, Durst, and LeFrak, to pension funds, international investment banks, and investors from Dubai wanted a chance to bid. Tishman Speyer and Blackstone were also registering as potential bidders. One executive called it "the ego dream of the world."[1]

Steinberg had also gotten an early morning call from Doyle, and I found an email from her waiting for me. "Wow, did you ever expect such a whopper of an issue your first year as City councilmember?" she asked. Bagli's *Times* piece was coauthored by Janny Scott. They speculated that a $5 billion sale would "lead to profound changes for many of the 25,000 residents of the two complexes, where two-thirds of the apartments have regulated rents at roughly half the market rate. Any new owner paying the equivalent of $450,000 per apartment is going to be eager to create a money-making luxury enclave." Bagli and Scott reported that MetLife hoped to have the deal consummated by November.[2] Honoring our embargo, the article made no mention of the Tenants Association's still-secret plan to make a bid.

The calls from nervous residents to the Tenants Association and to my office started immediately. "MetLife was the devil they knew," Steinberg recalled. "Tenants didn't know what the future was going to be. They didn't like the feeling of uncertainty. What's going to happen to us? Are we going to be able to stay? Are we going to remain rent regulated? People had no idea."[3] The TA's message service lit up with press inquiries from everyone from the BBC to the *Bergen Record*. But our own plans were still under wraps for a few more days, and I implored Doyle, other TA leaders, Quinn's staff, and Grunstein not to call back any reporters before September 5, the date of our announcement. We did our best to quietly reassure tenants that we would fight to protect their interests in any scenario and hinted that we were developing our own plan in response.

On September 1, the Friday afternoon before the Labor Day weekend, we started placing calls to elected officials, labor leaders, and key tenants, inviting them to our announcement, and explaining confidentially what we were up to. Some elected officials bristled that they were only hearing about this at the last minute. They were right to be annoyed, but an earlier briefing would definitely have leaked out, and we could not take that risk. That afternoon, I sent a letter to MetLife chairman C. Robert Henrikson, advising him that I was working with the Stuyvesant Town and Peter Cooper Village Tenants Association to put together a tenant-backed plan to buy Stuy Town. The letter asked him to give us access to the necessary financial materials, including "the bid book," to help us analyze the property's financials. My staff and Crotty helped me prepare remarks for the press conference, and the city council sent out a media advisory stating cryptically that "Speaker Christine Quinn and the New York City Council will make an affordable housing announcement on Tuesday, September 5th at 10AM." It declined even to note the location, lest we tip anyone off. On Sunday at 4 p.m., Harry Giannoulis, MetLife's lobbyist who had alerted me to the potential sale only six weeks earlier, called and left a message on my cell phone asking to know what exactly we were planning on Tuesday. I didn't return the call.

On Tuesday, September 5, our big day had arrived. Scott's *New York Times* article, which went online during my date, kicked off the news day, and by 9 a.m., dozens of tenants and Tenants Association leaders were out mingling on the corner of 16th Street and First Avenue. I had picked this spot for the announcement because it was known to have a continuous flow of people in and out of Stuy Town. I had spent countless hours shaking hands on that corner during the 2005 campaign, and since we were looking for attention, it was the natural place for us to convene. As we had hoped, the *Times* article had driven lots of interest to our announcement. When I got there, at least eight television cameras were set up, and print reporters from every New York newspaper were there. US senator Chuck Schumer, city council speaker Christine Quinn, the city comptroller Bill Thompson, Manhattan borough president Scott Stringer, and elected leaders at every level of government joined us. Ed Ott, the president of the New York City Central Labor Council, and Mike McKee of Tenants PAC also were on hand. The presence of Thompson and Ott sent the strong message that labor and pension funds were behind us, adding credibility to our announcement. Doyle and many TA leaders were there, too, as well as my mom, who came to check out the scene. Kevin Gallagher told the *Times* that the AFL-CIO was interested in being a financing source for the tenants. Because of the sheer number of units in Stuy Town, the AFL-CIO viewed this as "an opportunity to double their work in one project," Gallagher said. "What we're looking to do is to provide tools for them, and the money, so that the tenants can become homeowners and not worry about a middleman coming in and driving up the value."[4]

I stood alongside the many political veterans, most of whom did not realize that this was my very first press conference. I shook off my nerves, looked at the cameras, and declared that the tenants of Stuy Town were going to put together an investor group to buy the entire property. We needed to stand up for New York's middle class, and saving Stuy Town was critical in doing that. I reminded the crowd of the words of Mayor Fiorello La Guardia, who had said that Stuyvesant Town had "certain public obligations different from and greater than a like project financed entirely by private funds." Schumer, Thompson, Quinn, Stringer, and others chided MetLife for creating uncertainty for tenants and for turning its back on the core principles on which the East Side community was founded in 1943. We collectively warned that if we cannot save Stuyvesant Town, the symbol of New York's housing for middle class people, then there was no future for affordable housing in Manhattan.

I knew that the phrase "affordable housing" had lost most of its meaning to the general public. Most people don't even realize that there is a technical definition of "affordable" housing. The city has a variety of affordable-housing programs that are designed to be available to people based on their need, as defined by income. Those programs create opportunities for housing that is affordable to people who earn between 30 and 165 percent of the area median income. Of course, many apartments in New York City are not subject to any such programs (in fact, there is no income cap to be eligible for many rent-stabilized units in New York City), but they still may be considered affordable to an individual renter. Generally speaking, if you are not paying more than a third of your income for housing, you are not rent burdened, and it may be considered affordable—to you. But rent that is affordable to you may very well not be affordable to your next-door neighbors, depending on their income.

At Stuy Town, we were explicitly targeting our efforts at housing that was affordable to the ever-shrinking middle class of New York, but even the term "middle class" was itself murky. At the moment of our announcement, only 16 percent of New York City families were considered to have a "middle income"—one of the lowest rates for cities in the entire nation. That was down from 25 percent in 1970. There also was a corresponding decline in middle-income neighborhoods within New York. In 1970, those neighborhoods—where the typical family earned a middle income—comprised nearly half of all neighborhoods citywide. By 2000, only three in ten New York neighborhoods fit this profile.[5]

In the three years before MetLife's announcement, the city lost 205,000 units considered affordable to middle-class New Yorkers, like firefighters and nurses. While rent-stabilized units were not reserved exclusively for only middle-income people, much of Stuy Town and Peter Cooper was in fact occupied by people who fit that category. A *New York Times* analysis revealed that Manhattan's middle class fell somewhere between $45,000 and $134,000. But if you actually defined middle class by lifestyle, then in order "to accommodate the cost of living in Manhattan, that salary would have to fall between $80,000 and $235,000. That means someone making $70,000 a year in other parts of the country would need to make $166,000 in Manhattan to enjoy the same purchasing power." In 2005, the median household income in the Stuyvesant Town area was $76,010, and 25 percent of all residents fell into the category of "rent burdened," which meant that they paid more than 30 percent of their income in rent.[6]

We framed our announcement in this context—a defense of the middle class of New York. The coverage portrayed us as the scrappy underdogs, defying expectations and taking on the fat cats. Jen Chung of Gothamist wrote, "The underdog bidders to capture the public's heart of the sale might just be the tenants of STPCV themselves. Really." She went on to say, "Now, how a group of tenants will get billions ready for a bid is another question, but it'll be interesting to see how the tenants fight the sale of the complex." The *New York Observer* said, "Dan Garodnick is trying to put other people's money where his mouth is trying to raise public and private money to buy Stuyvesant Town and Peter Cooper Village and rent them below market rates to middle class tenants." The Tenants Association leaders were satisfied with the way the announcement turned out. It generated the attention we wanted, and it showed our community that we had a plan. "There was no backing down once we went and said it out loud," Steinberg recalled. "We were in it up to our necks and beyond. We had to put in a bid that was credible, and we knew it was going to be a fight to the last. We had taken a step that was so unusual that whatever happened, whether we failed or we won, our lives were never going to be the same."[7]

Figure 4.1. On September 5, 2006, we announced the tenant bid to buy Stuyvesant Town and Peter Cooper Village from MetLife. *From left*, Senator Chuck Schumer, New York State Assembly member Jonathan Bing, me, Manhattan borough president Scott Stringer, state senator Tom Duane, city council speaker Christine Quinn, state senator Liz Krueger, New York State Assembly member Sylvia Friedman, Congresswoman Carolyn Maloney (behind Friedman), and Central Labor Council president Ed Ott. Photo credit: William Alatriste.

Later that afternoon, city comptroller Bill Thompson, who was expected to be a candidate for mayor in 2009, called me to give further encouragement and support. Thompson had embraced our effort at the announcement that morning and believed it was appropriate for the city's public pension funds to invest in the tenant bid. "Dan, this is a defining moment in the city's history," he said, "and you are doing the right thing." He then told me that he hoped that a successful tenants' effort to preserve affordable housing in Stuy Town could be used as a model of activism that could be replicated throughout the city.

Mayor Bloomberg had a much more circumspect reaction. When asked whether the city might help out the tenants in our bid, he observed that while the property was "privately owned," the city would "have to take a look at it." Bloomberg added, "Most of the people in Stuyvesant Town or in Peter Cooper Village are protected by the rent stabilization laws. So even if it does change hands, most of them will not find their rents changing other than from whatever the Rent Guidelines Board say. But we have to take a look at it."[8]

I was surprised by the passivity of Bloomberg's comments, because his administration had regularly intervened in private deals in order to preserve affordable housing. In fact, it was the entire mission of his Housing Preservation and Development agency. In 2004, the Bloomberg administration had put forth a plan to create "an ambitious middle-class housing program for the twenty-first century." The plan intended to use city capital funding to build twenty-two thousand units of housing on large sites in all boroughs for citizens earning between $50,000 and $100,000—above the city's median of $42,000—financed through an agency that would issue bonds, speed up land development, and subsidize the affordable units with those renting at the market rate. His overall housing initiative grew to be a $7.5 billion plan to build and preserve 165,000 units by 2013. The administration had a variety of tools to achieve its goals, such as building on city-owned land or offering tax incentives, to spur private housing development.[9]

I wasn't the only one surprised to read Bloomberg's diffident words. Rafael Cestero, the deputy commissioner of Housing Preservation and Development (HPD), was already at City Hall when he saw the mayor's comment that the city might not intervene because the property was "privately owned" and went directly to the press shop to caution them. "You've got to be careful about positioning him saying things like that. We do that every day! We intervene in the private market to protect affordability all the time." Cestero had been part of a number of meetings about Stuyvesant Town, which explored whether the city had any meaningful hook to require long-term affordability in the community. Housing officials had dug up MetLife's original plans from 1943, the extension of its tax abatement in 1974, and concluded that it would be far too expensive for the city to try to eke out crumbs of affordability in Stuy Town. But as for Bloomberg's statement that the city was going to stay on the sidelines because it was the private market? That was HPD's bread and butter.[10]

In fact, only two years earlier, the city and state had blessed the deal at the West Village Houses, led by Grunstein. In that deal, in exchange for the owner agreeing to sell apartments to the tenants at a discount, the city forgave a $19 million loan and provided a tax exemption. Mayor Bloomberg had himself said that that deal would preserve affordable housing "in a neighborhood where tenants might otherwise have been priced out."[11] Why not in Stuy Town? Mayor La Guardia fought to create Stuy Town, pitching it as the ultimate public-private partnership. Now, it seemed to be barely registering with Bloomberg, who had thirty thousand constituents who needed his help.

Steve Cuozzo of the *New York Post* echoed Bloomberg's theme, questioning why the city would offer any benefit to middle-class tenants. Cuozzo mocked our announcement, which "can only give the impression that rent stabilized tenants (two-thirds of Stuyvesant's and Cooper's 25,000 residents) are at imminent risk of being driven from their homes and into the East River. Indeed, the mood conveyed by sob-story commentary is of city marshals massing on First Avenue to sweep through the complex with eviction notices and truncheons." He went on to object to any benefit to middle-class tenants, particularly city workers, calling them the "entitled labor class."[12]

Cuozzo did not note that the number of apartments affordable to households making 80 percent of the median household income in New York City had already dropped by a fifth between 2002 and 2005, and that as a result New York City had the lowest percentage of middle-class people of any large city in the United States. To Cuozzo and others, the middle class was doing just fine and did not need any extra help from the city.[13]

A day after the announcement, Senator Schumer called MetLife's chairman C. Robert Henrikson on our behalf. We had explained to Schumer's staff that we did not yet have the bid books necessary to make our own bid and that the speed of this transaction might make it hard for us to fairly compete. Schumer formally asked Henrikson to take the time to work with us, even if it meant slowing the process down. He reminded Henrikson of MetLife's having benefited not only from city tax benefits but also from eminent domain.[14] Nevertheless, Henrikson refused to delay, even for a minute.

MetLife's general counsel James Lipscomb reached out to City Hall for a meeting with deputy mayor Dan Doctoroff and Housing Preservation and

Development commissioner Shaun Donovan (who later joined the cabinet of President Barack Obama).[15] Commissioner Donovan called me before the meeting for a status check, and I told him that the tenants were working to assemble a bid but that MetLife had not given us what I had asked for in my letter: certain basic information about the property necessary to allow us to proceed. I asked Donovan to push MetLife to treat the tenants like any other bidder—and that included sharing the offering memorandum, or "bid book," with all of those relevant details. I was momentarily encouraged by Donovan's call to me. Having Mayor Bloomberg and his team on our side would have been a big boost, and despite the mayor's public comments, I hoped that Commissioner Donovan might find a way to help us from the inside. Donovan did not commit, but he said that he understood what we were after. "I don't think this should be a hard sell," Andrew Sullivan said to me in our council office. "Politically, saving Stuy Town is solid gold."

Lipscomb went to City Hall for the meeting, where he met Doctoroff and his team. Despite the fact that he was freelancing as my adviser, John Crotty was also invited to this meeting in his professional role as a member of the Bloomberg administration's housing team. Doctoroff introduced Crotty to Lipscomb as a Stuy Town resident, and Liscomb asked, "So, you're a spy?" "Yeah, pretty much," Crotty laughingly agreed. MetLife's public position was that it was at the beginning stages of its process and that it intended to conduct a process that "allows all potential buyers to make offers." Privately, Lipscomb now told mayoral aides that MetLife wanted to move fast. Doctoroff, hearing this, and echoing the mayor's public comments, assured Lipscomb that the city would not interfere with MetLife's ability to sell the property.[16] Rafael Cestero, his deputy housing commissioner, had presented one option to Doctoroff—unfortunately, not the one the tenants were proposing—which provided that, on vacancy, units would be rented to people who qualified as middle income. While this was a noble goal, the city would need to spend $900 million to accomplish it, which was the equivalent to the housing agency's entire capital budget for two years. To Doctoroff, there were other critical priorities that deserved the city's limited funds.

Crotty reported back after the meeting, confirming what we had suspected: that MetLife was moving fast and the city would not intervene. Our task of assembling a credible multibillion-dollar bid by October 5—the date that MetLife had set for bidders—was already challenging, to say the least. And we felt that the Bloomberg administration, by telling MetLife that the city was going to stay on the sidelines, was signaling that MetLife did not need to give the tenants' plan any consideration. After all, if the mayor wasn't going to endorse our effort—even conceptually—why should MetLife or any of the other bidders?

Green-lighted by the city, MetLife's broker Darcy Stacom proceeded to give buyers the opportunity to transform Stuyvesant Town and Peter Cooper Village into what we later learned the bid book called the "city's most prominent market-rate master community." The offering memorandum further said that buyers could expect to triple their earnings from the properties in ten years. Stacom also offered a variety of "creative strategies" for prospective buyers to wring more revenue out of Stuy Town. These included combining apartments for larger families, upgrading the retail stores, adding doormen to make the spartan buildings appear more luxurious, and developing "senior-friendly buildings." While the complex already had six garages, Stacom's materials said that a new landlord might also want to create additional parking—at premium rates—along the four interior "loop roads" that allowed cars to come in and out of Stuy Town's perimeter. Stacom was playing up MetLife's calm and quiet management of the property, in order to highlight the limitless upside. She and her team were making the case to bidders that MetLife had been a sleepy institutional player that didn't recognize that it was sitting on a gold mine.[17]

Despite the discouraging position of the city, and despite the fact that MetLife still had not provided us the bid books, as Crotty had predicted, our calendar was filling up with potential suitors. We set up meetings with major players in real estate: Steve Green and Marc Holliday of SL Green Corporation; Harrison and Richard LeFrak of the LeFrak Organization; Bill Dickey of ING Clarion Partners along with Jim Simmons of Apollo Real Estate; Richard Lerner and Anthony Orso of Credit Suisse; Ruby Schron of Cammeby's International; Dov Hertz of Extell Development Corporation; Mike Lappin of Community Preservation Corporation; Doug Eisenberg of Urban American; Christopher LaBianca, Rochelle Dobbs, and David Fallick of Bank of America; Jeff Blau of the Related Companies; and Steve Witkoff, with former speaker Gifford Miller representing him. Most meetings took place in the Chrysler Building at Grunstein's offices at Troutman Sanders, while the meetings with Related and Witkoff took place at City Hall. I attended most of the meetings with Grunstein and Maura Keaney, who represented Speaker Quinn.

While I was happy to see so much interest, the meetings were cursory, and I had the distinct sense that these firms were advising us of their plans and checking the box of having met with us, rather than truly seeking a legitimate partnership with the tenants. Some, like the Related Companies, flat out told us that the tenants' plan for homeownership was a mistake and something that they did not want to do. But nearly everyone who was interested in making a bid for the property reached out to us. Only one prominent institutional investor snubbed the TA entirely: Tishman Speyer Properties. Rob Speyer, Tishman Speyer's president and co-CEO, was quoted in the *New York Post* saying that "the opportunity to buy 11,000 units in Manhattan is what you live for," but did not make any contact with me or the Tenants Association. For his part, real estate tycoon Donald Trump said he would be sitting it out and predicted that it would be "a heated bid and that usually means somebody will overpay."[18]

Ten days went by, and MetLife had not given my September 1 letter the courtesy of a response, so Grunstein reached out to Darcy Stacom, MetLife's broker from CB Richard Ellis, and asked her for a meeting. On September 11, Stacom came to the Troutman Sanders offices in the Chrysler Building, where Keaney and I were waiting with Grunstein to greet her. She was all business, barely offering a smile when she shook my hand. Stacom turned to us with a cool "So, how can I help you?" Keaney and I looked at each other. This was clearly not how other prospective bidders were being treated by MetLife's broker. Grunstein politely expressed to her the Tenants Association's plan to find a partner and make a bid for the property. Stacom looked at us skeptically, took a few notes, and excused herself after about fifteen minutes. The next day, Stacom called Grunstein and told him that the tenants would not independently be considered to be a "qualified bidder" by MetLife. Stacom said that we were more than welcome to team up with another qualified bidder if we wanted to. She relayed the same information to Senator Schumer's staff. That meant that MetLife was not going to give us the information we needed, which was included in the bid books, necessary to assemble our own independent bid.

"You have got to be kidding me," Keaney said when she heard Stacom's comments. "*Of course* we are going to partner with another qualified bidder. What do they think we're going to do?" That part was beyond question for us, because other than the funds that tenants would contribute by buying their own apartments, we had no money. But to deny us the opportunity to evaluate the financials of the property and come up with our own detailed proposal put us at a real disadvantage, and it was also, as Stacom's demeanor showed, a slap in the face. After all that New York City had done for MetLife over the years—now they wouldn't even engage with the tenants and their city councilman, who wanted them to simply consider a proposal that we expected could be in the billions of dollars. "Strategically on their part, it was a terrible decision. They were going to have to reverse course. If they really thought we were so inept, why not just give us what we were asking for?" Keaney asked me later.[19]

Keaney and I then decided to plan a quick, but sharp, protest on the steps of City Hall to call out MetLife for abandoning its commitment to New York City. We wanted to publicly remind the company of the years of subsidies and guaranteed profits that MetLife had enjoyed in Stuy Town, which had been approved under a cloud of controversy in the building behind us sixty years earlier. With Keaney's help, I invited the entire city council to join me on the steps of City Hall to make this point and to demand that MetLife reverse course. Dozens of tenants, including Doyle, Steinberg, and Marsh, joined me and a handful of council members shouting "Shame on Met." "This is a company that has enjoyed every tax break known to man," I embellished to Sabina Mollot of *Town & Village* newspaper. "And now they are turning their backs on the tenants and the city." It was great political theater and got picked up by a variety of news outlets.

Hours later, Stacom called both Quinn and Schumer's staff to say that there was a misunderstanding and that they would be happy to provide us the bid books. Keaney quipped to me, "'Misunderstanding' seems to be a code word for 'we didn't realize you'd do a press conference demanding the books, and since we now look like idiots we are going to give them to you.'"[20] We cheered our early success.

All the same, we were billions of dollars away from making a credible bid, and while Grunstein was having productive follow-up conversations with potential partners, we had precious little time to pull anything together. MetLife had asked for bids to be submitted on October 5—which was only three weeks away. Crotty suggested that I look into whether there was any legislative strategy that could help protect tenants, and perhaps find a way to slow this whole process down. It hadn't occurred to me that I could use the legislative process like that, and it felt only marginally appropriate. But I rationalized that under emergency circumstances, pulling any political lever at our disposal was worth a shot. Keaney agreed that it made sense and called a meeting with the city council's legislative division to kick around some ideas.

As a result of Governor Rockefeller's unhelpful 1971 reforms, the City of New York did not have the right to strengthen rent-stabilization laws, only to weaken them. Named after Rockefeller's housing commissioner Charles Urstadt, the Urstadt Law of 1971 required that most tenant-friendly initiatives be passed by the New York State Legislature in Albany. Because the Republican-controlled State Senate opposed tenant protections, we knew that a state legislative remedy was unlikely. On the other hand, with the support of the new city council speaker, there was very little we could not pass through the council if we wanted to. Keaney and I met with the council's policy staff and reviewed a variety of ideas. Some were just arbitrary, unconstitutional, or just bad policy—like a 25 percent property tax increase on properties, like Stuy Town, that had been former urban renewal areas. However, one intrepid legislative staffer then threw out a promising idea: a local law that would require owners of properties with thousands of rent-stabilized units to give 120 days of notice to the city's housing department before they were sold. During that time, the city would have an obligation to assess the impact of the transaction on the overall stock of affordable housing and to recommend changes to the deal before it was finalized. This was neither groundbreaking nor transformative legislation, but if we could get it passed, it would give us enough time to come up with the money for our bid and put more public pressure on MetLife. There was of course no reason to believe that Mayor Bloomberg would sign the bill, but even if he didn't, we hoped that it might force him to engage more fully on the Stuy Town issues. There also was a substantive case for it—private transactions that had the potential to affect so many tenants all at once lost some of their exclusively private character, so I felt that some level of public review was appropriate. But mostly, we had very few options, and we needed some leverage.

Doyle was getting worried as every day passed that we would not have enough time to get our bid together, and when I told him about the legislation, he was very eager for us to pass the bill. I shared Doyle's urgency but also feared that if we passed it, it would be too easily dismissed simply as a naked attempt to aid the tenants' bid. I reached out to Rosie Mendez, the council member from District 2 just across the street from Stuy Town, to see if she would be willing to step in as the sponsor and put a little bit of official distance between me and the proposal. Mendez and I had been elected at the same time in 2005. Our districts shared a boundary along 14th Street and up First Avenue, and her district virtually surrounded mine in Stuyvesant Town and Peter Cooper Village. She agreed to be the prime sponsor, and we made phone calls, together with Keaney, to ask our colleagues to serve as cosponsors. In short order, we had thirty-two of fifty-one members of the city council supporting the bill.

While MetLife scrambled to figure out whether the city council was actually going to pass this legislation and effectively slow down the bidding process, Grunstein was hard at work reviewing the offering documents and preparing the details of our bid. One evening, with a pile of papers on his desk, Grunstein made a quiet discovery. He saw that MetLife had been taking a property tax break from the city for its renovation work on Stuy Town buildings. The tax break, called J-51, allowed an owner to abate its taxes for certain improvements it was making on the property. And the law provided that if you take the J-51 tax abatement, then you are not allowed to take units out of rent stabilization at the same time. Grunstein and everyone else seemed to know that MetLife had been using vacancy control to deregulate units for years, but not that it was participating in the J-51 program. Grunstein called me urgently and told me that if he understood the law correctly, residents of thousands of apartments that had already been deregulated—seemingly illegally—might actually have a right to sue MetLife and the future owner for damages for the amount of rent they overpaid. Grunstein explained to me that a potential legal claim like this could also add value to the tenants' bid. Other bidders could be shackled with this ongoing liability to tenants, while existing tenants could waive their legal rights in exchange for an opportunity for them to own their units. Moreover, if MetLife had illegally taken apartments out of rent stabilization, this could radically affect any new owner's business plan. Grunstein said that he and his colleagues at Troutman Sanders would quickly do more legal research and come back to me.

Meanwhile, the tenant leaders were hearing reports of lots of people in suits touring the property in groups. In a community like Stuy Town, even before social media, nothing escaped the notice of our neighbors. Some more bold residents would sidle up to the prospective investor groups and eavesdrop, hoping to pick up any tidbits of information about their plans that they could relay back to Doyle. For our community, the visitors in suits walking around represented the enemy camp—outside investors walking right into our home and scoping it out as a naked business opportunity. Seeing them around symbolized the change that nobody wanted.[21] Grunstein continued to field calls from potential partners. Others, like Ofer Yardeni, chairman and CEO of Stonehenge Partners, reached out to me directly and said that he was homing in on a "very compelling" proposal. Yardeni proposed keeping about 20 percent of the community as affordable housing for a twelve-year period, in exchange for a tax abatement.

Doyle and I were speaking daily, trading stories about what we were seeing and hearing. In the community, people were rather excited by the prospect of a Tenants Association bid. "Once our neighbors realized it was conceivable, they were just out of their minds with exhilaration," Steinberg said. "The idea that we could own the property and protect ourselves was quite powerful." Doyle and Marsh were fielding constant questions from neighbors about what it all meant. A couple of weeks away from MetLife's October 5 bid date, the pieces started to come together for us. Grunstein secured a term sheet from Bank of America, which was willing to lend us funds to buy the property; and the New York City Retirement System, the New York State Retirement System, and the Central Labor Council's Housing Investment Trust had each made verbal commitments to use their targeted investment dollars to make loans or to invest in equity in our plan. As we raced against the clock, both United States senators—Chuck Schumer, for the second time, and Hillary Clinton—called MetLife's chairman, directly arguing that he should support our bid, urging him to do whatever necessary to keep Stuy Town affordable.[22]

About 900 tenants tried to pack into the 330-person auditorium of Junior High School 104 on Saturday, September 16, to hear how the Tenants Association and its brand-new councilman proposed to come up with billions of dollars and give them a chance to own their apartments. This was my first Tenants Association meeting in my new role. Onstage in front of many anxious neighbors, I stood in the spot where I had for so many years watched Assemblyman Steve Sanders, Jack Lester, Susan Steinberg, and Al Doyle address the familiar but rowdy crowd. Now I was introducing myself for the first time in this context and explaining this most unusual plan. I was worried about how it was going to be received, and whether we would be able to answer the many questions that people had. Furthermore, I had to walk a fine line of explaining why we should be deeply concerned about MetLife's decision to sell, while also not unnecessarily scaring the many rent-stabilized senior citizens in the community. For the 73 percent of the tenants already covered by rent stabilization, they first wanted to know that their legal protections would stay in place.

I stepped to the microphone and explained why the Tenants Association had decided to make a bid to buy the property. You could hear a pin drop in the room as I explained that under our plan, rent-stabilized residents were free to remain as renters, protected by the rent-stabilization law. However, if they wished, they could decide to buy their unit. They were therefore going to be better off under our plan, I argued to the group, because we were adding options that they otherwise did not have. Market-rate tenants like me, who now represented 27 percent of the community, had even more reason to support the Tenants Association's objectives. Many of us had seen 20, 25, or even 30 percent increases in our rent bills when they had come up for renewal in recent years. And our legal protections were defined only by the terms of the lease rather than any government regulation. Market-rate tenants also generally were more affluent and able to pay market-rate rents, which were in some cases double, or even triple, what rent-stabilized tenants were paying. An opportunity to buy their unit, I argued, should be particularly desirable to this group. But it was hard to assess their interest in any meaningful way, because few of them turned out for the meeting, and as a result of the already high rents, many of them had little intention of staying in Stuy Town for more than a few years.

After laying out the plan, I introduced Grunstein—a new lawyer in this community that had only seen attorney Jack Lester onstage over the prior decade—to help explain how we were going to make a bid. Grunstein and his wife, both Sabbath observers who lived in Queens, had stayed in Manhattan overnight so that they would not need to drive to the Saturday meeting. When Grunstein got up to speak, he declined to use the microphone because it was the Sabbath—prompting some old-timers in the audience, not sensitive to his limitations, to demand that he "use the mike!" Grunstein politely demurred. Rather, he projected his voice and explained our plan to the uncharacteristically quiet audience. When we were done with our presentations, neighbor after neighbor stepped up to the two microphones stationed at the front of the auditorium, politely asking about every conceivable detail, like the cost of units and the risks to rent stabilization. We couldn't answer many of their questions, but we were able to say with certainty that if the tenants were successful, at least it would be our prerogative to collectively make the decisions. After all, people who owned shares in a cooperative had a right to elect a board, which effectively set the rules of the property.

The mood of the gathering was positive. "Most tenants left the meeting with a spring in their step," Justine Almada recalled. "The Tenants Association and this new councilman had a plan, and if they might deliver homeownership, this was worth a shot." Nearly everyone in attendance, representing 560 apartments, signed our "no buy" pledge. Marsh also signed up 193 volunteers to go door to door and approach neighbors to explain what was going on, and why we needed their support. Mike McKee, who did not ordinarily advocate directly to market-rate audiences, sent a pointed note on the electronic mailing list that Marsh and I had created for market-rate tenants: "Contrary to the assertion that the market rate tenants might be in an advantageous situation, the market rate tenants indeed are the most vulnerable and have the most to lose." They did not enjoy any rent protections, and their costs would inevitably be higher in any deal that the tenants were not endorsing. "Pull together, guys. Otherwise, you lose," McKee warned.[23]

On a conference call late in the evening of Sunday, September 24, I spoke with both Speaker Quinn and Senator Schumer about where we stood. Schumer intended to make another plea to MetLife's Henrikson and wanted to know how much progress the tenants had made, and what angle he needed to push. I briefed the senator about our plans for homeownership and told him that we expected to be able to put together a bid that was more than $4 billion, including debt from major banks that we suspected might include Bank of America, and equity investments from a variety of pension funds. But our chances of success, I explained, would be much greater if we had just a little more time to put it all together. Now armed with the information he needed, Schumer promised to push as hard as he could to slow it down and get MetLife to work with us directly.

To our amazement, Senator Schumer paid an in-person visit to Henrikson and relayed to him the seriousness of the tenants' effort. Henrikson emphasized his commitment to his own shareholders but promised the senator that he would give a close look to the bid when it came in. Unfortunately, that was as far as he was willing to go. Henrikson again flat-out rejected Schumer's call to slow the process down. If we wanted to buy ourselves time, the Mendez bill in the city council was our only option.

The next day, the city council held a hearing at City Hall on the Stuyvesant Town sale. I had asked Quinn to put a hearing on the calendar as a way to continue to focus attention on the importance of this community as an affordable enclave. She agreed immediately, and on the day of the event, Doyle led dozens of Stuy Town tenants to City Hall to argue that New York City should not allow Stuy Town to become luxury housing. Housing chair Erik Dilan welcomed Doyle to the witness stand. "We are not seeking a handout," Doyle said. "We are not looking for anything other than assistance already available to other similarly situated individuals or corporations who are looking to improve themselves, their communities and their city." He went on, "I am a second-generation Stuyvesant Town resident just like my neighbors: NYPD Chief Tom Sweeney who is raising his family here. Or Tom's brother, retired Firefighter Jackie Sweeney. Also Supreme Court Officer Chief Tom Wheeler, or his brother, much-decorated Port Authority Police Officer Jimmy Wheeler. And second-generation resident Councilmember Dan Garodnick." One popular senior citizen named Joy Garland, who had moved into Stuy Town in 1974, taught second grade at the local public school, and raised two kids in her apartment, pointedly asked the council: "Do we want Manhattan to only house the rich elite?"[24]

Grunstein was accumulating prospective partners and capital and told us that he was narrowing in on a $4.5 billion bid, a price that he felt was competitive and also would allow us to achieve our goals. At this price, where the initial loans would be paid down by unit sales, it was not over-leveraged, and there was no pressure to evict anyone in order to pay back debts, giving significant security to rent-stabilized tenants. Along with the AFL-CIO and the New York City Pension Fund, Grunstein told us, JPMorgan Chase had accepted our basic assumptions and was willing to put up a first mortgage commitment. Grunstein had also reached out to individual and institutional investors, who he believed would not only be acceptable to MetLife but also deliver a cooperative conversion plan for the Tenants' Association. Grunstein had loosely assembled a team of partners who agreed to put up the equity needed to close on the deal and assume the risk that we would successfully sell apartments to residents.[25]

Marsh and Doyle were floored by the price—it was, after all, well beyond what most people would expect from the Tenants Association. They quickly did the math of what that bid would mean for residents. With ten million square feet of space, and units that tended to hover around 1,000 square feet (a Stuy Town one-bedroom was 755 square feet, and a Peter Cooper two-bedroom was 1,223 square feet, for example),[26] $4.5 billion translated to an average of $450 per square foot, or around $450,000 for a unit. We were assuming that the market rate for a comparable apartment (there were no real comparable apartments, as Stuy Town is unique) was around $800 per square foot. Since the average price to buy an apartment in Manhattan in 2006 was nearly $1.3 million, that made our plan a great deal for Manhattan real estate. However, it was going to be challenging to explain to a rent-stabilized tenant that they should trade in their $1,000-a-month rental unit for the opportunity to buy a $450,000 apartment, no matter how good a deal it was. Regardless, I believed that we could find ways to help these New Yorkers buy their units if given the opportunity.

Grunstein projected that in the initial co-op offering, about 50 percent of tenants would opt to buy their apartments at discounted rates, which would bring in about $2 billion to pay down our debts.[27] There were some vacant apartments, which the group of equity investors, as sponsor, would be allowed to sell at market prices. The unsold apartments were to be retained by the sponsor and split into two groups. Twenty percent of the apartments in the complex were to remain rentals in perpetuity, with rents to be capped as affordable to people who qualified as middle class, up to 165 percent of the area median income. The remaining unsold apartments could be sold at market rates, over time, as the current tenants who had decided not to buy their apartment moved out.

The Tenants Association's plan, as envisioned by Crotty's team and fleshed out by Grunstein, would give every resident a choice between two purchase prices. If a resident opted for a deep discount, we would require that the unit be sold only to a person who could be certified as middle class. For residents who took a smaller discount, they would have an opportunity to sell their unit for increasing profit over time. For example, one year after the offering, they could sell the unit only for the price they had paid initially, whereas an apartment sold after five years could recover 140 percent or 150 percent of the cost. Eventually, the restrictions would burn off, and the apartment could be sold for the market rate. In this case, there would be no income restriction for the person buying the apartment.

Our hope from city government was that they would freeze property taxes at the current level in exchange for keeping the rental units affordable. (This would hark back to the 1943 legislation that created Stuy Town as a public good.) We also hoped that the city would convert the mortgage into bonds, which would give an additional tax benefit. Finally,

Figure 4.2. John Marsh was the organizing force behind the Tenants Association for fifteen years. He was a feisty, committed tenant advocate and was known to move around the community on roller blades, meeting volunteers and delivering materials building to building. He succeeded Al Doyle as president of the Tenants Association.
Photo credit: *Town & Village* newspaper.

we hoped to take advantage of existing state and federal programs that would help people to become first-time homeowners.

We knew that our bid was the only one that would accomplish any of these goals. In the final two weeks of September, Marsh sent dozens of volunteers into Stuy Town, every day, knocking on doors asking people to sign "no buy" pledges and explaining to our neighbors what the TA was trying to do. Marsh treated this project the way that he had treated the Peter Cooper electrical MCI, as a challenge, almost as a dare. "It reminded me of when I was a young activist. When Lenny [Grunstein] said we needed the unity pledges, I was like, *I can do that*. So we did."[28] By October 5, Marsh, along with board member Margaret Salacan and an army of volunteers, had signed up 5,601 apartments with a "no buy" commitment to the Tenants Association, more than half the units in the community.

On September 29, the entire executive board of the Central Labor Council wrote to Mayor Bloomberg and advised him that they, along with the TA and other private partners, had an "economically viable plan for MetLife to preserve their profit" in order to preserve Stuy Town. They asked that Bloomberg mediate a conversation among them, MetLife, and the tenants, to assist in delivering a positive outcome. Their plea did not move the mayor.

Bids were due by 3:00 p.m. on October 5. Proposals needed to include the purchase price, any conditions, and other relevant information. Grunstein submitted our bid documents at 2:53 p.m. with a bid price of $4.5 billion.[29]

REGROUPING AFTER THE LOSS

Charles Bagli, real estate reporter for the *New York Times*, had written the piece that announced the MetLife auction on August 30 and had followed the Stuy Town bidding process in real time. So I was not surprised when, three hours after the Stuy Town bids were in on October 5, Bagli called me for comment about the results. Of course, I didn't know the results yet, but Bagli did. I braced myself for the news. He already had learned with absolute certainty that the low bid was $4.3 billion, the high bid was over $5 billion, and that the Tenants Association's bid was in the mix, at $4.5 billion. By the next day, Bagli had reported the whole story. Top bidders were the Related Companies with Lehman Brothers, Ramus Capital with Apollo Real Estate, Tishman Speyer—and, to everyone's surprise, the Stuyvesant Town and Peter Cooper Village Tenants Association. And there was going to be a second round of bidding.

While it was unlikely that MetLife would select anyone other than the highest bidder, I held out hope that continued public pressure would force it to bend and either accept the tenants' plan or insist on some

long-term affordability protections (beyond rent stabilization) from another bidder. I told Bagli—and he reported—that the city council was moving forward on the Mendez bill, which still had the potential to postpone
MetLife's sale by 120 days and give us a little more time to build momentum in support of the tenants' plan. We hoped that if MetLife was left
hanging out in the wind long enough, its executives might feel compelled to
change course. And the politics of the situation were not good for Mayor
Bloomberg, who was being criticized for his hands-off approach; we still
hoped that the mayor would find a way to support the tenants' position.

Harry Giannoulis, MetLife's lobbyist, called me on October 6 to say
that he was "hearing good things" about our chances for making it to
the second round. He added that some people in the highest echelons
of MetLife are "praying that the tenants' proposal wins." He also asked
about the Mendez bill and whether I thought we would be moving it
quickly. "I think it's very important legislation, so that's my hope,"
I puffed. While Giannoulis was being polite about it, I knew from public
comments from real estate advocates that this bill had rankled them. Steven Spinola, president of the Real Estate Board of New York, called the
bill unconstitutional and promised it would be thrown out in court.[1]

On October 7, Darcy Stacom, the lead broker for CBRE on the deal,
called both Grunstein and Doyle in their respective offices to let them
know that we had in fact made it to the second round of bidding. Stacom
took the opportunity to express her displeasure at our legislative proposal,
saying it surprised her, "considering the sophistication of our team."
Doyle, despite Stacom's reaction, was extremely encouraged, and relayed
to me what Stacom had said. He also passed along our progress to the TA
board, which was giddy with excitement. Maura Keaney shared that view:
"Christ, this is like being picked for American Idol!" she emailed me when
I told her the good news.[2]

People in the community were excited but nervous, chatting around
the playgrounds and gossiping with their neighbors about how much their
apartment might cost and whether they would be able to get a reasonable
mortgage. While the Tenants Association was being bombarded with related questions, Grunstein cautioned us against dangling even hypothetical apartment prices to tenants because state law forbade us from doing
so until we put a formal offering plan before the New York State attorney general. The Tenants Association was also subject to a confidentiality

agreement with CBRE, which gave Grunstein the ability to access the financial information in their bid books and barred the Tenants Association from sharing information obtained through that process. Plus, in order to ensure confidentiality, Doyle and I decided to keep individual members of the board (and me) away from sensitive information, like individual apartment rents. We did our best to explain those limitations to tenants, but they pushed us every day for more information. Some read key details in newspapers and got upset when reporters seemed to share more information than we did. Board member Soni Fink was someone who wanted to see more details laid out to the board, and to the public. "You may be surprised to know that this is the first time I've been involved in a $5 billion investment," she cynically observed, "but I know the kind of information I require before I put $10,000 into a mutual fund."[3]

Meanwhile, things were moving very quickly on the deal. Finalists in the second round were asked to make their best and final offers by October 16 at noon, and it was reported that MetLife was preparing to close by November 15.[4] Anyone who has ever bought property, even a modest private home, knows that a thirty-day period from handshake to a closing is not just fast, it is warp speed. Doyle privately told me that he hoped we could raise our bid to $5 billion. Unfortunately, he and I both knew that every dollar we went above $4.5 billion would cost us real affordability. If we raised the amount of our bid just to win, we might not be able to deliver any new protections for future residents. And yet, if we didn't raise our bid somehow, we would also lose.

All of a sudden, my neighbors—many of whom I had known since I was a child—had started to treat me differently. No longer was I called "Danny," a nickname I had around my building, but they started, with gratitude, calling me "Councilman." I lay awake at night worried about what might happen next.

While we had, on any sober consideration, very little chance of winning against firms whose first-round bids were higher than where we felt we could end up, I had grown increasingly worried about what would happen if our bid actually did prevail. I had heard enough comments in community meetings that made it clear to me that our neighbors had different agendas. We had tenants with different profiles: some were covered by rent stabilization, and some were not, and each tenant's appetite to own his or her apartment varied. Some tenants believed deeply in our goals of preserving affordable housing for the next generation of residents; others did not. It was obvious to me that it would have been easier to simply say no to MetLife in protest, rather than to champion a certain goal. With anger and hostility, my constituents would have surely cheered my fighting spirit, and win or lose, I would bear no responsibility for the results. Saying yes to anything, on the other hand—and certainly by proposing something myself—would mean that I'd own the outcome and be responsible for any problems that might emerge later. I could hear the voice of Assemblyman Sanders, who continued to urge caution. "The whole matter is loaded with political landmines and big problems," he said to me. "It will be an albatross if not a waterloo."[5] I had not heeded his advice in August, and as I got reactions from my neighbors, which were all over the lot, it was becoming clearer to me that he was probably right: winning would likely create stark divisions in the community as we worked out all the details. But despite these trepidations, I felt we still had no alternative path. We had started the process because it was, and continued to be, our best move. Now we needed to see it through.

With only a week left before October 16, we made one last attempt at persuading Mayor Bloomberg to support our effort. Grunstein, Keaney, and I scheduled an appointment with HPD commissioner Shaun Donovan in his conference room at 100 Gold Street. At a bare minimum, we thought the mayor should call a press conference and remind MetLife of its relationship with the City of New York and the commitment it had made to middle-class New Yorkers in 1943. Donovan heard us out but still did not make any commitments on behalf of the Bloomberg administration.

Without any certainty coming from the mayor, Mendez formally introduced her bill on October 11, five days before the second-round bids were due, saying that a 120-day notice period would give all parties a chance to study "both the immediate human and public policy consequences of these sales." My colleague Alan Gerson, who represented a district in Lower Manhattan, got thirty-four members of the city council to sign a letter to Mayor Bloomberg demanding that the city honor its commitment to preserve affordable housing by supporting the bid of Stuyvesant Town and Peter Cooper Tenants. Speaker Quinn amplified the message, saying MetLife "should remember all the support" the city has given them historically "and the critical role they play in providing middle class housing in our city." She warned bidders that any new owner who failed to preserve significant affordable housing in Stuy Town could forget about any future rezoning help from the council.[6]

Despite this public pressure, MetLife totally brushed aside arguments about equity, made no mention of history, and rejected any suggestion that it had any continuing obligations to provide below-market housing in Stuy Town. MetLife's CEO C. Robert Henrikson even challenged the notion that Stuy Town could even be considered affordable housing. Outrageously, his spokesman John Calagna told the *New York Sun* that with a median income in Stuy Town and Peter Cooper Village of $78,000, "that doesn't sound to us like that is affordable housing for the middle class."[7]

While we negotiated the terms of the bill at City Hall, Grunstein ran the numbers again and again. He felt strongly that at $4.5 billion, we were at the highest end of what the property was worth. Any new owner who paid more than $4.5 billion would be forced to find ways to generate new revenue in order to pay back significant debts. In Stuy Town, that meant one of two scenarios, and neither of them was good for me and my neighbors. One way to generate revenue was to take advantage of the unused development rights in Stuy Town and build new buildings on playgrounds and green spaces. The other way was to try to evict people and use vacancy decontrol to raise rents on new tenants by getting apartments out of the rent-stabilization system altogether.

Three days before the second bids were due, MetLife suddenly and without warning asked the remaining group of bidders to submit a plan for how they intended to protect residents of the eleven-thousand-apartment housing complex.[8] We did not know if we had successfully pushed the affordable-housing issue into the conversation, or if this was just a cynical way to pacify us and lull the city council into tabling the Mendez bill. But it was the first sign of any movement by MetLife on one of our core concerns.

Doyle, Marsh, and I decided to make one final public push for the Stuy Town tenants on October 15, the day before the bids were due. The Tenants Association called a rally in Stuyvesant Cove Park, a spot on the East River that was historically significant to the residents of Stuy Town. In 1992, the tenants had defeated a disfavored massive real estate deal that had been proposed there called Riverwalk, which included multiple residential apartment buildings on the site, and this park was the trophy of their victory. The defeated developer in that case—Related Companies—ironically, was also now a second-round bidder to buy Stuy Town itself.

"Where's Mike?" the crowd of 750 agitated people bellowed at the absent Mayor Bloomberg. Yellow "Save Our Homes" signs dotted the crowd, and people turned out to express their anger at the mayor and at MetLife. In the crisp fall morning, we handed out flyers that encouraged people to call Robert Henrikson directly at MetLife's corporate office and Mayor Bloomberg at City Hall. "He's taken a laissez-faire attitude," Jim Roth, a Tenants Association board member, told the *Daily News* about the mayor. "He owes us more than that."[9]

We had set up a podium on a small stage outside of Solar 1, a not-for-profit environmental learning center on the East River. As I took to the stage before hundreds of my neighbors huddled together near the riverbank, I put on my game face. I hollered to the crowd, pointing my finger toward the ground: "We are here to say that the residents of Stuyvesant Town and Peter Cooper Village are drawing a line in the sand. We are standing up for ourselves, and we are giving hope to every community in New York City that seeks to preserve housing for the middle class." But then I also tried to manage expectations. "We are still hopeful to be the winning bidder, but make no mistake about it—in order to fully achieve our goals, we will need the support of the city to preserve the affordability of this community for the long term. That's why we need to continue to show our strength. And we need to encourage the mayor to stand with us."

Speaker Christine Quinn and Brooklyn congressman Anthony Weiner, who were both expected to be candidates for mayor in 2009, followed me at the podium. Quinn doubled down on her support for the tenants and our bid, calling on MetLife to do the right thing. Weiner said that the mayor should fight for tenants in Stuy Town, just like he had fought for Goldman Sachs to stay in the city. Behind the scenes, even as we gathered at Stuyvesant Cove Park, Grunstein was speaking to most of the remaining bidders and exploring last-minute partnerships. While few real estate experts gave the tenants much hope, *Daily News* columnist Juan Gonzalez observed that our bid, supported by city politicians and labor unions, was a "daring move to compete head to head with a dozen of New York's most powerful developers." While still the underdogs, the tenants, he said, had become "the most popular girl at the dance."[10]

On October 16, we were ready to submit our new bid to MetLife. We had increased the number to $4.55 billion, up nominally from $4.5 billion, and asked MetLife to allow the Tenants Association to lease the property for ninety-nine years, instead of selling it to us outright. Grunstein believed that such a lease structure would bring tax savings to MetLife because of its partnership with a not-for-profit organization. Under this scenario, MetLife would agree to defer some of its income over ninety-nine years, but increase by potentially billions of dollars its upside over that period. But other bidders were offering much more money, right then. He submitted our bid before twelve noon on October 16, and waited.

At 10:24 a.m. on Tuesday, October 17—less than twenty-four hours after the bid deadline—my communications director Dan Pasquini fielded a call to me from Rob Speyer, the co-CEO of Tishman Speyer Properties, at my 250 Broadway office. Pasquini emailed me a message that said that Speyer had "signed the deal to buy STPCV, and wanted to reach out before the public announcement later this morning."[11]

Tishman Speyer was a firm deeply involved in civic affairs in New York and was a known quantity to both MetLife and to Mayor Bloomberg, but less so to me. Only one year earlier, Tishman Speyer had bought MetLife's building at 200 Park Avenue for $1.72 billion. The elder Speyer, Jerry, was chair of the Museum of Modern Art, and the Partnership of New York City. His son, Rob, who was now calling me, had been appointed by Mayor Bloomberg to be the chair of the Mayor's Fund to Advance New York City. My hands shook as I called Speyer back. I reached him on his cell, and he immediately told me how excited he was to be part of the Stuyvesant Town and Peter Cooper community. I congratulated him on his victory and tersely asked what his plans were for preserving affordable housing for future middle-class people. Speyer promised that they were not planning on making any significant changes at Stuy Town and reminded me that my neighbors would be protected by the rent-stabilization law. But as for long-term affordability, Speyer told me that they had no specific plans beyond rent stabilization to preserve affordability there.

He was, I judged, weary from all-night negotiations, and I was angry—at him, at MetLife, at the mayor, and at myself. Speyer had never even reached out to the tenants in the prior months and now was acting as if

I had nothing to worry about. MetLife had enabled all of this, and the company was now walking away with billions of dollars. Tishman Speyer was poised to do exactly what Stacom had laid out for a new owner: shake things up to increase revenues, and to do it fast. The TA and I were going to be left on the sidelines to watch it all unfold. Speyer suggested that we make a time to meet later in the week, and I agreed.

Negotiations had indeed gone all night, and concluded about an hour before Speyer called me. We learned that Apollo had come in a very close second place at $5.33 billion. Overnight, Apollo had been in contact with Grunstein, exploring the possibility of an eleventh-hour partnership with the tenants. "It was beyond belief close," Grunstein later observed. "Most of the bidders thought that having tenants as part of the bid would make a difference. Everyone was straining to say that they were partnering with the tenants. But not Tishman Speyer."[12]

Later that day on October 17, Keaney paid a visit to Speyer's office in Rockefeller Center on behalf of Speaker Quinn to strongly urge Tishman Speyer to work with the city on an affordability plan.[13] Speyer bounded into the conference room to meet her. "You know, you shouldn't write off the tenants. Dan Garodnick is reasonable," Keaney said. "He doesn't have horns coming out of his head. Let's find a way to do something here that is tenable for you; you really don't want this political headache." Speyer acknowledged what she was saying, and seemed receptive to Keaney's perspective. ("I could have spoken to him in Gaelic, and he would have agreed," Keaney subsequently told me.) He did not rule anything out regarding affordability, and Keaney left the meeting hopeful that Speyer might still be willing to do something.[14]

It was officially the largest American real estate deal ever: "$5.4B!" shouted the headline in the *Daily News*. "My heart sank a little bit, mostly because of the amount of money they paid," said Eric Stedfeld, a twenty-eight-year resident of Stuy Town. "I'm concerned that because they're paying as much as they're paying, affordability is not in the equation." Grunstein himself felt like Tishman Speyer had gotten what he called "most favored nation" treatment in the deal. "The two final bids were not far enough apart that they shouldn't have prompted more conversations. It's hard to explain why they were the one buyer who didn't meet with the tenants."[15]

A couple of hours after my call with Speyer, I walked onto the steps of City Hall to talk to interested reporters and was surrounded by an array of television cameras as local news outlets looked for a reaction to this extraordinary real estate story. "Stuy Town was never intended to become a luxury, gated community—and must not be," I said. I then reiterated what I had demanded to Speyer: we needed to know how Tishman Speyer intended to ensure the affordability of the community for the next generation of residents. "We will want to know that Tishman Speyer does not intend to add additional development onto the historic property," I demanded to the cameras. "We will want to know that Tishman Speyer will be an owner whose benevolence will extend beyond the mere obligations of the law."

Soni Fink drafted a dire but determined missive that the Tenants Association sent to the community that same day. It began with the news that just about everyone had already heard: we lost. Signed by Doyle, Steinberg, and Marsh, it concluded defiantly: "The Tenants Association, strong to start with, has emerged stronger, more cohesive, and more determined to save this community than ever before."[16] We knew that nobody really expected us even to be in the game; even though we felt like we had just gotten manipulated by MetLife into believing we had a chance, we surprised a lot of people. Tenants groups do not ordinarily amass billions of dollars to compete in real estate deals. Doyle's Tenants Association was stronger than ever, but the immediate contest had been lost, and we were now forced to search for a second strategy.

The criticism of Mayor Bloomberg was fierce after October 17. Housing advocates agreed that losing Stuy Town created a dangerous precedent for the city. The Tishman Speyer win created the impression that the Bloomberg administration was only willing to support affordability in new housing construction—but not to protect existing rent-stabilized units. This was a "dark day for affordable housing," Michael McKee of Tenants PAC told the *Times*, explaining that Stuy Town would never have even been created without eminent domain and favored tax treatment. "It's disingenuous to say there's no public interest in what happens to this housing," John H. Mollenkopf of the Graduate Center of the City University of New York told Bagli. The Tenants Association had worked so hard to get Mayor Bloomberg to throw us even a crumb of support, and Grunstein later confessed that he had walked away feeling like the mayor and his agencies were just not interested. "It appeared that the mayor believed that special efforts did not have to be taken to preserve middle-income housing in prime locations in Manhattan. The mayor's efforts were directed at creating major new middle-income housing developments in the boroughs. There seemed to be a clash of philosophy here at a deep level."[17]

Bloomberg did have one substantive point in favor of his hands-off position: preserving Stuy Town would have come with a cost. Bloomberg's New Housing Marketplace Program—which he called the most ambitious housing plan ever developed—had a goal of creating or preserving 165,000 units of city-subsidized affordable housing over eleven years. It was expected to cost $8.5 billion, not including city-financed bonds, and would serve half a million "low income and middle-class New Yorkers." So, while it anticipated spending significant sums to create and preserve affordable housing, the Bloomberg administration had to make some choices. Deputy Mayor Dan Doctoroff explained to Keaney and Quinn that, for the same price, they could build twice as many outer borough

Figure 5.1. I enjoyed a good working relationship with Mayor Michael Bloomberg but was deeply disappointed that his administration decided to stay on the sidelines during the 2006 Stuyvesant Town sale. Photo credit: William Alatriste.

units as they could save in Stuy Town. "To save Stuy Town, it would mean they needed to create a tradeoff in their plan," said Keaney. "To them, this was core Manhattan, and core Manhattan is just unaffordable."[18]

Seemingly in an attempt to deflect attention from what had happened in Stuy Town, the Bloomberg administration on October 20 announced its plans to create "the largest middle-income housing complex built in New York City in more than thirty years" at Queens West, on the Queens waterfront in Long Island City. The city had purchased the land from the Port Authority and hoped to create five thousand middle-income rental units where a family of four earning between $60,000 and $145,000 a year would pay $1,200 to $2,500 a month in rent.[19] I read the stories about this and shook my head with irritation.

The *New York Times* reported the Queens deal but noted the continued criticism of the way the mayor had handled Stuy Town: "Even as tenants pulled together a bid with support from the City Council, the mayor stayed on the sidelines, drawing rebukes from housing activists who questioned his dedication to affordability," wrote Damian Cave. Asked about the loss of Stuy Town at the celebratory press conference for Queens West, Doctoroff repeated what he had told Keaney and Quinn: they could build two units in Queens for every unit preserved in Stuy Town. Mayor Bloomberg, willing to go on the record for Cave, said, "You must remember that a lot of the housing units in Stuyvesant and Peter Cooper Village are affordable and will stay affordable for many, many years." Housing advocates did not agree. "This is a blind spot on the part of the mayor and the administration," said Mike McKee of Tenants PAC. "They are stubbornly refusing to recognize that they are taking one step forward, three steps back." Rob Speyer, however, was ebullient. "The opportunity to buy 11,000 apartments in a terrific neighborhood in this city doesn't come along very often, maybe once in a generation," he told the Associated Press for a piece that also ran on October 20. "You live for opportunities like this one."[20]

At 9 a.m. on Friday, October 20, I went directly from my Peter Cooper apartment to the Tishman Speyer offices in Rockefeller Center. "Just a couple of young gun-slinging real estate tycoons in the ultimate stare down," my chief of staff Andrew Sullivan emailed me just before the meeting, doing his best to lighten the moment. When I got to Rockefeller Plaza, I noticed that the seventh floor waiting area was stark white, with large colorful works of valuable modern art adorning the walls. The receptionist brought me to a square conference room with a glass wall on one side and a view of St. Patrick's Cathedral on the other. Several minutes later, Speyer walked in, also alone, and we shook hands. He was charming and unassuming in manner and acknowledged with great humility that it was a difficult bidding process.[21]

We were about the same age and had both grown up in New York City, attending competing high schools. In spite of myself, I liked him personally, and he reminded me of many of my own friends. The meeting was brief and friendly. I politely suggested that we find a way, together, for Tishman Speyer to develop a plan for long-term affordability in Stuy Town beyond what the rent-stabilization law required. He said he was open-minded and expressed a sincere desire to do right by the tenants but said he would need governmental help to do anything like what I was asking. It was an opening, and like Keaney had felt after her conversation with Speyer, I thought there was an opportunity. As I left the office, I immediately emailed Quinn to tell her that we should continue to push the Speyers on affordability. In my gut, I felt certain that Rob Speyer surely would want to do something, anything, to smooth over the fact that the new owner had just beaten out the local Tenants Association in a bidding war.[22]

Keaney and I quickly organized fifteen elected officials, including Senators Schumer and Clinton, to join me and Quinn on a letter—which we sent on October 24—to demand that Tishman Speyer step up and agree to do something specific to go beyond rent stabilization to preserve long-term affordability in Stuy Town. We did a lot of demanding in those fall days of 2006, without a whole lot of authority. "Tishman Speyer has the opportunity to preserve these middle-class apartments for generations to come, and to be part of stemming this affordable housing crisis," the letter said. It went on to say: "We believe this should not be limited to the existing rent protections." Tishman Speyer was too distracted working its own public relations campaign to pay much attention to our demands. The day after he won the bid, Rob Speyer dropped a letter under each of the doors of the community expressing how "honored and excited we are to become a part of your outstanding community." The photocopied letter went on to note that Tishman Speyer is a "business with deep roots in New York, a true love of our city and a great respect for the neighborhoods that make it special. We are committed to maintaining the unique character and environment that have made Peter Cooper Village and Stuyvesant Town such a wonderful place to live for so long."[23]

Unfortunately for us, the structure of the deal told a story different from the one Tishman Speyer's letter suggested. Speyer had paid an awful lot of money to buy the property, and borrowed the extraordinary sum of $4.4 billion to close the deal. It had borrowed from a variety of sources, including the government of Singapore, SL Green, the Public Pension Funds of California and Florida, and the Church of England. The rest of the purchase price was made possible by a variety of pension funds and other institutional lenders. Tishman and its partner BlackRock each contributed the relatively small amount of $112 million. Tishman Speyer, with MetLife's support, had led these investors to believe that they could increase the net operating income from $167.4 million to $252.4 million in three years—and up to $504 million in ten years—and cash in. The only way to do that was by raising rents on existing units or by building on open spaces in order to create new ones. Tishman Speyer had some interest in protecting the open spaces, because they were an amenity for high-rent-paying tenants. That meant that Tishman Speyer most likely needed to develop a plan to use vacancy decontrol to get rent-stabilized tenants out of the community, to renovate their vacated units, and to find a way to entice into the community people at a higher income level who could afford to pay much more. Simply put, they would need to transform this largely middle-class community into a luxury product. And, indeed, it quickly became apparent that this was their plan. Tishman Speyer and its lenders had privately projected that approximately three thousand rent-regulated units would be deregulated within five years. This was a 33 percent tenant turnover rate that housing advocates felt certain could only be achieved using illegal harassment.[24]

Beyond being an offensive strategy, it also was destined for financial and political failure. Adam Rose, who was managing the property, saw Tishman Speyer's projections and just could not understand how they were going to make it work. He had spent years pursuing tenants who he felt were gaming the system. A particularly straight talker, Rose told the new Tishman Speyer executives at a Rockefeller Center staff meeting that there was simply no way to get so many tenants out of their apartments in the time frame they had imagined. They were projecting 15 percent turnover in the first year and a 12 percent turnover in the second. Rose told them they were wrong, and that their best-case scenario was 4 to 5 percent annually. The Tishman Speyer team smiled and did not pay Rose any mind. "How arrogant," Rose later commented. "They spouted off about how many apartments they were going to turn over, and how they were going to make the deal work. I told them it was ridiculous." Rose, a real estate veteran and politically a liberal gay-rights advocate, concluded, "We have already gone through the entire property and dealt with all the egregious cases. This huge population that you think you are going to get rid of doesn't exist." Rose was replaced within two months.[25]

Tishman Speyer's business strategy was becoming the norm in New York real estate. Much like what had happened when vacancy decontrol first went into effect in 1971, efforts to get rent-stabilized tenants out of their apartments were now in full swing all across the city. Vacancy decontrol took a bite out of the rent-stabilization system from 1997 to 2006; the very first year it was in place, at least three times the number of apartments in New York City were deregulated as had been the prior year. Landlords certainly had enough loopholes in the rent-stabilization laws to make widespread displacement a viable financial strategy. It gave rise to a new business opportunity, which was politely called the "repositioning" of multifamily buildings. The aggressive entry of investors into the working- and lower-middle-class real estate market began to strike Central Brooklyn—and then the South Bronx, East Harlem, and Washington Heights. Practically every New York neighborhood with a concentration of rent-stabilized buildings was on the target list for real estate investors. Because many were institutional players with lots of capital, these new owners could afford patient, relentless eviction proceedings and tenant buyouts in a way that most previous owners, who often owned single buildings, working with a different set of profit margins, could not.[26]

From 2005 to 2009, private-equity-backed developments bought about one hundred thousand units of rent-regulated housing—about 10 percent of all regulated units in New York City. In most of the cases, the purchase price was not supported by the rents that were then being paid, which meant that profit levels could only be achieved by creating vacancies and displacing tenants. Tenant advocates coined a new term for all of this: "predatory equity" in housing. A report by the Association for Neighborhood and Housing Development stated that residential real estate

rent-stabilized tenants, Tishman Speyer also needed to make significant property improvements and add amenities to attract people who would pay higher rents.[31]

Days after the announcement, Speyer shrewdly invited tenant leaders Doyle, Jim Roth, and Susan Steinberg to a meeting within Tishman Speyer's headquarters. They too took note of the crisp white walls, the modern art collection, and the impeccably dressed receptionists. I had spoken with Doyle before his meeting and encouraged him to keep pushing Speyer on an affordability plan. Speyer and David Dishy, one of Speyer's associates, came out to meet them. Speyer knew the tenants were on edge and was doing his very best to make them feel comfortable. After listening to Speyer's expression of enthusiasm for Stuy Town, and a commitment not to make any sudden changes, the tenants were getting increasingly uncomfortable. They felt that there was a deep disconnect between Speyer's optimism and their own feelings of alienation from the bidding process and the result.[32]

Tired of the pleasantries, Doyle politely asked Speyer to explain what his plans were for long-term affordability. Speyer and Dishy stopped their pitch, exasperated by the question, which they were hearing more regularly now. Speyer took a breath and again assured Doyle that he and the other tenants would be happy in a year about how they turned things around. "We pride ourselves on service," he said to Doyle. Steinberg told Speyer that this was cold comfort for tenants, who were happy enough with the current service and wanted assurances about their, and the community's, future. Dishy and Speyer worked to calm their new residents and even tried to establish goodwill by inviting the tenant leaders to the Christmas tree lighting in Rockefeller Center—another property owned by Tishman Speyer—the following week. Steinberg bristled at the invitation. She felt like Speyer was trying to buy them off. Doyle and Roth felt the same. When they left the meeting, Roth looked at Doyle and Steinberg and said, "If any of you goes to the tree lighting, I'm going to get everyone in the world in front of your building to tell them that you've been bought." None of them went.[33] Not realizing that the tenant leaders had drawn a line in the sand, Zoe and I accepted our own invitation.

The Stuyvesant deal closed on November 18, 2006. Ten days later, on November 28, Grunstein called me urgently. He wanted again to talk

about MetLife's use of the J-51 property tax abatement program to reno-
vate units. During the bid process, Grunstein had discovered that MetLife
was applying for the J-51 break even while taking apartments out of the
rent-stabilization system. This was not allowed, based on his understanding of the law, and in the rush to assemble the bid, he did not have a
chance to fully explore it. Now, with more time on his hands, Grunstein
had done more research and believed that MetLife and the entire real
estate industry had made a monumental mistake. We had lost the bid,
but challenging this even after the fact, he speculated, had the potential to
preserve and even expand affordable housing, not just in Stuyvesant Town
but throughout the entire city.

As part of their own due diligence on the deal leading up to the
bid, Tishman Speyer executives had surely uncovered what Grunstein
had found: MetLife was getting a J-51 property tax abatement for rehabilitation work on the property. The J-51 law provided that apartments that became rent stabilized "by virtue of" the J-51 tax abatement
needed to stay rent stabilized for as long as the owner was using that
tax break. In Stuy Town, the units had not become rent stabilized by
virtue of J-51, but rather by the 1974 Emergency Tenant Protection Act
(ETPA), years before MetLife had ever applied for a J-51 abatement.
MetLife had long taken the position that because Stuy Town became
rent stabilized by the ETPA in 1974, and not by J-51, the property was
not stabilized "by virtue" of the abatement, and MetLife could simply
follow the rules of rent stabilization and continue to deregulate units as
they became vacant.

There was some history behind MetLife's interpretation. In the early
1990s, Sherwin Belkin, MetLife's leading lawyer, had approached the
state housing agency and asked it to confirm that MetLife could deregulate its Stuy Town units because the property had not become rent stabilized *by virtue of* the J-51 benefit.[34] This was a difficult argument to make.
Stuy Town was not only protected by the rent stabilization law, but it was
also receiving the J-51 tax break, which independently required that these
units continue to be rent stabilized.

However, in January 1996, Belkin found a sympathetic official named
Darryl Seavey, who wrote a private opinion letter stating that Belkin's
interpretation of the J-51 rules offered "a feasible alternative." In his letter to Belkin, dated January 16, 1996, Seavey, an assistant commissioner

of DHCR, the state housing agency, cited Webster's dictionary to analyze the "by virtue of" language and applied "a lexicographical definition to those words," pronouncing that an owner should feel free to deregulate units unless "the receipt of [J-51] is the sole reason for the accommodation being subject to rent regulation." While informal and not binding (and Seavey expressly warned in the letter that his opinion should not be treated as a "substitute for a formal agency order"), the letter was spread throughout the industry, which eagerly grabbed onto this very generous interpretation. As a result of this nonbinding letter, landlords receiving a tax break from the city—which explicitly barred deregulation while receiving that benefit—now felt that they had another avenue to take units out of rent stabilization using vacancy decontrol. It was a gift to the real estate world, and they were going to act on it immediately. Five years later, in December 2000, during the administration of Republican governor George Pataki, the state DHCR formally amended its own regulations to be consistent with the letter. New York City's Housing Department unsuccessfully opposed the change, saying that the new interpretation violated the intent of the State Legislature. By 2006, Rob Speyer and most bidders in Stuy Town had not wasted a lot of time focusing on the J-51 issue, which they believed was long resolved.[35]

Grunstein, however, believed that there was no basis in the law to support this interpretation by DHCR. The whole practice of deregulating units in Stuy Town was illegal, Grunstein told me. "Wait, you're saying that MetLife was illegally deregulating units? C'mon," I said, not believing what I was hearing. "Yes," Grunstein said, and paused for effect, before explaining that while a landlord is receiving the J-51 tax abatement, deregulation is completely forbidden—and that every unit in Stuy Town and Peter Cooper was covered by this provision. If Grunstein was right, Speyer's entire business plan that relied on deregulating units was dead on arrival.

Grunstein felt strongly that the Tenants Association should immediately sue MetLife and Tishman Speyer on the grounds that deregulation of units was not allowed. This made many of the tenant leaders, including me, deeply uncomfortable. We certainly didn't want to antagonize the new owner—or to embarrass ourselves—with a bogus claim. Board members like Marsh and Roth strongly urged moving forward with a lawsuit, while others like Frank Rinaldi and now-retired assemblyman

Steven Sanders felt it was very unlikely that we would succeed in court and would surely alienate Tishman Speyer. The rest of the board watched the lawyers on the board fight it out by email, unsure of what exactly they should do. I stayed on the fence for quite a while myself. It was hard to imagine that all the bidders in Stuy Town had simply missed this issue. In fact, MetLife had been using J-51 for years. It was an insurance company, which in my mind was hardly the type known to take enormous risks by playing fast and loose with the rules. After several rounds back and forth with Grunstein, I was persuaded that he was right on the law, and if we had even a distant shot to lock in rent stabilization in Stuy Town and other communities around the city, we needed to take it.

The message board that Marsh and I had created as part of our Market Rate Residents Network had become over the years the primary place for tenants to share their lease renewal experiences. It now was fertile ground to find tenants who lived in the units that had previously, and unlawfully, been deregulated. One resident, Amy Roberts, posted in December 2006 on the TA's message board about her worries of an unreasonable rent increase. Roberts was a single mom who had moved into Stuy Town in 2004 and was about to negotiate her own lease renewal, which included a significant rent hike. She asked about others' experiences, explaining that she was trying to decide what to do before moving out. Marsh and Roth had been keeping an eye on the posts on the message board and sent her a note. They let her know that there was a lawsuit being contemplated that would impact the rent hikes and gave her the contact information of the lawyers, if she was interested. Roberts was certainly willing to hear more and had nothing to lose, so she made the phone call. Roberts was frustrated about her experience in Stuy Town and felt that the case was worth pursuing. "You just have to have a little bit of willingness to put yourself out there," Roberts later told the *Times*.[36]

Grunstein's firm had a conflict, so he called his friend Stuart Saft at Wolf Haldenstein and asked him to take on this case. On January 22, 2007, led by Amy Roberts, who became the lead plaintiff, a group of tenants filed a lawsuit claiming that MetLife—and its successor Tishman Speyer—had illegally deregulated more than three thousand apartments in the complexes because state law required that units covered by the J-51 tax abatement be kept rent stabilized. The suit accused the company of "wrongfully pocketing nearly $25 million in New York City tax benefits." Roberts and the other class representatives stood for ten thousand present and former market-rate tenants of Stuy Town and Peter Cooper, like me, who argued that they should never have been paying a market-rate rent to both MetLife and now Tishman Speyer.

In Stuyvesant Town, the filing of the lawsuit barely registered. Residents had other more pressing matters on their minds as the new owners came in and began making changes immediately. What we didn't know was how this long-shot lawsuit, coupled with the impacts of an over-leveraged property, would ultimately doom Tishman Speyer's business plan.

PUSHING BACK AGAINST
A NEW OWNER

Within weeks of closing, Tishman Speyer unfurled huge advertising banners down the sides of the plain redbrick buildings on First Avenue and Avenue C loudly proclaiming "Luxury Rentals." John Marsh saw the signs and thought, "These guys are out of their minds."[1] The nondescript buildings in Stuy Town were sometimes confused with public housing; they had no doormen, no amenities, and they were built to be basic, not "luxury." I braced myself for the change that was coming—it was clear that Tishman Speyer was about to give the place a makeover.

They coined the slogan "A Park Runs Through It" and trumpeted the ample green spaces. They took down all the chain-link fences that for years had kept teenagers off the grass and instead invited people onto the long-forbidden lawns. They changed the no-pets policy that dated from the 1940s and welcomed dogs and cats. They undertook a massive planting program to beautify the landscape and converted a local supermarket to a gym. Other new amenities were provided in the middle of Stuyvesant Oval, all for a fee. Branded "Oval Amenities," these benefits promised members exclusive access to a small movie theater, an indoor playground, a place to host parties, and a quiet place to work. On one hand, the improvements were arguably a benefit to the community, despite the fact that some carried a fee above and beyond one's rent. On the other hand, it was obvious from the improvements that Tishman Speyer had a rather different vision of the type of residents who they hoped would be populating Stuy Town. By adding amenities and remodeling apartments—and inviting in new residents—Speyer could make Stuy Town hospitable to what Gabriel Sherman of *New York Magazine* called "the new armies that were increasingly populating Manhattan, the recent college graduates with jobs in marketing and finance who worked long hours and wanted a full-service experience." Sherman referred to it as a "clash of the utopias," where traditional rent-stabilized properties were being transformed into "lifestyle communities," which are essentially a cross between a hotel and a spa. Buildings that promised a "kind of post-frat lifestyle where every moment not spent at work was spent cocktail in hand amid nonstop hilarity."[2]

Marsh and Steinberg were both alarmed by Tishman Speyer's changes. Before long, Tishman Speyer had invited the rock band Fountains of Wayne to Stuy Oval, and hundreds of people from around the city had turned out to hear them belt out "Stacy's Mom," right in the heart of Stuy Town. With its concert series open to the public, Tishman Speyer created an opportunity to showcase Stuy Town's new flowers, its "luxury" buildings, and its lifestyle offerings. "They called us fuddy-duddies and asked 'what's wrong with a little music on the Oval?' It was all part of their marketing plan, and they really needed this stuff to promote themselves," Marsh recalled. Visitors stomped on the grass, made noise, and left their mud and garbage behind. Twenty-somethings filled the buildings in greater numbers, subdividing apartments to allow for extra bedrooms. As more people occupied units, my office received many more complaints about noisy neighbors with parties, pizza boxes tossed in hallways, and a more common smell of marijuana in the buildings. "These buildings were built for families, not as dorms," Marsh complained.[3]

I tried for a period to keep an open mind about the new owners. As a resident, I didn't mind the new amenities, and even joined the new local gym. I understood the objections to the growing number of pizza boxes and concerts, the over-planting, and the bogus airs of luxury, but I was far more concerned about a weightier problem that was developing. After Tishman Speyer won the auction, I had expressed my continuing concern about the lack of an affordable-housing plan, but at that time I did not fully appreciate what the structure of the deal would force them to do to current residents. I wanted to believe that well-respected New York institutional players would not resort to doing bad things to New Yorkers. I was wrong. Soon after the transfer of ownership, my office started getting calls from concerned rent-stabilized tenants—many who had lived in the community for years—who said that Tishman Speyer's lawyers had served them legal notices informing them that their lease would not be renewed because the unit was not their "primary residence."

New York's rent-stabilization law gives renters a legal right to a lease renewal, but only if they are actually living in their rent-protected apartment. And if you are not actually living there, an owner has the right to evict you. To do so, an owner sends a "Golub notice" rather than a lease renewal, between 90 and 150 days before the lease expires. To prove their case, landlords must have evidence that the tenants in question do not actually live in their apartment—giving landlords incentives to dig into the private background of their tenants. With the introduction of vacancy decontrol in 1994, this incentive was compounded. "It created an industry of investigators, lawyers, who started looking into rent-regulated tenants," said Sam Himmelstein, a tenants lawyer and partner at the law firm Himmelstein McConnell, which saw its volume of cases multiply by eight times from 1997 to 2008, primarily because of vacancy deregulation. Landlords suddenly were hiring private investigators to uncover the true whereabouts of tenants—sometimes by questionable means. One of Himmelstein's clients received a package at his weekend home in the Catskills from a fake delivery man sent by his landlord trying to secretly record him admitting that he didn't actually live in his apartment in the city. "Tell me about the house, how much time do you spend around here?" the "delivery man" asked as he used an audio recorder to capture secretly the conversation for the benefit of the landlord's lawyers.[4]

Short of employing such extraordinary means, landlords and their investigators commonly used other legal but intrusive tactics to make their case. Investigators searched data about car registrations, voter registrations, or taxes; they questioned other tenants about a neighbor's activities, and scrutinized video cameras in public hallways and electronic key card data from the front doors to monitor the presence (or absence) of a tenant. Some owners even added cameras in hallways—motion activated and trained on tenants' doors—in order to capture the evidence they needed. Lawyers representing owners were known to come to court with shopping carts of VHS tapes to make their case.[5]

Following this well-established playbook, Tishman Speyer hired a lawyer named Fred Knapp, who worked as a private detective and whom the *New York Times* profiled in 1988 as the "scourge of illegal tenants." "Minus Bogie's trench coat, and armed only with his knowledge of the law, Mr. Knapp spends his days in damp basements and dusty side rooms of county courthouses, scouring documents that might prove conclusively that a tenant really lives somewhere other than in his rent-controlled or rent-stabilized apartment," Alan Finder wrote. Knapp had gone into this business as a young lawyer in 1984, appalled at bad tenant behavior. "I see apartments that rent for $180 a month and the tenant is subletting out rooms at $300 a month," he said. "I see so many abuses here. Investment bankers who keep a pied-a-terre in New York and bought four acres in Greenwich." Knapp's techniques included looking in public records like election boards, the New York State Department of Motor Vehicles, and other, more obscure documents. "We got somebody on a dog's license once," he told the *Times*. "To get up in the morning and hit the courthouse—I like it," Mr. Knapp said. "To me, it's a hunt. And when you hit, it feels good."[6]

The hunt was now on in Stuy Town, with Knapp as the leader. The problem for Tishman Speyer was that the great trove of untapped "illegal tenants" that they planned to evict in order to make their business plan work simply did not exist. Adam Rose had warned the Tishman Speyer team when they took over that MetLife—like most owners of rent-stabilized apartment buildings in the city—had regularly kept up with evictions.[7] That didn't stop Tishman Speyer from starting to deliver Golub notices to residents. The receipt of these notices was frightening—even for the overwhelming majority of tenants who were in their apartments legally—and forced people to hire lawyers to defend themselves. Some tenants chose not to fight and just left rather than spend the resources and time they would need to stay in their apartments. Others fought, but with a significant financial and emotional toll.

"They are fishing, deep-sea fishing," Marsh said to me after a few of these cases crossed our desks. "This is nuts." Pursuing tenants for illegal behavior was only appropriate where an illegal act was present. Yet for so many tenants of Stuy Town, they were suddenly on the receiving end of claims that were surprisingly weak. Himmelstein marked the starting point of these abuses as early 2007—just months after Tishman Speyer bought the property. And it continued for the next two years, mostly un-abated. The Tishman Speyer cases "were the flimsiest ones we had ever seen," Himmelstein said. "All they came up with was the mere existence of an alternate address, and they would claim that it was your primary residence. Like with any group of cases, the facts varied. But in the vast majority of cases, it wasn't true."[8]

"Today you'd call it 'alternate facts,'" recalled James Fishman, a part-ner at Fishmanlaw PC, another firm representing tenants. "It was as if they were making stuff up. Not only was there this much higher volume, but also a much lower level of legitimacy. There was just a lot of either totally bogus allegations, or flimsy allegations, or both." One of Fish-man's clients was a Stuy Town resident who got a Golub notice claiming that she was actually living in Naperville, Illinois. Not only had she never been to Naperville; she had never even been to the state of Illinois. But a quick Google search revealed that there was a person of the same first and last name who lived in Naperville. "They were putting people in a name search and finding people of the same name living somewhere else," Fish-man said. "That's how crazy it got."[9]

In December 2007, Amy Lamy, a legal secretary and a ten-year resident of Stuyvesant Town, opened her mailbox to find a Golub notice from Tishman Speyer that accused her of living in a four-hundred-square-foot apartment in Brooklyn rather than Stuy Town. Lamy was surprised to see the notice. She had bought that studio apartment for her mother and had never lived there herself. Lamy's notice also cited another Manhattan address—but she had not lived there for fifteen years. She spent four months working with a lawyer and assembling bank and credit-card records that proved she lived in Stuyvesant Town before Tishman Speyer relented and renewed her lease.[10]

In many cases, Tishman Speyer also wouldn't drop the claim when tenants brought evidence of their legal residence. One Fishman client provided forty-seven pieces of documentation to prove that she lived in Stuy Town—but Tishman wouldn't withdraw its claim.[11] Yet another tenant wrote to my office asking for help because Tishman would not accept proof of her twelve years of employment at the Peninsula Spa in Manhattan, her rent checks, and her passport. "Do I need a lawyer?" she asked me plaintively. I did my best to keep up with cases like these and to make the case personally to George Hatzmann, Tishman Speyer's point person. If I successfully intervened, it would help tenants avoid having to spend several hundred dollars per hour on a lawyer. The process of getting one of these cases dismissed, even without a court appearance, would likely cost a tenant around $2,000. This was big money for a lot of Stuy Town tenants, and neither Stuy Town leases nor the law had any provision for the landlord to pay a tenant's lawyers' fees if the tenant won the case. Tishman Speyer simply was allowed to make a claim based on its own "information and belief" that tenants were not legally living in their units. This is an extremely low bar and meant that cases like these were very hard to get dismissed early in the process.

Tishman Speyer was serving plenty of Golub notices but also was making other moves to challenge rent-stabilized residents. This included denying nearly all requests for subletting, and rejecting most cases where a family member claimed a right to take over a deceased relative's apartment. Some tenants received neither a Golub notice nor a lease renewal—rather, when it was time to renew their lease, they just got radio silence.

Of course, while the vast majority of rent-stabilized residents did not own second homes, some did. And as long as the second home was not their primary residence, they were doing nothing illegal or improper under New York State law. It's worth noting here that this reality is part of the complexity of fighting for the interests of middle-class people. They are—by definition—not impoverished, and may have amassed some amount of money. Along with taking family vacations, paying for some of your child's college education, and putting money away for a comfortable retirement, owning a home is one of the dreams of middle-class people. Tishman Speyer used the "second home" rationale to not only pursue residents, but also to amplify their argument that these tenants did not really deserve to live in a below-market unit. And it forced me to make the politically unappealing, but legally correct, argument that the people with summer homes also deserved to be free from harassment.

I spoke with Doyle and Marsh and discussed our strategy to fight back. They had already been networking with potential allies like Tenants PAC, the New York State Tenants and Neighbors Coalition, the Metropolitan Council on Housing, the NYC AIDS Housing Network, and the Coalition for the Homeless. Together they plotted an enormous tenant rally at Stuy Town against predatory practices in housing more generally. Because Stuy Town had been recognized as the most prominent example of this problem, the group announced that on May 23, 2007, the coalition would come to Stuyvesant Town with some ten thousand people to form a human ring around the community. This gesture was intended to show their support for Stuy Town tenants and to demonstrate the strength of the tenant movement. The Tenants Association, led by the organizing muscle of Marsh, drove Stuy Town residents to the perimeter of the property, to join hands with our tenant allies from around the city. On the corner of 14th Street and First Avenue, I met many pro-tenant members of the city council, and we hollered into bullhorns that we would not allow communities like Stuy Town to fall apart on our watch.

Over only seven months, in 2007, Tishman Speyer had sent out 507 Golub notices, out of 3,380 lease renewals. Our rallies and declarations of public support were strong, but Doyle and I agreed that we needed to provide the tenants actual tools to defend themselves. I had allocated funds in the city budget that passed in June 2007 to support a free legal hotline for tenants, hosted by a lawyer named Harvey Epstein and his team at the Urban Justice Center, and eagerly passed the number on to residents needing help. We huddled with Fishman, Himmelstein, and other tenant lawyers and contemplated filing a lawsuit against Tishman Speyer's lawyers themselves, for propagating lawsuits that we believed had so little merit that they might have constituted an ethical violation. I also personally implored Tishman Speyer's George Hatzmann and Rob Speyer to send letters—instead of legal notices—to people whose tenancy they were questioning. When I spoke to them about it, they seemed to be open-minded, but once they took it to Sherwin Belkin, their lawyer, the conversation ended. Belkin explained to me, "Based upon the phalanx of case law, I believe that I would be doing a grave disservice to my client were I to endorse the sending of a letter prior to the services of the Golub notice, which letter might, even arguably, cause a tenant to assert a claim of

Figure 6.1. On May 23, 2007, thousands of tenant advocates from around the city formed a human ring around Stuyvesant Town and Peter Cooper Village to vocally push back against landlord abuses. This photo was taken from the roof of Beth Israel Hospital, looking north toward 20th Street and First Avenue. Photo credit: *Town & Village* newspaper.

confusion or other basis to vitiate the Golub notice. The owner already goes beyond the legal requirements by including a note with the Golub notice."[12] In a cynical attempt to be "responsive" to my request, Tishman Speyer instead sent a letter to *every single tenant* in the community, not just to tenants they suspected of using their apartments improperly. The letter invited everyone in a friendly and a seemingly nonthreatening way to "come in and talk to us" and to bring in their personal documents with them if they were at all concerned about their legal status. This letter just added to people's worries that they too were going to lose their apartment.

Inflamed by this move, Doyle publicly urged all tenants to simply ignore Tishman Speyer's invitation. "While this letter says it is intended to ease fears, it is actually creating them," the Tenants Association stated in a sharp press release. The icing on the cake was when John Marsh—lifelong resident and leader of the Tenants Association—opened the mailbox in his building lobby on December 13, 2007, and found his own Golub notice. Marsh called me up. "Dan, you're not going to believe this. I got one of the Golubs. Ha! Is this for real? They know who I am. They see me all the time fighting with them," he said to me. But the fact was that Marsh had a modest New Jersey cottage in his family's name since 1969. And now they were coming after him. I reached out to George Hatzmann and gave him a heads-up that Tishman Speyer was about to cause itself even greater embarrassment. This time recognizing their error, they dropped it quickly, and Hatzmann apologized to Marsh.

Tishman Speyer's relentless pursuit of tenants continued well into 2008. On July 22, 2008, I called a press conference with the tenant leaders to again demand that Tishman Speyer stop its pursuit of tenants and that it impose a moratorium on its campaign of Golub notices. As we stood on 16th Street, I called out a variety of other ways that Rob Speyer could do right by tenants, like paying for tenants' legal fees in situations where Tishman Speyer had pursued a tenant in error, and by committing to not trying to evict people year after year for the same issue. I had raised these issues directly to Speyer by letter on both March 24 and July 17 but got no response and saw no changes in Tishman Speyer's official policy. Between 2006 and July 2008, Tishman Speyer used Golub notices to decline to renew 870 of 6,679 rent-stabilized leases.[13]

We were getting nowhere with Tishman Speyer and had few remaining options. Life had gotten considerably more complicated for me personally, too. Zoe and I had gotten married on May 10, 2008. We had moved the date of our wedding up because we were increasingly worried about my mom's health. After she had been diagnosed with multiple myeloma, a blood cancer, in 2003, each month we waited to see her test results with dread. On January 2, 2009, my dad, Zoe, and I checked in my mom to New York-Presbyterian Hospital, where she was going to have a stem cell transplant. She had harvested her own cells years earlier, and the doctors were going to blast her with chemotherapy, destroy her existing cells, and then reintroduce her own stem cells, with a hope of slowing this terrible cancer. It was a successful procedure, but she suddenly was too weak to eat, or move much, and Zoe and I spent most of our days at the hospital, keeping her (and my dad) company. She was discharged after a couple of weeks, and my dad took care of her in their Peter Cooper apartment as she slowly recovered. Since I lived only two buildings over, I visited them frequently whenever I had a minute during the day, or before I headed home at night. My worry for her pervaded my every day and followed me as I went from meeting to meeting, event to event, juggling my responsibilities as a city council member and my desire never to be away from my parents for too long.

As I balanced my personal and professional life, and the tenants scrambled to defend themselves, Tishman Speyer was running out of liquid assets. Their debt obligations far outpaced what they were generating in rent.[14] Because rent-stabilized leases were all either one or two years, by the end of 2008 Tishman Speyer already had been able to scrutinize every single lease when it came up for renewal. They had successfully pushed out only half the tenants they went after and now no longer even had the prospects of raising significant revenue by driving out additional tenants. Golubs began to drop, from a high of 15 percent of all renewal leases down to about 3 percent. Tishman Speyer then tried offering incentives to get new high-rent-paying residents in the door: a free month of rent, gift cards or cash when existing tenants referred friends, and they actively promoted the new amenities. They were also raising rents on the existing market-rate tenants by a significant amount—in some cases up to 33 percent. At the same time, we started to hear talk about Tishman Speyer and BlackRock having to raise more money to keep the Stuy Town operation alive.

There was one thing that could truly push them off the cliff: if the court were to find for the tenants in their J-51 lawsuit and prohibit any deregulation of units whatsoever. For 2007 and most of 2008, that seemed unlikely, in any event. In August 2007, Justice Richard Lowe III of the New York Supreme Court (not, despite its name, the highest court in the state) had dismissed out of hand the *Roberts* case, the class action named after lead plaintiff Amy Roberts, reasoning that the "clear and unambiguous language" of the law said that MetLife and Tishman Speyer were allowed to deregulate units because they had not become rent stabilized by virtue of participating in the J-51 program. (Stuy Town had become subject to the rent-stabilization law fully eighteen years before MetLife had even applied for J-51 tax benefits.) Justice Lowe interpreted the law to mean that because the units did not become subject to rent stabilization *solely* by virtue of receiving J-51 benefits, the owners could continue to take units out of rent stabilization through vacancy decontrol.[15]

A new member of Wolf Haldenstein's class-action practice, Alex Schmidt, had not even heard of the *Roberts* case while it was being litigated in 2007. At that point, it was being handled by his firm's real estate department. Schmidt, a soft-spoken graduate of Brooklyn Law School, had spent the first twenty years of his legal career doing general commercial litigation at other firms. He joined Wolf Haldenstein in 1999 doing general litigation and joined the class-action group in 2005.

After Justice Lowe dismissed the *Roberts* case in August 2007, Dan Krasner, the surly chair of the firm's class-action team, walked into Schmidt's office with the dismissal order and threw it on his desk. "We lost this," he said. "I wanted to see if you could do anything with it." Schmidt shrugged. He had lived in a rent-controlled studio in his first year of law school but didn't even bother to read the lease, let alone learn anything about rent regulations. He had a full plate in late summer 2007 but agreed to take it on. A quick look at the file revealed that it was full of dense statutory references—all foreign to Schmidt—and he was relieved that another law firm, called Bernstein Liebhard, was also working on the case as co-counsel. The lawyer at Bernstein Liebhard had agreed to write a first draft of the appeal brief. The final version wasn't due for nine months, so Schmidt put it on a pile on his desk and waited for Bernstein Liebhard's draft to arrive.[16]

In the spring of 2008, Schmidt looked at his calendar and saw that the deadline for the *Roberts* appeal was coming. He pulled the case file out from his growing pile to give it a more careful read. As he waded through the statutory references, he was struck by how simple and clear the tenants' argument actually was. MetLife took a tax break that barred deregulation of rent-stabilized units. That was basically it. The state housing agency had said something different, but state law was determinative. Could it be that simple? He read the papers again and felt certain that Justice Lowe was simply wrong to have dismissed it. Schmidt carved out some time, rolled up his sleeves, and told his co-counsel at Bernstein Liebhard that he would draft the appeal brief himself. Schmidt summarized the tenants' position this way: when MetLife decided to take the J-51 benefits, it now had not just one, but two mandates to keep Stuy Town units under rent stabilization. Stuy Town residents were entitled to the protections of rent stabilization because state law had required it in 1974, and now the existence of the J-51 tax abatement protected them a second time. He submitted his papers on May 30, and on September 11 he marched down to Madison Square Park to argue the appeal at the grand white marble building of the Appellate Division's First Department at 27 Madison Avenue.[17]

Schmidt bumped into lawyers from Skadden Arps during the walk to the courthouse and recognized Jay Kasner, a powerhouse partner who represented Tishman Speyer. He introduced himself to Kasner and his colleague, Scott Musoff, and the lawyers chatted politely as they walked the last few blocks of Madison Avenue together. At the time, Kasner was best known for his recent US Supreme Court victory in *Dabit v. Merrill Lynch*, which stopped state law securities fraud class action claims on the ground that they were preempted by the Securities Litigation Uniform Standards Act of 1998. He was one of New York's most feared litigators, and he entered the building with the confidence of a lawyer whose client had won decisively at the lower court. The entire gallery was filled with sharply dressed men and women in suits, energized by the probability of another win.[18]

Off the bat, the five judges seemed to understand, and accept, Schmidt's argument that the state legislature clearly did not intend for apartments to be deregulated when getting this tax break, no matter what. They tossed softballs at Schmidt, and he handled them easily. When Kasner rose to the podium, he parried questions from the justices who were aggressively challenging his position. Kasner was skilled, and held his own, but the judges had shown their hand. They did not agree with the lower court. When the arguments were over, Schmidt saw the Tishman Speyer and MetLife legal teams huddled in groups both in the lobby and out on 25th Street, quietly conferring with each other.[19]

All those involved knew that a loss in this case would be devastating to Tishman Speyer, but they, as well as other owners of real estate, had other, bigger problems brewing. Days after the argument before the appellate court, on September 15, 2008, Lehman Brothers, the nation's fourth-largest investment bank, filed for bankruptcy. With $619 billion in debt, Lehman had just made the largest bankruptcy filing in US history. The roots of Lehman's collapse were in the overinflated housing market that gave rise to the Stuy Town deal. Mortgages had been bundled into securities and sold to eager investors who wanted to take advantage of the returns that the US housing market had produced regularly for the prior seventy years. Firms like Lehman held on to large positions in subprime and other lower-rated mortgages while they were bundling and selling shares in products connected to those underlying mortgages. At the same time, rating agencies like Moody's and Standard and Poor's were giving high marks to these mortgage-backed securities, sometimes favoring them with ratings as good as US Treasury bonds. When the underlying mortgages started to fail, the securities that were backed by those mortgages suffered huge losses; and the firms that held them, like Lehman Brothers, lost an extraordinary amount of value. This was a terrifying moment for the US economy. The stock market dropped 4.4 percent in a single day, at the time the largest decline since the terrorist attacks of September 11, 2001 (the nearly 13 percent drop in a single day of trading in March 2020, owing to coronavirus fears, has since topped it), and some $700 billion vanished from retirement plans and other investment funds. The panic that followed plunged the US economy into a severe downturn, now known as the Great Recession.[20]

Only six months earlier, the Federal Reserve Bank of New York had bailed out Bear Stearns, and the weekend before the Lehman bankruptcy, the US Treasury Department had seized control of mortgage giants Fannie Mae and Freddie Mac.[21] By September 16, 2008, US treasury secretary Henry Paulson had bailed out insurance giant AIG for $182 billion. Later that same week, Paulson and Federal Reserve chairman Ben Bernanke asked Congress for a $700 billion bailout measure to rescue all other banks, which promptly passed. It was signed into law by President George W. Bush on October 3, 2008.[22] All of this spelled serious trouble for Tishman Speyer and its quieter partner, BlackRock. With the collapse of the entire housing market, Stuyvesant Town was worth a fraction of its initial value. Tishman Speyer had failed to raise revenues as they had hoped, and their reserve fund to pay for debts was nearly gone. And then, a panel of judges of the Appellate Division had given the distinct impression in their questioning of Tishman Speyer's lawyers that they might rule for the tenants in the *Roberts* case, which would mean that Tishman Speyer's entire business plan, in addition to not working out as they hoped, was also illegal.

On Thursday, March 5, 2009, Schmidt was sitting at his desk and saw the "First Department" come up on his caller ID. It was the clerk of the court calling to advise him that a decision was coming later that day. He had never gotten a call like that before, so Schmidt asked tentatively if it was OK for him to ask who won. The clerk told him that the panel had reversed the lower court. It was a tenant victory. When the decision arrived by email one hour later, Schmidt eagerly printed it out. Judge Eugene Nardelli—with the support of each of the other judges on the panel—had concluded that while receiving the J-51 tax break, MetLife and Tishman Speyer had been barred by law from deregulating even a single unit in Stuy Town. Schmidt took a moment to savor the win. But for him, it was a legal victory only—and not one that had any broader political or real estate implications. He was only marginally aware of the battle currently being fought in the community over tenant rights, or what this would mean for Tishman Speyer and their backers who had just invested billions of dollars in this deal.

For the tenants, and for Tishman Speyer and their investors, however, the *Roberts* win created shock waves. Tishman Speyer and MetLife could have to pay up to $200 million in damages to the ten thousand current and former tenants whose rents had gone up illegally under both of their tenures, and they might even need to return three thousand apartments to rent stabilization.[23]

Harvey Epstein from the Urban Justice Center emailed my staff the decision, and we passed it along to the Tenants Association. Once we had a chance to review it, we were exuberant. It was particularly meaningful to those market-rate tenants who were suffering from enormous

rent increases, because it meant that their units likely were still rent stabilized and they could be entitled to damages for having paid too much
over the years. "Victory is sweet. Thank goodness," Marsh wrote to me
that afternoon.[24] But he and Roth were already thinking about how real
estate lobbyists might try to get the state housing agency to cancel the
tenant win, and wanted me to help fortify public support. I drafted a
quick public statement, reaffirming our view that these units should never
have left rent protection—and checked in with Doyle before sending it
out. "Tishman Speyer needs to do something unheard of in this town:
re-regulate apartments that have been lost as affordable housing," the
statement proclaimed. "Tenants who have been wronged by their landlords' double-dipping are owed rent overcharges and significant damages,
and they should collect." We went out into the community the next day,
on March 6, to hand out flyers to share the news of the tenant win, and
started planning a press conference to celebrate it.

When I got to the office, I called Schmidt to introduce myself and to
congratulate him on the victory. Schmidt had never gotten a phone call
from an elected official, and he didn't know how to react. I thanked him
for his hard work and invited him to a rally that we were holding on Sunday morning to cheer on his efforts down at Stuy Town, on the corner of
16th Street and First Avenue. "A rally?" Although he had attended political events in the past, Schmidt had never been to a client's rally before; it
is not what lawyers usually do, and he hesitated. I told him how excited
everyone was to meet him and that we were certainly going to celebrate
him whether or not he joined us. After some gentle cajoling, he agreed to
make an appearance.[25]

That Sunday, March 8, Schmidt, wearing a blue blazer and khaki pants,
walked up to the growing crowd on Stuy Town's perimeter, and I grabbed
him and shook his hand vigorously. "This is the man who just won the big
case," I hollered to nobody in particular. Doyle, Marsh, Steinberg, Fink,
Roth, and many other tenant leaders gathered to congratulate Schmidt
and to thank him. Schmidt smiled uncomfortably and quietly said hello to
people one by one as they came up to him. As the media pressed forward
to the temporary podium, he positioned himself at the very back of our
press conference, with arms behind his back, tentatively, trying to avoid
any attention. "Because he was so soft-spoken, it was hard to believe he
had just won such a big victory," Steinberg recalled. Schmidt watched

Figure 6.2. Stuyvesant Town and Peter Cooper Village occupy eighty acres next to the East River, sandwiched between the East Village, Gramercy, Flatiron, and a corridor of hospitals on the East Side of Manhattan. Map credit: Bill Nelson. Based on map from Mack Scogin Merrill Elam Architects.

as, one at a time, elected officials like Congresswoman Carolyn Maloney, Borough President Scott Stringer, Senator Tom Duane, and Assemblyman Brian Kavanagh came to the podium to celebrate his win and denounce MetLife and Tishman Speyer for daring to take a tax break while taking apartments out of rent stabilization. He saw tenants' signs calling out Tishman Speyer for their bad behavior. Watching the crowd, and hearing the commentary, it started to sink in for Schmidt how meaningful the case was for the people of this community. Schmidt sneaked a peek at his Blackberry and saw telephone messages from Charles Bagli of the *Times*, Eliot Brown of the *Wall Street Journal*, and from Reuters, the *Real Deal*—and even the *Sacramento Bee*.[26]

Meanwhile, the real estate world reeled from this decision. "Landlords may have to give back thousands of dollars in rent, which in turn could lead to lower building values and a drop in tax revenues for the city," complained industry advocate Joe Strasberg, who orchestrated the vacancy decontrol legislation in the city council in 1994.[27] The industry was boggled by how the courts simply could ignore the fact that they had all relied on a 1996 letter opinion and 2000 formal rule from the state housing agency. How could tenants claim to have paid too much for rent when they had willingly paid it?

Tishman Speyer and MetLife sought an expedited appeal to the Court of Appeals—and hoped to keep the decision from becoming effective until the state's highest court sorted it all out. Arguments were set for September 10, 2009, and Schmidt felt like he needed to present a fresh angle. When he had briefed the case at the Appellate Division, he was new, and a bit rushed. Now he had a command of the case and the law and had time to dig a little deeper into the legislative history of the J-51 tax abatement. While the text of the law was clear enough, he wondered whether, during the debate over the law, any legislators had explained what they actually *intended* to do. As it turns out, finding legislative history and transcripts of floor debates, like so many other things in Albany, is difficult. Schmidt's associate Michael Liskow figured out that you could buy New York's legislative histories from a private service. So, Wolf Haldenstein's office invested $3,000 and ordered the history of the Rent Regulation Reform Acts of 1993 and 1997. Liskow started plodding through the text.[28]

Almost immediately, the words jumped out. Republican senator Kemp Hannon, the sponsor, had said clearly and repeatedly in the debate that because J-51 was a "public benefit," under no circumstances would the J-51 tax break go to a building that was deregulating units. Liskow excitedly ran the text into Schmidt's office and read him a July 7, 1993, colloquy between Senator Hannon and Senator Olga Mendez. Mendez had pushed Hannon repeatedly on whether a building could ever be deregulated while receiving J-51, and Hannon repeatedly affirmed that it would not. Hannon's comments were going to be the nail in Tishman Speyer's coffin, Schmidt thought.[29]

As both a former litigator and as a politician, I was excited by this case and decided to cosponsor with Doyle and the Tenants Association a September 29 event at the Stein Senior Center on East 25th Street to watch the live-stream of Schmidt's argument before the Court of Appeals in Albany. I was also in the midst of my first reelection campaign. I did not have any challengers in the primary, and unlike my first election, Doyle and the Tenants Association leaders were mostly supportive of my candidacy. I gave some introductory remarks to the sixty seniors assembled from Stuy Town, explaining why this was so important, then took my place on a folding chair around a small television set and watched Schmidt and Jay Kasner taking questions from the seven-judge panel. Over the intervening months, I had gotten the city council—with the complete support of Speaker Quinn and thirty-five other council members—to submit an amicus brief in support of the tenants. Borough President Scott Stringer, a regular at the TA meetings at the local public school, had done an amicus brief of his own, too. MetLife and Tishman Speyer had once again brought their top legal talent for the occasion: Kasner and Scott Musoff of Skadden, Arps, Slate, Meagher & Flom appeared for Tishman, and Alan Mansfield of Greenberg Traurig was there for MetLife. Behind these two formidable lawyers sat probably twenty to twenty-five associates and junior partners on one side of the courtroom, scurrying around, writing notes.[30] Kasner stood up to make his argument, and I was struck by how good he was. He was a natural—a big, dominant personality, who addressed each of the judges by name and filled the courtroom with his loud and clear presentation.

Schmidt was outgunned in terms of moral support. His team at the podium included just Ron Aronoff of Bernstein Liebhard and his partner

Dan Krasner. Schmidt's wife, Barbara, had also come up and was in the audience. When it was Schmidt's turn, the judges were firing questions at him almost faster than he could process. He responded cogently but was tentative with questions that he did not anticipate. Schmidt hoped that he got his points in, but in the excitement of the moment felt that he did not; he left the argument feeling deflated. When he passed by the Tishman and MetLife legal teams in the lobby of their Albany hotel, Schmidt felt worse. With ties loosened, and enjoying a few drinks, they were in a celebratory mood.[31]

Schmidt got in the car with Barbara to drive home and finally calmed himself down once they were on the New York Thruway, well south of Albany. He replayed the argument in his mind. Each of the judges that questioned him had expressed skepticism or concern about different issues, but he realized that he had heard nothing that challenged his most important point: the plain meaning and legislative intent behind the J-51 tax abatement. Despite knowing that he hadn't matched Kasner's dominating presence in the courtroom, he turned to Barbara and said, "I think we're going to win."[32]

Over the next month, Schmidt braced himself. Any day could bring news of the court's ruling. On October 22, 2009, at 9 a.m., Schmidt looked at his Blackberry as he walked through the Port Authority Bus Terminal on his way to work from his home in New Jersey. There it was—the decision from the Court of Appeals. He stopped right in the middle of the sidewalk, forcing rush-hour commuters to weave around him. He quickly skimmed the decision. He could feel the blood pounding through his veins as he read the words and realized that he had won. The Court of Appeals found that MetLife and Tishman Speyer had violated the "plain text" of the 1993 law that prohibited the deregulation of any building receiving J-51 tax breaks from the city. The court affirmed the Appellate Division and ruled that MetLife and Tishman Speyer had acted illegally when deregulating units in Stuy Town and Peter Cooper. It was a complete victory for the tenants.

I had started my day at 7:30 a.m. at the Mandarin Oriental Hotel on Columbus Circle at an early morning breakfast in support of the Mount Sinai Adolescent Health Center with Diane and Fin Fogg, parents of one of my closest friends from high school. After the event was over, I jumped in a taxi to head down to City Hall and looked at my email. At 9:32, Schmidt had forwarded the Court of Appeals decision to me and my chief of staff Justine Almada with the subject line "FW: Stuyvesant Town Affirmed!!!" I called Almada. "This is nuts! We need to get everyone out in front of Stuyvesant Town this afternoon to celebrate this. Please get the wheels in motion, quickly," I told her, knowing that every politician in town would be calling us asking us to tell them where they should be, and when.

At 9:42 a.m., a *New York Times* breaking news alert popped up on phones announcing the tenant victory. Bagli had somehow already posted a 1,110-word story on the *Times* website, saying that the court had dealt a potentially "crippling blow" to the owners of Stuy Town and Peter Cooper. Bagli's piece cited industry experts who predicted that the ruling could affect as many as eighty thousand apartments citywide and that Tishman Speyer, BlackRock, and MetLife, as the former owner, could be liable for an estimated $200 million in rent overcharges and damages owed to tenants of the deregulated Stuy Town and Peter Cooper apartments. At the time of the decision, 4,352 of the 11,232 units had been deregulated, of which Tishman Speyer and BlackRock had been responsible for 1,163. The rest of the 11,227 apartments—still 61 percent—had never been taken out of rent stabilization.[33]

Frank Innuarto, president of Realpoint, a credit rating agency, called the decision, which came just three years into Tishman Speyer's ownership, "the last shoe to drop" for Stuy Town's owners. The partnership between Tishman Speyer and BlackRock originally had set aside $890 million in reserve funds to pay the difference between rent revenues and the monthly debt payments on the property. As of the moment of the decision, there was only about $24 million left in the kitty, and because Tishman Speyer and BlackRock were burning through about $16 million of the reserve per month, they had less than two months before they ran out of money. Tishman Speyer called it "an unfortunate outcome for New York."[34]

Tenants, however, saw this as a very fortunate outcome for themselves, and middle-income New Yorkers specifically. "I was screeching in my apartment. I was like yes! I called everybody I could think of including people who couldn't care less," said Arlynne Miller, a tenant activist. Susan Steinberg remembered her own astonishment: "I thought the real estate industry had such a firm grip on this issue that it ultimately was not going to be winnable for us." Justine Almada had gathered the Tenants Association leadership, and I invited the elected officials for the neighborhood to a quick celebration on 16th Street and First Avenue the very same day at 2:15 p.m. The crowd was made up mostly of rent-stabilized tenants who were unaffected by the ruling but happy to score a victory against their landlord. "It's unbelievable that the courts finally sided with the tenants rather than the owner. They really emptied out a lot of middle-class families, so this is a good verdict," said Myron Reingold, a longtime resident.[35]

Comptroller Bill Thompson (whose name would be on the ballot for mayor against incumbent Michael Bloomberg in two weeks), Borough President Scott Stringer, Congresswoman Carolyn Maloney, state senator Tom Duane, and Assemblyman Brian Kavanagh all dropped everything to join us that day on 16th Street and First Avenue. We tenants cheered the demise of Tishman Speyer and BlackRock, saying that they deserved everything they got. "The era of affordability in Stuyvesant Town is far from over. This community will continue to be the center of affordable, middle-class housing in New York City," I crowed. "The court made it clear that you cannot pocket millions in taxpayer dollars while pushing rent-stabilized tenants out of their homes." Schmidt graciously congratulated me with a note later that afternoon. "This has been your issue from the start, so you must be immensely proud and satisfied with the results thus far."[36] Boosted by the results of the *Roberts* case, I won my first reelection to the city council with 75 percent of the vote, against a Republican named Ashok Chandra.

Privately, however, I started to worry about what it would actually mean for the community, and about all the other uncertainties that lay ahead. If Tishman Speyer failed, we had no idea what would happen next. Did it mean that the banks would foreclose on the property? Who were the banks anyway? Would Tishman Speyer and BlackRock file for bankruptcy? Would a new owner come in with the same financial demands? There was also still the question of damages. The Court of Appeals had sent the question of damages back to Justice Lowe of the Supreme Court. If the decision were applied retroactively, tenants might be entitled to compensation; it was also possible that the court would apply the decision only prospectively. We did not know how much money tenants were going to be paid, if anything, and whether their rents were going to be rolled back.

Even if a court concluded that damages should be retroactive, calculating them was going to be complicated. If a tenant was paying $4,000 per month for a market-rate apartment, and the legal rent-stabilized rent should have been only $2,500, that tenant was overpaying $1,500 a month. However, the legal rent for every apartment in the entire community was different, based on the number of times it had become vacant and the value of improvements the owner had made to the unit. Under rent stabilization, an owner was entitled to a 20 percent vacancy bonus every time the unit turned over, so if a unit had a series of one-year leases, and tenants vacated after every one of them, the legal rent-stabilized rent could be quite high. Calculating the rents would take months, and this was no easy task. The new question for the parties, and the court, was how many—if any—of these vacancy bonuses should be included in determining the legal rent-stabilized rent.

After the Appellate Division decision back in March, Schmidt and Kasner had entered into an interim agreement on behalf of their clients that put a portion of rents into an escrow account, under court supervision. These funds—which had grown to $16 million by December—were set aside to pay for potential damages to tenants down the line. Now that the tenants had won at the Court of Appeals, Schmidt and Kasner reached an agreement whereby Tishman Speyer would start lowering rent bills. For the first time in history, rents were actually going down in Stuy Town.[37]

7

Preparing for an Uncertain Future

Even before the *Roberts* decision came down, the *Wall Street Journal* was already reporting in October 2009 that Stuy Town, one of the "biggest, most high-profile deals of the commercial real-estate boom was in danger of imminent default," and predicted a wave of commercial property failures in its wake. Rather than raising the net operating income up to $252 million by 2009, as MetLife had promised could be done, Tishman Speyer was stuck at $139 million. RealPoint LLC, a credit rating agency, also estimated that the property was now worth only $2.1 billion—less than half the purchase price from three years earlier. One tenant emailed over the *Wall Street Journal* article to me and the Tenants Association with the ominous note: "I think now would be a good time to get stuff fixed, because in about six weeks we are going to be on our own."[1]

Tishman Speyer and all owners of real estate were feeling the impacts of the recession, which had been precipitated by a collapse in the inflated housing market. In early December, Tishman Speyer defaulted on a package of loans that it used to finance the $1.72 billion purchase of six office buildings in Chicago's Loop. They had made that deal just after Stuy Town, buying it from the Blackstone Group. Like so many others, these buildings had lost much of their value amid the broad decline in the commercial real estate market. Shawn Mobley, executive vice president of the real estate firm Grubb & Ellis Co., told *Crain's New York Business,* "Virtually all the assets bought between '05 and '07 cannot be refinanced today without a significant capital infusion." This was true in both the office and residential markets.[2]

In Manhattan, apartment prices had fallen sharply as 2009 wore on. Closings had fallen more than 50 percent, and prices were down in some categories by as much as 25 percent compared to 2008. Larry Gluck, the owner of Stuy Town's sister community, Riverton, built by MetLife in Harlem during the peak of its racist rental policies, had also defaulted on his loans in 2008. Gluck had a $225 million mortgage and, pursuing a business plan that mirrored Tishman Speyer's, failed to convert enough of the property's 1,230 units from rent stabilization to the market rate to pay back its debts. Gluck also defaulted on $550 million in loans in San Francisco's Park Merced, a third property built by MetLife in the 1940s.[3]

After the *Roberts* decision, the situation for Tishman Speyer became only more dire. The idea of Stuy Town becoming a zombie community, with maintenance requests going unanswered and buildings falling apart, was deeply concerning. And I was selfishly worried that if that happened, some blame would be cast on me and the Tenants Association for the *Roberts* decision. Yet, in this moment of turmoil, there was also an opportunity. Three years after the sale to Tishman Speyer, in the context of a restructuring or bankruptcy, it looked like we would have another chance to push for long-term affordability protections—and even homeownership—in Stuy Town. I sat down in my living room after the *Roberts* decision, with a pad and pencil, and scratched out a list of long-standing principles—or demands—that we wanted to see achieved: long-term affordability for middle-class people, adequate maintenance, and the protection of open spaces. I added a fourth principle: keeping Stuy Town and Peter Cooper as a unified whole, since we had worried that a new owner might decide to separate Peter Cooper out from Stuyvesant Town. If there was anything else fundamental that mattered, I couldn't think of it. The Tenants Association had called a "Unity Day" rally on Saturday, November 14, in Stuyvesant Cove, and I thought that would be the right time to road test those principles with our neighbors. Doyle had agreed with what I had written, and the Tenants Association formally adopted them as their own.

In advance of the rally, the Tenants Association put out a statement that said, "Three years ago, Tishman Speyer Properties, L.P. and Black-Rock Realty Advisors bought Stuyvesant Town and Peter Cooper Village for $5.4 billion, premised on the notion that they could quickly turn rent-stabilized apartments to the market. They engaged in aggressive tactics toward tenants, including serving legal notices on many long-time, perfectly legitimate people who had lived in the community for a generation. We fought back at every turn, and they did not achieve their goals."[4] It went on to state that "the tenants of this community will insist—either through partnership with a benevolent new owner, or through a tenant-initiated bid—that their interests be protected in any restructuring."[5]

In a post–Tishman Speyer world, we were going to have another opportunity to fight to protect Stuy Town and Peter Cooper as affordable housing for middle-class New Yorkers, and we were determined to put all our collective energy toward that goal. Over time, the neighborhood had become home to a wide range of New Yorkers, including skilled construction workers, civil servants, law enforcement officers, firefighters, teachers, judges, and other professionals. Because of the predictability of rents under rent stabilization, families put down deep roots, raising children alongside newer arrivals who were also attracted to its stable atmosphere. Tishman Speyer's business plan had directly challenged that stability, and if they were going to default, we wanted to push for a restructuring plan that would keep Stuy Town accessible to middle-class people and stop its march toward "luxury" housing.

Marsh and the Tenants Association board had turned out hundreds of tenants at the Saturday rally, energized and carrying signs that read "Save Our Homes," and "We Are Not for Sale," "No Bailout for Predators," and "Will Freddie Mac Have Our Back?" As a light drizzle came down on us, the Tenants Association handed out postcards for tenants to mail to CWCapital Asset Management, which had been named the "special servicer" that could take over if Tishman Speyer defaulted, and to Fannie Mae and Freddie Mac, which we had learned were significant bondholders in the trusts that held Stuy Town's first mortgage. The postcards demanded that they "work with my elected officials and the Tenants Association to protect this community as affordable housing, to provide adequate maintenance, and to preserve the historic configuration of this property." Before turning over the microphone to Speaker Quinn, Borough President Stringer, Public Advocate-elect Bill de Blasio, and other elected officials, I taunted Fannie Mae and Freddie Mac for their participation in the Tishman Speyer deal. To any future owner, I had this message: "This is a community of people, some older, some younger, some richer, some poorer, and we are not a tranche of a loan. We cannot be simply bought and sold and shuttled between bank accounts, or tossed about like pawns in a game." The rest of the speakers amplified the message that tenants deserved a seat at the table. The *New York Post* covered our list—the headline read, "Stuy Town Tenants Set List of Demands"—which we publicized widely to the press and to tenants.[6]

On December 15, Rob Speyer called and asked me for an urgent meeting, which I agreed to have the next day. I was well aware of his precarious position from news reports. (Days earlier, Deutsche Bank, in an analyst's report, had called a bankruptcy and restructuring the most likely outcome here.)[7] After years of fighting, I could not imagine what he wanted from me. So I went to the meeting with a list of my own issues and the Tenants Association's newly stated principles at the ready. I was also eager to ask Speyer whether he intended to move toward bankruptcy, or whether a sale was on the horizon.

This time, Speyer and Hatzmann came to my office at 250 Broadway in Lower Manhattan, where I hosted them in the council speaker's conference room. After some quick pleasantries, Speyer turned to the purpose of the meeting. He told me vaguely that Tishman Speyer was working on plans with their lenders, looking to renegotiate the terms of their debts, and was hoping to make peace with the tenants. He asked me if I could give him a full rundown of all outstanding tenant quality-of-life concerns that they might be able to address. I paused, wondering whether this was a sincere request. We had an extremely long list of grievances, and while they were not easily corrected, I saw no harm in itemizing them, beginning with the Golub notices that they had been filing against tenants for two years. I then walked them through a litany of maintenance problems.

Speyer had fired Adam Rose as the property manager soon after he had taken over, and Tishman Speyer had taken on the maintenance of the property itself. Speyer and Hatzmann expressed genuine concern when I told them there was a prevailing view among tenants that they had managed the property poorly.

Hatzmann and Speyer scribbled notes, periodically conferring with each other. "We can fix these things," Speyer said optimistically. He then said that they were open to giving tenants an opportunity to own their apartments (which, of course, the Tenants Association and I had pushed in 2006) and were ready to start disbursing the escrow that they were holding from the *Roberts* case. He even expressed a willingness to explore ideas to deliver long-term affordability in Stuy Town. As the meeting wrapped up, Speyer thanked me for the information that I had shared with him and explained that he was planning to add a considerable amount of new money into the deal, which he hoped would allow him to renegotiate with his lenders and give Tishman Speyer a chance to stick around.[8] He also said that he wanted to do right by the tenants and start fresh, even if he did ultimately need to turn the property over to his creditors. Speyer and Hatzmann thanked me for my time, and I showed them to the elevator bank on the eighteenth floor. All of this was very positive but, after years of constant confrontation, surreal.

Outside my view, Speyer was negotiating with special servicer CWCapital, which had stepped in on November 7, 2009, to represent the lenders in the $3 billion first mortgage as Tishman Speyer catapulted forward toward default. Most residents, including me, had never heard of them, and yet in the wake of so many catastrophic real estate failures in 2008 and 2009, special servicers were now playing an increasingly critical role in the operations of multifamily housing. Servicers generally are named when the initial loans are made, as a precaution, with the expectation that they will take over in the—hopefully unlikely—event of a default. "For very little investment, special servicers got themselves inserted in all these loan deals, with no expectation that they would ever swing into action. Their role ordinarily included eliminating liens, finishing capital work, making improvements, basic real estate 101 stuff," Adam Rose explained to me. CWCapital had been selected as the servicer in the 2006 deal.[9]

At the time of our meeting, Speyer was already negotiating with CWCapital and hoped to demonstrate the improvements that he intended to make to benefit the property and, relatedly, the tenants, to convince the special servicer to go along with his plan. Speyer had offered to inject $250 million into the deal in exchange for the lenders' agreeing to voluntarily reduce the first mortgage from $3 billion to $1.8 billion and allowing Tishman Speyer to continue in its ownership position. He was still waiting for a response.[10]

On January 7, at a few minutes after noon, Rob Speyer called me to let me know that Tishman Speyer was going to miss a loan payment the following day, which would put his firm in technical default on its mortgages. Hatzmann made a similar call to Al Doyle on January 8.[11]

With the default now official, Chuck Spetka, the chief executive of the special servicer CWCapital, representing the $3 billion first mortgage, was now in the driver's seat. He—along with CWCapital's new parent company Fortress Investment Group—had the power to accept or reject Tishman Speyer's plans and to determine what was going to happen next. Notably, Fortress had announced its plan to acquire CWCapital six days before the Tishman Speyer default was official. Press reports described Fortress's move as "another example of how creative some real estate players are in trying to get access to distressed properties." Fortress was not the only real estate player to do this. Related Companies' senior executives Steve Ross, Jeff Blau, and Bruce Beal Jr. had formed a bank, called SJB National Bank, in late 2009, with an eye toward buying other failed banks to assume control of distressed properties. It certainly looked to me like this was just a play by Fortress to acquire Stuyvesant Town.[12]

I cold-called Spetka to introduce myself. Spetka came quickly onto the line and, after exchanging a few pleasantries, invited me to his office for a meeting. Based on the speed of the invitation, I figured it was going to be a one-on-one exchange, so I went alone, without any staff or TA leaders, to CWCapital's headquarters at 1540 Broadway, in Times Square, on January 13. I was eager to convey to Spetka that while the tenants could create public headaches for him, we were tired of volatility and conflict and wanted to be part of the solution. As I walked into the conference room, I stopped briefly when I saw that there were about a dozen people in suits around a conference table, who stood up when I walked in. Spetka was there, and he introduced me to, among many others, Dave Iannarone,

CWCapital's president, and Greg Cross of the law firm Venable—who had come up from Baltimore for this meeting.

As they went around the room explaining their roles at CWCapital, I could feel them sizing me up, and they seemed as uneasy as I was. Bankers, lawyers, and restructuring professionals were generally not in the business of meeting local elected officials, and for many of them I was their first direct exposure to the Stuy Town tenant body. Special servicers in particular preferred to operate quietly and below the radar; CWCapital's own website even said, "Due to the confidential nature of special servicing contracts and functions we can not discuss any details related to properties within our special servicing portfolio." This was a high-profile assignment for CWCapital, and they needed no reminding that the Tenants Association and I had played an outsize role in fighting back against Tishman Speyer. This meeting was not a time for conflict, but I did want to clearly set the expectation with CWCapital that they needed to work with the Tenants Association. "Frankly, we expect you to chart a better course, with our support and partnership," I said to the group, with more bluster than I was entitled to as I sat alone on one side of the conference table. The CWCapital executives asked a lot of questions about Tishman Speyer's management and failures. I told them about the efforts to create vacancies by evicting tenants, the culture of conflict that Tishman Speyer had created, and laid out a variety of the tenants' maintenance concerns. They took notes as I spoke and thanked me politely as they shook my hand when I left. The next day, Spetka dropped me a conciliatory email, saying, "It was a pleasure to meet you. We look forward to working with you to reach a satisfactory conclusion." This was a refreshing change for us, as we had spent years feeling ignored, or attacked, by Tishman Speyer. I sent it off to Doyle, who wrote back simply: "Wow."[13]

On January 22, Spetka wrote me a letter saying that while his primary responsibility was to deliver a repayment of $3 billion to the first mortgage holders, he was committed to better understanding residents' concerns and to work with us to a satisfactory outcome that was "fair and just."[14] I leaked the letter to the *Commercial Observer*, which observed that the "taciturn financial firm that controls the senior mortgage" at PCV/ST "has broken its public silence." The article noted that Spetka's letter concluded "by lavishing some praise on Mr. Garodnick for his leadership on the issue—never a bad move with an elected official, particularly one who was a thorn in the side of Tishman Speyer."[15]

Spetka had rejected Rob Speyer's offer to invest more money and to remain in control. Instead, Spetka offered him the opportunity to simply stay on as property manager, which Speyer declined. "Our investors had experienced a tremendous amount of pain," said Speyer, as he explained his thinking. "It's not appropriate for Tishman Speyer Properties to create a new profit center out of their pain." On Sunday, January 24, Speyer huddled with his lawyers and concluded that it was not worth having a protracted legal battle playing out in full view of New York's tabloids and politicians. On his way home in a taxi from the offices of his lawyers at Fried Frank in Lower Manhattan, Speyer called Spetka and told him that he was prepared to turn the property over to CWCapital.[16]

On Monday, January 25, my cell phone rang—before 8 a.m.—as I was having a cup of coffee in my Peter Cooper apartment. It was Rob Speyer on the line. I was not surprised to hear from him: thirty minutes earlier, I had shown Zoe the Stuy Town–related breaking news alert that had popped on my phone from the *Wall Street Journal*. It said that Tishman Speyer and BlackRock had decided to turn the property over to its creditors. Speyer sounded worn out, his voice gravelly. He told me that they were "turning over the keys" to CWCapital but that they weren't going to just pick up and walk out, and that he would ensure a seamless transition. I wished him the best, got dressed, and hurried to the office to figure out how I was going to balance this new Stuy Town emergency with all the other demands of my East Side district.

We had come to learn that the biggest holder of bonds in the first mortgage happened to be Fannie Mae and Freddie Mac. These two quasi-public entities owned more than $2.1 billion of Stuy Town debt, and based on their seniority in the deal, they had the potential to be major players in any restructuring plan. In late 2009, I had organized a letter from East Side leaders—which included Congresswoman Carolyn Maloney, Borough President Scott Stringer, Senator Tom Duane, and Assemblyman Brian Kavanagh—to Fannie and Freddie, dripping with hostility and sarcasm about their participation in the Tishman Speyer deal that was so harmful to tenants. "As investors, we are certain that you were intimately aware of the ultimate goal of the investor group," we chided, and demanded that

Fannie and Freddie use their influence to protect us and the city. "No debt restructuring plan should be considered separate from that which serves the public interest," we wrote. Fannie and Freddie had recently gotten about $187 billion in public funds to bail them out of financial trouble from the 2007 financial crash, and we felt that the bailout had created for them an additional obligation to look out for the public interest.[17]

Senator Schumer offered to help us with Fannie Mae and Freddie Mac. Schumer knew that Fannie and Freddie had negotiated deals to help preserve affordable housing in other distressed properties, such as in Starrett City in Brooklyn and Ocelot in the Bronx. In Ocelot, Schumer had worked with local and federal officials to create a sale process that ensured that a new owner would emerge who had a track record of protecting affordable housing. Schumer thought that Fannie and Freddie had an obligation to actively insert themselves into the negotiations in Stuy Town, and in particular to make sure that the buildings did not fall into disrepair during this period of uncertainty. "This would seem like chaos, but there's a silver lining on this cloud," Schumer told the *Daily News*. Both privately and publicly, he was urging the agency heads to craft a sale process in Stuy Town that would ensure affordability into the long term.[18]

The TA invited Senator Schumer to join us on an icy cold Sunday morning on January 31, at high noon, on 18th Street and First Avenue for a press conference. Senator Schumer was well known for his regular Sunday press events, and as one of our biggest boosters he gladly accepted our invitation. The Tenants Association, with tongue in cheek, had sent out a cheerful message to the entire community about the Schumer event: "With the TV cameras rolling, Senator Schumer will publicly announce his support for an affordable Stuyvesant Town and Peter Cooper Village. We need a crowd on hand to let the world and prospective owners know—via TV coverage—that we tenants are united in our determination to protect and maintain our homes." We asked the public safety force to close down the loop road off First Avenue to accommodate the crowds of people who were expected. That morning, Schumer shook hands with hundreds of tenants as he made his way to the makeshift podium we had set up.[19]

Schumer eventually made it to the middle of the crowd where I was waiting with Speaker Quinn, Borough President Stringer, Senator Duane,

Assemblyman Kavanagh, and TA board members. I thanked him for his support and kicked off the speeches. "Are we united?" I hollered. "Are we organized? Are we ready to defend our homes?"

"Yes! Yes! Yes!" came back the response from the crowd. I called out the investors who had lost money in the deal and then said, "But imagine our surprise to learn that lurking deep in the background, this transaction was supported by Fannie Mae and Freddie Mac—two entities charged with preserving affordable housing in this country."[20]

Schumer stepped up to the podium. "At the end of the day we have to put the needs of thousands of middle-class residents and the need for New York City to maintain middle class housing first," Schumer said, his gloved hands in fists punching the air. "They were caught up in a high stakes real estate gamble that ended up going bust. Now Fannie and Freddie must guide this process to a conclusion with the least amount of

Figure 7.1. Pictured here with Al Doyle, Assemblyman Brian Kavanaugh, and City Council Speaker Christine Quinn, on January 31, 2010, Senator Chuck Schumer came to Stuyvesant Town to express his intention to push Fannie Mae and Freddie Mac to help us develop a solution. "This would seem like chaos, but there's a silver lining on this cloud," Schumer told the *Daily News*. Photo credit: *Town & Village* newspaper.

impact on current tenants and families. I am going to watch them like a hawk to make sure they do just that."[21]

My contact with Spetka picked up in the following weeks. I learned that he was one of my constituents on the Upper East Side, and we developed an easy rapport. Spetka told me that he was bringing back Adam Rose, who had been first hired by MetLife, and then fired by Tishman Speyer, as the property manager for Stuy Town. Spetka installed him as a "transition consultant" to CWCapital. Having invested countless hours of time and energy in Stuy Town, Rose was still smarting from his experience with Tishman Speyer, but the high-energy, garrulous copresident of Rose Associates was delighted to be back. Almost immediately, Rose saw that things were different from what they were under MetLife. Tishman Speyer had planted trees everywhere, which blocked security cameras, and morale was low among the staff. And, unlike when he had managed Stuy Town previously, Rose was getting constant phone calls from prospective buyers like David Bistricer and representatives of Appaloosa asking him for pretextual "get to know you" meetings. When Rose sat with them, the conversation would inevitably turn to Stuy Town, and they asked for tidbits of information about CWCapital's plans.[22]

Bringing Rose back was a safe move by Spetka. Rose had the necessary experience and a good personal reputation. It also did not upset the apple cart—no investor in the Stuy Town deal could possibly object to CWCapital engaging a well-recognized New York firm, with an experienced team, which had previously managed Stuy Town and Peter Cooper. Spetka continued to engage me about possible next steps, which I relayed in real time to Al Doyle. A week after sending me his supportive letter, Spetka called me to ask if I knew of any way to reduce the property's transfer tax obligation if CWCapital were to join in a partnership with the Tenants Association. That was exactly the question I wanted CWCapital to be asking me, but I was uncertain of the precise answer. I told him I would look into it. As optimistic as I was feeling, I realized that we were again unprepared for the next phase of our advocacy. Being outgunned in the CWCapital offices on January 13 had perhaps been harmless. For it to happen again was going to make me, and the tenants, look foolish. We needed professionals at our side who knew what they were talking about, and fast. Unfortunately, the Tenants Association had no meaningful funds to pay anyone, so any firm would need to take us on either pro bono or on a contingency basis.

I talked to Doyle, who agreed with my assessment and encouraged me to go looking for help. I solicited proposals from a handful of law firms, including Wolf Haldenstein, which served as the lawyers for the tenants in the *Roberts* case. I had also hoped that Paul, Weiss, Rifkind, Wharton & Garrison LLP, one of New York's top law firms, with a great real estate practice, would consider taking us on because of my personal history as a lawyer there. I had worked at Paul Weiss for nearly four years before running for the city council and had gotten to know Meredith Kane, the co-chair of the real estate department. I had approached her when we made our first bid to MetLife in 2006, but she had cited a conflict at that time and turned me down. Anticipating the default, I had reached out to her in December 2009, and she turned me down again. Now, one month later, I wanted to try one last time, and called her office to make one final plea.

Kane's real estate clients were a who's who of the biggest property owners in New York City, such as Vornado Realty Trust, Rockefeller Group Development, the Metropolitan Transportation Authority, the New York Public Library, and the City University of New York. She did acquisitions, sales, financing, and developments—and was regularly honored as one of the most important and powerful real estate lawyers in the city. "Dan, great to hear from you!" she said cheerily as she picked up the phone. "Listen, Meredith. I know you have already turned me down a couple of times, but I really need someone to help the tenants figure out what the options are, how to engage, how to do this," I said, practically begging. "And we need someone to show us how we can make this happen." Paul Weiss generally would not do a major transaction like this pro bono, but she knew how important this situation was to the tenants, the city, and to me personally. She wondered out loud whether her firm might consider getting paid only if we successfully consummated a deal. Even if she could determine that there were no internal conflicts among the firm's other clients, she feared that her partners would not sign off on a compensation structure that was so speculative. She got off the phone with me and called her well-respected partner in the bankruptcy department, Alan Kornberg, and explained the situation.[23]

"Well, this could very well go to a bankruptcy," Kornberg told her, encouragingly. That alone could allow for Paul Weiss to justify its time and to allow it to get its fees paid, he argued. In a bankruptcy, the lawyers for the various parties tended to get their fees paid as part of the court-sanctioned outcome. Real estate transactions rarely made it to bankruptcy, but this one was highly unusual and could be different. Even without a bankruptcy, Kane and Kornberg agreed that the whole deal was centered on the tenants, which meant that we likely would be part of the solution. "We realized, just like all the suitors realized, that if you want to be successful, you need to be with the tenants," Kane said. "They were in the deal no matter what." Paul Weiss took a leap of faith that someone would figure out how to pay their bill, and Kane and Kornberg agreed to be considered as lawyers for the TA board.[24]

Within two weeks, on January 28, I had added two other options for legal representation, both of them firms willing to represent us without any upfront retainer fee. I presented them to the TA board and left the meeting to allow the group to consider its options. Each firm had its own strengths, but I was very happy and not at all surprised when the board voted to retain Paul Weiss. In order to support their new client, Kornberg and Kane rounded out their team with Brian Hermann, a more junior partner in the bankruptcy department. Doyle and the Tenants Association were beyond enthusiastic. They now had one of the best law firms in the world on their side, which was important for the substance of what we wanted to achieve but also to show CWCapital and other real estate players that we had the heft to be taken seriously.

Kornberg recommended that we also bring on a banker or restructuring specialist—a numbers cruncher—who could help us to analyze deal proposals as they emerged.[25] To find the right person, Kornberg tasked Hermann with setting up a series of meetings to allow the Tenants Association board to meet with firms that could guide us through a bankruptcy, a recapitalization (where new money was introduced into the deal), or a sale. Hermann quickly got to work and set up the first meeting on February 17, on the twenty-ninth floor of Paul Weiss's offices at 1285 Avenue of the Americas, in its largest conference room. On one side of the table sat Doyle, Marsh, Steinberg, and board members including Soni Fink and Jim Roth, as well as me and my staff, and the Paul Weiss lawyers.

We were brimming with enthusiasm as we anticipated hearing presentations from the world's biggest and best restructuring advisory firms, invited by our Paul Weiss lawyers, each seeking to work for the Tenants Association.

Discarded plates and food boxes littered the table by the end of the first day of meetings, as one firm after another came in with binders of presentation materials to make its case. Miller Buckfire, Alvarez & Marsal, Goldin Associates, Citigroup, Alix Partners, Perella Weinberg, Zolfo Cooper, Blackstone, and Moelis & Company filed into the conference room to show off their credentials and their vision for how to protect the tenants of Stuy Town. "It was great—we had never seen anything like that before," Kane said. "Firms that make thousands of dollars an hour now saw the tenants' role as central to the process. The best presentations showed us that they were basically there to support what we wanted to do."[26]

The presentation from Alex Rubin and his team at Moelis & Company stood out. Rubin himself had spent much of his childhood in Stuy Town, at 505 East 14th Street, one of the first buildings to have been completed by MetLife. His parents got divorced in 1977 when he was in fourth grade, and Rubin spent alternating weekends with his dad in this Stuy Town apartment. It was an unrenovated rent-stabilized apartment, with no air conditioning. Rubin's father referred to Stuy Town as the "campus" because everything was so orderly and neatly laid out, and both Rubins appreciated that the maintenance staff seemed to take pride in keeping the property immaculate. Alex Rubin graduated from Cornell University in 1989 and spent a short period back in Stuy Town with his dad before he got his own place. In 2009, Ken Moelis recruited Rubin from Citigroup to work for his relatively new firm.[27]

Rubin was a picture of professionalism. He looked the part of a banker—with perfectly coiffed hair and rimless glasses. His speaking style was direct and deliberate, conveying his message in the fewest words necessary. Alex Rubin and his partner Bill Derrough led the very large team from Moelis & Company, which included a handful of sharp associates. "They have an army, I love it," I whispered to Steinberg. After a brief introduction from Alan Kornberg of Paul Weiss, Derrough—who went on to become treasurer of the Democratic National Committee—took us through the team's credentials in complex credit restructuring, bonds, and real estate. He then took pains to distill the complicated information about how this deal could be unwound into easy-to-digest pieces. If Rubin was careful with his language, Derrough was the opposite, speaking in analogies and anecdotes. "You guys are the prettiest girl at the dance," he proclaimed. "Everyone is going to want to partner with you." Meredith Kane grimaced, but like the rest of us, she was very impressed with this talented, albeit colorful, group.[28]

Then they turned to the tenants and—in contrast to most of the other groups that came in—actually asked what we felt we needed from this transaction. Al Doyle spoke on behalf of the group and explained how Tishman Speyer had used vacancy decontrol as a weapon and why we had decided to take steps to control our own future. Steinberg injected that we were determined not to allow this to happen to the community ever again. Other board members chimed in about why our guiding principles were so important to us and what we were fighting for. The Moelis team listened closely, and both sides asked a few more questions in a casual and conversational style. "We believe that the tenants are the central path to success," Rubin said directly. Between Derrough's humor and charisma and Rubin's substance and poise, the Moelis team made a very positive impression with the group. You could feel the energy in the room change as they spoke. "Moelis blew it out of the water," Steinberg said. "They were so impressive, they had numbers, they were wonderfully responsive, and spoke in a way we could understand."[29]

Rubin and Derrough also left the meeting motivated and energized by their interaction with the tenants. Just as the *Roberts* lawyer Alex Schmidt had felt when he came out to our press conference celebrating his victory, the contact with the Tenants Association made them even more motivated to support us. "What struck all of us was here were real multigenerational New York City families for whom this was not a series of financial transactions," Rubin recalled. "Their homes were caught up in these larger trends that had played out, and they were staking out as best they could to get well represented legally and financially in order to influence the outcome. We all thought it was laudable and bold."[30]

The stress of these meetings was taking its toll on the tenant leaders. Steinberg was having trouble sleeping, as she mentally ran through the presentations from all the distinguished professionals. One of her closest friends told her that she looked "haggard." Steinberg confided what was going on and expressed her worry that she could not handle the pressure related to this high-stakes endeavor. "Do you realize," Steinberg asked her friend wearily, "that my decisions will affect twenty-eight thousand people? You would look haggard, too, and you wouldn't sleep, either, if you had that responsibility."[31]

The tenants voted unanimously on February 24 to retain Moelis, with a similar fee structure as Paul Weiss—they would get paid only when a deal was consummated. Rubin and Derrough invited us in for a celebratory meeting at their headquarters at 399 Park Avenue. Ironically, this restructuring firm was housed in the space of the former Lehman Brothers, which had filed for bankruptcy only two years earlier. When I arrived in the Moelis offices with a dozen members of the board of the Tenants Association, we navigated enormously long hallways, which extended hundreds of yards, and proceeded to a cluster of conference rooms at the end of the hall. Ken Moelis, the firm's founder and former president of UBS Investment Bank, was on hand to welcome us. With a warm smile, he shook hands with me and every one of the tenants, and thanked us for the opportunity to collaborate with us. Imagine that—he was thanking *us*. And the team—which included Bill Derrough, Alex Rubin, Larry Kwon, and others—was there in force to make us feel comfortable and to show its commitment. Investment banks often give internal names to their projects, which are anonymous and don't, by their name alone, reveal details if inadvertently disclosed. Kwon, a member of the team, had set up a group email list and named it "Project David." "The Tenants Association was taking on billions of dollars of securitized debt, and seeking to influence the outcome," Rubin observed. "They were David, in a David and Goliath story."[32]

"Tenants groups in New York are notoriously disorganized, but that isn't true about the one representing tenants of Stuyvesant Town and Peter Cooper Village," the *Wall Street Journal* reported, recognizing that we had "lined up some big names as advisers." Even billionaire David Tepper of Appaloosa Management, whose firm owned a piece of the $3 billion first mortgage, called the homeownership plan by the tenants "the best solution."[33]

On March 13, 2010, we called a community-wide Tenants Association meeting to introduce our new professional advisers and to talk about some possible next steps. An overflow crowd turned up at Baruch

College's Mason Hall, which included both of my parents and Zoe. Everyone was excited and nervous; nobody knew exactly what the outcome was going to be. The meeting was attended by Public Advocate Bill de Blasio, Speaker Quinn, Borough President Stringer, Assemblyman Kavanagh, and Congresswoman Maloney. *Roberts* lawyer Alex Schmidt was also on hand, as were Rafael Cestero, who had succeeded Shaun Donovan as the New York City commissioner of housing preservation and development (HPD), and Adam Rose, the new property management consultant appointed by CWCapital.

Neither Doyle nor I had thought it was likely that Cestero or Rose would show up when we invited them to give remarks and to take questions. Property managers and bureaucrats tend not to like to face the firing squad like that, particularly with so much uncertainty swirling around the property. However, both were new on the scene and good on their feet, and we figured they might each like a chance to make a first impression on a large group of Stuy Town tenants.

The question of whether Cestero should accept our invitation was hotly debated not only within HPD but at the top levels of City Hall. Bloomberg's staff had reservations about homeownership (as opposed to keeping the property as rentals) and understood how angry people were at the mayor for his inaction when MetLife put the property up for sale in 2006. Nevertheless, because of the importance of the moment to the community, the city agreed that Commissioner Cestero would attend, although he would stick to a careful script: the city was there specifically to protect against conditions deteriorating at the property. Cestero was not particularly excited about the meeting because he knew people were upset and wanted answers, but there were no easy or simple answers to offer. "I knew people wanted more from us, and I wasn't in a position to provide more," he recalled.[34]

Rose also accepted our invitation, though he too was worried about how he would be received. With over a thousand passionate Stuy Town residents expected to attend, he was concerned about his own physical safety. Many equated Rose with unpopular MCI charges and the later years of MetLife, when it started filing Golub notices. So, just to be safe, Rose hired three armed off-duty NYPD detectives, who sat in the audience, playing the role of concerned tenants but were prepared to usher him out if things got wild.[35]

With Cestero and Rose sitting onstage, along with all the elected officials from our neighborhood, I looked out to the overflow audience with a feeling of dread. It was going to be extremely difficult to explain to this audience the role of CWCapital, and the uncertainty of the future, without a specific plan to organize around, and to keep the competing personal and political interests of the group in sync. Steinberg welcomed the crowd to this important gathering and turned the microphone over to me. After updating people on the current state of play, I promised to work with our professional team in order to come up with a new plan of attack. I also pleaded with my neighbors to appreciate how complicated it was going to be to come to a consensus in a group of thirty thousand tenants and why every individual interest could not possibly be fully satisfied. In anticipation of this challenge, the TA board had already tapped John Marsh to gather "unity pledges"—much like the "no buy" pledges that we had gotten in 2006—which were an informal commitment of solidarity among our neighbors. I took pains to impress on the group that the TA had already gathered thousands of signed unity pledges, which proved that, no matter our differences, we were in this together.

"The biggest players in the real estate industry recognize that the road to Stuyvesant Town goes through the tenant body. They recognize that when we are united, we can be constructive in getting a deal done, *or we can be a real problem for them*," I said. "I feel confident that we can band together as a community—that we can first embrace our overarching belief that we would rather be working together toward our goal than sitting back and watching as this property falls into the hands of one hedge fund or another, and allowing the mistakes of the past to be repeated."

All the speakers, remarkably, echoed those themes. After Alex Schmidt gave an update about the *Roberts* case, we turned to Meredith Kane from Paul Weiss. Kane shielded her eyes from the lights and saw a sea of New Yorkers in the audience. "In all my years as a lawyer, I will never forget what it was like to try to communicate to a large group of people with different interests in a way that was fair and thoughtful and clear and basic and down to earth," Kane recalled. We were happy that one thousand people were there, but that also meant there were still twenty-nine thousand people who were not going to get any direct update from us. With people lining up to the microphones, questions came fast. "What about rent stabilization?" "How about succession rights?" "MCIs?" "How much will I be able to buy my apartment for?" Kane urged patience on these subjects. People wanted to understand what was happening with their specific apartment, but Kane cautioned that we were not yet in a position to make any decisions: "These are issues we will be dealing with, but first we need to get a hold of this thing!"[36]

Commissioner Cestero then got up to face the crowd. "Where's the mayor?" several people shouted from the crowd. "*I'm* here," Cestero responded. Cestero made a brief statement and focused his comments on his commitment to ensuring that there was no decrease in services to tenants during this uncertain period. It was safe territory for him, since it was far from clear that the Bloomberg administration would ever intervene in this process. I then welcomed Adam Rose to the stage and needled him that since the tenants intended to be the owners of the property, this was basically a "job interview" for him. A good sport, Rose answered questions and did an impressive job parrying pointed statements of concern from residents. He expressed his strong desire to do a much better job than the Tishman Speyer management team in addressing quality-of-life issues on the property. Since Rose had not been officially hired to run the property, people asked when that might become official. "If I am tapped to run the property, you all will be the first to know, right after I call my mother," he said. The tenants laughed, and I breathed a deep sigh of relief that we had all survived the meeting.

Coming out of the March 13 meeting, I was convinced that we had the right advisers, but one issue continued to nag at me: a potential challenge to the legitimacy of the Tenants Association itself. The board, for example, was almost entirely composed of tenants who paid rent-stabilized rents. The board had also, over time, dwindled to only eight members. As a result, in 2006, when we announced our first bid, some tenants had rightly questioned how the Tenants Association could speak for them. Not every tenant, after all, was a thirty-five-dollar-dues-paying member of the organization, and Al Doyle, who was known as "Fidel" by many for the length of his service, had not held an election among all members in years. Disgruntled neighbors would periodically demand to see the TA's bylaws or the membership lists—requests that Doyle would politely ignore. It didn't really matter much because, for years, the Tenants Association had been a loosely organized group of volunteers who assembled to fight back against MetLife, to challenge MCIs, and to advocate for renewal of the state rent-stabilization laws. People were mostly grateful that board members were volunteering their time for that effort. But now the board was aspiring to become a player on the largest stage, and to propose a plan that would affect every single tenant's bottom line. Our credibility in the real estate world came directly from our ability to claim that the TA was a group that was duly elected, representative of the community, and could negotiate in the name of all Stuyvesant Town and Peter Cooper tenants. Anyone with a different agenda—whether disgruntled tenants or competing bidders—would have their knives out, looking for any weakness. It was high time to call an election.

Despite the fact that I had grown up in a rent-stabilized apartment where my parents still lived, Zoe and I were *Roberts* tenants, which meant that our apartment had illegally been taken out of rent stabilization, and our rent was now being negotiated under the supervision of a judge. Young professionals without kids, at the time, we resembled a lot of the newer people in the community who likely would have little interest in volunteering their time to a local tenants group. One night over dinner, I told Zoe that I needed to find some newer tenants for the board and asked if she had any interest. Zoe had just started a new job in the general counsel's office of Planned Parenthood Federation of America and quickly dismissed any thought I might have had of drawing her into this. But she agreed to reach out to a friend of hers, a lawyer at the ACLU Women's Rights Project named Julie Ehrlich. At the same time, I decided to approach a neighbor named Steven Newmark, a litigation associate at Orrick Harrington, who was politically active and had moved into a market-rate apartment in Stuy Town in 2007. Both Ehrlich and Newmark, despite being busy people, agreed to help us out at this critical moment.

Doyle recognized the board's weakness and appreciated that I had found two new prospects who paid the market rate. He eagerly and quickly pushed the approval of Newmark and Ehrlich onto the board. They represented a new generation of tenants; each was a young professional, a lawyer, and a breath of fresh air for the Tenants Association. Along with Jim Roth, another lawyer on the board, they took the lead in working with our Paul Weiss lawyers to set up a fair election process, and spent the next several months reviewing the TA's bylaws and debating provisions such as the terms of office and election procedures. Ultimately, they decided to expand the board to fifteen members, with staggered four-year elected terms, and called an election for June 12, 2010—giving all dues-paying members an equal chance to get on the ballot. They set up a two-tiered process for running for a seat on the board. One way was to be nominated by the board itself, and the other was to gather thirty-five nominating signatures from neighbors. A number of residents expressed interest in being nominated to the board, so the Tenants Association formed a nominating committee and began to interview prospective candidates.

There hadn't been a Tenants Association election in some time, and it generated a number of candidates. One of those candidates, John Sheehy, had served for a number of years as chair of the litigation department at Rogers & Wells, one of New York's most prominent law firms. He and his wife, Morna, had moved into Stuyvesant Town in 1965 when he was an assistant district attorney under Frank Hogan. After a stint working for Governor Rockefeller in Albany, he returned to Stuy Town and in 1983 moved into an apartment at 6 Peter Cooper Road. Sheehy had worked at Rogers & Wells for over twenty years before taking an early retirement in 1996. He had followed the Tenants Association's efforts to buy the property in 2006 and took note of our surprising victory in the *Roberts* litigation. He wondered how that might affect his unit, which itself had been deregulated many years earlier. He also kibitzed with neighbors when Tishman Speyer defaulted. "Wow," he thought, "there is a lot happening here."[37] Much like Steinberg, Sheehy had pulled the *Town & Village* newspaper from his mailbox in the lobby and saw a posting from the Tenants Association. It announced the expansion of its board of directors and called for new candidates to participate in the election. Sheehy was not a typical resident. He had the means to afford one of the community's very few market-rate three-bedroom apartments and in fact had a second home in East Hampton. But he had deep roots in the community, and he wanted to help. He decided to respond to the advertisement, wondering if he should add this to his growing roster of volunteer activities.

For his board interview, Sheehy walked through Peter Cooper's manicured paths, just two buildings over, into the apartment of Soni Fink, now one of the board's most senior members. Her pseudo-adopted son,

John Marsh, joined for all of the meetings, as did Julie Ehrlich and Jim Roth. Sheehy was tall, athletic, and good looking, with an assured but not cocky manner. Fink immediately thought that he was dignified and projected a command of the issues. She felt that the new board, facing more complicated challenges, would need people like Sheehy. Not only was he a *Roberts* tenant, but it certainly would not hurt to have another lawyer, and someone of his stature, in the group. Fink and the committee decided to put him on the board's "recommended" slate. The board considered all the applications and decided to recommend a slate of five new directors, which included Sheehy, as well as Kevin Farrelly, Jennifer Kops, Judith Preble Miller, and Jonathan Wells.[38]

Along with the five candidates on their slate, three additional candidates got on the ballot by gathering thirty-five nominating signatures. In the first electioneering that the community had ever seen in a TA election, the TA took out full-page ads in *Town & Village* on June 3 and June 10, complete with a group photo, urging tenants to vote for the slate of ten incumbents and five newly nominated directors. The TA also hosted two gatherings in the Community Center and invited neighbors to meet the candidates and ask them questions.

On Saturday, June 5, at 11 a.m., I decided to walk over to the Community Center to meet the candidates for the TA board. I had enjoyed a very close relationship with the existing group, and I did not want that to change when the board grew to fifteen members. In that sense, I was there campaigning, too. Standing in the middle of the room, I saw a new face in the crowd, with a name tag that said "John." "It is an honor to meet you," Sheehy said, assuredly, as he took me through his impressive professional bio. "I hope we have a chance to work together to fix this mess," he added. I did too. As a commercial litigator by training, he had the sort of professional chops that we needed on the board, and he later played a key role in helping us get on a successful path.

As we got closer to the election, we started to hear more divergent—and vocal—views about the course the Tenants Association should be pursuing. The plan for converting Stuyvesant Town to homeownership was not on the ballot, but it might as well have been. While the TA had not yet developed a new plan, tenants were still focused on the two-tiered homeownership structure, with restrictions on the ability to sell units, that we had proposed in 2006. As I knew would be the case, with thirty thousand residents, including plenty of accomplished lawyers and bankers and real estate professionals, there were at least thirty thousand opinions. To some, we were not acting fast enough, and we were getting lapped by the competition. To others, we were a bunch of socialists who wanted to restrict profits on apartments to the detriment of existing tenants. "I know that 'restrictions on profits' sounds nice in theory, but I really think it will be fatal to getting any tenants to buy into the plan," wrote one resident to Al Doyle in an email. "The reality of our community is that people who live here don't have a lot of money—Therefore, you have to allow for the opportunity of a profit if you want any of the 11,000 tenants to make an investment decision and buy into a risky real estate asset."[39] There were even rumblings about an "Owner's Association" forming, to protect the interests of people who saw this purely as an investment opportunity.

To address the increasing number of inbound suggestions, the Tenants Association decided to set up a committee for people to interact directly with Paul Weiss and Moelis, the Tenants Association, and with me. Residents with real estate and finance backgrounds were invited to participate and to offer their expertise. We felt that this forum was a better place for any disgruntled voices than on blogs, or Facebook, which were growing in popularity as forums for local politics.

The TA called the board election for June 11 at Baruch College's Mason Hall on 23rd Street and Lexington Avenue. I stood up on the stage and took the opportunity to brag to my neighbors about the strength and legitimacy the TA was projecting in the real estate world. "On January 1 of this year, Tishman Speyer had not defaulted," I observed from the stage. "We had no professional team, no Paul Weiss, no Moelis. Six months ago, not a single unity pledge had been signed, and most of us had never heard of CWCapital. Today, a mere six months later, we have a world-class team," I declared. "We are organized, with floor leaders, building captains, zone and community leaders. We are unified. We have just held an election for a new board of the TA. We are motivated and we are determined to get to our common goals and we will not be deterred."[40] And, I noted, John Mash had already gotten 65 percent of the entire community to sign unity pledges. All of this, I thought, was good news and reflected well on the ten incumbent board members.

Three thousand five hundred two votes were cast, and the top fifteen vote-getters were elected to the board. Doyle, Marsh, and Steinberg were

at the top of the heap, followed by *Roberts* tenants Ehrlich and Newmark. The Tenants Association's preferred slate also was approved by the
voters. Mark Grayson, a proponent of a purely market-rate conversion
of the property, came in sixteenth, missing a spot on the board by 201
votes.[41]

Back in 2006, when MetLife put Stuy Town up for sale, our neighbors
were constantly griping about the "suits" walking around, calculating
what our home was worth, looking right past tenants and dreaming of a
big payoff. On June 28, 2010, I invited the Paul Weiss and Moelis teams,
as well as the newly constituted TA board, to my apartment for Ess-a-
Bagels and a tour of the neighborhood. It was partially a substantive exercise to educate our advisers about the community, but it was also part
political theater, and I proudly paraded *our* suits around as we waved to
our neighbors with excitement.

As a first step, Rubin and Kane recommended that we privately engage
Chuck Spetka at CWCapital and offer him a plan, well in advance of
any auction. Their theory was that if CWCapital could see the benefit of
bringing the tenants into the fold, we could then jointly set out parameters
of a sale. Rubin thought that this strategy could very well be in CWCapital's interests because it would not only allow them to fully pay back the
bondholders they represented, but also keep the tenant group happy and
eliminate the considerable political risk and uncertainty of an auction. To
me, a private approach was perhaps a reasonable business plan but, unless it worked out quickly, a terrible political strategy. Quiet approaches
to CWCapital meant that we could not share with our constituents what
we were doing. When our neighbors didn't hear from us, they generally
did not assume that we were diligently having successful arms-length negotiations. They assumed that we were sitting on our hands, or plotting a
secret course of action that was contrary to their interests, and over their
own dinner tables complained that the TA was incompetent and did not
know what it was doing.

Spetka continued to tell me that he believed the right deal was with the
tenants, but he was clearly worried about taking any unusual moves that
might throw his process off course. There were a lot of deep-pocketed
investors in the deal, and CWCapital was vulnerable to a lawsuit from
a number of them, no matter what action they took. For example,

CWCapital had already filed a motion for foreclosure—the first step in the process of selling the property—and Appaloosa's David Tepper immediately sued to intervene in the lawsuit. Tepper argued that the decision to pursue foreclosure, instead of a bankruptcy, would unnecessarily cost $200 million in transfer taxes. Spetka was asking for my patience and assured me that he was committed to an outcome where "everybody wins." For the first time, on July 10, he raised a concern that I had long anticipated: the complexity of working with tenants. "How do you deal with eleven thousand units?" he asked me. "What happens when CWCapital has an agreement with the TA but there are groups that peel off and object or want to do their own thing?" It was a fair point, and while I was happy we had just held the TA board election to bolster its legitimacy, I was quite worried about tenant unity too.[42]

As we thought about how best to engage Spetka, we were also having conversations with the city's housing commissioner Rafael Cestero and his team. Because I chaired one of the city council's subcommittees that oversaw the housing agency and approved its development projects, Cestero and I had occasion to speak early in his tenure. On our very first call in 2009, just before Tishman Speyer's default, he brought up Stuy Town himself and told me that he was keeping a close eye on it. I also appreciated that he had come to our March Tenants Association meeting in person, even though City Hall had imposed significant limitations on what he could say. As I got to know Cestero better, I started to feel like I was talking to a co-conspirator who was sincerely interested in helping us figure it all out. He was honest and did not overpromise to me, but was clearly motivated to find a reasonable solution. By May 2010, before the TA election, I was talking regularly to Cestero, and the HPD team was in direct contact with our professionals at Moelis.

I asked Cestero whether—or which—city programs could help us ensure long-term affordability in Stuy Town. "Normal programs don't work here," he explained to me. "Stuy Town is a program in itself." He candidly shared with me that he was skeptical that our conversion plan would work because he did not believe that rent-stabilized tenants paying the lowest rents would ever opt to buy their apartments. "Once you add carrying charges to their mortgage payments, you are basically doubling the average rent—and people won't do that," he told me. "I don't see an easy incentive for the low-rent people to buy that doesn't involve the city rolling up an eighteen-wheeler full of cash to Stuyvesant Town." I didn't agree, but did not want to discourage him from exploring options that he felt were feasible. Cestero was pushing his staff to work to determine what city incentives might support a plan that preserved long-term affordability in Stuy Town, with or without a homeownership option, and that itself was real progress.[43]

A variety of outside investors had begun to circle the complex—such as the Related Companies, and a partnership between the LeFrak Organization, Centerbridge Partners, and Wilbur L. Ross, which was interested in stepping in to both own and operate the property. The tenants had interacted with Related and LeFrak in 2006, when they had explored bidding in MetLife's auction. Harrison LeFrak, who was running the LeFrak Organization with his father, Richard, and brother, Jamie, touted his firm's credentials as an owner and operator: "I don't think there exists another firm with our capabilities," he said. In language eerily reminiscent of the Tishman Speyer deal, Wilbur Ross said, on behalf of their partnership with LeFrak, "We are not really capital-constrained, so we can put up whatever is needed. We're prepared to go all the way." Donald Trump also expressed his interest in buying Stuyvesant Town and Peter Cooper Village, prompting the *New York Post* to speculate that the community could one day be called "TrumpTown." "People have asked us if we would get involved in running it or buying it. We are looking at it right now very seriously," Trump said. He added, "No one has a better track record running properties."[44]

By 2010, there were signs that after the collapse of the American economy, the housing market was becoming more stable.[45] Even beyond stability, the real estate world was starting to have an excited tone that resembled 2006, and we were worried that CWCapital could very well opt for a quick sale that simply excluded us. The satisfaction that we felt in June, bringing on the Paul Weiss and Moelis teams, had already evaporated. I did not have a relationship with any of these real estate players, and most of them viewed me skeptically, watching me, for years, attack Tishman Speyer for their bad acts. One exception was the LeFrak family. Harrison LeFrak, or "Harry," as I knew him, was a friend of mine from Trinity School. We had met in the second grade in 1978 and graduated together in 1990. I did not know whether the LeFrak Organization would be the right fit to own Stuy Town, but I felt certain that Harry would, at a minimum, be honest in his dealings with me. I could not say the same about anyone else.

Among the interested parties, there were few people who had more closely studied the ways to maximize value at Stuy Town than Andrew MacArthur. MacArthur was a flinty New Englander in his mid-forties, who never wore a tie. He had a taste for the drama of politics and relished walking into meetings with Democratic elected officials like me and setting a copy of the conservative-leaning *New York Post* on the conference table just to watch our reactions. MacArthur and his father-in-law, Bill Dickey, had approached MetLife with Apollo Real Estate Advisors and ING Clarion in 2005 to try to buy Stuy Town even before it went up for sale, but was rebuffed. His group ended up being the second-place bidder in the 2006 auction. MacArthur was someone not to be dissuaded by the messy or contentious backstory at Stuy Town.

On the cusp of Tishman Speyer's default in December 2009, MacArthur had gotten a cold call from Dave Iannarone, the president of CWCapital. Iannarone and Spetka at CWCapital had just stepped in as the special servicer in Stuy Town, and knowing MacArthur's experience, they asked to talk to him about the deteriorating situation. Tishman Speyer was careening toward a default, and Iannarone needed someone to help CWCapital look after its interests. Over breakfast at Iannarone's hotel in Times Square, Iannarone told him that "it looks like this thing is going to go sideways, and we need someone who can oversee the foreclosure." But, he cautioned, "Step one is to get control of the asset. We won't be able to execute until we get control." Iannarone made MacArthur an offer to become the lead in Stuy Town on behalf of CWCapital, which he accepted. MacArthur's first task was to find a way to ensure CWCapital's control over the property and to not be distracted by the bidders, or the tenants.[46]

As a legal matter, Tishman Speyer still owned the property, but the right to make decisions was in the hands of CWCapital—which now meant Andrew MacArthur. MacArthur was the new face of the owner of Stuy Town. It was unclear to us whether he would be the villain or savior in the story of Stuy Town, but we were certain he was going to be right in the middle of all the action.

8

Suddenly the "Prettiest Girl at the Dance"

When most people buy a house, they usually take out a loan from a bank, which helps them to pay the full purchase price. When Tishman Speyer bought Stuy Town, the purchase price of $5.4 billion was so large that there was not a single bank, or other investor, able to make a loan of such a significant amount. That was hardly a problem at the height of the market in 2006, because banks and other firms were wildly eager to invest money into new real estate opportunities. Doug Harmon of Cushman & Wakefield described the exuberant mood like this: "You go to a casino, and your friend gives you $1 million. He says, go, have a good time—if you lose it, don't worry about it, you don't need to pay me back. If you win, you can keep 20 percent. But if you don't gamble *at all*, you need to give it all back." Enthusiastic investors looking to cash in on the real estate market lent Tishman Speyer and BlackRock what they needed to buy Stuy Town from MetLife. Now, in 2010, an appraisal put the value of Stuy Town and Peter Cooper at $1.8 billion—$3.6 billion less than the purchase price—which meant that there were a lot of lenders about to lose a lot of money.[1]

As is the custom in deals like this, lenders had all signed a contract that defined who would be paid back, and in what order, in the event of default. In Stuy Town, the $3 billion first mortgage was the primary loan that paid for the property, and when Tishman Speyer defaulted, these lenders were entitled to be paid back before anyone else. They had accepted a lower rate of return in exchange for a higher likelihood that they would get repaid if things went south. Like so many financial products in 2006 connected to real estate, the $3 billion first mortgage had been packaged (in this case by Wachovia Bank) into five sets of other mortgages around the country and sold to investors as bonds. These securities were called "commercial mortgage-backed securities," or CMBS. Fannie Mae and Freddie Mac owned $2 billion of the $3 billion in Stuy Town CMBS, a point that we had already called out publicly with Senator Schumer's help.[2]

Just behind the first mortgage in seniority were $1.4 billion in "mezzanine" loans. Mezzanine loans are usually made based on an owner's ability to repay them from the cash flow. Accordingly, these are riskier loans than the first mortgage, but the deal terms had included a bigger payout if the venture were successful. In the Stuy Town deal, the mezzanine loans were divided into eleven different individual loans. They included the government of Singapore, also known as GIC ($575 million), SL Green ($200 million), DG Hypo ($100 million), Hartford ($100 million), CWCapital ($90 million), Bracebridge ($75 million), JER ($60 million), Fortress ($50 million), AIB ($25 million), Brascan ($25 million), NY Credit ($25 million), and Winthrop ($25 million).[3]

Finally, at the bottom of the stack was the equity—the actual owners of the property, who would benefit the most in a successful venture, but who also took on the most risk if the deal were to fail. They included Tishman Speyer ($112 million), BlackRock ($112 million), as well as the California Public Employees' Retirement System ($500 million), the California State Teachers' Retirement System ($100 million), the Florida Pension Fund ($250 million), and—notably—the Church of England ($70 million). Together, they had invested over $1 billion in the deal.[4] The agreement between all the parties, called the intercreditor agreement, designated CWCapital as the special servicer, whose job would be to manage the payouts in the event of default and specifically to protect the interests of the bondholders of the first mortgage.

The public pension funds at the bottom of the stack were, unsurprisingly, deeply unhappy with how things had turned out. Between the California and Florida pension funds, nearly $1 billion of the hard-earned money of state employees in California and Florida had just evaporated. The Government of Singapore Investment Corporation, which made a $575 million mezzanine loan, also stood to lose it all. The Church of England was in there too, prompting a snarky headline in Curbed, a New York real estate blog network: "Even God Losing Money on Stuy Town."[5]

Moreover, because a good portion of the Stuy Town debt had been sold as commercial mortgage-backed securities to investors throughout the country, and because it was so large, some speculated that the deal's failure had the potential to slow the nation's overall economic recovery. Some $700 billion worth of CMBS were issued during the boom years, but the impact of a failure of this size was untested. This single deal had the potential to rattle the market for apartments, offices, hotels, and other commercial properties everywhere. Analysts called Stuy Town the poster child for the entire housing bubble. "If you owe the bank a million dollars, you're in quite a bit of trouble; if you owe the bank a billion dollars, the bank is in quite a bit of trouble," observed Chris Cornell, a real estate commentator.[6]

After the default, regrets from real estate investors were starting to burst through to the surface. Carl Schwartz, chair of Herrick Feinstein's real estate department, told the *Real Deal* that in 2006, the buyers, the sellers, and their lawyers were all happy. "Now," he said, "very little is celebratory. A celebration for the client now is more in the nature of, 'I dodged a bullet.'" The *New York Times* cited an unnamed member of "one of New York's more prominent real estate duchies," who spoke only on the condition of anonymity for fear of displeasing the mayor: "Letting the market rule there was one of Bloomberg's very worst decisions. A mayor's voice matters in setting out the parameters." Even Deputy Mayor Doctoroff expressed qualms about the administration's decision not to get involved. "Maybe we should have pushed back harder on MetLife. Maybe we could have found a way to partially subsidize tenants based on income. Honestly, I'm not sure," he wrote in his memoir. Senator Chuck Schumer observed that Tishman Speyer's business plan was "one of the most despicable acts of corporate greed I have ever seen." As we started thinking about the future, we hoped that the failure of the 2006 deal might prompt investors to exercise more caution in 2010; perhaps Mayor Bloomberg, who was still in office, might even see reason to support us.[7]

With Andrew MacArthur in place at CWCapital, we needed to find a way to develop a relationship with him. I asked Chuck Spetka if he would make an introduction to this new member of his team. On July 21, 2010, Alex Rubin and I sat down for granola and eggs at Blue Fin in Times Square with Spetka and MacArthur. MacArthur was polite, but cool and all business. Rubin suggested to him that the tenants and CWCapital work together to develop a term sheet that would guarantee financial recovery to CWCapital's bondholders, while also delivering on the tenants' goals of a conversion plan.[8] It was a simple proposal that seemed entirely uncontroversial to me. It also was within the realm of what Spetka had been saying to me about CWCapital's own goals since he himself came on the scene. However, despite months of engaging with us, Spetka was a little more circumspect with MacArthur at his side. He told us that some partnership could be possible down the line, but, citing litigation between the creditors, that it was premature to discuss it before CWCapital was formally in control of Stuy Town, which they kept calling "the asset," to my great annoyance. I probably should have taken their unwillingness to engage with us as a sign of what was to come, but I still had reason to be hopeful. Unlike the rapid-fire auction in 2006, with a faceless insurance company calling all the shots, and a slap-dash effort by the tenants to make a bid, we were in a much different position now. We had professionals on our team, and a counterparty that was actually sitting with us over granola.

While he was not prepared to make any affirmative commitments to us, over the next two weeks MacArthur had one meeting and multiple calls with Larry Kwon of Moelis, to talk about entering into a memorandum of understanding with the Tenants Association. MacArthur explained that CWCapital was first planning to foreclose out the junior lenders by mid-September, and that by the end of 2010 it would likely be prepared to start a sale process.[9] Our objective was for MacArthur to include our affordability and homeownership goals as a requirement for any bidder. While Moelis was working on proving to MacArthur that this would give CWCapital a full recovery for its bondholders, Meredith Kane drafted the memorandum of understanding and sent it to him on August 4 for his review.

As we explored our options with CWCapital, the Tenants Association was being actively courted by a who's who of the real estate world. When a representative of the People's Republic of China reached out to Kane about partnering with the tenants, I was not surprised. Our own city council phones were ringing fast and furious; email invitations were coming in: Silverstein Properties, the owner of the World Trade Center. Apollo Global Management, the private-equity giant. The Qatar Investment Authority. Related Companies. Investor Wilbur Ross. Harrison LeFrak. Carmel Partners. Time Equities.

On Saturday, August 7, four days after we circulated our draft memorandum of understanding to MacArthur, I got a phone call from Jon Silvan of Global Strategy Group, one of the city's most prominent public affairs and political strategy firms. Silvan was a friend of mine whose firm had done polling for my campaigns. He wanted to tell me that his client, Bill Ackman, was going to announce publicly on Monday that he was "planning on buying Stuy Town" and that I would hear from him directly. Ackman is a handsome, press-savvy financier, and just about anything he does tends to generate front-page news in the business section. He had made a name for himself buying stakes in companies that he viewed as undervalued and then taking aggressive and public steps to boost their stock price. Most recently, in 2008, Ackman had made a bet that General Growth Properties, the second-biggest mall owner in America, would file for bankruptcy but would emerge even stronger. Ackman bought up shares at twenty-five cents in 2008 and advocated for the company when it filed for bankruptcy. The result was an extraordinary $1.6 billion return on a $60 million investment.[10]

Ackman called me personally at noon that Monday, August 9, to introduce himself. He breezily described the fact that he and Michael Ashner of Winthrop Realty had formed a joint venture to buy the senior-most mezzanine loans—originally valued at $300 million—for $45 million. He told me that he had spent time studying the priorities of the tenants and felt that our goals were achievable. Ackman asked if we could get together so that he could just "listen and learn." I couldn't help but think how easy it seemed for him to bet tens of millions of dollars hoping that it would yield a big payoff in the form of owning Stuy Town. Nevertheless, I found Ackman extremely charming and was encouraged by his stated desire to support our goals of an affordable, non-eviction co-op. "All constituencies need to be happy with the outcome," he said reassuringly.[11] Ackman encouraged me to review his work on General Growth Properties and, on a personal level, said that I could ask about him with an ex-girlfriend who apparently worked with Zoe at Planned Parenthood. I promised him I would do my due diligence and told him that the tenants of the community were going to need to come out on top in any deal. "Don't start out as an adversary, you will fail right out of the gate," I suggested. Ackman said he understood completely, and told me that CWCapital did not yet know about his deal with Michael Ashner—but that he expected that it would become a public matter the next day.

Bill Ackman had been on vacation in Nantucket in July when Ashner called him to propose this partnership.[12] Ashner, a self-described "barnyard dog" and shrewd real estate veteran, had for about eight months been promoting his own plan to take control of Stuy Town. Winthrop Realty, a New York Stock Exchange–listed real estate investment trust, owned $25 million of the $300 million in senior mezzanine loans in the Stuy Town deal, which meant that he would be paid back for his loan after the $3 billion first mortgage bondholders, who were now represented by CWCapital. Ashner theorized that he had the right to foreclose out the interests of all the mezzanine lenders junior to him, to work with the tenants, and to take control of the property.

Ashner had cold-called my city council offices to introduce himself on January 12 and to lay out the beginnings of what would ultimately be the plan he and Ackman were now promoting. He told me then that he was angry at Tishman Speyer, not only because they had struck a terrible deal in 2006, but also because they were not consulting mezzanine lenders like him while they were attempting to restructure the debt with CWCapital. Of course, in an ordinary homeowner default, the lending bank simply forecloses the interests of the homeowner and becomes the owner. In Stuy Town, there were so many lenders, each of which technically had a right to foreclose out the interests of everyone who held a position junior to theirs in the deal. Ashner told me that because of his position, he could wipe out Tishman Speyer and BlackRock, as well as everyone else, and not only restructure the debt but also set out a more stable future for the tenants. He was worried, however, that such a foreclosure would trigger a big $180 million transfer tax obligation, which he did not want to have to pay. "I thought Stuyvesant Town had value, long term," Ashner said.

"It was worth fighting over, as opposed to some one-hundred-thousand-square-foot building in Kansas."[13]

Over the phone back in January, Ashner had excitedly served up a most unusual proposal, and as he spoke, I took notes as fast as I could. He suggested that the Tenants Association create a 501(c)(3) corporation, which would allow for it to receive tax-deductible contributions. Once we had that set up, Ashner planned to donate $10 million (of his $25 million) in mezzanine debt as a gift to the Tenants Association. By owning a senior portion of the Stuy Town debt, Ashner believed that the Tenants Association itself would then have the right to foreclose out all the other junior lenders, as well as Tishman Speyer and BlackRock's interests, in the capital stack. That meant, arguably, that the Tenants Association, in partnership with Ashner's Winthrop Realty, would become the owner of the property and assume an obligation to repay the $3 billion first mortgage, and the remaining $290 million of mezzanine loans. According to Ashner, because we would do all of this as a tax-exempt organization, we would reduce the tax liability from $180 million to $14 million, and it would be a "home run" for the Tenants Association.[14]

The Tenants Association would not only own the property, he argued, but could also decide what they wanted to do—"own their units, build a park, whatever." He claimed to be agnostic on what we actually did, but was absolutely certain that this was the best move for us, and for him. He currently was facing the possibility that his interests would be wiped out, so anything that helped him hold on to some or all of his $25 million investment was beneficial. "I'm not a freedom fighter, nor am I a terrorist," he said to me without further explanation. "Work backwards," he said, "and you control your own destiny. A landlord's job is to make as much money as possible; the tenants' perspective is different."[15] I didn't yet completely understand the mechanics of the capital stack, and how the tenants could foreclose out everyone else's interests. I really needed a tutorial from Rubin and Kane before I could respond, so I invited Ashner down to City Hall for a meeting a few days later. On January 21, Ashner was—without any entourage, but brimming with boyish excitement—sitting across from me and my chief of staff, Justine Almada, in one of the city council's drab windowless conference rooms at 250 Broadway. With a salesman's determination, he was again pitching me on the idea of giving the Tenants Association $10 million and to have them foreclose and become the owner. I took notes and tried to interrupt with a few questions. He was still smiling with a determined look when he shook my hand to conclude our meeting.

A novel opportunity, perhaps, but even after our second meeting, I was still skeptical and knew this would be a tough sell to my neighbors. After all, a "foreclosure" or "being in foreclosure" to most tenants had an overwhelmingly bad association and was what we thought we were supposed to be most worried about, not instigating. To most of us, it symbolized a property in disarray, where services would stop and buildings would start falling apart. It would be difficult for me to lead the charge for a foreclosure, but I certainly was not going to reject it just because it was difficult to explain and had negative connotations.

I had shared Ashner's idea with Doyle, as well as Rubin and Kane, on the day Ashner first reached out. I had also made a late-night call to the city's housing commissioner, Rafael Cestero, and let him know what Ashner had proposed. Everyone agreed that it was a highly risky strategy, because in a foreclosure, a mezzanine lender might be obligated to pay off the entire $3 billion first mortgage before proceeding; but Rubin observed that it was not entirely without precedent. Just one year earlier, a partnership bought the mezzanine debt in Boston's John Hancock Tower, the tallest building in New England, and put the property into foreclosure. At the auction, the partnership won the tower with a bid of $20 million, and took over its $640 million first mortgage. Mezzanine lenders had also recently foreclosed on the W Union Square Hotel and 100 Church Street, both in Manhattan. Never, however, had a tenant group stepped into the shoes of a mezzanine lender, and done it on a residential property. After considerable discussion with Kane and Rubin, I explained it to Doyle and the tenant leaders, who agreed that because it carried such risk, it was not the right route for us. We held off Ashner by telling him that we were not prepared to move forward with a partnership, yet.[16]

I wasn't the only one on Michael Ashner's dance card, however. After he did not get an immediate positive response from us, Ashner went on to meet with CWCapital, AREA Property Partners, and others. He was liberally sharing his plan to partner up with the tenants group, which was getting reported back to me second and third hand. Ashner's continued advocacy for this plan both unnerved and perplexed me, because we had expressly declined to embrace this risky concept. When Ashner pitched it to Ackman, however, Ackman loved it almost instantly. By early August, without any assurance from the tenants that they would be supportive, Ackman took the gamble and formed a joint venture with Ashner, and for $45 million, together they bought Stuy Town's most senior mezzanine loans.[17]

On Sunday, August 8, the day before Ackman reached out to me directly, Ackman and Ashner published a notice of foreclosure in the *New York Times*, with a date of August 25. Very few people actually saw it, but those who did understood it as a direct challenge to CWCapital's authority. If Winthrop and Pershing Square were successful in foreclosing out all junior interests, they could have the legal right to trigger a bankruptcy, which would take decision-making power away from CWCapital. They also would have to pay a transfer tax, which Ashner still hoped to avoid by partnering with the tenants. Complicating matters, CWCapital had already gotten its own order of foreclosure from a court in June—on behalf of the $3 billion first mortgage—giving it the right to foreclose out everyone else (including Ashner's position), but because of the tax implications had not yet taken the final step of finalizing it. Kane told the TA that we could expect CWCapital to go to court to stop Ashner and Ackman from proceeding with their August 25 foreclosure.

Meanwhile, Ackman and Ashner issued a public press release that was extremely solicitous of the Tenants Association: "We share the Tenants' Association objective to complete a non-eviction, affordable, co-op conversion of the property." Ashner added, "We understand the importance of this property in providing housing for moderate income New Yorkers. Among our goals is the continued supply of affordable housing for its residents for years to come." Ackman and Ashner said that they were proposing the "largest co-op conversion in history," in partnership with the tenants. Ackman publicly made the case that we had been making to MacArthur privately, that he could do a conversion to homeownership for current tenants, pay off the first mortgage, and still make a profit. "It's a $3 billion real estate transaction," Ackman said. "They need help. They need us, we need them. I think that's the right way to look at it, and there's plenty of room to make a deal where everyone's happy." Doyle and the tenant leaders enjoyed watching these titans expressing their deep commitment to supporting affordable housing, and to delivering on the Tenants Association's top priorities. The *Times*'s Charles Bagli called on

August 9 to ask me about Ackman and Ashner, and I thought I heard some bemusement in his voice. He made passing reference to the memorandum of understanding that we had been trying to negotiate with MacArthur at CWCapital, which had not been finalized. I didn't know how he knew about it, but I hoped that he would not write about it. I suspected that the scrutiny that came with any publicity would make it harder for CWCapital to actually do it.[18]

Over coffee at the Brooklyn Diner on West 57th Street, on August 11, I met with Bill Ackman and Carolyn Tiffany, president of Winthrop Realty. Ackman said that he hadn't asked for the meeting to present any grand plans but rather just wanted us to get to know each other. But he did get to the point: he and Tiffany wanted the tenants' help in keeping CWCapital from fighting this out with them. "Lawsuits will come right out of the tenants' pockets," he said. Ackman observed that they didn't need to foreclose on August 25, so long as CWCapital would work with them. On the other hand, if CWCapital foreclosed first, his interests would be wiped out entirely. That meant that he needed to beat CWCapital to the punch, regardless of whether the strategy was cooperation or competition with them. He told me that he had spent the prior weekend walking anonymously around Stuyvesant Oval, talking to residents, and said how much he had loved the experience. I pictured Ackman in a baseball hat and sunglasses, snooping around Stuy Town and casually striking up conversations with some of the seniors sitting on the benches.[19]

The TA and all Stuy Town tenants were suddenly, as Bill Derrough of Moelis & Company had promised, "the prettiest girl at the dance." We were flattered that an entity with not only money, but actual legal rights in the capital stack, was looking to team up with us. Yet for most Stuy Town residents—including me—Ackman was an unknown quantity. To Doyle and the tenant leaders, no matter how good it sounded, partnering with a hedge fund manager looking to seize control of the property, to foreclose, and to trigger a bankruptcy did not feel like the direction we were supposed to be heading. We were looking to keep Stuy Town affordable and maintain the quality of life in our community, not be a big real estate wheel.

It did not help matters that Ackman was musing out loud about his plans to the *New York Times*. He speculated that he could sell a Stuy Town apartment at $600 a square foot, for around $546,000. We had studiously avoided talking about specific prices in the community, so when Ackman floated them, people took notice, and not in a good way. For that price, residents figured that they might have to come up with $110,000 cash—around 20 percent—for a down payment. With a 6 percent mortgage and $1,500 for maintenance and taxes, their monthly burden would be $4,100. As Housing Commissioner Cestero had warned us, that number was well beyond the means of most Stuy Town residents, and much higher than the current rent of many. Almost immediately after I read Ackman's comments, I got a phone call from Doyle and Marsh, together. They were very concerned about how the numbers would be received, and whether our constituents would latch on to them as a reason to oppose any homeownership plan. To make matters worse, Ackman was quoted in the *Times* saying that he had "other ideas for profiting from Stuyvesant Town, but he does not want to disclose them."[20]

Ackman's optimism about working with the tenants seemed inflated, given our own concerns, and his plans to strike a deal with CWCapital still needed to be realized. "I think CWCapital will welcome us. We are peacemakers," Ackman told *Crain's*. As with the tenants, this optimism proved unsubstantiated. A week after Ackman's plan emerged for Stuy Town, on August 18, CWCapital filed a lawsuit in New York State Supreme Court seeking to keep Pershing Square and Winthrop from foreclosing on the property. CWCapital was now parroting comments the TA and I had been making for years; the complaint said that "the future of this iconic enclave in the borough of Manhattan is in imminent jeopardy." CWCapital argued that their bondholders were owed not just $3 billion, but with interest and fees it was $3.66 billion, and that they needed to be paid off completely before any such foreclosure could take place. Ackman's lawyers responded that they had the absolute right to foreclose out lenders junior to them, while assuming the obligation to pay all the interest owed to CWCapital's bondholders when the notes came due. Justice Richard Lowe of the New York Supreme Court quickly halted Ackman's foreclosure sale and asked the parties to come in for oral arguments on September 2. CWCapital's spokeswoman Beth Orcutt—breaking months of public silence by her firm—called Ackman's action an "imminent breach of the intercreditor agreement to which it was bound." Ackman said that CWCapital's position that it needed to be paid in full before any foreclosure could take place was "ludicrous."[21]

The tenants didn't know if this infighting was good or bad, and with Soni Fink out to dinner when the news broke about Justice Lowe's decision, Marsh asked Sheehy to quickly draft an explainer for the TA to put on its website. Bankruptcies and foreclosures could bring terrible uncertainty, and we were worried that our quality of life might deteriorate in any period without a clear owner. "The creators of this property would feel no pride in the fact that the home to 25,000 New Yorkers is being treated like a pawn in a financial chess game," I said in my own statement. But, to the extent that there was fighting among creditors, we hoped that they each might seek to gain an advantage by cozying up to the tenants. And, in fact, after Justice Lowe scheduled his oral argument, *both* Pershing Square (and Ashner's Winthrop, through Pershing Square) and CWCapital were now actively wooing the Tenants Association. On August 25, after weeks of silence following the delivering of our draft memorandum of understanding, Andrew MacArthur suddenly sent a letter to Rubin expressing CWCapital's commitment to each of our principles, and to working with us. He noted Ackman's "attempts to challenge our rights under the mortgage documents" but said that CWCapital would work with us to achieve all the tenants' fundamental goals. MacArthur instructed his lawyers at Kramer Levin and Nixon Peabody to communicate directly with our lawyers at Paul Weiss to begin sharing information and to explore formulating a proposal together.[22]

MacArthur called me the next day to reiterate the point, saying that CWCapital intended to migrate Stuy Town "into a long-term affordable structure, which will serve as a paradigm for other properties in New York City." He added, "The only way to do that would be in cooperation with the tenants."[23] I thanked MacArthur for his helpful sentiments but expressed that I was disappointed we had not been able to show any progress publicly prior to this point.

This burst of generosity toward the tenants as soon as Ackman appeared on the scene spread throughout the real estate world. Seemingly out of nowhere, Stephen Ross and Bruce Beal of Related Companies called Rubin to express their continued interest in working with the TA to implement a rental-only solution. They also offered to assist us in "defending" against Ackman and Ashner. "This gets more interesting by the day," Rubin observed to me. Richard and Harrison LeFrak, Lance West from Centerbridge, and Wilbur Ross, who later became President Trump's secretary of commerce, asked for a meeting with me to talk about Stuy Town. I agreed, and we convened with Rubin in one of Moelis's corner conference rooms facing Park Avenue. Ross observed that the uncertainty created by the litigation was creating a unique opportunity for the tenants. With so many unresolved legal questions, Harrison, the junior LeFrak and my childhood friend, argued that the tenants should have a partner who could influence this entire volatile process. I smiled as Harrison spoke. I had been to his bar mitzvah, and we worked together on the *Trinity Times*, our high school newspaper. We studied for Modern European History exams together by phone, which mostly involved Harry lecturing to me out of the textbook from his Upper East Side apartment, and me frantically taking notes at my apartment, in Peter Cooper. I had always been impressed by his ability to take complicated concepts and make them more accessible—so listening to him do an analysis of the Stuy Town capital stack brought me back.[24]

LeFrak, West, and Ross proposed a deal with the tenants, whereby the property would stay completely as rentals, but tenants would have the right to buy shares in a Stuy Town corporation, where we would all share in any upside growth. They warned us that we needed a partner like them because CWCapital would not likely make a deal with us if we were operating on our own.[25] I was intrigued by the idea that we could give tenants an equity stake in all of Stuy Town even in a scenario where the property remained as a rental.

After the meeting, Rubin and I felt energized by the opportunity. If we weren't going to foreclose on Stuy Town in partnership with Ackman, we now had another option: a chance to securitize it. When we discussed it with Kane, though, she raised immediate concerns. If market-rate neighbors owned shares, for example, they could be driven—just as Tishman Speyer was—to push out their rent-stabilized neighbors. It could generate income for people, without a doubt, but shareholders would make a lot more income if their neighbors were paying $3,500 rather than $1,500 for their apartment. The proposal Harrison articulated was novel, but, Kane argued, it built in an unnecessary conflict among neighbors. Kane was clearly right. She persuaded us that our homeownership plan, where individuals were able to make their own decisions, regardless of their neighbors', continued to make the most sense. This was also the reason that Kane had directed us in our homeownership plans away from a cooperative (where everyone would be connected to each other as share-holders) and toward a condominium structure, where there was more in-dependence. "We concluded that the fewest conflicts were in just owning your own apartment. Buy your apartment. American dream. *Condo*," she recalled.[26]

Doyle and Marsh were certainly enjoying the full-scale courting of the tenants that we were getting from the real estate world, but they were worried about the deals potential partners were proposing. They agreed with Kane's assessment of the LeFrak and Centerbridge plan. And they were hearing worries from tenants about Bill Ackman, too. Not only was he openly musing to the *Times* about sales prices that were well beyond the reach of many tenants, but he also made clear that he intended to as-sume the existing mortgage and to restructure it at a value even greater than $3.66 billion. Tenants had been hearing that the property value was down to $1.8 billion, so this price felt like an unnecessary bailout of the very lenders in the deal that had done so much damage. Doyle and Marsh wanted me to draw a line in the sand and make it clear that this number was not representative of the Tenants Association's plan—and that we did not support giving such a gift to CWCapital's bondholders. I agreed and sent Ackman a letter saying so on September 1, the day before Justice Lowe's scheduled court hearing. In the letter, I challenged his plan to restructure Stuy Town for more than $3.66 billion, as well as his proposed unit sale price of $600 per square foot. I also expressed concern about the amount of debt he intended to keep on the property, and whether that might continue to create pressure to evict rent-stabilized tenants. "Whether they are paying through reduced maintenance levels, or through higher sale prices, or by funding litigation costs of intercredi-tor disputes," I wrote, "it is the tenant body that is going to be paying the price, as they always do."

Ackman's advisers quickly reacted to the letter, quite concerned that, if leaked to the public in advance of the September 2 hearing, it could in-fluence Justice Lowe's thinking about the merits of Pershing Square's case. Justine Lapatine of Global Strategy Group called me to ask that I not release the letter until after the hearing the next day. I had no intention of interfer-ing with the court process, and agreed to shelve it for one day. I did, how-ever, decide to go down to 60 Centre Street to watch the proceedings myself. The case had been assigned to Justice Lowe because he still had jurisdiction

Figure 8.1. A retired litigator, John Sheehy joined the Tenants Association board in 2010. Sheehy was a strong voice in support of homeownership, and he brought a level of pragmatism to the process. His business sense was critical in helping us to strike a deal in 2015. Photo credit: *Town & Village* newspaper.

over the *Roberts* case (he was the judge who decided against the tenants initially, and had been reversed). Nobody knew what was going to happen in Lowe's courtroom or exactly what it would mean for the tenants. In preparation for the hearing, my office had drafted two press releases—one in case CWCapital won, and one in case Pershing Square and Winthrop emerged triumphant. In both versions, we declared victory for the tenants.

John Sheehy arrived at the New York Supreme Court building on Thursday, September 2, about forty-five minutes before the hearing. He spotted Ackman and went over to introduce himself. After an exchange of pleasantries, and basic personal information, Ackman asked Sheehy directly, "Is the Tenants Association truly representative of the community?" Sheehy was prepared, and responded that ten members of the board were from Stuy Town, and five were from Peter Cooper. Ackman did not ask the more complicated questions of how many residents actually were dues-paying members of the Tenants Association, or how many board members were rent stabilized versus paying the market rate. Sheehy decided to take the occasion to give me a boost as the TA's chief negotiator, warning Ackman that no matter what happens, he would be well advised to follow my lead.[27]

Ashner was also there early and spotted me as I walked in. Unlike Sheehy's pleasant exchange with Ackman, Ashner approached me aggressively. "You don't think we can get this done at 3.66 billion?" I guessed he had seen my letter as well as some comments I gave Bagli at the *Times* that had questioned the benefit to tenants of the Ackman and Ashner plan. "It depends what you mean by 'getting it done,'" I responded. And then added, "No, no I don't. Not if you intend to keep it affordable for current or future tenants." Ashner started to argue, warning me that if I thought that CWCapital would actually work with the tenants, I had it all wrong. As Ashner and I spoke to each other in increasingly raised tones, Ackman came over, wrapped his arms around Ashner, and with a deliberate smile on his face as he faced me, slowly pulled him away. My irritation with this exchange reminded me to email Bagli, who was sitting across the courtroom from me, to tell him I had a letter that I wanted to share with him after the hearing.[28]

Along with Sheehy, Steinberg, and Newmark from the TA, Bagli and all the reporters covering Stuy Town were sprinkled around the wooden benches of the courtroom. Oshrat Carmiel of Bloomberg News, Kaja Whitehouse of the *New York Post*, Sabina Mollot of *Town & Village*, Cindy Rodriguez of WNYC Radio, Eliot Brown of the *Wall Street Journal*, and Teresa Agovino of *Crain's* were all in attendance. Adam Rose and Andrew MacArthur were also there. At 9:45 a.m., the court officer bellowed "All rise!" and, as Justice Lowe appeared, the packed courtroom of tenants, real estate interests, lawyers, and journalists stood up in unison. Justice Lowe heard the arguments, each side making the case that not only was their action supported by the law, but it was also *better for the tenants*. At the conclusion of the hearing, Lowe decided to halt all the foreclosure actions—both Ackman's as well as CWCapital's—but did not issue an immediate ruling on whether Ackman had a right to foreclose without paying off the entire $3.66 billion first mortgage. Unfortunately for my staff, with no side winning, neither press release they had prepared would be accurate.

After it was over, and I was standing at the back of the courtroom with my chief of staff Justine Almada and Steven Newmark of the TA board, Ackman came over and asked us if we had time for coffee. Surprised and intrigued, we accepted. We walked right past MacArthur and the CWCapital team huddled on Centre Street, and I waved to them as they watched us walk out with their adversary. Once we were situated by the window at the Starbucks on Lafayette Street, Ackman self-interestedly observed that CWCapital had been ignoring the tenants until he came on the scene—and predicted that if he were gone, they would surely go back to ignoring us again. He made an analogy that we were now re-alizing was common in the traditionally male-dominated real estate industry: Ackman compared our situation to being in high school, where the pretty girl doesn't pay any attention to you until your dad buys you a BMW. He strongly felt that CWCapital would not be able to make a deal with us because of their strict limitations as a special servicer. Anyway, he asked, "Who do you go with, the girl who liked you all along, or the girl who only likes you now?"[29]

It was clear that Ackman was feeling less confident of his legal position after the hearing, but he maintained a calm and cool demeanor. He matter-of-factly observed that the letter I had sent to him, once public, would likely influence Justice Lowe. Ackman politely asked if we could hold off on making our letter public until after Justice Lowe had made his decision. I said no, but that I would be careful to make clear that the tenants did not have a horse in this particular race. I asked Ackman if he would appeal if he lost. "That depends," he said, "on whether I have to post a $3 billion bond."[30] Our coffee ended, and I went back to my office. At 1:30 that afternoon, Spetka called me to see what I thought of the hearing.

The tenants had reached peak influence. Ackman was asking me for coffee, Spetka was calling to check in. Bagli posted a *Times* story under the headline "Tenants Are Wooed": "The last time the mammoth Stuyves-ant Town and Peter Cooper Village complexes were sold, their tenants were largely ignored. Now, two lending groups battling in court for control of the sister complexes on the East Side of Manhattan are both trying to curry favor with the 25,000 residents." "The tenants' political influence has grown," Harvey M. Shultz, senior fellow with the Citizens Housing and Planning Council, told the *Times*. "You certainly don't want to antag-onize them until the last possible moment." "It's nice to be courted," Doyle said.[31] Ashner's son was very unhappy with Bagli's article, telling his father that he and Ackman looked desperate. "The Tenants Association appears to hold all the cards," he said. "Garodnick and Rafael Cestero look like they are calling the shots with the Tenant Association."[32]

As I was sitting in my office the next day, recounting to my staff the story of meeting with Ackman at Starbucks, the phone rang, and it was Ack-man on the line. "OK, I have a proposal that I want the TA board to ur-gently consider," he said, as I busily pulled out my legal pad. Ackman then proposed forming a joint venture with the Tenants Association, whereby he would give the tenants half the ownership of the property *immediately*. After Pershing Square and Winthrop earned a 15 percent return on their investment, they would split profits with the tenants fifty-fifty, and he sug-gested that we could use our portion to keep purchase prices down. We would share control of the board—with four representatives from their end, and four from the Tenants Association. "Today, the tenants own zero. Tomorrow, you own half the complex," he said. "Here's the thing, Dan—we want to close this down this weekend," he told me. (I suspected he was hoping to show the court that they had struck a deal with the tenants.) "What do you think?"[33]

As a former law firm associate, I felt my heart go out to the junior law-yers and bankers whose Labor Day weekend Ackman had just proposed to ruin. I also did not see any way that the Tenants Association would want to partner with Ackman before the litigation was resolved. "This is an interesting idea, but maybe it's better made after the court rules?" I asked him. After all, he was offering us half of the property, but he could have offered us half of the Brooklyn Bridge. If he wasn't able to claim ownership of it, where was the value? "No, Dan. Now is the moment." I told him that I would need to circle back with our team and get back to him.

Rubin and I spoke, and we set up a quick conference call with the TA board—explaining to them what Ackman had just proposed. Rubin and Kane shared my concern about any rushed partnership before Justice Lowe's decision. The Tenants Association leaders agreed and quickly declined to authorize a weekend-long negotiation with Ackman for this purpose. After the call, Rubin reached back out to Ackman and Ashner and told them that the TA was not presently interested in proceeding with a joint venture. Rubin encouraged them instead to get into a room with us and CWCapital to try to work out a satisfactory outcome. While Ackman was unconvinced of the merits of a summit meeting with CWCapital, he did ask to meet with the TA board, and me, on the Tuesday after Labor Day. We agreed to set it up.

Despite our rejection of their proposal on Friday, by Saturday, Ackman was again pushing his case. Zoe and I were spending our Labor Day weekend at the wedding of her law school friend Meredith Osborn in Gouldsboro, Maine, a coastal town fifty miles south of Bangor, with very little cell service. We were getting dressed for the wedding when one email managed to sneak through my spotty service—and it was from Ackman. The subject line said, "The Clock is Ticking." I had so little service that I couldn't get the full text of the email to load. As Zoe looked on with a mix of amusement and annoyance, I scurried from corner to corner of our hotel room, trying to get it to come in. Seeing my stress, and eager to join her law school friends downstairs, she finally encouraged me to go look for a signal elsewhere. I got in the car and drove five miles, where the email finally loaded. Ackman impatiently reiterated the "generous offer" that he had made one day prior and cautioned against the "risk associated with the passage of time." He warned that nobody else would ever make as good an offer, and that while we might be criticized for making any decision, the Tenants Association also could "be scrutinized for opportunities for which it chose to pass or otherwise for which it let the clock expire for fear of making a decision." In the email, Ackman asked Rubin to revisit the question of partnership with the TA, and for us to share his thoughts with the entire TA board. My heart raced as I tried to get Rubin or Kane on the phone. Ackman's note was designed to make me nervous that I was jeopardizing the Stuy Town tenants' one chance for success, and it was working. I was stranded in Maine on Labor Day weekend, without the ability to actually do anything, with my wife, four months pregnant with

our first child, waiting for me to go to a wedding that was starting immi-
nently. Driving to every corner of Goldsboro, I managed to find consistent
cell service and spoke with Rubin. Rubin, in his patient style, assured me
calmly that there was no reason to change course and that we could wait
to hear from Ackman and Ashner directly on Tuesday.[34]

Reaction to Ackman's "Clock is Ticking" email was fierce from the
TA board. "I don't respond particularly well to pressure tactics," said Jim
Roth in a group email exchange. Soni Fink agreed: "Like Jim, I have the
distinct shadow of threat in Ackman's letter—go with us now or else. I get
bad vibes from this." Other members, like Newmark and Sheehy, were
more open. "This whole process is imbedded with urgency," Sheehy said.
"The tone of the email may have been harsh," Newmark said, "but it is
imperative that we evaluate Ackman's proposal on the merits." Privately,
I had conferred with Doyle, and he shared my deep discomfort with the
notion of making a quick deal with Ackman. By the end of the weekend, Ackman had already briefed Housing Commissioner Cestero about
the proposal to line up with the tenants, and encouraged Cestero to
get himself invited to the Tuesday meeting with the TA board. Cestero and
I spoke on Tuesday morning, and I told him he was welcome to join us if
he thought that was valuable. "Ackman doesn't realize that I'm on your
team, I guess," Cestero quipped to me.[35]

Cestero chose not to join us and instead decided to pay Ackman a
personal visit at his office at 787 Seventh Avenue. An assistant offered
Cestero a sparkling water, which she placed on a dense coaster on the
conference table. Cestero sipped it as he looked out at spectacular views of
Central Park. After a few minutes, Ackman walked in with two copies of
*Confidence Game: How Hedge Fund Manager Bill Ackman Called Wall
Street's Bluff* under his arm, and put both on the table, sliding them over
to Cestero. "I thought I'd give you a couple of copies of the book that
I wrote that predicted the Great Recession," Ackman said. "I signed one,
and gave you another in case you want to share it with a friend." Cestero
looked down at the books, quietly wondering why Ackman thought it
was a good idea to start a meeting with the housing commissioner like
that. Cestero listened to Ackman's pitch on how he would make money
on a quick turnaround, while getting a good outcome for tenants. "He
was talking like a trader," Cestero recalled. "It was not the right mental-
ity about owning multifamily housing. I did not think it made sense for

tenants to partner with him, and did not think it would end well if it went that way." Cestero expressed this opinion, in milder terms, to Ackman, while scanning Central Park at the peak of late summer.[36]

"We're not your typical hedge fund," Ackman insisted at his presentation to the TA board around the Moelis conference table, with Ashner also present, on September 7. I caught Marsh's eye and saw him repress a smile. Ackman told us about his success at General Growth Properties (GGP), which ran malls across the country and had gone into bankruptcy. He explained that the tenants of GGP—the stores that filled their malls— were very much like the tenants of Stuy Town concerned about their future as their landlord careened toward insolvency. For GGP, bankruptcy gave them a chance to successfully restructure and to raise new capital. The result was that GGP's market value had increased by more than $10 billion. "A similarly successful outcome here would ensure tenants have long-term access to affordable housing," Ackman argued. He then went on to call CWCapital—and special servicers like them—nothing more than "robotic auctioneers," who were uninterested in affordability or a speedy outcome, and lacked the flexibility to work with us, no matter what MacArthur was saying. "CWCapital is incapable of and will be unwilling to make a better deal for tenants," he said in his presentation. Ackman pushed his case as someone who could make a deal now, offer us a real seat at the table, with real standing in a bankruptcy. "Nobody else, current or future, can offer the tenants this deal," he said.[37]

Ackman explained that he believed the law required Justice Lowe to consider "broader public interests" in making his ruling and hoped to reduce his company's litigation risk by firmly aligning itself with the Tenants Association. If we partnered with him, and he lost the litigation, he argued, the tenants would be no worse off than they are today. But, he said, "You would permanently change the state of play, having anchored the expectations of any other alternative future owner."[38]

The TA was tough on Ackman and Ashner at the meeting. Our goal was to preserve the long-term affordability of Stuy Town and to protect middle-class tenants. This financial dealing all felt pretty far afield for us. "How do you think a possible alliance with the TA would help your position with Justice Lowe?" Steinberg challenged him. Others jumped in. "What is your understanding of the affordability issue?" "How do you plan to price the units for conversion?" "Do you really believe that it is realistic to expect us to come to a definitive agreement on this matter with the prospect of a ruling by Judge Lowe looming over this?" "How far have you thought this through?" Ackman and Ashner urged them just to take a leap and make a quick decision, promising that any remaining substantive issues could be worked out later. There was reason for their urgency; Justice Lowe's ruling on CWCapital's lawsuit was expected any day.

After the meeting, Fink observed that Ackman and Ashner were hoping to achieve a 15 percent return. "Are we talking about $7,500,000 per year that they would take off the top? If so, I want in on their half of the deal," she quipped. "During the 1970s," she continued, "just before Paul Volker took over at the Fed, anyone who had savings was walking around with a grin because the money markets were paying 14 percent. That's the last time anyone has seen returns like that except for Bernie Madoff." An active debate took place among Tenants Association leaders. Some, like Sheehy and Newmark, were open to Ackman's argument and wanted to explore it further. Others, like Roth, expressed concern that tenants would get "raked over the coals by a guy who is in it only for the money."[39]

The Tenants Association board ultimately concluded that if Ackman were to win his legal case, he still needed the active support of the TA, which meant that embracing Ackman and Ashner now had plenty of risk but little upside for us.[40] With that in mind, the board again declined to embrace a quick partnership with Ackman, but formally authorized Moelis and Paul Weiss to continue talking with him. I strongly agreed that we should slow down and reevaluate the issue after the court's ruling. Rubin communicated the board's decision to Ackman and explained that the TA needed to stay neutral in the litigation, but recommended that Ackman send a formal letter, expressing support for what the TA was trying to do. To MacArthur of CWCapital, Rubin relayed the "aggressive" outreach that Ackman was making to the TA board and encouraged him to make his own appearance before the group before too much time passed.

On September 12, Ackman and Ashner took Rubin's advice and wrote to Doyle, Kane, Derrough, and Rubin, thanking the board for giving its "authorization" to explore a partnership with Pershing Square and Winthrop. They promised to provide the equity capital necessary to recapitalize the property and fund a non-eviction co-op conversion plan. Ackman's team gave the letter to Bagli and to Speaker Quinn, and pushed it out to other press outlets, giving the impression that the TA had "authorized" something other than continued conversation. Teresa Agovino of *Crain's New York Business* called me for insights on what Ackman was trying to pitch to her; she told me that he had been teeing up a promise of a big story all weekend long. I told her it likely was the letter that Pershing Square and Winthrop had just sent us—and also to her. I made it clear that there was no partnership at all, and seemingly nothing to report. "That's it?" she said to me. "Ackman needs to dial it down."[41]

Jon Silvan of Global Strategy Group, Ackman's PR firm, called me to express his clients' disappointment with my lack of enthusiasm for their proposal. Silvan told me that he would be reaching out to Quinn, Stringer, and Mayor Bloomberg, to make them aware of the deal that Ackman and Ashner had proposed. Silvan's team circulated talking points to the elected officials, which said that Ackman's plan "seems to offer an end to the uncertainty and gives tenants a level of control over their own future that we have not seen from any other prospective owners." Since the TA board had not authorized any partnership with Ackman, I was worried that these talking points might prompt elected officials to inadvertently endorse the Ackman proposal in the press. I quickly called them all personally and warned them against doing that.[42] The public relations wrangling was short-lived, however, because Justice Lowe delivered his ruling only four days later. On September 16, he found in favor of CWCapital, saying that Pershing Square and Winthrop could not take control of the property unless it paid off the entire $3.66 billion mortgage first.

A week later, I was invited to serve as a panelist at the Museum of the City of New York in a discussion called "Can Stuyvesant Town Be Saved for Affordable Housing?" As I squinted past the lights from the stage, I could make out two men in crisp suits and no ties, sitting right in the middle of the audience, eight rows back. It was Ackman and Ashner. I waved to them from the stage. They stood out awkwardly in the midst of my middle-class Stuy Town neighbors and museum members who had come out for the event. Not deterred by Lowe's ruling, they had filed an appeal and were continuing to pursue the tenants while the litigation remained pending. Ackman and Ashner had again met with Rubin and his colleagues at Moelis earlier in the day, discussing ways to ensure long-term affordability in Stuy Town. At that meeting, Ackman had confidently guaranteed that, despite the setback from Justice Lowe, he would ultimately win the litigation, but noted that the parties likely would settle earlier. I watched them in the audience as they listened, poker faced, to my description of Tishman Speyer's bad acts, and why it was important to preserve Stuy Town as a middle-class affordable complex. "They wanted to have fun with this," Kane recalled regarding Ackman and Ashner. "They were going to pick it up for a song and have a great time with it. They were going to get it for so cheap they could both make a deal with us, and make a pile of money for their investors."[43]

Despite Ackman's bold assertions, the Appellate Division swiftly affirmed Lowe's decision on September 28. Alex Rubin got two inbound emails, five minutes apart. From Ackman: "We lost. No written decision."[44] Then MacArthur: "We won again." The bid from Ackman and Ashner was over. As CWCapital was now the last entity standing, my public statement that same afternoon reminded them that "the only route to financial stability was through partnership with the tenants of this community," and we looked forward to collaborating with them "toward a more stable future." Ackman's Pershing Square bitterly lamented that the decision may have the effect of keeping his firm and the tenants from "participating in the restructuring of the ownership of the property and implementing a permanent affordable housing solution."[45]

CWCapital was now free to foreclose out all the junior interests in order to completely eliminate interference from Ackman and Ashner. MacArthur scheduled the foreclosure auction for October 4, creating an opportunity for anyone to come out of the woodwork and make a bid. However, pursuant to Justice Lowe's ruling, interested parties would need to show up with a check for the total amount of the first mortgage and interest, or $3.66 billion. CWCapital itself had the ultimate advantage to emerge successful at a foreclosure auction. It was allowed to simply bid what it was owed—in a process called a "credit bid"—and take ownership of Stuy Town without actually putting up any money. There was, to me, nothing sadder than the thought of a small handful of people trading some papers as the title of my childhood home was transferred in a cold, empty rotunda of the federal courthouse downtown.

A foreclosure was not CWCapital's preferred route, however, because it triggered a large transfer tax obligation. CWCapital reached a quick settlement with Ackman and Ashner and bought out their mezzanine position for $45 million. The deal allowed Ackman to essentially break even on his investment and gave CWCapital the tools necessary to take control of the property without a foreclosure or tax. CWCapital simply replaced Ackman and Ashner's directors with its own and became what is called a "mortgagee in possession." It meant that, as a practical matter, there was nobody left to challenge CWCapital's authority, and they were able to make all the decisions. The deal done, and their position secured, CWCapital simply canceled its October foreclosure altogether.

Doyle and I felt that this whole dynamic was getting too hard for us to explain to tenants by email. I proposed that he and I situate ourselves for a few hours in the middle of the Stuyvesant Town Oval, next to its important central fountain, and make ourselves available to answer questions from any tenants who had them. Doyle thought it was a good idea, and on October 16, 2010, we did just that. Publicized by the Tenants Association, the occasion drew people out by the dozens, gathering around us in groups and waiting their turn to ask every imaginable question—but most focused on the legal status of the property. Who exactly owned it? What was going to happen? What was our plan? I shared what I knew with rotating groups of neighbors until my voice was raw and hoarse: Ackman and Ashner were gone, CWCapital was fully in control and, we hoped, now freer to work with us without the specter of litigation to deal with. That of course did not mean that they *would* work with us, but we were going to try to force the issue. Charles Bagli was out there too, listening. He also brought a photographer who was taking pictures for a book that he was writing about the collapse of the Stuy Town deal. My feet ached from hours of standing in the Oval; Doyle and I had answered questions for three straight hours.

Ackman felt that his legal team had gotten "outgunned" by CWCapital's but was still interested in putting in a bid to buy the property with Winthrop if and when it ever came up for sale. "A serial winner, Wily Bill was still not entirely satisfied with his results," the *Observer* noted in a piece called

"Ackman Breaks Even on Stuy Town, Still Wants to Own the Place."[46] The next day, after the settlement was announced, Ashner formally reached out to request a meeting with the Tenants Association board to explore a new partnership in making a bid to CWCapital. Shaken by the excitement of the prior few weeks, we demurred and promised to keep him posted as we started our formal process of trying to get CWCapital to embrace the Tenants Association.

9

Finding a Partner

Balancing himself carefully as he climbed up on top of the reception desk of the management office at 317 Avenue C in Stuy Town, Adam Rose looked down at a handful of colleagues gathered at his feet and smiled mischievously. In his hands, he held a crowbar, and his gaze was fixed on the Tishman Speyer logo in front of him. With the crowbar, he tugged at the sign until it came crashing down to the ground. After being summarily dismissed by Tishman Speyer in 2007, Rose had now officially returned at the request of CWCapital's Chuck Spetka. He laughed as he looked at the Tishman Speyer logo on the ground. "Rose is back!" he announced to the assembled crowd. "There's a new sheriff in town."[1]

Rose was eager to find ways to make his mark on the quality of life in the community—and to show how he could do a better job than the hated Tishman Speyer, who many tenants felt had allowed maintenance to deteriorate. Andrew MacArthur was the boss, but since he came without the institutional memory for the property and without the full team that Rose brought to the table, he gave Rose significant discretion over property management in those early days. Rose got right to work. In his first three months, he increased the public safety force by 12 percent and promised to grow the number of employees who answered calls from residents by 30 percent to reduce on-hold times for maintenance requests.[2]

Together, Rose and MacArthur also brought in a man named Jim Yasser as the property's managing director. The Tenants Association looked forward to having a new point person, someone who could politely and seriously engage with tenant concerns. During much of MetLife's tenure, the property manager had been Bill Potter, who not only lived in the community but had a reputation for helping tenants in difficult personal situations, like a divorce, or a parent who died. Mr. Potter, as he was known, was spoken of adoringly by residents because he cared about their well-being and acted on it. Meredith Kane knew Yasser and told me that he was more of a "deal guy" and expressed some surprise that he had been tapped to handle tenant complaints. Nevertheless, Doyle and the tenant leaders were happy to give anyone a chance to make things right in Stuy Town.

CWCapital invited me and the TA board to meet Yasser on November 16, 2010, in a conference room in the management office at 317 Avenue C. Doyle, Steinberg, Sheehy, Fink, and I showed up with a handful of other board members, as well as Samuel Ditter from Moelis. Ehrlich and Anne Greenberg participated by phone. With Ackman and Ashner out of the way, we were happy to have a chance to engage with CWCapital and wanted to use this meeting to reiterate our position that we wanted MacArthur to link arms with us. By the fall of 2010, the only potential bidder publicly clamoring for attention in Stuy Town was the Tenants Association, and many saw our plan of conversion to homeownership as the most likely outcome.[3] We were eager to begin this conversation.

MacArthur, Yasser, and Rose, however, had another meeting in mind. Rose enthusiastically jumped in to tell us that things were going to be different under his leadership. He ticked off a number of issues on his agenda, including a new system for handling noise complaints, and removing nonstructural walls that had been put up to subdivide apartments so more tenants could live in them. Across all issues, he promised to be fair, and quick to respond.

This was obviously welcome news, and Doyle acknowledged it as such. "We look forward to enjoying a much better relationship with you than we had with the last management company," Doyle said to Rose once he had finished. But as important as this conversation about quality-of-life issues was, we were determined to keep this group focused on our long-term goals. Doyle turned directly to MacArthur and said that it was time for all of us to roll up our sleeves to resolve the long-term questions about property ownership. "We expect to be your partner in that," Doyle said. In front of the group, Doyle reminded MacArthur of the letter he had written us three months earlier, while in the heat of battle with Ackman and Ashner, in which he promised regular discussions with the Tenants Association and to share the rent rolls and other information necessary for us to formulate a bid.[4]

Much as Ackman had predicted, none of this had actually come to pass once he was off the scene and the pressure was gone. MacArthur listened stone-faced to Doyle's appeal. When Doyle finished speaking, MacArthur responded impassively that his only immediate goal was to settle the *Roberts* case before 2010 was over. He then frowned and said that if the case were not settled, the tenants would be in for a long, arduous battle. Most members of the assembled group were not even affected by the *Roberts* case. Of all the TA representatives, only Ehrlich, Newmark, and I were even in the class of litigants, and we were not among the formal class representatives making decisions about a settlement. It was surprising that MacArthur was talking tough with the TA about *Roberts* at this moment in a meeting we had thought was meant to be a feel-good kickoff to a new relationship, and that concerned all of us.

MacArthur's combative tone and seeming unwillingness to engage with the tenants about the long-term future of the property was only one of our many new challenges in the fall of 2010. Charles Bagli called me on September 28 to talk. He tended to have two modes: sometimes he called because he was writing a story; sometimes he was calling just to chat, and his entire tone of voice and demeanor would be different. After years of practice, I could tell immediately which kind of call it was. This one was all business. He said that he was writing another piece on Stuy Town, trying to explain what likely would happen next, now that Ackman and Ashner had lost their court case. I explained to him that we were still continuing to pursue a home ownership plan, which would include rules to keep the community affordable for middle-class people into the future. The conversation was fact-based, but Bagli left me with an unusual impression that his piece might expose some possible fault lines in the community. "Going to be tough to keep people united," he said to me.[5]

As usual, he was a step ahead. While his piece turned out the way I expected, almost immediately after it was posted later that day, one of the brand-new TA board members sent me an email, challenging me on its contents. He quoted to me Bagli's words: "The tenant association wants the complex to retain its historical role as an affordable, middle-class enclave by setting aside some apartments as rentals and others with restrictions on resale prices"—and provocatively asked, "Do you know when this was decided . . . ?" He went on: "Seems to have been decided by someone or the NYT is wrong? The TA keeps saying nothing is decided yet reports continue to be contrary. Something isn't right here," he went on, accusingly. I sat up in my chair, alarmed. I wrote back that while nothing was decided, having restrictions on sales of apartments was one certain way to achieve long-term affordability for future middle-class residents. I bit my tongue and did not observe that I was just parroting the plan that we had been discussing for at least four years.[6]

In reality, the board member was surfacing a much bigger issue, to which I didn't know how to respond. A homeownership plan with resale restrictions, while not formally adopted by the board in 2010, was so fundamental to the direction that the TA had been pushing for four years that I didn't think I was out on a limb to confirm it for Bagli. But the email's unspoken point was that there was a new board of directors, that I did not have the right to speak for the Tenants Association and that I was beyond my authority to have floated this. This was the first time in four years that a member of the board had made such a critique, and I was shaken. We had spent months in 2010 calling an election to ensure the legitimacy of the TA board, and now my own legitimacy was in question. I conferred with Marsh, Doyle, and Steinberg, who all assured me that this was a minority view on the board and that I had their full support.[7]

This criticism of me, and my office, provoked a raw back-and-forth at a board meeting on October 7. A second new board member agreed with the first and felt that I had crossed a line by speaking for the Tenants

Figure 9.1. Susan Steinberg, the longtime vice president of the Tenants Association, protesting against CWCapital outside the leasing office as Steven Newmark looks on. She was elected president of the Tenants Association in 2015. Photo credit: *Town & Village* newspaper.

Association, not just to the *Times*, but all the time. Others like Marsh were puzzled by what he perceived as a fake controversy. He and the longer-serving board members felt that they were only in a strong position because of my work over the course of five years. Three days earlier, Marsh had participated in a press conference—called by the TA and my office to demand that CWCapital give us a seat at the table—where every elected official, including me, praised the Stuyvesant Town Peter Cooper Village Tenants Association for its work and perseverance. The TA had gained much of their strength because of its close relationship with the elected officials, and me in particular. Marsh retorted to the objecting board members, "We need the electeds and will continue to need the electeds. It is this symbiotic relationship that makes each other so strong." He cited Bagli's article, which said that investment groups "have conceded, the tenants have proven to be a potent political and legal force" and that "they want to work with the tenants' association rather than risk the ire of elected officials."[8] Most agreed with Marsh, but a couple of the dissenting board members insisted that the TA board needed to find its own voice.

I was incredibly frustrated. I had for years been tapped as the TA's surrogate and carefully never did anything without consulting Al Doyle. At this point, I was not only working seven days a week on these matters, but I was also helping the Tenants Association to manage its own internal operations, to call an election, and to be their liaison to Paul Weiss and Moelis. And I was doing all this while still managing my other responsibilities as councilman for the entire district, and doing my best to prepare with Zoe for the birth of our first child, and to support my mom, who was fighting progressing multiple myeloma. I realized that I needed to be understanding, but I did not have the energy to manage this problem.

In order to find a way to resolve the brewing conflict, the board tasked Julie Ehrlich and John Sheehy—two calm and diplomatic people—with reaching out to me to make sure I understood that there were board members who were raising concerns about my role. At Sheehy's apartment at 6 Peter Cooper Road on the afternoon of October 17, I met with the two of them, who uncomfortably raised the questions concerning my role that had been so fervently debated at the board meeting. They thanked me for my work dealing with the press, for taking the initiative to advance the TA's interests, and for vetting all material with Paul Weiss and Moelis. They delicately explained that there was a small contingent on the board who felt that I should take greater efforts to elevate the TA's public profile. I obviously knew whom they were referring to, and I readily agreed to help smooth out the situation. It burned me to hear the critique, because I was *constantly* working to elevate the TA. I was motivated to be supportive of them for altruistic reasons; they were, after all, my partners and my constituents. But I also knew that without the TA, I lacked authority to speak for the community. I acknowledged to Sheehy and Ehrlich that I understood the issue, and promised to do more to put the Tenants Association up front in public matters. Sheehy and Ehrlich felt that they had done what they were tasked to do, and Sheehy told me to consider this matter concluded. He reported our conversation to

Doyle, and then threw himself between me and the angry board members by email: "If anyone has a problem with this resolution the fault or blame is mine—not Dan's." Doyle supported this solution and resolved to discuss it again at the next in-person board meeting.[9]

Against this background, we convened a number of conference calls with Paul Weiss and Moelis for the TA board to consider what to do next. I was an active participant in the calls but for a while tried to be a little quieter and more deferential to TA board members. There were a few ways for us to proceed, and none guaranteed success. We debated just sitting back and waiting for CWCapital to state their plans and to then use our outsize voice to react to whatever they did. By not offering a specific proposal, we could keep our large and unwieldy community united around a general set of principles. On the downside, the Tenants Association would be among the last groups to be consulted, if we were even consulted at all. Another route was for us to develop our own proposal for CWCapital to consider. That would allow us to dictate the pace and to set the market expectations of what the tenants wanted, but it also left us vulnerable to attack by our own neighbors, who surely would have varying opinions of the details of our plan. Our final option was to seek out a third-party partner to help us to develop and propose a plan for CWCapital to consider. Finding a partner who had money and expertise, and whom we could bring to the table with us, would give us increased leverage. That option ran the risk of alienating CWCapital.[10]

In any scenario, we were determined to create at least a perception of unity, because without it, nobody would ever feel like it was necessary to work with the Tenants Association, or me, in developing a solution. "In order to have legitimacy in the marketplace you have to speak with one voice, and bring along the community. The difficulty with dealing with a tenants association is the existence of splinter groups," said Meredith Kane. "The minute you have that dissent to the outside world, the outside world throws up its hands and says there is nobody to negotiate with on the other side."[11]

After some debate, the TA board decided that it did not want to wait to react to whatever CWCapital decided. We had been burned in 2006 because we did not anticipate MetLife's sudden auction. We were unprepared, and had resolved not to let that happen again. Rubin and Kane recommended that the tenants develop a so-called strawman proposal. A strawman, in business jargon, is a draft proposal that is intended to generate a discussion. The tenants had already articulated a broad set of principles, but Rubin and Kane felt that it was time for us to give potential partners a more detailed plan to react to, but something that was flexible enough to allow us to pivot, depending on community reactions. The TA called a community meeting for October 30 at Baruch College to start soliciting feedback about what should go into our plan.

As we had come to learn, even within the newly reconstituted TA board, not everyone embraced a homeownership plan that had any restrictions on tenants' ability to resell their unit down the line. And, on the other end of the spectrum, there were tenants who objected to any plan that deliberately took even a single unit out of rent stabilization. One resident, John Dillon, left a message with the Tenants Association on October 5, attacking the TA's plan, which he called "the first step to luxury housing." Dillon argued that all TA board members should have to state publicly whether they intended to buy their units. Dillon claimed to have spoken to hundreds of residents and that a very specific 93 percent of them said that they did not want to buy their apartments. Two days before our community meeting on October 30, Dillon posted on Facebook that a group of tenants who were opposed to the plan "to bail out the slimy investors who ruined our quality of life" were going to organize a brand-new tenants association. Dillon's group announced a protest outside the meeting hall, but ultimately fewer than five people gathered. In contrast, over one thousand residents came inside to hear from me, Kane, Rubin, and a host of elected officials, as we walked everyone through the complicated state of play. It boiled down to this: it was time for us to work with CWCapital directly on our homeownership plan, and we were going to develop a strawman proposal for them to consider.[12]

After the meeting, Rubin and Kane worked to fill out the details, which they planned to present to the TA board at Moelis's offices on Park Avenue on December 20, 2010. As we prepared for that discussion, it was filtering back to me that some of the newer members were still challenging the work that I was breaking my back to do. I wanted this issue

resolved immediately and consulted with Doyle and Sheehy on how best
to handle it. We agreed that we would address it directly with the group
at the December 20 meeting.

When we were all settled around a massive conference table at Moelis &
Company, I asked for the floor. I explained to the newer board members
that about a year earlier, the board had deputized me to serve as a liaison
with Paul Weiss and Moelis, to strategize, and to take meetings on their
behalf and report back to Doyle. "I have tried very hard to do all of those
things, carefully, respectfully, and in a way that I thought reflected well
on the community," I said. I acknowledged that some board members
had raised questions about my role, and asked that the board "make
any directional change that is necessary—*or to simply reaffirm what the
board has asked me to do in the past.*" With some drama and a share
of irritation, I then said that I would excuse myself and wait for their
instructions.

Within ten minutes, they invited me back in, and the meeting proceeded without any explanation to me. Kane and Rubin shared the details
of their strawman proposal, which closely resembled the homeownership plan we had been discussing for years. It allowed for apartment
sales with two levels of pricing offered to tenants. One was a discounted
price, offered to current residents, which would be subject to a flip tax to
prevent short-term profiteering from the sale. The other price was even
more discounted, but would allow future sales of the apartment only to
people who were middle income, earning up to 165 percent of the area
median income. And for tenants who had no interest in buying, they
could remain in their rent-stabilized rental units. Since we were creating
different opportunities based on the choices that individual tenants might
make, Kane recommended that a condominium structure—as opposed to
a cooperative—would best allow us to direct certain rules and benefits to
individual units.

I learned later that while I was out of the room for those ten minutes,
the critical board members expressed displeasure at having the issue of
my role sprung on them in front of their advisers. The group had decided to punt on the issue until the next night, at a board meeting that
had been previously scheduled.[13] At that meeting, the board reaffirmed
my role as an adviser to the Tenants Association, officially ending the

controversy but certainly not changing the views of the dissenting members. The board also approved the strawman proposal and encouraged Rubin and his colleagues at Moelis to start shopping it around to potential partners.

On January 23, 2011, Zoe and I welcomed our son, Asher, into the world. Asher, who grew into an easygoing, reasonable, and all-around charming kid, did not start out that way. Together at Mount Sinai Hospital, we were overjoyed, but a little concerned that Asher did not take easily to eating. A lactation consultant gave us a ritual of trying to feed him every three hours, throughout the day and night. That meant that Zoe and I had to set our alarm clock at midnight, 3 a.m., and 6 a.m., and each time it took us about an hour to feed him before we put him back to bed. We got two hours of sleep at a time, if we were lucky, and Zoe kept threatening me with divorce, or worse, if I spilled an ounce of breast milk that she had meticulously pumped. Through the haze of sleep deprivation we struggled to teach this colicky baby how to breastfeed, how to sleep in a crib, and how to calm himself. Our neighbors in the building likely heard sounds of hair dryers, stove vents, and white noise on our iPods coming from our apartment, all of which we used to get him to calm down. Usually, we resorted to bouncing him up and down until our legs were sore.

As I adapted to my life as a new parent, Adam Rose was hard at work. Like a winning political candidate, on February 7, 2011, Rose even issued a first "100 days" report. He was particularly eager to reverse what he believed were Tishman Speyer's most egregious mistakes, starting with the way they handled legal claims against tenants. To send a message that things were different, he personally took over reviewing the difficult cases coming out of the legal department. Fred Knapp, who had been responsible for bringing Golub cases under the Tishman Speyer years, was still there. His instructions under Tishman Speyer had been to evict rent-stabilized residents in order to create vacancies, and, it seemed, to give no benefit of the doubt to tenants. This had caused years of friction with us, terrible press, and, ultimately, a black eye for his bosses. "It pissed everyone off and created a feeling of unreasonableness," Rose said. But now, all decisions about claims related to succession, sublets, and evictions were to be approved by Rose personally.[14]

"Tishman Speyer sent notices to everyone and wouldn't talk to people no matter what. They got a reputation for spurious actions," Rose told me later. "For those people who called us up and could show us that we made a mistake, we would drop it immediately." Adam Rose invited Marsh up to his office to discuss his new priorities on Golubs, subletting, and succession. Tishman Speyer had been famous for denying subletting requests, as well as for challenging claims to succeed an elderly relative in a rent-stabilized unit. On those succession claims, Rose told Marsh, "If someone wants a rent-stabilized apartment so badly that they are willing to live with their grandma without knowing how long she'd be around, then give them the apartment immediately! Anyone who can live with a grandparent for that long is entitled to it!"[15]

While our relationship with the property manager was getting better, we were still hitting a wall with CWCapital on the larger question. MacArthur continued to cite the resolution of the *Roberts* case as the main reason CWCapital could not embrace our strawman proposal or even negotiate with us. As months went by without resolution, Rubin and Kane felt that the time was right for us to find a big-name partner who could help us nudge CWCapital to the bargaining table. There were a variety of potential partners for us. Bill Ackman had already shown up, as had LeFrak, Ross, and Centerbridge; surely there could be others. We had already heard from Michael Ashner, who had disentangled from Ackman but now was working with Apollo Real Estate Advisors. Initial conversations with Brookfield Asset Management, Silverstein Properties, Belvedere Capital, Westbrook, and many others were under way, too. Kane and Rubin began assessing the proposals with an eye toward presenting a handful of options to the TA board. As an elected official whose reputation was on the line, I was very concerned about the optics of picking a single firm as our partner. We also needed a rationale as to why we chose certain firms to meet with. With that in mind, Kane and Rubin widely circulated our strawman proposal for many firms to evaluate—and started taking meetings, nearly seventy of them, with separate firms, each willing to explore partnering with us in one way or another.

We got a range of responses. In March, Lance West and Vivek Melwani of Centerbridge told a Moelis associate that our conversion plan was "too complex" and that any investors would want broader latitude to pursue their own economic interests.[16] Michael Peloquin of Black Eye

Capital called to say that they had retained Willkie Farr & Gallagher and Skadden Arps to negotiate the purchase of the Fannie and Freddie portions of the commercial mortgage-backed securities notes. Peloquin said that there were a lot of vultures circling but that Black Eye would have a "foot in the door real good" once they bought the notes. Pricing, he told us, was $1.5 billion, and a closing was imminent. Even the City University of New York—New York's public college system—had circulated a survey to professors, saying that CUNY was "considering participation in the ownership" of Stuy Town and Peter Cooper and gauging interest.[17]

On March 14, 2011, Alex Rubin had lunch with Barry Blattman, a leader of the real estate practice at Brookfield Asset Management. Rubin and Blattman knew each other from the time when they were partners in the real estate group at Merrill Lynch. Each had left to go to other firms, but they had stayed in touch. Rubin described the dynamic at Stuy Town and the considerable interest that the tenant group had drawn. Rubin told Blattman that we still had not found the right "well-connected New York City–centric capital partner" for the Tenants Association, and observed that Brookfield uniquely fit the bill. Blattman was intrigued. He was aware of the situation in Stuy Town and had a preexisting relationship with CWCapital's Dave Iannarone and Chuck Spetka, as well as Randy Nardone of Fortress, which was now CWCapital's parent company. Brookfield had the heft and resources to be an effective partner to the tenants, but because of the charged environment created by the tenants, Blattman said he would need to understand more about the politics before getting too invested. Rubin said that he would introduce Blattman to me and that we could explore those questions together. Blattman agreed.[18]

Rubin came out of the lunch and excitedly called me to share his conversation with Blattman and the possibility of a Brookfield partnership for the Tenants Association. After having met with many potential suitors, Rubin had concluded that Brookfield could be among the very best partners for the tenants, because it was not only deep-pocketed but also well respected. Rubin also thought that Blattman and I would hit it off on a personal level.[19] I reported this positive development to Doyle and confided that I was worried about boxing ourselves in with a single partner and leaving no room to negotiate with others down the line. Doyle encouraged me to not worry about resolving all the issues at once and to just go meet with Blattman.

I walked from my Lower Manhattan office on April 13 to City Hall Restaurant on Duane Street, where Rubin was sitting at a round table in the middle of the restaurant with Blattman, who stood up to introduce himself. Blattman had a friendly but understated demeanor, much like Rubin. Once we placed our orders for lunch, Rubin suggested that I take a few minutes and describe to Blattman the political dynamic at the property, and what the tenants were trying to achieve. Taking my cue, I explained that tenants had felt attacked by Tishman Speyer, and now felt ignored by CWCapital. We needed an institution, with money, that could develop a bid—on our terms—that would force CWCapital to react to us. I also shared my worry about locking in with a single partner. Tenants, political opponents, and even competing real estate firms would surely criticize our decision to partner up with anyone, so the tenants needed to retain the ability to drop our partner if a better deal for us or the city came along. Rubin had explained to me before the lunch that it was not uncommon in deals like these for there to exist an escape hatch to ensure the best possible terms. There was even a term for this in industry parlance: it was called a "go shop" provision, which essentially meant that we would have a chance to shop our deal around to other partners to see if we could do any better. Blattman listened carefully and did not even flinch at anything I was saying.

Much as Ackman had done, Blattman asked me about the TA and whether there were competing groups in the community. Ignoring the recent challenges to my authority from new board members, and the flare-ups of dissent, I told him that the TA had remarkably kept the community united behind its efforts and recently held a community-wide election. Blattman wasn't particularly worried about being replaced in a go-shop scenario. "Brookfield is a company that has its future very much tied into its reputation in New York. There really were no historical blemishes, and we had a lot of capital," Blattman recalled. "It would be difficult for others to jeopardize our opportunity because there weren't a lot of others with our level of capital."

As we discussed the possibility of a partnership, I tried to picture him standing onstage at Baruch College in front of a thousand nervous tenants. Blattman was patient, engaging, and very appealing; with $500 billion in assets under management, it was obvious that his firm had the heft and commitment that we needed, and he was enthusiastic about helping us achieve our goals. I hadn't scared him away with my candor. He seemed even more excited about the challenge when we shook hands and parted at the end of the meal. Privately, Rubin reiterated to me his strong view that if we could land Brookfield as a partner, we shouldn't hesitate even for a moment. I enthusiastically reported the details of our lunch to Doyle.[20]

Blattman was also satisfied with our meeting and was intrigued by the opportunity that a partnership with the tenants presented to Brookfield. He went back to the office and summoned a team—including Lowell Baron, John Moore, and Lauren Young—to start working on financial models for the possible acquisition of Stuy Town. Days later, over breakfast with MacArthur at Petite Abeille on 20th Street, I told him—without naming names—that we were having productive conversations with potential partners and that the tenants intended to put together a bid. He shrugged and told me to keep him posted.[21]

At Rubin's suggestion, Doyle invited Barry Blattman to meet with the TA executive committee on May 9. Blattman brought with him John Zuccotti, the former New York City planning chairman and now senior Brookfield executive, and associate Lowell Baron. Blattman touted Brookfield's $500 billion of assets under management, its public listing on two stock exchanges, and long history of successfully restructuring complicated deals. It had recently recapitalized General Growth Properties for $8 billion and restructured and acquired the Babcock and Brown Infrastructure for $2.5 billion, so Brookfield was well versed in resolving complex matters. Board members like Steinberg, Marsh, and Jim Roth grilled them about their goals, and Blattman carefully explained that his firm was willing to embrace all our principles: allowing for homeownership, protecting the open spaces, ensuring long-term affordability, and keeping Peter Cooper and Stuy Town together. Blattman noted his personal relationships with both CWCapital and Fortress, which impressed the board. Blattman felt that the tenants were best advised to find a way to preemptively negotiate with CWCapital rather than to wait for an auction, and proposed that we join forces and put together a plan within forty-five to ninety days.[22]

We could not believe our good fortune. Rubin and Kane felt strongly that there were only two firms who credibly could partner with us on the terms we had outlined. One of them was the Blackstone Group, which had told Rubin that they were not quite ready to jump into such a highly charged political atmosphere. The other was Brookfield. "They are dominant in a way that no one else is in a close third," Rubin told us. To Rubin, the right call was to go with Brookfield, and not delay. On May 25, 2011, the board voted to select Brookfield to be our partner. Our plan was to sign an exclusivity agreement (with the requisite go-shop escape clause for the TA) with Brookfield, as part of a letter of intent. Only after the letter of intent was agreed to would we publicly announce our partnership, and we expected that would be later in June.[23]

The political environment in Albany in 2011 continued to be highly unfavorable to tenants. That year, Republican control of the Senate was made

Figure 9.2. Stuy Town tenant leaders showed up at a fund-raiser for Governor Andrew Cuomo demanding stronger rent laws. "Real Estate Is Devouring Affordable Housing," said one sign, created by the Tenants Association. *From left,* Susan Steinberg, Al Doyle, Margaret Salacan, Anne Greenberg, Kirstin Aadahl. Copyright © 2015 by Anne Greenberg.

possible by a breakaway group of Democrats, who called themselves the Independent Democratic Conference, or IDC, and allied themselves with the Republicans.[24] Republicans in the State Senate not only prevented pro-tenant reforms from being enacted but also constantly looked to chip away at tenant gains. One of the most significant tenant victories in years was the *Roberts v. Tishman Speyer* case, and the landlord lobby was pushing their Republican (and IDC) allies in the Senate to help them out. In its written opinion in *Roberts*, the Court of Appeals had said that if the J-51 statute created too much of a burden on landlords, then they should petition the state legislature to change the law. That is exactly what they did. In the spring of 2011, real estate interests got the State Senate Republicans to introduce a bill that significantly curtailed the damages that tenants might hope to achieve from the decision.

Advocates for the real estate industry were whispering to state legislators that these Stuy Town tenants, who had been voluntarily paying $3,000 to $5,000 per month in rent, didn't really need or deserve damages. Rumors were buzzing around Albany that a compromise could be in the works that would render the court's ruling functionally meaningless by making damages *prospective* only. Former assemblyman and Peter Cooper resident Steven Sanders, now a lobbyist, local legislators Brian Kavanagh and Tom Duane, as well as Senator Liz Krueger, whose district included Stuy Town years earlier, were working the phones trying to shore up the tenants' position. We all knew that in Albany bad things happened at the last minute, often in the middle of the night. Compromises were reached, and deals were frequently revealed to the public once they were done and wrapped up in one big package of inscrutable legislation. Senator Krueger, Tenants PAC's Michael McKee, and other tenant leaders were telling me that we needed to be vocal and aggressive.

On June 1, the Tenants Association assembled on buses to go up to Albany to fight for the renewal of rent stabilization and to push back against this effort to kill *Roberts*. To draw attention to our effort and to build interest in the trip, I agreed to hold "rolling town hall meetings" on the buses and to answer questions from tenants all the way up to Albany. At each rest stop on the way up the New York Thruway, I would dash out of one bus, board the next bus in the convoy, and pick up the microphone. Tenants were cheerful and determined and had lots of questions for their councilman. For many of the two hundred rent-stabilized residents on the buses, a three-hour trip to Albany was old hat, but the questions about J-51, our conversion plans, and our complex path to making another bid to buy the property were new. (The fight to maintain the *Roberts* decision was legally and financially distinct from our homeownership plans, but not in the minds of the tenants.) I was hoarse from talking for hours when we arrived in Albany and met with friendly Senate and Assembly members, as well as senior staff of the Cuomo administration. Ultimately, the rent laws were renewed, and *Roberts* survived the legislative session. Later that month, we got even more good news from court when the Appellate Division ruled that damages in the *Roberts* case would be applied not just on a going-forward basis but also retroactively.[25]

Once back home, I took note of the unique power of the Tenants Association. Not only could they motivate grassroots activism, with tenants on buses loudly demanding results from state legislators, but they were now equipped to sit across the table from real estate powerhouses like Brookfield and Blackstone and be taken seriously as a potential partner. And that was fortunate, because if we were going to be successful in this complicated negotiation, we needed to be able to do both well.

Calling a Tenants Association partnership with Brookfield unconventional would have been an understatement, as tenant groups do not ordinarily make deals with real estate giants. We knew that throughout the city many were going to be skeptical of our move, and I asked Brookfield to hire a public relations shop not only to help the TA build support for our plan, but also to keep tenant and broader public opinion galvanized behind our effort. Seeing the value in a coordinated public campaign, Brookfield retained Berlin Rosen, which tapped Mike Rabinowitz and Jen Shykula to help us craft our official announcement, which had already slipped well past its original June date.

Charles Bagli was still working on his book about Stuyvesant Town. He asked me if I would sit with him for an interview in August 2011, and I gladly agreed. We decided to meet for sushi at Hane, a Japanese restaurant on 20th Street and First Avenue, steps away from where John F. Kennedy held his rally for president in October 1960. We got settled, and Bagli pulled out a shiny new Mac that he had bought for this project. As he turned on his device and pulled out a pad and paper, he casually said, "I hear you've got a deal with Brookfield and are approaching CWCapital next week." I paused and looked at him blankly. "I'm not writing right away, but I want the story," he said, planting his flag in the ground, as he poked at his keys without making eye contact. "Um, OK," I stammered.

Like so many of our initiatives, the Brookfield partnership could be jeopardized if revealed prematurely. We had a handshake with Brookfield, but we were far from formalizing our letter of intent—a *New York Times* story at that point would have been very harmful. I shared no details and quietly hoped that Bagli would be too distracted by his book to worry about writing newspaper articles for the time being. After dinner, I sent off a quick note to Rubin and Kane, incredulous: "He knows the whole situation. We probably need to bump up our public timeline," I told them.

In reality, things were already slipping out, and not through Bagli. Rubin had run into Phil Rosen on the street. Rosen was the head of real estate for Weil Gotshal & Manges, a major New York law firm. "How are things going with Brookfield in Stuy Town?" he asked, to Rubin's great surprise. Michael Ashner had also emailed Kane, disappointed to learn that the tenants had not chosen him as their partner: "The most and suddenly worstest aspect of this is someone just informed that the anointed group is Brookfield—a company that has beaten us badly thruout the year. Oh Well." Kane sent the note around to the team: "Oy!!! Unbelievable!! How does this info get out???" she asked. No matter the leaks to the financial world, the news had not yet gotten out into the community, and tenants were demanding that Doyle share some information about what the TA was up to. In response, Doyle was urging me to move the team along, and I was in turn trying to prod Rubin and Kane and our new partners. Time was of the essence, and Kane sped up her efforts at negotiating the terms of our letter of intent with Brookfield.[26]

Even though we had not yet finalized the terms of that agreement, on August 11, at a meeting at Moelis's offices, Blattman asked the Tenants Association for permission to make his first official approach to CWCapital as our soon-to-be partner. Blattman and his associate, Lowell Baron, walked us through the materials that they intended to present to CWCapital. As they explained it to us, Brookfield would make the case that only a Brookfield / Tenants Association partnership would allow a successful conversion to homeownership, secure approval of the plan from the attorney general, settle the *Roberts* case, and ensure support from the state and city government. I was frustrated that the presentation to the TA board did not include a contingency plan of what they would do if—as I anticipated—CWCapital did not respond affirmatively. Blattman told us that he hoped we would not need such a plan B, and that we would all cross that bridge if and when we came to it. While we were all eager to allow Blattman and Baron to approach CWCapital, it felt odd considering the fact that we had neither formalized, nor announced, our partnership. I was worried that Brookfield would be getting all the private benefit of being our partner, without giving us the public momentum (and transparency) that we needed in the community. Nevertheless, because we were all so desperate to jump-start the process, the TA decided to let Brookfield take a meeting with CWCapital on our behalf and hoped that they would have more success than we did on our own.[27]

On September 9, 2011, Blattman met with Dave Iannarone and Andrew MacArthur of CWCapital and made his case for CWCapital to work with Brookfield and the tenants. When immediate reports of the meeting did not come back to me, I figured it was bad news. "They were good listeners and we had an active dialogue," Blattman eventually reported to us, but made it clear that CWCapital was not in any hurry. The CWCapital team had said that they planned to review their position in Stuyvesant Town twice a year, and they promised to evaluate our proposal at that time. There was no courtesy offered to Brookfield because of its partnership with the tenants; in fact, we got the message that we were just going to be processed like any other bidder. MacArthur called me the next day, with some positive feedback: "Of all the cast of characters you could have lined up with, Brookfield is a good choice," he said. However, MacArthur told me that he had left his conversation with Blattman the way he had left it with everyone else: once they settle *Roberts*, they'd like to talk, but not before then. Our partnership with Brookfield had not moved the needle at all with CWCapital.[28]

Too many months had gone by without any substantive report to our thirty thousand neighbors from the Tenants Association or me, and we were all feeling enormous pressure to say something out loud about our progress. We were on the cusp of being partnered with one of the few real estate entities in the world that could actually consummate a deal in Stuy Town, but nobody knew about it. But Meredith Kane urged patience. She preferred for the TA to do things in the right order and sign the formal letter of intent before we made any public statements.

Jen Shykula and Mike Rabinowitz of Berlin Rosen sketched out a two-month strategy for October and November 2011. We would announce our partnership and then launch an organized public campaign to push CWCapital to the bargaining table. We wrote out our talking points, prepared detailed briefings for elected officials, and planned to hold community meetings to inform people what was going on.

I had been waiting since June, so I figured that staying quiet for just a few more weeks probably wouldn't hurt. Additionally, at that particular moment, Brookfield's name was all over the news, every day, because hundreds of anticapitalist protesters had decided to occupy Zuccotti Park, named after Brookfield's John Zuccotti, who had visited the TA in May. Zuccotti Park was a private space that Brookfield owned but which was publicly accessible, and now was the home to hundreds of Occupy Wall Street protesters, with tents, who seemed to have no intention of leaving. Brookfield and the Bloomberg administration were eager to get the protesters out but needed to do so carefully, as this group had attracted not only support from the city council but also international support and attention. Along those lines, I had publicly signed a letter with twelve council colleagues calling on the mayor to respect the protesters' right to free speech. I did not know how it was going to turn out and was worried that Brookfield might get a black eye from this episode, further complicating our partnership once it became public.[29]

Just blocks away from the protests, Brookfield's Lowell Baron and MacArthur met for a round of drinks on November 9, at P.J. Clarke's in the World Financial Center.[30] With two additional months of work under his belt, Baron was hopeful that with more details about what Brookfield would be able to offer to CWCapital, MacArthur might shift his position a bit. He didn't. MacArthur told him that he appreciated the outreach but again reiterated his position that the property was not currently for sale.

On November 15, the city evicted the Occupy Wall Street protesters from Brookfield's Zuccotti Park, and Eliot Brown of the *Wall Street Journal* started placing phone calls to CWCapital, to me, and to others, looking for information about the TA-Brookfield partnership. We had already promised the story to Bagli, but we still couldn't announce anything until the letter of intent was finished. But given the press interest, we needed to move faster. If Brown's story came out before we were ready to back up our plan with a clear and simple explanation to our community, we knew we'd get pilloried by our neighbors.[31]

As Rubin pored over a nearly final draft of the letter of intent on November 27, he saw the "11111" sequence displayed on his caller ID. That was the sign that the *New York Times*—and inevitably Charles Bagli— was calling. We were close to wrapping up our agreement, and Bagli and Brown were writing stories in real time. I had been helping Bagli to assemble the details for an exclusive story to be published just after the agreement was finalized, and Brown was at the same time calling and emailing everyone involved. It was clear that Brown had the rough outlines of what was happening, but he did not know the timing, and seemed to understand that he was likely being scooped by a rival paper. "What, your constituents don't read the *Wall Street Journal*?" he griped to me as I dodged his questions about whether the tenants had in fact selected Brookfield as its partner.

Having negotiated the final issues in the agreement, including the Tenants Association's ability to shop the proposal to other partners before formally moving forward with Brookfield, the TA board voted to approve the letter of intent on November 29. The *Times* story was finished and filed at the same time. Bagli posted his story before anything leaked out—and Brown followed him only by a short while. "Tenants Trying Again to Buy Stuyvesant Town and Peter Cooper Village," said Bagli's *New York Times* story, posted online at 7:15 p.m. on Tuesday, November 29. "This time," he wrote, "the tenants have a deep-pocketed partner, and they are hoping that the lenders who control the property will sell it to them, rather than to another heavily leveraged owner who might try to displace longtime residents in favor of higher-paying tenants." Blattman was quoted on behalf of Brookfield as saying that the Tenants Association was eager to "take matters into their own hands." Given the difficulty in obtaining financing for large real estate deals today, he said, the condominium structure, in which tenants buy their apartments, might be the best way for CWCapital to get the highest price for the property now. "This is the beginning," Al Doyle told Bagli. "We're trying to take control of the destiny of Stuyvesant Town and Peter Cooper in order to keep it an affordable property."[32]

The Tenants Association sent out an advisory to the community explaining why they had selected Brookfield, and why it was important. We knew this was going to take a bit of massaging, and we turned to Berlin Rosen for their help crafting the right language. "Brookfield is a highly respected global real estate and investment manager, with extensive expertise in complicated transactions like this one," the Tenants Association said. "Most importantly, they also share our goals." The Tenants Association also noted our agreement was flexible enough to allow for us to entertain alternative concepts and proposals as we developed our bid. With Brookfield on our team, we stated, it was our hope that CWCapital would find it extremely difficult to continue to ignore us.[33]

Finally, we were able to hold a press conference on Wednesday, November 30, on 16th Street and First Avenue, announcing the TA's partnership with Brookfield. With about one hundred neighbors joining us, we announced that we had found a well-respected firm, with plenty of resources, that was going to help us in our efforts to preserve Stuy Town as an affordable middle-class community. Only five years earlier, we had stood on the same corner, aspiring to be a bidder. Now we were in a position to preemptively shape the process. Blattman came out and made his case for Brookfield not only as a partner but also as an enthusiastic booster of the Tenants Association. He did a good job— personable, sincere—and we felt lucky to finally have him at our side. Nobody asked about the Occupy Wall Street controversy, to my relief, and we projected confidence about our position. Blattman was energized and repeated his performance before a packed house of tenants on December 3 at Mason Hall of Baruch College. The Tenants Association's leaders and I had made it through a choppy period, and even though CWCapital was still holding us off, we now felt that we had everything we needed to meaningfully negotiate with them.

CHALLENGED FROM THE OUTSIDE

Doyle and I were satisfied with how our announcement had gone. We had again surprised our neighbors—and the public—with how commercially savvy this Tenants Association could be. Importantly, it also explained to our neighbors our months of silence, and gave us an opportunity to catch our breath. We now had a partner who could carry some of the burden of getting us the result we wanted. I was hoping to have a reprieve from the intense focus on Stuy Town, to be able to devote my attention to other matters I had been working on in the rest of my city council district, like introducing faster-moving bus lanes, trying to move Upper East Side buildings away from dirty heating oil, and introducing new consumer protections in my role as the chairman of the council's Consumer Affairs Committee.

But my break from Stuy Town matters was short-lived. Almost immediately, a new area of complication emerged for us. Days after our Brookfield announcement, every resident's mailbox received a colorful missive from Gerald Guterman, a real estate speculator, that attacked and directly undermined the TA and Brookfield.

Guterman had been trying to engage the Tenants Association for well over a year, without success. He had approached me soon after Tishman Speyer's default and proposed a partnership with the tenants. He cited his unique experience, which he said would be necessary for us to do a successful conversion. The TA had promised to review his plan in due course. When Guterman did not hear from us for two weeks, he got impatient and called me directly. "I can do this in my sleep, Councilman," he insisted. Only five days later, he left a message in the Tenants Association's general mailbox asking for a call back and said that he had the capacity to "back the whole thing." I invited him to a meeting with me and Meredith Kane in my district office. He was full of bluster and confidence that he could do the deal, telling us that he would make it so easy for tenants to buy their apartments that there would be bankers with folding tables in the Stuyvesant Town Oval granting mortgages one after the next.

He described his plan as "simple and direct," namely, that he would convert the property to a co-op and sell units to tenants at $130,000 per unit (the average sale price for a one-bedroom Manhattan co-op in 2011 was $588,985; a two-bedroom was $1,504,747). This was by far the lowest number that we had ever seen—by hundreds of thousands of dollars per unit. In response, I had asked him to explain how he could get apartment prices that low. He responded that he couldn't show us the plan unless we were partners, because he'd be afraid that someone would steal the idea. Weeks after meeting with me and Kane, Guterman sent a letter to Al Doyle, Kane, and Bill Derrough of Moelis, with a copy to me, dated September 20, 2010, setting forth his plan. He also conveyed that he was planning to move forward with an offer directly to CWCapital later in the week.[1]

The details of Guterman's plan, as laid out in his letter, sparked an anxious debate about who—in any plan—would become the owner of units that were not sold to the tenants who lived in them. For example, Guterman intended to sell occupied rent-stabilized units to individual outside investors. Longtime rent-stabilized renters like Soni Fink objected to any scenario where her individual unit could be sold out from under her. "Let's give a thought as to who the guy might be who chooses to buy my inconveniently occupied 2 bedroom, 2 bath river view apartment. This is not some guardian angel who has decided to take under his wing a sweet old lady, who wants to live out her days within easy reach of Manhattan's cultural and entertainment goodies and, should she no longer be able to enjoy them, happily gazing out her window. This is an investor who has looked into the actuarial tables and decided that given the odds, the apartment might become vacant just in time to sell the house in Mamaroneck when his youngest child goes off to college."[2]

In consultation with Moelis, we had concluded that we would not give Guterman special attention over other potential partners. Not only was his model one of short-term ownership, but it also lacked any long-term affordability protections. Marsh had also uncovered, in a basic internet search, some of Guterman's past business practices, which sounded lots of alarms for us.

Guterman was best known for buying rental buildings and converting them into cooperatives and condominiums in the 1980s. He offered a discounted, insider rate for tenants who wanted to buy their units. For the units that were not bought by the people who lived in them, Guterman offered outside investors an opportunity to buy these occupied apartments at an even steeper discount. With a lot of conversions happening in the early 1980s, there was an active market to sell units that were still occupied by residents, and Guterman made a bundle. Guterman had attracted considerable attention in 1986 when he chartered the *Queen Elizabeth 2* cruise ship, along with a crew of six hundred, for his thirteen-year-old son Jason's bar mitzvah party. "Jason Guterman did not merely come of age last week, he *arrived*," quipped the *New York Times*. In attendance at the event were numerous politicians and real estate figures, including New York City Council president Andrew J. Stein—formerly the assemblyman for Stuy Town—and the city comptroller, Harrison J. Goldin. The ship set sail at 6 p.m., though helicopters continued to touch down on the sports deck to drop off latecomers, including Ivan F. Boesky, the stock and investment speculator.[3]

Since the 1980s, however, it had not been smooth sailing for Guterman's business. Thirty-six of Guterman's co-ops later experienced serious cash-flow problems after their operating accounts were temporarily frozen by the Bank of New York. The Stanhope, an Upper East Side hotel Guterman had been renovating at an estimated cost of $26 million, filed for reorganization under Chapter 11 of the federal bankruptcy laws. In addition, the management division of Guterman's Hanover Companies had to vacate its twenty-three thousand square feet of office space on Marcus Avenue in Lake Success, New York, after being sued for failure to pay rent since the first day of its lease.[4]

Most concerning was Marsh's discovery of business practices that also had drawn the attention of the New York State attorney general. When Guterman sold occupied rental units to outside investors, he naturally understood that the sooner people moved out of their apartments, or died, the better the investment would be. So, in his marketing materials, Guterman identified key details about the tenants who lived in them: "Single female in her 70's," "30-year-old single male," "couple in their 30's," his ads said. Tenants complained that the descriptions—aimed at letting would-be buyers know that the apartments might well become available in longer, or shorter, time frames—jeopardized their personal security. "It's not in very good taste," said Fred Mehlman, chief of the bureau of real estate financing in the New York State attorney general's office, which demanded the withdrawal of the advertisement. Marsh and I recognized this tactic. It smacked of what Tishman Speyer had tried to do. "People need to know about this," Marsh said to me. We conferred with Kane and Rubin and with the TA board. We did not favor Guterman's plan in any event, because it lacked a long-term affordability component. These additional data points solidified that view, and everyone agreed that with or without his questionable history, we could not partner with Guterman.[5]

When Guterman read about our partnership with Brookfield in the newspapers, he was enraged. His letter to all tenants attacked Brookfield as a "corporate bottom feeder" and promised that the deal he was proposing was going to be "better" than what the TA and Brookfield were offering—and even better than the stabilized rents that people were paying. An anonymous muckraking blogger called *Stuyvesant Town Report* gleefully posted Guterman's letter, saying "I'm not a fan of any condo/co-op proposal, but it is interesting to see how people are already screwing each other in private, non-transparent deals that concern all of us residents. Let the fighting begin!" Commenters on the blog, and on Facebook, started to pick up Guterman's narrative and called into question the motivation of the Tenants Association and me, vowing to fight back against our partnership with Brookfield. Some demanded to know how we picked Brookfield, calling the TA and me corrupt and questioning our motives. "The voices on that blog were negative, cynical, and strident. It was a way to scream and yell and call people names," Marsh recalled. "We couldn't tell who was saying what, and it gave them an oversize voice that didn't really fit." Guterman said that he was prepared to send letters to tenants every week if he had to. "I'm entitled to do this. I'm not a kid," Guterman told the *New York Post.*[6]

Rather than reveling in the excitement of our own Brookfield announcement, we were already on the defensive. Guterman's well-funded counternarrative was that there was a better deal out there for us but the TA wouldn't pursue it. Some members of the TA board thought it best to ignore Guterman as an unwelcome nuisance, but Marsh strongly disagreed. "Guterman is a bare-knuckles—or mallet-to-the-forehead—fighter. We can't afford to be pussycats," he argued. I agreed with Marsh. To me, every day that we gave Guterman a chance to attack us without any rebuttal was a day we risked losing the confidence of our neighbors. So many people were already—and understandably—dissatisfied with our own lack of transparency and communication that we decided to respond as forcefully as we could. "They're like the ads on late night TV—extremely misleading and designed to sow mistrust and doubt," I said to Bloomberg News about Guterman's communications to the tenants as part of a media counterattack.[7]

In response to Guterman's letter, the TA also sent a direct message to tenants, describing our process for picking Brookfield over Guterman and others. It explained that we had met with Guterman and his representatives, as well as dozens of other potential partners. "We decided to select Brookfield Asset Management over all the others because they have both the credibility in the real estate market and the commitment and ability to live up to principles and goals of the Tenants Association." The TA also attacked the Guterman-Westwood proposal, saying that they lacked the ability to raise the amount of capital necessary to purchase the property, that they intended to make this a short-term investment, and that their plan to do a cooperative—as opposed to a condominium, which Kane had been recommending—would increase the chance of "systemic financial distress" that could impact every resident in the community.[8] We were tempted, but decided not to share what Marsh had learned about Guterman's advertisements that had caught the attention of the attorney general.

At the Tenants Association meeting on December 3 at Baruch College, which we had called to introduce Brookfield to the tenants, we emphasized all these points. After Susan Steinberg called the meeting to order, she turned the microphone over to me. I explained the TA's long and laborious process to select a partner, and how we had landed on Brookfield. I also thanked Barry Blattman, whom we had welcomed onstage, for stepping up to support us. I also spent some time addressing Guterman's supposed "offer of a lifetime." I had the stage, and addressed his plan directly: "Just remember that if something sounds too good to be true, it probably is. Their plan is based entirely on profiteering. It is based on a concept that would have a sponsor come in, convert the property, take a profit, and leave. It does not seek to preserve even a single unit of

Figure 10.1. On December 3, 2011, the Tenants Association convened a meeting at Baruch College to introduce residents to Barry Blattman, who represented our new partner, Brookfield Asset Management. *From left*, Alex Rubin, tenants attorney Tim Collins, Barry Blattman, Meredith Kane, me, and Assemblyman Brian Kavanagh. Virginia Rosario and Al Doyle sat behind us onstage. Photo credit: *Town & Village* newspaper.

affordable housing in Stuyvesant Town. We are done with people who view this property as a piggy bank."[9] When it was Blattman's turn at the podium, he calmly introduced himself to the assembled crowd, and to polite applause publicly committed to delivering a formal bid to CWCapital by no later than April 15, 2012.

Contemporaneously with Guterman's approaches, we were hearing increasing criticism from traditionally rent-stabilized tenants who themselves opposed a conversion plan entirely. Organized under the banner of a group called "Save Stuy Town," they curiously spared Guterman from criticism, even though he too was pushing a conversion. Instead, they saved their ire for me and the Tenants Association. "If you're a real rent stabilized tenant then you have no reason to thank the TA," wrote an anonymous poster on the *Stuyvesant Town Report* blog. "They have sold out the real Rent Stabilization people." We bristled at this accusation because not only did most members of the TA board occupy rent-stabilized units, but we had been meticulous in protecting the rights of rent-stabilized tenants and creating only positive opportunities for them. Their support was critically important to our effort, and we could not afford to alienate tenants in those units. Under any Tenants Association–led plan, rent-stabilized tenants had the right to remain in their apartments, without harassment, even if they did not want to buy their units. Our plan also advanced the cause of long-term affordability of the community, and the city, because we wanted to test people's incomes before allowing them to occupy future units, to ensure that middle-income people were going to live there. And yet, the Save Stuy Town group was promising a lawsuit to remove the TA leadership and "take off the gloves and call out the former Tenants Association and their patron saint Dan Garodnick." MacArthur amusedly shared with me a five-page anonymous manifesto that he had received complaining that "the Tenants Association and our elected officials do not have OUR best interests at heart for ALL the tenants concerned." It went on to say, "They are good for photo-ops and nothing more. They do not speak for ALL the tenants concerned."[10]

On another front, a war of letters to the editor in *Town & Village* erupted. Our supporters made the case that the Tenants Association's conversion plan was the only viable way to save affordability in Stuy Town and Peter Cooper Village, and that the Guterman plan was smoke and mirrors. Others anonymously took aim at our plan, claiming that they were not consulted and that future buyers would find that owning their units would be less affordable than renting in the long term. "Now, all of a sudden, we are being urged to buy apartments, at a cost of hundreds of thousands of dollars. Yes, that's how much they will cost. Do you think for a moment that they will be sold below market rates? In addition, if you buy, you will no longer have free utilities (gas and electric), free maintenance (painting, plumbing, elevator and grounds). You will pay dearly for every one of these."[11]

One of the more vocal critics of the TA was a young, market-rate Stuy Town mom who called herself Jill. She was adamantly opposed to homeownership and was vocal in online forums. Marsh later discovered that her picture was from a cooking blog run out of Texas and that she was not who she claimed to be. This was a time before bots and fake media identities, and we could not tell whether these loud voices represented more than a few disenchanted residents. Because they were loud, and hostile, we felt like we had to pay attention and to respond to every criticism. "Are we fighting a phantom army? How many people are actually behind this? People were running multiple identities on Facebook," recalled Berlin Rosen's Jen Shykula, who had been helping organize tenants in support of our bid. "It was incredible how a contained group of people could hijack the conversation online."[12]

I shook my head. "How are we going to deal with this?" I asked my chief of staff, Justine Almada. First, we were responding to Guterman pushing a conversion allegedly faster and cheaper, and now we were shadow boxing with a group of people (including at least one fake personality) who objected to a conversion altogether. Our moment of peak influence suddenly felt like a distant memory. The real estate blog network Curbed ranked Stuy Town as the third property on its "shitshow list." The *Village Voice* put the tenants' and Guterman's plans on the same level of desirability, asking "whether the tenants or Guterman Westwood Partners has a better shot at buying the complex and converting part of it into cheap condos." Guterman also posted on the blogs that he was on the cusp of doing another mailing to tenants about his plan and preparing an interactive website, which he later, in January 2012, announced with great fanfare. Residents would pose questions on Guterman's user-friendly site about his plan, and Guterman would respond personally, the same day. The Tenants Association did not have the manpower to do that and was unable to keep up. At our request, Brookfield agreed to assign someone to that task, but our neighbors were increasingly doubting our efforts.[13]

Shykula had her hands full. She had been charged with helping the Tenants Association build support for the Brookfield partnership. The urgency of this organizing effort was becoming clearer with every dissenting voice. Shykula worked with Marsh to map out an all-out blitz of public information. Her effort had turned from sharing relevant information to waging a full-on campaign. It started with the large-scale tenant meeting to introduce Brookfield in December, and she teed up dozens of house parties to introduce people to our effort. Shykula also planned a community-wide telephonic town hall meeting, the first of its kind in our neighborhood.

Crammed into the Berlin Rosen conference room on Maiden Lane on January 27, Senator Duane and Assembly Member Kavanagh joined the Tenants Association for our very first telephone town hall. Susan Steinberg, the TA vice president, welcomed people to the call, and we watched the computer screen excitedly as the number of participants went from 100 to 500, over 1,000, and then up to 2,425.[14] We again explained why we felt we needed a capital partner and why we were so encouraged by having an entity like Brookfield on our team. Senator Chuck Schumer called in from a Chinese restaurant, where he was having dinner, to reaffirm his commitment to Stuy Town as a bastion of middle-class housing in New York City. He said that he was pushing Fannie and Freddie to work with us, and committed his full support to the Tenants Association.

The anonymous *Stuyvesant Town Report* blogger was listening in and later observed that we had made a "valiant" effort to defend our plan and to stave off interruptions from other real estate entities. However, he said that we had failed to explain how we could claim to stand up for the middle class and affordability when our conversion plan "means that people will voluntarily give up their rent stabilized status and enter the market rate, with a significant mortgage (despite being drawn from an insider price), high maintenance fees, high real estate taxes, etc." I understood the concern about homeownership but was frustrated that this blogger and others gave absolutely no recognition to the fact that nothing about our plan forced these tenants to give up their units, or their rights, and that we were addressing the affordability concern for both current *and future* residents.[15]

The January call was useful for solidifying our position with our neighbors, but it in no way changed the static situation with CWCapital. Blattman had dinner with CWCapital's president Dave Iannarone later that month and was left with the distinct impression that CWCapital was still in no rush. They were perfectly satisfied to be collecting special servicing fees for the time being and were focused on a price of over $3.5 billion for Stuy Town and Peter Cooper. Frustrated by the lack of movement by CWCapital, I thought that we needed to loudly, and publicly, announce that a bid—of a specific amount—had been initiated by the tenants and Brookfield and was sitting on CWCapital's desk. Doing so would pressure CWCapital, and help me and the TA to keep the community united behind a single goal. I dreamed of reading a story in the *New York Times* under the headline "Tenants Put Massive $3.5 Billion Bid on CWCapital's Desk; Bondholders Made Whole." Blattman asked for patience and countered that the most promising route for us would be for him to continue to make his case to Iannarone privately and told me that there was "likely very little value to putting a bid on their desk that they will reject or use to test the market." What Blattman was saying made sense, but I suspected it was difficult for him to appreciate how hard it was for us to manage the dissenting voices in the neighborhood.[16]

The Tenants Association board invited me to join them in late January for their meeting at the Stuy Town Neighbor Services Room on East 18th Street. After Doyle dispensed with some preliminary business, we turned to a discussion of our progress. The board was eagerly awaiting the official contours of a bid from Brookfield, which Blattman had promised at our community meeting, to deliver to CWCapital by no later than April 15. Now it seemed like Blattman was retreating from any public approach to CWCapital, and the uncertainty was creating anxiety for all of us. While we had just announced our partnership with Brookfield, many tenants were already eager to know what would happen next. And if tenants knew what the board knew (that we had already been unsuccessfully working to get CWCapital's attention for months), they would have been even more frustrated. At the board meeting, Sheehy complained about how "slow moving" the process was and how difficult it was to get this point across to tenants. Only seven weeks after our announcement of our partnership with Brookfield, one tenant, trying to be supportive, emailed me and the board under the subject line "What happened?" Citing the misinformation that was coming from our adversaries, the note pleaded, "The TA had great momentum going for a while and it's a shame to lose that and not give tenants what was promised. The TA started the conversion ball rolling and it's up to the TA to keep it going, for the sake of tenants and for the sake of the TA's credibility."[17]

With Marsh and Shykula leading the charge, we doubled down on our grassroots organizing. From the days fighting for civil rights, to the battles over MetLife's expiring tax break, collective action was in the bloodstream of Stuy Town. Usually, the mission had been to fight against an injustice, or a pending crisis. This time, it was the tenants who were looking to control the conversation, to educate people, to answer their questions, and to move them toward consensus in a complex real estate transaction. Shykula and Marsh started activating building leaders to host small gatherings to help explain the plan in an informal setting. The vision was for neighbors to invite people into their homes to meet with a tenant leader, or me, or both, to hear about our plans. "This was how real organization happens and power gets built," Shykula said in retrospect. "People opened their homes. They would invite people they knew, and also others who had expressed interest directly to the Tenants Association in attending a meeting. Neighbors were meeting each other. Market raters, young families, a young professional crowd." These were the sorts of things that no other bidder could possibly do.[18]

Board members like Steven Newmark and Julie Ehrlich were very helpful in bringing younger residents to the meetings. Ordinarily, Marsh, Steinberg, Sheehy, or Margaret Salacan would facilitate the discussions, and I was asked to attend about a third of them, particularly where Shykula and Marsh felt a difficult issue might be presented. As we broadened our reach, Shykula ran training sessions with TA members on how to host house meetings themselves. In the meetings, we asked people what they hoped to see in a tenant-led bid and did our best to answer questions. Perhaps most significantly, people wanted to know the price of their units, which we still could not answer. Some expressed concerns for people who wanted to stay as renters. Others feared that Brookfield might be well intentioned but also might sell the property to a third party who could then evict people.[19]

We supplemented the house meetings with literature under doors, a website, and a telephone hotline that was staffed by volunteers. When we wanted to distribute a flyer to all 11,232 units, John Marsh set up a system of delivering them to several pickup spots around the community—including Oval Concierge, a concierge service based in Stuy Town—and alerted his building leaders by email when there was something to pick up. They in turn would stuff the flyers under the doors in their buildings. Sometimes Marsh would rollerblade around the property, leaving bags of flyers on people's apartment doors, including mine. Our tenant outreach plan from fall 2011 through spring 2012 had been impressive. Some 1,100 tenants had attended our community meeting to introduce Brookfield; 2,402 tenants had participated in our telephone town hall; 1,188 individual questions were fielded through the website, the hotline, comment cards, house meetings, and the town hall; 192 tenants had been recruited as volunteers to help, and we held sixteen intensive small-group discussions in apartments.[20] Plus, Marsh and his team of organizers had collected thousands of unity pledges, where individual residents committed to working with the Tenants Association in support of our effort. All this was in preparation for our bid, which we hoped to formally give to CWCapital with full community support—and equally importantly, to publicly announce—in April 2012. In the interim, I tried to keep pressure on CWCapital—demanding that they work with us, and questioning their stonewalling. As we engaged the community, we became more confident that the dissenting voices were a vocal but small and disgruntled group, and that we continued to enjoy the support of the vast majority of our neighbors.

As we ramped up our grassroots and public negotiating efforts, CWCapital had ceased to be indifferent and was getting increasingly hostile. It did not help that Alex Schmidt, the *Roberts* counsel, had quietly proposed to MacArthur that CWCapital try to settle the *Roberts* case as part of a broader deal with the tenants and Brookfield. MacArthur was outraged by the notion that the *Roberts* settlement might be used to clear a path for Brookfield. In response, MacArthur curtly told Adam Rose to advise the Tenants Association that they no longer would be given the courtesy of distributing any literature out of the management-run spaces, like the Oval Concierge office. MacArthur called me to say the same thing, and used some threatening language about how it was lucky that he didn't "trigger defcon 5." I asked him what he meant by that, but he chose not to explain, and said that he "already said too much."[21]

On April 3, 2012, just before we expected to see a formal bid proposal from Brookfield, I publicly announced that I was going to be a candidate for city comptroller the following year. I had talked about it with Zoe, and with my political advisers like Micah Lasher, Jonathan Rosen, Valerie Berlin, and Alex Navarro-McKay, and we believed that this office was not only a good fit but also the right opportunity for me. In a video released that day (but contemplated for several months), I stood in front of my building in Peter Cooper and promised a drama-free comptroller's office, where audits were driven by facts and not politics. I expected that John Liu, the current comptroller, would be a formidable candidate, but I believed it was also possible that Liu would jump into the mayor's race and not run for reelection as comptroller, leaving an open seat. As I navigated my work representing my East Side district, I started to make visits to colleagues around the city, trying to build support. I needed to raise money fast, and I asked friends and family to help me raise contributions of $175, which the city matched with public funds at a rate of 6 to 1. My ailing mom, ever in my corner even as she continued to battle cancer, sat at her laptop in Peter Cooper and emailed everyone she knew, including her doctors, with the subject line "My son the Comptroller???"— shaking out a number of contributions for me.

With the election over a year and a half away, I still had capacity to continue to support the TA as usual. We were all quite excited to hear from Brookfield about the formal, detailed bid that they had prepared to give to CWCapital. On the evening of April 30, 2012, the entire fifteen-member board of the TA was navigating the lobby security at Brookfield Place in Lower Manhattan. This was the moment that we were finally going to see the precise contours of Brookfield's proposal. We already knew the basics, because we had negotiated most of the details in our letter of intent. What this document was supposed to do was to formalize it all and finally allow us to show CWCapital that we had more than a vision, but actual dollars behind it. As we gathered with Kane and Rubin in a conference room with breathtaking views of the Statue of Liberty and New York Harbor, all of us were optimistic about the possibilities that lay ahead. The offer, aside from the number itself, was to me as much a political document as it was a business plan. It showed our strength, our perseverance, and our resolve. The mere existence of a multiple-billion-dollar bid by the tenants in partnership with real estate giant Brookfield—all done on our terms—was itself a victory.

Lowell Baron took the group through the bid that Brookfield intended to present to CWCapital. Brookfield proposed offering $3.25 billion to CWCapital, consisting of a $500 million upfront cash payment to their bondholders, which included all transaction costs, $2.5 billion of restructured debt—including $1 billion as a temporary "bridge facility" that would be paid off quickly from condominium sales, and $1.5 billion that would be a first mortgage loan. The TA board members were nodding their heads as Baron detailed the plan.

Then Blattman gave a summary of the informal approaches he had already made to CWCapital, expressing his frustration that MacArthur and Iannarone had not been more open to Brookfield's early entreaties. He hoped that with the formality of a more detailed offer that would make their bondholders whole, their perspective might change. Blattman explained that waiting much longer would carry some risk for CWCapital, because they did not know if future property values were heading up or down. By passing up a legitimate offer—which could very well end up being the very best price CWCapital could achieve—they could be subject to litigation from the very bondholders they represented. On the other hand, he acknowledged, to accept an offer, without a formal process, would always leave open the question of whether they could have done better, which was also a litigation risk.

Blattman told us that he did not know what CWCapital would say in response. He hoped to once again privately, and quietly, invite them to partner with us, give Brookfield a chance to conduct several months of diligence, and then enter into an agreement. Blattman reluctantly acknowledged that if they did not accept our invitation, then we would need to pivot to a more aggressive posture—which I strongly supported—which we were calling Plan B. That would consist of taking our case directly to the bondholders that CWCapital represented, to CWCapital's parent company, Fortress, and to the public. In that scenario, Brookfield and the TA, with the help of Berlin Rosen, would announce to the world that we were giving CWCapital an opportunity to get a full recovery for their bondholders, but that they were ignoring that opportunity. Based on their recent posture, I strongly suspected that CWCapital would not respond to another private approach and expressed to the board and Blattman that we should be prepared for the inevitable Plan B. Blattman again pushed back delicately against my combative posture, urging continued patience. Brookfield wanted to negotiate with CWCapital, not go to war with them; but based on what we all were hearing from MacArthur, I knew we were going to have no choice.

As we watched the sun begin to set over New Jersey, board members started to feel (not for the first time) that we were fighting a losing battle. We walked out of Brookfield's office and through the cavernous Brookfield Place, and shared cabs back to Stuy Town. The mood was somber. "I was a bit bummed out," said Steinberg. "I wondered if all of our efforts to get ahead of the situation would slip away because of an obdurate special servicer—who had no business holding on to the property in the first instance."[22] Board members openly wondered, as they chatted in backseats, what would happen next, and how we could get CWCapital to engage with us. One thing was obvious to everyone: if Brookfield was still getting shut out, it did not bode well for our chances of success.

As planned, Blattman and Baron set up a time on May 11, 2012, to sit with MacArthur quietly and without fanfare. They gave him a draft offer letter and asked him what he needed to formally open a dialogue with us. MacArthur was, as usual, not in the mood to make any commitments, and said blandly that he would consider it and "take it back" to others at CWCapital. Blattman and Baron left the meeting deflated. Chuck Spetka, CWCapital's president, called Blattman later in the day and told him that CWCapital was simply not going to sell Stuy Town until 2013 or 2014, at the very earliest. They were placing a bet that the property value was increasing to a point where CWCapital would not only be able to pay off the $3 billion first mortgage but also keep for itself up to $700 million in default interest, which they believed they were entitled to under the 2006 deal. Darrell Wheeler, an analyst for Amherst Securities Group LP, was now predicting that the value of the property could reach $4 billion, which would vindicate CWCapital's decision to hold on to Stuy Town. CWCapital was banking on Wheeler, and others who were bullish regarding the real estate market, being right.[23]

This put the Tenants Association and me in a bind. We could not just wait until 2013 or 2014, and Brookfield was still resisting the more aggressive Plan B public strategy, unless they felt they truly had no alternatives.

By the time of the TA board meeting in June 2012, the board members had lost all patience with CWCapital, and even with Brookfield. "We are way behind in schedule," the group observed dejectedly in the minutes of its June 27, 2012, meeting. The group noted that our detractors were calling us out on blogs, questioning our approach, and asking what we were doing behind closed doors. Board members like John Sheehy were outraged by CWCapital's intransigence, and the board unanimously agreed that we could not wait any longer: it was time for us to publicly challenge them.

In a final attempt at partnership, on August 13, 2012, Blattman and I paid a visit to CWCapital's offices at 555 Fifth Avenue for lunch with Chuck Spetka, to try one last time to urge him to work with us. He politely but firmly told us that they were not ready to start a sale process, and that doing so prematurely was harmful to their interests. Blattman repeated to Spetka what I had been arguing for months: that the thirty thousand people in the community were going to need to hear from the Tenants Association leadership about where we were headed, and that it was critical for us to find a way to show progress with CWCapital. If we couldn't say anything that would show movement by CWCapital—or anything at all—the tenant body would continue to splinter, and it would eliminate any chance of our keeping people united. Perhaps that was not important to CWCapital if they had no interest in making a deal with us, but we argued that a fragmented and hostile tenant body had the potential to scare bidders away. I told Spetka that if we could not tell our constituents that CWCapital was willing to work with the tenants in developing a plan, the only alternative for us was to point out publicly that CWCapital was ignoring a credible bid that was already on their desk. "It is entirely up to you," I said, doing my very best to present it as an effort at transparency, rather than a threat. Spetka thanked us for coming and repeated that they would consider their options.[24]

Clearly, I failed. MacArthur called me the next day, and he was even more curt than usual. He reiterated that CWCapital was just not interested in the Brookfield proposal and that the CWCapital leadership was deeply unhappy that I had used the threat of political pressure to get them to move. I tried to explain that I had not intended a threat, but rather was trying to candidly explain my options. "Why is Brookfield even involved in any of this?" he barked at me. "What do you mean?" I asked. "They add cost to

the deal," he huffed. As his voice grew louder, MacArthur proceeded to attack the Tenants Association and Brookfield partnership, claiming that we
had offered him no details on our plan, like which tenants were expected
to buy their units, when, and at what price. CWCapital lacked sufficient
details and transparency to react to us, he told me. I was surprised at the
sudden need for information from us, since we had been trying to have
this level of engagement with CWCapital for months. "Fine, I said. How
about we have a summit meeting between CWCapital and the Tenants
Association's advisers to allow us to make a more formal presentation to
you?" I asked. MacArthur paused for a moment and then said he had to
get off the phone. "A light at the end of the tunnel exists," MacArthur said
before he hung up in a huff. "But it's post-*Roberts*."[25]

Admittedly, putting public pressure on CWCapital was not our ideal approach, because cornering one's counterparty in a negotiation is a bad
strategy. Attacking CWCapital could very well end our relationship and
make it much harder to work together. On the other hand, because we
saw little evidence that CWCapital was going to embrace us anyway, the
far bigger risk was losing the support of the tenant body, which would
make it impossible for us to succeed. I huddled with Rubin and Kane,
as well as Brookfield's Blattman and Baron, and everyone now agreed
that the TA should publicly share the bid that we had already made to
CWCapital and show their bondholders what they were passing up.

At the anxiety-filled TA board meeting in the Stuy Town Neighbor
Services Room on September 4, 2012, Kane, Rubin, and I were invited
to talk about next steps. In the meeting, Rubin explained that the longer
CWCapital kept the loan outstanding, the more they were going to collect in default interest. The enormous upside from default interest—which
could rise to a billion dollars or more—plus the bet that property values
were going up, was prompting CWCapital to hold out as long as possible
before doing an auction. With apartment improvements and MCIs, net
operating income in Stuy Town was expected to rise between $5 million to
$10 million every year and had already risen from $135 million in 2010 to
nearly $170 million in 2013. CWCapital had also decided to replace Rose
Associates as the property management company with its own subsidiary,
called CompassRock, a move that boosted its fees further, and it was now
taking in $625,000 a month from just overseeing the operations of Stuy

Town and Peter Cooper. CWCapital had already earned $26 million in servicing fees since first becoming involved with the property in 2009.[26]

Rubin noted that this dynamic was allowing for a potential conflict of interest to develop between CWCapital and the bondholders that they represented. While CWCapital had an interest to collect fees and hold out as long as they could, the bondholders' only priority was a full payment of their loans. That opportunity was presently on the table, by way of the tenants and Brookfield. Unfortunately, because the bondholders that CWCapital represented were divided into five different securitized trusts, no one entity was in a position to force CWCapital to embrace our proposal. Sheehy wondered aloud if CWCapital had to disclose to their bondholders this dynamic.[27]

As we mapped out our communications strategy, we were able to determine that TIAA, Hartford Life, and Principal Financial Group held sizable positions in the debt and had large exposure in Stuy Town.[28] Appaloosa had already identified itself as a bondholder by suing CWCapital in 2010. Other than these entities, plus Fannie and Freddie, we did not know who else was even an interested party. A carryover from the 2007 financial meltdown, these bondholders owned shares in securities that were grouped with many other mortgages in them. We concluded that the only way to talk to them was simply by speaking to the press. After all, these sophisticated investors surely followed closely the news about their assets.

As we geared up for our next move, Al Doyle was getting busier at work and felt that it would be prudent for him to step down from his position as TA president and turn the reins over to the next generation. Without much fanfare, and without missing a beat, the board elected John Marsh to succeed him in the role. Marsh, who was much more aggressive in nature, was eager to execute the public attack on CWCapital. Marsh and I each sent off letters—mine to Spetka, Marsh's to the Stuy Town community—with a sharp critique of CWCapital. "Despite having teamed up with word-class legal and financial advisors Paul Weiss, and Moelis & Company, and a highly credible capital partner, Brookfield Asset Management, and communicating in multiple ways with CWCapital, it consistently declines to engage with us," Marsh wrote. "CWCapital is not willing to work with the tenants of this community in any way other than they would work with any multinational real estate conglomerate eyeing ST/PCV as their next asset to acquire. It is time for CWCapital to go."[29]

In my letter, I reiterated the point directly to Spetka—pointing out that CWCapital was wrong not to accept our bid of over $3 billion, including a significant immediate cash paydown. "While you may not share a commitment to this community beyond your short-term interests, I would expect that you would not willfully pass up an opportunity to satisfy your bondholders." We were at a breaking point. After decades of peace in Stuyvesant Town and Peter Cooper Village, the last six years had brought conflict, upheaval, and instability. "While we cannot point fingers at CWCapital for creating the problem, we certainly can fault you for prolonging it," I wrote. I advised Spetka that we were going to attempt to raise this issue with CWCapital's bondholders; with Wells Fargo, the trustee and master servicer of the CMBS trusts; with Fortress, their parent company; and with the relevant rating agencies. "To the extent that CWCapital cannot see the wisdom of having this conversation with an organized community that has secured a capital partner prepared to get you a full recovery, perhaps these others will." We leaked both letters to the press.[30]

Press headlines reflected our impatience: "Tenants Would Just Like Stuy Town to Be Sold Already"; "Stuy Town Tenants Cut Out Middleman in Bid to Buy Complex"; and TA's own community blast, which crowed, "Tenants Association to CWCapital: It Is Time for You to Move On."[31] The *Structured Credit Investor*, an industry magazine, shrewdly observed, "Although the tenants intend to approach CMBS bondholders directly, they cannot negotiate the resolution with anyone other than the servicer. Meaning that their campaign would appear to be more about putting pressure on CWCapital than about taking any formal or legal action."[32]

Perhaps feeling some pressure, MacArthur made a round of visits to elected officials like council speaker Quinn, to firm up his position. MacArthur told Quinn's staff on October 25 that CWCapital was not ready to sell the property and disputed that the tenants' plan would give them a full recovery, claiming that CWCapital and its bondholders were owed closer to $4 billion, not just $3 billion. After all, they were claiming that nearly another $700 million was due to CWCapital for advances and default interest. The council staffers saw what was happening very clearly: as ordinarily happened, the long game here would favor the real estate interests, and not the tenants.[33]

11

UNDER WATER, ACTUAL WATER

As we continued to badger CWCapital in the press, my mom's health began to take a turn for the worse. She had been fighting multiple myeloma, a blood cancer, since 2003, and at the time it had an average life expectancy of three years. By 2012, she had been through a number of treatment options, including a stem cell transplant and a variety of cocktails of anticancer drugs. She was weak, and we had been back and forth to the hospital with her every few months. I spent every day worried about her health, and the numbers that every test result would bring. She and my dad continued to live in Peter Cooper, but as her health deteriorated, we spent more and more time at New York-Presbyterian Hospital on the Upper East Side. If I thought life couldn't get more complicated as I scrambled to care for my mom, support my dad, and raise a toddler with Zoe, all the while working to address constituent issues from all over the East Side of Manhattan and find a way for us to get CWCapital to engage with us, right then, Hurricane Sandy struck.

There had been few community-wide emergencies in Stuy Town and Peter Cooper Village in its history. There was the 2003 suicide attempt by a man distraught over the end of a relationship, who sealed his kitchen door with packing tape, turned on the oven gas, and prepared to kill himself by asphyxiation. The resulting gas explosion ripped through his top-floor apartment at 21 Stuyvesant Oval, forced the evacuation of more than a hundred other residents, and injured eight people. There was the former city police officer who shot off his service handgun out his Stuy Town window one fall day in 2002, wounding a preschool teacher walking with children and sending tons of residents scurrying in every direction. In 1996, a water main behind 11, 15, and 17 Stuyvesant Oval ruptured during the night, leaving residents without water. Mayor Giuliani came to Stuy Town to observe the situation firsthand.

I had personally experienced only two small-scale emergencies in my forty years in the community. When I was about six years old, I was awakened in the middle of the night by a police officer at the front door of our apartment at 431 East 20th Street, yelling that the water tank on the roof was leaking and that we might need to evacuate the building. Fearing a building collapse, the NYPD told us to stand in our doorways and to be ready to escape at a moment's notice. Looking into the rectangular windows of the elevator doors, I could see the unnatural sight of water cascading down. This was in the pre-9/11 era, and like many people, we were under the impression that buildings didn't just come down, so my parents and I stood patiently at our door until the police told us it was safe to go back inside.

On Christmas Eve 2005, I came home to see a guard sitting outside my door at 3 Peter Cooper Road. There had been a fire in the apartment just below mine, and while I was out, the New York City Fire Department had broken down my door and smashed my windows in its effort to contain the fire. A lonely Stuy Town public safety officer was sitting on a folding chair outside my apartment door, waiting to greet me when I came home.

Major weather events were similarly rare—there was Hurricane Gloria in 1985 when schools were closed, and a nor'easter in 1992 that flooded the Stuy Town garages, destroying many cars. And the blizzard of December 2010, when the city—and Stuy Town—was not able to deal with the volume of snowfall, trapping many New Yorkers in their apartments.

But no previous weather event compared to Hurricane Sandy, which charged toward the East Coast in the final days of October 2012. The weather reports had been predicting a significant storm, but a year earlier, the ominous Hurricane Irene had done less damage than expected. With that backdrop, New Yorkers were hearing the warnings about Hurricane Sandy but not really listening. Peter Cooper Village and Stuyvesant Town—despite being only one hundred yards from the East River—were not officially in an evacuation zone, so people were encouraged to shelter in place. To his credit, unfazed by the public relations hits he took after Irene, Mayor Bloomberg ordered a mandatory evacuation of low-lying areas on Sunday, October 28—which for my council district included Waterside Plaza, just two blocks over from Stuy Town on the East River, and the public housing community at Stanley Isaacs and Holmes Towers, uptown on 93rd Street and First Avenue. Bus and subway service was shutting down across the whole city beginning on Sunday night, and schools were going to be closed on Monday.

I sent out an email blast to my constituents about how to protect themselves during the storm. I also told my staff—most of whom lived in Brooklyn—that we would work remotely from Monday until transit service was restored. I reached out to friends and lightheartedly reminded them to take showers now and fill bathtubs for later, before power and water were no longer an option. Zoe and I put our one-and-a-half-year-old, Asher, to bed, prepared our flashlights and our "go bag," and put batteries in a transistor radio. We watched the news reports on television and tracked the storm online.

At 9 p.m. on Monday there was a massive flash of light outside the bedroom window of our apartment overlooking the East River. The entire sky lit up for four seconds, and then it stopped. It was bluer and brighter than lightning and filled the entire sky. We did not know it, but there had been an explosion at the Con Edison substation on 14th Street, which sits right next to Stuy Town. A few seconds after the flash, we heard the hum of power fade out, and our apartment lights went dark. Zoe and I flipped on our flashlights and hoped that we would continue to have cell phone service. We didn't. We had no way of knowing that all of Stuy Town and Peter Cooper—as well as about a quarter of New

York City's homes and businesses—were now without power, and many of them also were without water. As Asher slept in his crib, Zoe and I took turns visiting our neighbors Ryan Garner and Andrea Kebis on the twelfth floor, because they had a window that faced out onto East 23rd Street. From that vantage point, we could see the East River steadily moving up the modest grade from its banks bordering the FDR Drive. Waves slowly and quietly submerged cars on the street, some of which had hazard or other lights flashing. The cars parked closest to the river were completely underwater. I took the flashlight and walked down ten flights of stairs to the basement, which was still, for the moment, lit with emergency power. I had to stop in my tracks on the street level. I couldn't even go further; the basement of 510 East 23rd Street was completely full of water.

The next morning, Tuesday the thirtieth, there was still no power, heat, or hot water in our apartment or anyone else's in Stuy Town. At 6:30 a.m. I left Zoe and Asher in our apartment and went to see how everyone in the neighborhood had fared. Immediately upon stepping out of the building, I saw cars scattered in every direction on the street. One car sat, as if waiting for a traffic light to turn, with a fifteen-foot wood pillar from a construction site perpendicular on its crushed hood. I scanned everywhere but could not see where it could have fallen from—and then realized that it had not fallen; the pillar likely had floated in from the East River. One of the 23rd Street gas station pumps lay face-down on the ground, pummeled by the force of the river. The management office of Stuy Town, on Avenue C, was destroyed. Four of the community's five parking garages were flooded. The Manhattan Kids Club II day care center at 655 East 14th Street, where Asher went, was totally wiped out.

On my tour, I walked up the thirteen stories to check on my parents in their apartment a few buildings over from mine. I described what I saw outside and strongly encouraged them to leave Peter Cooper and go to a safer spot. My seventy-six-year-old dad initially told me that I shouldn't worry; he and my mom would be fine, because he could walk up and down the stairs to get whatever they needed. I strongly preferred my parents to be somewhere I didn't need to worry about them, because I knew that I was going to be busy helping my neighbors. I persuaded my parents that they would be safer and more comfortable out of town. That afternoon, my dad slowly and carefully walked my frail mom down the staircase and into their car. They drove out to Westhampton, New York, and I followed with Zoe and Asher later in the day. We planned for them to remain out of town until things were back to normal in Peter Cooper. My parents helped with Asher while his Stuy Town day care center was still underwater, and Zoe was able to work remotely.

While I was moving my family out of Manhattan, I called Andy Kane, MacArthur's deputy at CWCapital, to offer my help, but did not get an immediate response. City maps were inaccurately showing that there was no power outage in Stuy Town or Waterside, just to the north. I emailed both Kane and MacArthur to make sure they knew that there were a lot of stranded seniors in Stuy Town, who had stayed in place because that is what they were told to do. Without elevator service, these residents were functionally trapped. As I waited on Kane and MacArthur, I spoke to Assemblyman Brian Kavanagh, whose district included many public housing units on the Lower East Side (completely without heat and water), and he suggested that we start knocking on doors to check on people who were shut in. He had many more affected constituents than I did, and I thought that was a very smart idea. Still out of town, I started to organize our door-knocking effort in Stuy Town, Peter Cooper, and Waterside Plaza. Waterside was in the worst condition because it had no water at all, and the buildings there are forty stories high.

On Wednesday, October 31, I left my family and drove back to the city at 5 a.m. to beat the rush hour traffic, only to join one of the worst traffic jams in New York's history. The subways were not running, and the East Midtown Tunnel was flooded, sending all traffic over the bridges. I inched over the Queensboro Bridge, with one bar of power on my iPad, trying to communicate with my chief of staff, Ilona Kramer, who was in her Brooklyn apartment. The traffic into Manhattan was so severe that Mayor Bloomberg later that day announced restrictions on single-occupancy cars entering Manhattan. Still not able to connect with MacArthur and Kane, Assemblyman Kavanagh and I decided to start door knocking at the fourteen-hundred-unit Waterside Plaza late Wednesday afternoon. We met Peter Davis, the manager of Waterside, and his senior staff in their dark management office. Together, we began the process of trekking up forty flights of stairs and then descending, floor by floor, as we checked on people in each of the four buildings in the complex. Along with Senator Tom Duane, Assemblyman Kavanagh and I each took responsibility for a building, and as we knocked, we found a number of stranded residents who needed help. We brought them water and took note of where they were, so that we, or more likely Davis, could follow up with them in the following days.

That evening, Kane finally responded, and we agreed to convene together in Stuy Town on Thursday, November 1, at 8 a.m. to strategize about how we could work together to help people in their apartments. I asked Marsh to get out an email to the Tenants Association's list. "If you are physically fit, and can help, please report to Oval Study starting at 8 a.m. tomorrow. This effort is being coordinated with CompassRock, the Tenants Association, and every elected official office in the area, and will be directing volunteers through the entire property," he posted.

Stuy Town still had cold water, and after taking an ice-cold shower in a cold and empty apartment, at 8 a.m. on Thursday, I met a concerned-looking MacArthur and Spetka, as well as CWCapital's property management team in Stuyvesant Oval. "I am here to help," I said, and suggested that they give me a space to coordinate a volunteer operation. They conferred privately for a moment. My friendly overture was, after all, a sharp departure from my calling them out publicly as self-interested double-dealers. But they could tell that my offer was sincere and, looking at the complexity of the situation they were in, must have realized that they needed the support. MacArthur directed me to set up in the Stuyvesant Town Community Center, just off 16th Street. Volunteers, mostly from the community, started to show up, and we began dispatching them out to buildings to knock on doors. I sent my staff to the leasing office, where we got our hands on hundreds of property maps and started to give people assignments as they came in. On a master map, I crossed off each building to which we had sent volunteers. When they returned, they reported what people needed—things like batteries for their flashlights, prescriptions filled, or even messages delivered to worried relatives. We kept a careful list and circled back with deliveries. With the help of many volunteers, on the first day, we knocked on all 11,232 doors in Stuy Town and Peter Cooper Village.

Figure 11.1. In late October 2012, Hurricane Sandy devastated the East Side of Manhattan, including this car, which had been parked in front of Stuy Town. In a brief reprieve from our conflicts, we partnered with CWCapital and organized volunteers to check on our neighbors. Photo credit: *Town & Village* newspaper.

On Friday, day two, we had even more volunteers. Hundreds of them. New York Cares had put Stuyvesant Town on a list of volunteer sites, and, working hand in hand with CWCapital, we sent them out to visit our many stranded neighbors. A group of nurses and doctors from Stuy Town showed up and offered to help, so we set them up in the back of the community center. When reports came back about seniors who looked frail, or who described a concern about a medical condition, this team would pay them a visit. My district office was getting calls from as far away as Dubai asking us to check on relatives living in Stuy Town. We did and reported back about their condition. MacArthur and Kane were appreciative of what we were doing and gave us daily written updates for our volunteers to distribute in buildings.

By November 1, mass transit north of 42nd Street had been restored, but power still had not come back to anyone south of 39th Street on the East Side.[1] Zoe, my parents, and Asher were still in Westhampton—and

I was still sleeping in our cold, dark, empty Peter Cooper apartment. When I returned home from a day managing our door-knocking effort, I walked across the eerily dark and mostly abandoned community. There were no lights in the windows or streetlights to guide the way. As time went on, many tenant leaders, and residents generally, had found other accommodations, but I was still there with the most elderly and infirm residents who had no ability to get out.

Inside my building, I pushed open the front door, no longer protected by electronic keycard access, and walked up the completely dark staircase, using a flashlight to guide me. In my apartment, I had no cell service or light, so I would get quickly into bed and cover myself with as many blankets as I could find. In the morning, I would wake up frozen, take a cold shower, and get dressed to take on the day. This repeated itself for several days. By the end of the fourth day, on Saturday, November 3, I needed a break and asked my friends Andrew Ehrlich and Tania Brief, who lived on the Upper West Side, if I could stay with them. Things were entirely normal north of 39th Street, and I was desperate for a hot shower. I got in a cab after 8 p.m. to head to their apartment but did not get far; I looked down at my phone and saw an email describing an emergency situation and possible evacuation of 6 Peter Cooper Road due to a sudden carbon monoxide problem.

I quickly turned around and hurried over to 6 Peter Cooper Road to find Andrew MacArthur pacing back and forth on the scene, with fire trucks everywhere. He told me that Con Edison had reintroduced power to twenty buildings before Stuy Town management was ready to receive it, which created a carbon monoxide condition in 6 Peter Cooper Road. The Fire Department was debating whether to evacuate the building as a precaution. I stood with MacArthur outside the building watching the scene, when several manhole covers on Avenue C exploded with such a loud noise that it shook the ground and made us duck for cover. As we stood watching firefighters dart in and out of 6 Peter Cooper Road, MacArthur explained to me that Con Edison's workers on the scene were now refusing to *turn off* the power, which was continuing the dangerous situation. I offered to help and called council speaker Christine Quinn, who had situated herself in the command center of the Office of Emergency Management, and asked her to communicate to Con Ed what MacArthur had told me. She spoke with senior officials at Con

Ed in the command center, and, just after midnight, Con Ed cut the power to all the buildings again. MacArthur expressed his appreciation to me, and I was happy to have found a way to make myself useful. I left at 12:15 in the morning and went to the Upper West Side and collapsed from exhaustion. It was not until several days later, at 3:45 a.m. on November 7—eight days after the power went out—that all buildings at PCV and Stuy Town finally had power. Steam heat started to come back shortly thereafter.[2]

The damage had been severe, and residents slowly returned to the affected buildings to find that their basements (and laundry machines) destroyed, their intercoms not working, and unsightly recycling bins now located right in front of their front doors, rather than tucked away in the basements. CWCapital decided to give a modest credit to residents on their rent bills for the days in which we were without either heat or power—but not for many other basic services that had been slow to return. By late November, many residents were still unable to use laundry machines or intercoms to let guests into their buildings. Recycling bins were frequently spilling over with garbage as CWCapital, which had appointed itself the property manager, struggled to get things back to normal.

The Tenants Association and I were sensitive about criticizing MacArthur for anything related to Sandy. I had hoped that our collaboration in responding to the storm would engender a better working relationship and translate into a partnership. However, when MacArthur advised me that fifteen of the buildings would be without laundry services for a full year, we all felt that it was not fair for residents to pay their full rent. I made that argument to MacArthur, but he rejected the idea of doing anything more than he had already done.

With the moment of collaboration during Sandy now clearly over, the TA returned to the more familiar place of fighting with CWCapital, this time for basic services. The TA decided to file a legal challenge against MacArthur's decision not to grant a rent reduction for the reduced services. To be eligible for a rent reduction, every single aggrieved tenant needed to sign on to a formal challenge before the state housing agency. If they did not, they were not eligible for any relief. By this point, Marsh could mobilize tenants in his sleep, and he had a very strong Tenants Association infrastructure to work with. He and TA board member Margaret Salacan organized the necessary forms in cardboard boxes in Soni Fink's apartment and got to work door knocking and collecting signatures. It is hard to imagine that we would have so eagerly engaged in another conflict with CWCapital if MacArthur had agreed to work with us on a long-term affordability plan; but since we were still getting a cold shoulder from him on that point, we felt we had no reason to hold our fire.

As we opened a new front in the battle with CWCapital, my campaign for comptroller had hit a speed bump. John Liu had in fact decided to vacate the comptroller seat to run for mayor, but Scott Stringer, who had previously announced his candidacy for mayor, decided to run for comptroller instead. Bill de Blasio, one of Stringer's rivals, called me and told me immediately that he was endorsing Stringer for the comptroller's post. I could see the makings of a political deal—and it did not include me. I spent a few weeks exploring whether I had a path to run a race that included Stringer, another reform-minded Manhattanite, in it. Rather than force this issue, I decided on November 28, 2012, to drop my own quest to be the city comptroller and instead run for reelection to the city council. A number of colleagues had asked me to consider running for city council speaker instead, and that suddenly felt like a more viable option for me.

Zoe was pregnant again and working full time in the general counsel office at Planned Parenthood Federation of America but still supportive of my plans to be a citywide candidate. The speaker vote would be held at the council's first meeting in January 2014, so I had only a year to earn the votes of my fifty council colleagues. I tended to have good relationships with them, and that was important, but winning a speaker's race would involve piecing together a patchwork of support from labor unions, Democratic Party bosses, and other influential New Yorkers.

The day after I dropped out of the comptroller race, on November 29, 2012, MacArthur and Alex Schmidt, on behalf of the tenants, reached a $145 million settlement in the *Roberts* case. The settlement was broken down into two parts. First, CWCapital agreed to pay directly to the *Roberts* class members a total of $68.75 million for the amount they overpaid on their units between 2003 and 2011. Second, CWCapital agreed to forgo the $76 million the landlord had given up during the years of the "interim agreement," when many of the *Roberts* class members were paying dramatically lower rents than the negotiated "legal" rents for their apartments. They had already enjoyed all the benefit they were going to get; their rents were going to go up. As usual, Bagli reported the story in the *Times*.

Schmidt, who had inherited this case knowing nothing about landlord-tenant law, delivered this extraordinary and unusual tenant payout, which also included $18.9 million in fees to his firm, Wolf Haldenstein Adler Freeman & Herz, and to his co-counsel, Bernstein Liebhard. Most people were ecstatic when they started getting checks in the mail to compensate them for their overpayments. Such a thing was unheard of and deeply satisfying to Stuy Town residents. But others were surprised to see their rents go up as part of the settlement. MacArthur had for years worried about the dynamic that Tishman Speyer set up with the "interim agreement." MacArthur felt that Tishman Speyer had lowered rents too much just to avoid conflict at the time. Now, the negotiated rents were in many cases at levels higher than the interim agreement had prescribed. "Everyone had forgotten that they had been paying a much higher rent before," MacArthur recalled.[3]

As it goes in public life, you rarely hear from giddy constituents who received $10,000 checks in the mail. Those neighbors were delighted at their good fortune and kept it mostly to themselves. Those we did hear from were unhappy either because they thought their checks were too small, or they were surprised by their new legal rental rate—or both. Nevertheless, it is fair to say that tenants were mostly grateful for the resolution. It was the first class action of that size that a tenant group had won in court; and with regular efforts to reverse it in the state legislature, few people really believed that they would ever see a penny in their pockets until Schmidt's negotiations had finalized the settlement. The TA worked hard to answer questions from tenants, and we hosted another telephone town hall out of Wolf Haldenstein's offices to explain how the settlement worked.[4]

For years, CWCapital executives had thrown at us the lack of resolution in the *Roberts* lawsuit as the reason it had kept us at arm's length. Now we would see if this was true, or just an excuse for refusing to enter into the next phase of engagement with us. Deutsche Bank observed that the settlement "removed the last significant obstacle which needed to be cleared before a sale could take place." Marsh told Bagli that CWCapital "now had no reason to delay negotiating with the tenants over their proposal to buy the complex as part of a condominium conversion intended to preserve its middle-class character."[5]

The timing was quite bad for a productive negotiation with CWCapital, of course, as we were right in the middle of challenging its poor performance after Sandy. We continued to push for a rent reduction and continued door knocking and asking our neighbors for support. It was already February 2013, and people in flooded buildings (including Zoe and me) still had not had access to their basements and laundry machines for three months. It did not seem to matter to MacArthur that people were paying full rent for their building services, like laundry or intercoms, and not getting those services well into 2013. All of the TA's regular detractors came together for the moment, rightly focusing their hostility on CWCapital as we tried to get compensation for basic services for our neighbors.

CWCapital's failure to do right by tenants, and its continuing to hold the TA-Brookfield bid at arm's length, were the top issues on my mind when I invited MacArthur and Andy Kane to my district office on February 12, 2013. MacArthur showed up in a surly mood. After dropping his *New York Post* on my conference table, he briefly explained how they were getting the property back in shape. I told him the tenants were still pressing their rent reduction claim for services that were still unavailable. "Why should people pay for a laundry room if they can't wash their clothes?" I asked. MacArthur waved me off and turned the conversation to me and my own advocacy. "Dan, we're finding it difficult to separate you from Brookfield," he said, effectively accusing me of merging my role as a public official with that of a bidder. "You've gotten sideways with my organization." He directly accused me of making a fuss about the post-Sandy quality-of-life issues as a way to boost the tenants' partnership with Brookfield. "Look," he said, wrapping up what was clearly a rehearsed statement, "I might have been inclined to have broader discussions about the future of the property, but I can't do it now. You are acting like a bidder, too linked to Brookfield." His argument that he could not work with me because I was no longer functioning as a public official, but rather as the agent of a Stuy Town bidder, rang hollow to me. I shook my head and smiled incredulously. For years, the obstacle was the fact that the *Roberts* case was not resolved, and now that it was settled, he was pointing to the tenants' partnership with Brookfield. MacArthur also warned me in passing that going to his bondholders was not the right route to create pressure on CWCapital, because the "bondholders are pretty happy with the current structure."[6]

I was damned if I did and damned if I didn't. In the 2006 auction by MetLife, the process had proceeded without us, even though we had made a rather impressive bid to buy the property. In 2012, not only had we put a $3.5 billion bid on CWCapital's desk *before* any auction had even been announced, but we were also accompanied by a credible capital source. In response, I was told that I was acting too much like a "bidder." Newly elected state senator Brad Hoylman had an introductory meeting with MacArthur and reported back: "Seems to me that CWCapital is pretty hostile toward this Brookfield partnership."[7]

I took this up with Alex Rubin and Meredith Kane and asked for their advice. "Based on your description," Rubin said, "it seems like some elements of pressure are beginning to register on Andrew."[8] Kane and Rubin agreed that behind his tough talk, MacArthur seemed quite worried about Brookfield's presence. For MacArthur to get someone to pay top dollar in a sale, they explained, he wanted as little disruption as possible in the market. Rubin speculated that because Brookfield was aligned with the tenants, that functionally made any other bidder *adverse* to the tenants, which could limit the willingness of other bidders to make competitive offers.

Kane and Rubin convinced me that our Plan B strategy of public pressure and our partnership with Brookfield were making an impact. After twelve hundred tenants of Stuy Town and Peter Cooper filed claims against CWCapital for a rent reduction for Hurricane Sandy failures, the TA board decided to renew our exclusive partnership with Brookfield, even if it risked alienating MacArthur and CWCapital further. Unless CWCapital—or its parent company Fortress—ultimately decided to forgo a sale and hold on to Stuy Town themselves, we were going to need a capital partner to be by our side in an auction, and we had a good one. Feeling less confident about our approach, but still believing it to be our best option, we powered on.[9]

One of the more controversial outcomes of the *Roberts* settlement was the fact that it gave CWCapital the right not only to adjust rents up to the new levels, but also to do so immediately. That meant that tenants could be subject to a rent increase in the middle of their lease term. Months earlier,

Schmidt had quietly warned me that a settlement might allow CWCapital to do such a thing, but I could not imagine that MacArthur would ever dare to take such a step. The public blowback would be enormous, because nobody who has ever signed a lease expected that a material term—like the amount of rent—might change in the middle. Regardless of the fine print in any lease, I was certain that few people believed that their rents could actually go up mid-lease. I also strongly suspected that leasing agents had told prospective renters that they shouldn't even worry about it. Months earlier, even before the settlement was final, I had sent a letter to MacArthur, warning him against raising rents in the middle of a lease and cautioning him about the destabilizing effect that mid-lease increases would have on individuals and the community at large.[10] "We are deeply skeptical of the legality of such a right, if exercised, and urge you not to take advantage of it," said the January 25, 2013, letter, which was cosigned by city, state, and federal representatives, including Senator Schumer, Congresswoman Maloney, Speaker Quinn, Public Advocate de Blasio, and Borough President Stringer. MacArthur did not respond.

MacArthur knew, because we warned him, but also through his own political instincts, that raising rents in the middle of a lease would be very unpopular.[11] Yet, as a special servicer, he also had a job to do to get the Stuy Town property in order for a sale. CWCapital could not market the property until the property revenues—meaning rents—were settled. Waiting to the end of all the lease terms would have slowed him down by up to two years, after every lease had been reviewed. Ultimately, the marketing expediency trumped good political judgment, and in mid-May 2013, just as notices were going under doors, MacArthur called me to tell me that CWCapital was going ahead with plans to raise rents on over a thousand tenants in the middle of their leases. "Are you kidding me?" I shouted at him.

This felt like a particularly low blow. The Tenants Association put out a statement calling the move "despicable," "outrageous," and "nothing short of heartless." The Tenants Association invited residents to a press conference on May 15, "to go public with CWCapital's abuse of power." MacArthur had not even given us the courtesy of a response to the letter from a half dozen elected officials—including a US senator—back in January. (When asked about the letter, he claimed not to recall receiving it.) "The sums are astounding, and people are seething," I told *Crain's*. This was well over an acceptable line of adversarial landlord-tenant interactions, but MacArthur seemed unconcerned about the politics or optics of what he was doing. In fact, to us, it felt like he was actually angling for a fight. I was beyond tired of MacArthur and his combative approach.[12]

My phone started ringing as soon as residents had seen MacArthur's letter under their doors. They objected on principle, but also many of them, just as I suspected, had been promised by leasing agents that their rents would stay fixed throughout their leases—regardless of how the *Roberts* case had resolved. I instructed my staff to put me on the phone with a few of the residents, and I heard the stories myself. I spoke to people who had seen the term in their leases that said their rents could *possibly* go up if the *Roberts* case were settled. They had asked leasing agents about what it meant—and were told, in substance, don't worry about that legal mumbo jumbo, we will never raise rents in the middle of a lease term. A number of people sent over the actual emails that they had gotten from leasing agents, with direct evidence of those empty promises. I called MacArthur again and let him know what the leasing agents had been saying to prospective renters, and he brushed it off—reminding me of his favorite fact, which was that many of the complaining tenants had already agreed to pay much higher rents when they moved in.

I again organized a group of elected officials and wrote formally to MacArthur asking that he discontinue these increases because they were based on a fraudulent premise. MacArthur knew he had a PR problem and potentially even a legal one, but sent over a salty response that quoted back to me my own supportive comments about the *Roberts* settlement being "a historic win" for tenants. "It is for this reason that we are surprised that you now object to a material term," MacArthur wrote. Accusing me of manufacturing a fake issue, he continued, "We are concerned by the accusation in your letter that leasing agents made representations that mid-term increases would not be enforced as part of a settlement and court order."[13] And in response to inquiries on its website, CWCapital was explaining that the "recent increases were a result of the *Roberts* settlement." I felt that this was misleading. While it was true that the settlement gave CWCapital the *right* to raise rents to the agreed-upon level in the middle of a lease term, it had no *obligation* to do so. No matter—MacArthur and I saw the world differently, and I had no possibility of persuading him to change his plans on rents.[14]

On May 21, I called Mike Meade and Micah Lasher in the office of the New York State attorney general, Eric Schneiderman, and asked for help addressing this apparent fraud being perpetrated on my neighbors. I was hopeful that an ambitious attorney general, with strong pro-tenant credentials, would be interested in learning how the tenants of the city's largest rental complex had been duped into ignoring key lease terms. Schneiderman's staff conferred internally and asked me to send them direct evidence of the alleged misrepresentations to help them evaluate what to do. I quickly compiled what we had—notes of phone calls and emails from leasing agents saying that rents would not go up mid-lease. I also asked people at public meetings, and on social media to share information with me if something similar had happened to them. One typical email from a leasing agent said, "Management has no intension [*sic*] of increasing the rate of your renewal during the course of the lease term."[15]

Schneiderman's staff summoned MacArthur to a meeting in the attorney general's office at 120 Broadway and presented him with the evidence. While the attorney general's right to intervene in a matter like this was unclear, his political weight was enormous. Nobody wanted to antagonize the attorney general, and certainly not a special servicer working to eliminate litigation and other uncertainties in order to allow for a sale. MacArthur was not happy to be summoned by the attorney general, and he knew I was behind it. In the meeting, MacArthur flashed his frustration with me and directly accused me of manufacturing a bogus issue. After a week of back and forth with MacArthur and his lawyers, the attorney general and CWCapital reached a settlement, which required CWCapital to withdraw the mid-lease increase if a tenant could establish that a leasing agent had in fact made a misrepresentation. On June 13, Fred Knapp, the lawyer who had for years been responsible for the Golub notice program on behalf of Tishman Speyer, sent a community-wide letter that whitewashed the offense. "In a limited number of cases," he said, tenants "claim that they were told" by leasing agents that they would not be subject to a mid-lease increase. He instructed those tenants to fill out an affidavit, which was attached to Knapp's letter, with details of the statements made to them, including emails or other documentation, if available. For those tenants, their rents would stay fixed until the end of their lease.[16]

My office had records of thirty-nine known tenants who said they were told, inaccurately, they wouldn't be getting a mid-lease increase, but I had no idea how many people in the community were going to file an affidavit with CWCapital. "We appreciate this strong step taken by the attorney general. There was clearly an issue here that affected many people and any misrepresentations will now not be able to stand," I said.[17]

Meanwhile, MacArthur continued to refuse to grant rent rebates for lost services from Hurricane Sandy, no matter that many residents still did not have access to their basements and laundry rooms, were complaining about failing intercoms, no longer had access to storage rooms, and in some cases had only a single working elevator in their buildings. Instead, MacArthur publicly accused the Tenants Association of "attempting to use a natural disaster, Hurricane Sandy, for financial gain." CWCapital directly attacked the Tenants Association as "petty and mean spirited" and said that "tenants seek to transform these events into an opportunity to profit."[18]

John Marsh read MacArthur's statement accusing the tenants of profiteering and shot back, "This from the people who are raising residents' rents mid-lease by hundreds, even thousands of dollars, forcing many residents who love living here to disrupt their lives and either pay up or seek another home in a mere two months in a city with a razor-thin vacancy rate. Could anything be more heartless, petty and mean spirited?"

Marsh then emailed MacArthur's statement out to the entire community and encouraged people to read it for themselves and then to write to MacArthur directly. Tell him "that you resent the characterization of tenants as profiteers and find ridiculous the red herring attempt to suggest that legitimate tenant complaints of lost services are meaningless when compared with Sandy's more spectacular damage. Tell him you are tired of his treating the residents of this community like an ATM machine. Tell him you want him to do the right thing and roll back mid-lease rent increases, and compensate residents for the lack of services."[19] In this climate, a deal with CWCapital seemed not only unlikely, but impossible.

12

A NEW START

As the 2013 election drew near, I was spending every spare moment I had focused on my race to be the next speaker of the city council. The speaker is chosen by his or her colleagues in the council, so one way to generate votes in a speaker race is by supporting current council members running for reelection, as well as other candidates whom you expect to become your colleagues. That meant I was spending my time helping council candidates raise money and make contacts. It also meant a fair amount of one-on-one time with them, usually while handing out flyers or door knocking in support of their elections. During the summer of 2013, I made a mad dash around the city along with Genevieve Michel, a member of my staff and a Berkeley, California, native who did not drive, but relished hardball politics. It was hot, my mom was suffering from the effects of another round of chemotherapy, Zoe was in her last trimester of pregnancy with our second child, and Asher was now an energetic two-and-a-half-year-old.

When Zoe's maternity leave ended after Asher was born, my sister-in-law Stacy Segal-Reichlin moved in to help us for a month, and then I took off the rest of the summer to be Asher's primary caregiver. Now, however, I had less time to focus on my family and also on Stuy Town. But as I ran for speaker, the tenants of the community were very much there for me. Marsh and other residents went en masse to districts all around the city as my proxies, to help support my preferred council candidates. For Stuy Town, having me in the role of council speaker would add considerable weight to everything we did. Even MacArthur was intrigued by it, and I got the feeling when we caught up over beers that he was rooting for me, despite our many public differences.

In the early afternoon of September 9, the day before primary election day in New York City, I was planning to drive out to southeastern Queens to make some campaign phone calls side by side with Donovan Richards, a new councilman who was running for reelection. Zoe, now nine months pregnant, called me to say that she thought she might be having some early labor pains. I told her I was going to skip my trip and come right home to be with her. Zoe had scheduled an afternoon of conference calls to wrap up before her maternity leave and pushed me to carry on. "Nothing is happening fast," she told me, reminding me of the twenty-eight hours it had taken for Asher to emerge. "Go finish up. I will too, and I'll see you at home later," she said, much more matter-of-factly than I expected. I questioned this decision, because, as I explained to her, I was about to drive literally as far away from her as I physically could be while still in the jurisdiction of New York City. But she was confident that nothing was happening anytime soon, and so I ended up going. I drove forty-five minutes, past Kennedy Airport, to meet up with Richards in his campaign office. As Richards and I sat together and called voters to remind them about the primary election the next day, I took a break and called Zoe to see if the labor had progressed. Everything was status quo, and she told me to stay, but Richards—who is now the Queens borough president—had overheard the conversation and looked at me half amused, half terrified. "Wait, your wife is in labor *right now*?" he asked incredulously. "You gotta get outta here!" Anxious to be near her even if she didn't think anything was progressing, I thanked him for his understanding, wished him good luck in his primary the next day, and returned to Peter Cooper Village.

Zoe was right, and we had plenty of time. At home, my mother-in-law Maddy Segal, who had come from Boston to help with Asher, had made a meal for me, Zoe, and Zoe's college roommate Katriona MacIver. Everyone other than me was surprisingly calm during dinner, but we went to bed early because we figured we wouldn't be sleeping for a while. By 6:30 a.m.—at my insistence—Zoe and I were on our way to Mount Sinai Hospital. Midafternoon, we became parents for the second time, as Devin Randolph Garodnick was born on primary day, September 10. His middle name is the same as mine, after Gandolfo Riotto, my Sicilian grandfather, who died before I was born. My mom, whose condition was deteriorating, and who was never shy, had dropped some rather strong hints that she would appreciate it if that was the middle name we landed on. The next afternoon, I picked Asher up from day care and brought him to meet his baby brother at the hospital, where he helped me wheel him from the nursery to Zoe's room. In one of my favorite life moments, I watched as Asher tickled the feet of his "baby brudda," as Zoe held a sleeping Devin in her arms. For that moment, there was nothing else happening in the world for me.

My mom was now at the Mary Manning Walsh Home on the Upper East Side, where she was getting physical therapy to build up her strength. To her great disappointment, she was not able to come to Mount Sinai Hospital when Devin was born, but as soon as Zoe was released, we drove right to her. On a warm afternoon on September 12, my dad pushed my mom in a wheelchair out onto York Avenue, and we introduced both of them to their new grandson, right there on 72nd Street. My mom smiled as she carefully held him in her arms.

After two weeks off with Zoe and Devin, I was sleep deprived and shuttling between the campaign circuit and visiting my mom. Every day we hoped that a new chemotherapy treatment would work a miracle, and each time we had moments of hope, and then severe disappointment as her health deteriorated further. Sometimes I made calls to my colleagues from my mother's bedside at the hospital or at home. She seemed to enjoy the distraction and liked to see me at work.

My campaign to be the next speaker was in full swing, and after primary day, most of the future members of the 2014 city council were already known. I had solid support, but my candidacy faced a new potential challenge. In a somewhat surprising turn of events, Bill de Blasio had won the Democratic primary for New York mayor. De Blasio and I had a complicated relationship. I had met him in 2005 when I was first running for the city council, back when he was running for council speaker. He was quite helpful to me and my campaign, and we developed a positive rapport as he spent many hours handing out flyers with me outside the Stuy Town supermarket on 14th Street. I was one of very few truly "independent" votes for speaker, which meant that I did not owe my position, or my vote, to a labor union or party organization, or any other single person. As a result, both de Blasio and his opponent for speaker, Christine Quinn, spent a lot of time offering their guidance, support, and even fundraising help, with the hope that they might earn my vote. When I won my election, to de Blasio's disappointment, I decided to support Quinn to be the council speaker.

Eight years later, de Blasio was the Democratic nominee to be mayor of New York City, and I was a leading candidate to be the city council speaker. Ordinarily, speakers were elected by building a coalition of members from Queens, the Bronx, and Brooklyn, with a few independent Manhattan members, who would cast their votes together as a group. That was how the two most recent speakers, Quinn and Gifford Miller (both of whom had been term-limited from their positions), had won their races, and it was the path that I was trying to take. This year, however, there was a different dynamic—de Blasio was poised to be the first Democratic mayor in twenty years, and there was a group of twenty-two council members who had formed a bloc of their own, hoping to influence the race. This group, which called itself the Progressive Caucus, had not existed before, and there was no way to predict how this new dynamic would play out. The election had come down to me and Melissa Mark-Viverito, the council member from East Harlem, who had endorsed de Blasio for mayor early on and who also was part of the so-called progressive bloc. I had stayed neutral in the mayoral primary, which had included Quinn, former comptroller Bill Thompson, Comptroller John Liu, and Congressman Anthony Weiner.

Now the nominee, de Blasio came to shake hands with voters one afternoon in October at 16th Street and First Avenue, right outside Stuy Town. I had endorsed him for the general election the day after the primary (admittedly not a bold move for a lifelong Democrat) and came out to give him a boost with my constituents. I had very little experience with mayoral politics and was awed by how many people wanted to shake his hand or take a photo. One Stuy Town resident patiently waited her turn, and when she got to the front of the line, asked him, "Do you support the Tenants Association's homeownership plan?" De Blasio pulled me over and good-naturedly said that he needed to consult with his "chief adviser on Stuy Town." During the primary campaign, de Blasio had met with some of the Tenants Association's leaders and, perhaps not realizing the precise ownership structure, remarked, "Over my dead body is any private developer going to get his hands on Stuy Town."[1] Standing on 16th Street that October day, he told my neighbor vaguely that he supported a plan that included long-term affordability, and that together we would figure out the best way to make it happen. Two weeks later, on November 5, 2013, de Blasio won the general election over Republican Joseph Lhota.

When the election for council speaker was still a couple of months away, most New York political players had traveled to the Somos El Futuro Conference in Puerto Rico to network, to gossip, and to build partnerships. The speaker's race was still up for grabs, and I was getting positive signals from the Queens and Bronx leaders. While in San Juan, I also had breakfast with Mayor-elect de Blasio's chief aide Emma Wolfe, who told me that it was highly unlikely that de Blasio would get involved in the race. And yet, in the subsequent weeks, the Democratic county leaders started to be concerned that de Blasio was in fact going to assert himself in support of Mark-Viverito. Once back in New York City, I asked for a meeting with de Blasio to make my case. At Berlin Rosen's offices on Maiden Lane—in the same conference room where we had hosted the Tenants Association's December 2011 community-wide conference call—I urged de Blasio to stay out of it. Giving him political advice that he hadn't asked for, I argued that it was politically perilous for New York City's chief executive to get involved in an internal city council election, because it would mean that he would be held responsible for everything that the city council did. De Blasio was friendly but unpersuaded, expressing his desire to run an "interventionist" administration. "It's what we do," he told me.

On a tense phone call on December 16, leaders of the Queens, Bronx, and Brooklyn county organizations grilled me on which council members from each of their boroughs were truly in my corner. I did my best to give my candid assessment, feeling uncomfortable about my ability to predict what any politician would do at the end of the day. It must have been a satisfactory performance, because after we got off the phone, they decided that they would unite behind my candidacy for speaker and called the council members from their respective boroughs and asked them to support me. Historically, the support of these county leaders was the conclusive route to victory in the speaker's race. I had worked hard to make the case to them that I was honest, steady, and someone they—and my colleagues—could work with, and was on the cusp of victory.

The next evening, as I was about to walk into Brooklyn Borough Hall for an event with the borough's Democratic leader, Frank Seddio, my friend Michael Woloz called me to tell me that de Blasio had started to reach out to council members on behalf of Melissa Mark-Viverito. Maybe I was on the cusp of victory before, but I suddenly found myself in the middle of an all-out war between the mayor-elect and the city's Democratic county leaders. The editorial boards of the *New York Times*, the *Daily News*, and the *New York Post* had all jumped in to support my candidacy. Congressman Joe Crowley, the Democratic leader of Queens, and Assembly member Carl Heastie, Democratic leader of the Bronx (and today speaker of the Assembly), stood firm in support of my candidacy despite the mayor's pressure. They encouraged the council members from their boroughs to stick with me, and on the evening of December 17, *City & State* posted an exclusive story titled "Big 3 County Leaders Appear to Have Votes to Make Garodnick Speaker." It accurately reported that the three Democratic county leaders—Crowley of Queens, Heastie of the Bronx, and Seddio of Brooklyn—had coalesced around my candidacy. The article noted that de Blasio had been personally calling council members in support of Mark-Viverito and that my selection "would debunk the notion that the county leaders are losing political clout."[2]

At around 6 p.m. on December 18, my phone rang in my pocket, and I saw the name "Bill de Blasio" pop up on the screen. "Listen," he said, "I just wanted to let you know that I have started to make some calls for Melissa. I wish you well, but I wanted you to know." I expected he'd call, but it was still hard to hear. "I understand," I said, sounding much more conciliatory than I felt. "We'll see you out on the campaign trail." I hung up, and started to digest a new reality of trying to win a legislative leadership race, with the first Democratic mayor in twenty years working against me.

Later that night, in a back bedroom at lobbyist Joni Yoswein's annual Chanukah latke party in Brooklyn, Seddio, the Brooklyn Democratic leader, and Frank Carone, the law chair, pulled out of the alliance with their Queens and Bronx colleagues and struck a side deal with the mayor to support Mark-Viverito. By the next morning, everything had changed. My allies in Queens and the Bronx suddenly couldn't get our Brooklyn colleagues on the phone, and we knew something was not right. If you added the handful of Brooklyn votes to the twenty-two votes already committed to the progressive bloc, which we expected would defer to the mayor-elect, that would be enough to give Mark-Viverito enough votes to win the speakership. We spent several weeks trying to claw back a few votes but ultimately were unsuccessful. On the day of the vote on January 8, 2014, rather than force a divisive vote in the council that I was bound to lose, I conceded and offered my support to Mark-Viverito. My dad, Zoe (with Devin asleep in a baby carrier strapped to her), and my friend Andrew Ehrlich came to the council chambers to be supportive of me. We tried to set my mom up with a live feed on an iPad from her bed at New York-Presbyterian Hospital, but she didn't have the energy to get the internet to work. Mark-Viverito and I quickly put the campaign behind us. My working relationship with the new mayor, however, was very much in doubt.

It was important to the success of Stuy Town tenants that we have a new mayoral team that was prepared to help, and we were hopeful that things would turn out that way. Days before his inauguration, de Blasio appointed Goldman Sachs's Alicia Glen as his deputy mayor for economic development. Before Goldman, Glen had served as assistant commissioner for housing finance at the Department of Housing Preservation and Development, and in her new role she was charged with creating and implementing de Blasio's affordable-housing program. Glen then recruited James Patchett, the vice president of Goldman's Urban Investment Group, to join her. The hard-charging Glen and more soft-spoken Patchett complemented each other's styles well.

At Goldman, Patchett and Glen sought out deals that made money, but also satisfied important policy goals. Glen called it the "mission-money matrix." They had seen a lot of investment plans cross their desks that sought to buy up portfolios of housing that promised "a lot of churn," which Patchett regarded as a polite way of saying that tenants would be

Figure 12.1. In 2013, I became a candidate to be speaker of the city council in an election among the fifty-one members of the council. After a year of campaigning, on January 8, 2014, I conceded the race at City Hall to Melissa Mark-Viverito, and she and I are pictured here. Photo credit: William Alatriste.

shown the door. Much like what Tishman Speyer had done in Stuy Town, these investors argued that prior owners had not really understood how the system worked. "When someone told us 'we know how to create value,' in these situations it usually meant that 'we know how to kick people out of their rent stabilized homes,'" Patchett said. Glen and Patchett generally saw two types of affordable-housing proposals. On the one hand, there were those with a legitimate goal of preserving affordable housing, which included a commitment to work with the city in exchange for some level of benefit. On the other were plans simply to eliminate rent-stabilized units and to turn them over to the market quickly. "All you had to do was look at the turnover percentage," Patchett explained to me. "Usually for rent-stabilized housing, it is 1 or 2 percent. If they were assuming 5 to 7 percent, you needed to call into question how they were doing that." On February 10, 2014, the day of Mayor de Blasio's State of the City speech at LaGuardia Community College in Queens, Patchett formally joined the administration, and he and I sat in separate parts of the audience as the new mayor reiterated his commitment to preserve or construct nearly two hundred thousand units of affordable housing in ten years and promised to deliver a plan to do so in only two and a half months.[3]

I had told Marsh and Doyle that I was hoping the de Blasio administration would dedicate a specific number of units in his overall housing plan for the preservation of Stuyvesant Town. If it was in the mayor's publicly stated plan, I reasoned, then it would lock in the mayor's support of some form of public intervention.

Four days after de Blasio's first State of the City speech, on Valentine's Day, I brought my mom up to her dialysis treatment, which she now needed four times a week at New York-Presbyterian Hospital. My dad, Zoe, and I took turns sitting with her for hours at a time, powerless to do anything more to help her. I gave her a card while she was plugged into the machine, and she smiled but was too weak to even read it. By early March, her doctors told us that we had no more treatment options for her multiple myeloma, and I was numb from exhaustion and sadness as we brought her home to her Peter Cooper apartment for hospice care. Our family and friends visited with her and consoled each other in the living room. I frantically and emotionally cooked her all of her favorite meals, and she fought through fatigue to give Devin, who was now six months old, his first spoonful of solid food from her bedside. I watched as she held Devin, realizing that she was not going to get to see him grow older. My mom was my guiding light, and her love and support gave me and my dad so much strength. She passed away with my dad at her side in the early morning of March 14, 2014.

As I mourned the loss of my mother, and worried daily about my dad in his Peter Cooper apartment all by himself, I distractedly settled into my third and final term in the council. I got adjusted to my new reality as someone with a higher profile because of the speaker's race, but very much the same role as I had before. My term had four years, and I had no obvious next office to pursue, so I needed to move fast on key issues that I wanted to see resolved. Not only was Stuy Town an open question, but we also had to recalibrate Mayor Bloomberg's failed East Midtown rezoning plan. Just months before the end of Mayor Bloomberg's term, the city council—at my encouragement—had halted his plan to change the zoning in Midtown Manhattan to promote more commercial development. I felt that his plan gave too much of a benefit to real estate developers, without enough certainty to the public on what it was going to get out of the deal. In November 2013, I had recommended to my colleagues that we vote against Bloomberg's plan. Rather than watch it get voted down, Bloomberg withdrew his proposal. In 2014, Stuy Town and East Midtown both needed a rational solution from local government, so despite our rocky start, I was set up to be a natural ally for the brand-new de Blasio administration on both housing and zoning.

I tried to distract myself from my sadness about my mother by throwing myself back into work. Glen, Patchett, and the new housing commissioner, Vicki Been, had worked overtime in the prior two months to put the details on Mayor de Blasio's plan to "build or preserve" 200,000 affordable rental units throughout the five boroughs by 2024. The preservation part of the plan aimed to keep 120,000 units that were already affordable from passing into the unregulated market. While Mayor Bloomberg's affordable-housing plan included a goal of preserving affordable units, de Blasio's aspired to "adopt a more strategic approach to preservation," which included proactively reaching out to building owners, financing partners, governmental agencies, and community groups to identify opportunities. The administration also hoped to design and target its preservation tools in a way that would address the needs of properties that existing housing programs currently were not serving. "The 200,000 units was a big goal, and it was our belief that in order to reach that objective we needed to succeed in some of the biggest ones that had gotten away. Stuy Town and Peter Cooper was *the* example of that," Patchett told me, alluding to the Tishman Speyer deal.[4] Patchett felt that you couldn't in good faith be the "affordable-housing administration" and not successfully deal with Stuy Town.[5]

Along with my chief of staff, Ilona Kramer, I went across the street to City Hall for our first meeting with Glen, Patchett, and Been. Both Stuy Town and East Midtown were on the agenda. Once past the security desk on the mayor's side of City Hall, we settled in the New Amsterdam Conference Room, a small space with a big window facing out onto the desks of a number of mayoral staffers. Glen came in and immediately and sincerely expressed her commitment to helping us get to a favorable result in Stuy Town. I always felt like I had been forcing myself on Mayor Bloomberg and his senior team and had never heard that level of encouragement from a mayoral official.

Glen threw out ideas, in rapid succession, of the various tools that we could use to allow for affordable homeownership. She first suggested an Urban Development Action Area Project, which gives a twenty-year property tax exemption in exchange for the preservation of affordable units, or an HDFC structure with an Article 11 tax exemption, which could preserve unsold rental units for people earning at or below 165 percent of the area's median income (the median in 2014 was $52,996). Glen also wondered aloud if the city could require a sponsor to keep a certain number of units affordable in Stuy Town in exchange for new development rights somewhere else on the East Side. Everything that came out of her mouth came out fast. Not all the ideas were practical, given legal and policy constraints, but everything Glen said was for affordability and pro-tenant.[6]

More the professorial type, Been asked for additional data about the units covered by the *Roberts* case, the current composition of the tenant body, and opportunities for end-loan financing for those who might want to purchase their units.[7] Her questions lightly tapped the brakes on Glen's grand planning, but the point was made: the deputy mayor and housing commissioner were ready to help us find ways to protect the long-term affordability of Stuy Town. Kramer and I left the meeting wildly enthusiastic and immediately got on the phone with Alex Rubin and Meredith Kane to try to track down the information that Been had requested. I also called John Sheehy, who was skeptical of all of the conversations about affordable housing that were happening outside the view of the TA, but who trusted my instincts and relayed all the details to the TA board.

Glen had also asked that the "bankers and lawyers" for the Tenants Association come to City Hall on Monday, April 14, to explain the tenants' plans in detail. I was away in Boston with my in-laws Maddy Segal and Abby Reichlin for Passover. Rubin and Kane attended in person, and I participated by phone while looking out at Fenway Park from my in-laws' guest bedroom. Alex Rubin walked Glen and Patchett through the current capital stack and explained the dynamic with CWCapital. He also expressed his growing concern about Fortress, CWCapital's parent company, coming in and making a quick—and unstoppable—play to buy Stuy Town. Glen listened carefully and agreed to allow us to bring our partners from Brookfield Capital Management in to meet with her and her team a few days later.

Our next parade of visitors to Glen included Brookfield Property Group's Ric Clark, Barry Blattman, and Lowell Baron, who gathered with me, Kane, and Rubin on the steps of City Hall on May 22. We briefly went over to the members' lounge on the city council side of City Hall to talk about our strategy. Blattman and Clark were among Brookfield's most senior officials. Baron, their trusted junior, quickly walked us through the deck that they intended to present to the mayoral team. It was essentially a rehash of our proposal to CWCapital but included the rationale for the TA-Brookfield partnership and details on how we were uniquely positioned to preserve long-term affordability in Stuy Town. The Brookfield team wanted to show Glen that CWCapital was earning enormous fees from property management, special servicing, and perhaps default interest, which were already creating a windfall, as well as the opportunity for another opportunistic buyer at the expense of future affordability of units.[8] They also wanted to warn Glen that by 2024, because of vacancy decontrol, only 23 percent of the property would have rents that would qualify as affordable to low-, moderate-, or middle-income New Yorkers, down from around 55 percent in 2014.[9]

We made our way to the Governor's Room—one of the building's most impressive and distinguished spots—where the governor of New York historically would receive guests when he was in town. We sat at a polished conference table, surrounded by paintings by John Trumbull and steps away from a desk used by George Washington. When Glen came in with Patchett by her side, she got right down to business. "So Brookfield is partnered with the tenants?" she asked. "How does *that* work?" Blattman explained that Brookfield had come in to support the goals that the tenants had so clearly articulated, and that their plan, if effectuated, would preserve thousands of units of affordable housing, both through homeownership and rental subsidies.[10] Blattman showed how 3,430 units would remain as rentals, which would be affordable to low-, moderate-, or middle-income New Yorkers; 1,683 units would be permanently affordable condominiums; and 3,367 units would be sold to current residents at a discount, with a long-term flip tax to maintain stability.[11] As Glen listened, Blattman said that this would allow us to satisfy the tenants' goals of homeownership, the city's goals of maintaining affordability, and CWCapital's need to deliver a full recovery to the CMBS bondholders. Unfortunately,

Blattman explained, CWCapital had been unwilling to engage in discussions with us, and he speculated that because they were earning so much money in fees for special servicing, they were in no rush to make a move.

Glen pushed Blattman for the bottom line. He told her that with CWCapital still acting uncooperative and unreceptive to the TA-Brookfield offer, there were a number of ways that the city could support our effort, like the real estate tax exemptions that were generally part of the city's tool box, as well as relief from transfer and mortgage recording taxes. Blattman also noted that there could be value in transferring seven hundred thousand square feet of unused development rights off the property, as a way not only to create value but also to ensure permanent protections for the open spaces.[12] Glen was open but did not commit herself. After the meeting ended, Glen pulled me aside and said, with urgency, "You need to quickly explore every possible legal and legislative option that we have at our disposal."[13] Glen felt strongly that, even with a well-intentioned partner like Brookfield, the city needed to find its own points of leverage to ensure that we got the best outcome.

I reported back all of these meetings to Marsh and to Sheehy, in his role as the chair of the TA's conversion committee. Everything suddenly seemed to be moving. Not only were senior mayoral officials fully engaged, but in April, the Tenants Association had struck a $30 million deal with CWCapital to settle a flurry of outstanding claims for major capital improvement charges, which had been filed by Tishman Speyer years earlier and had carried over to the new proprietor. The Tenants Association and MacArthur—despite the aggressive public sniping—had also resolved the Hurricane Sandy claims, which delivered a one-month rent reduction of 15 percent to residents of the seventeen buildings that were most affected by Sandy. It was another win for the Tenants Association and for the fifteen hundred residents who had filed claims.

Sheehy observed that MacArthur was checking off outstanding items, and—despite the personal animosity that had developed over the years on both sides—he now had even fewer reasons to avoid working with us. We wondered if CWCapital was on the cusp of starting a sale process in earnest, with or without the tenants.

It was time to put all the conflict behind us, Sheehy thought. He appreciated, in a way that many of our constituents and even some of the most frustrated board members did not, that if the tenants were going to have any level of success, CWCapital was going to be central to the outcome. After all, no matter how angry we were with MacArthur, CWCapital controlled the time, place, and manner of the disposition of the property. Sheehy called me up in mid-April and said, "Dan, we need to find a way to work with these guys." He asked if he could host a breakfast, very informal—and his treat—with tenant leaders, me, and MacArthur. "Naive on my part?" he asked rhetorically in an email to Kane and Rubin. "Regardless of the past nearly four years of inertia, I remain optimistic."[14]

I thought it was a great idea and certainly could do no harm. MacArthur and I had maintained a regular channel of communication over the years, regardless of the level of hostility we were projecting to each other, both publicly and in formal private meetings. We generally met quietly at Petite Abeille on 20th Street, and over cold Stellas we covered subjects ranging from local politics to Stuy Town, to some details about each other's personal lives. No matter the tensions of 2012 and 2013, it was important that we find a way to work together. Sheehy reached out to MacArthur, who also liked the idea of connecting with the broader group. We set our first meeting over breakfast at a local Gramercy Park restaurant on May 14.

With MacArthur and Andy Kane representing CWCapital on that Wednesday in mid-May, Doyle, Marsh, Steinberg, Sheehy, and I sat around a round table and, over eggs and toast, talked about the status of Stuy Town. So much tension had built up over years of battling each other, publicly and privately, but as we sat casually over breakfast, it had a familiar and even comfortable feeling, as if everyone were just tired of fighting. In reality, as Sheehy anticipated, CWCapital was opening up to the real estate market. MacArthur had called me the day before to advise me that CWCapital was planning on June 13 to do a so-called UCC foreclosure of the mezzanine loans, which he called a "clean-up action."[15] Over breakfast, he gave us a road map of what to expect. Since there had been a default, and CWCapital owned some of the mezzanine loans, under a UCC foreclosure federal law allowed CWCapital to foreclose the interests of the junior lenders in the deal without going to court. Assuming that the other mezzanine lenders (or others) were unwilling to pay the full amount of the $3 billion first mortgage, by foreclosing CWCapital would formally be in control. MacArthur explained to us that in the

UCC foreclosure sale, CWCapital would open its doors to the real estate market to inspect the property data, and that if parties like Brookfield wanted access, they would need to sign a confidentiality waiver to see the information.

Sheehy and Marsh asked MacArthur what his plans were *after* the foreclosure. MacArthur anticipated the question, of course, and explained that the next steps were uncertain, both as to form and timing. Sharing details with us for the very first time, he said that he had two different options: conduct a closed auction, or solicit public bids. He emphasized that he would do whatever he needed to in order to enhance the value to his bondholders. "Stay alert," he said. "It could happen later in 2014." I asked whether Fortress, CWCapital's parent company, might find a way to emerge as the owner of Stuy Town. After all, public reports in the spring of 2014 were saying that Fortress had designs on the property and that CWCapital "could be poised to give parent company Fortress the inside track." After all the work we had put into this, we worried that CWCapital would simply sell the property to Fortress, its own parent company, at a discount, so long as the senior bondholders got paid what they were owed. Real estate experts speculated that Fortress could borrow up to $2 billion from Freddie Mac to do exactly that.[16] MacArthur seemed legitimately to not know what Fortress would do. But, while he acknowledged that anything was possible, he did not think that Fortress would attempt to take control through the foreclosure on June 13. "They will likely be a participant in the next step," he said. "Then again, they don't tell me everything." Around the table over breakfast, I felt the frozen positions of the past two years begin to thaw.[17]

Unfortunately, MacArthur's hostility to Brookfield was still palpable, and he now told us directly that the tenants had made a mistake by picking a partner. He explained that if Brookfield was not the high bidder in any process, they would not win, regardless of their partnership with the tenants. "Stay flexible, be open," he told us. He repeated what he had said to me a year earlier—this time more politely: that because of our partnership with Brookfield, when the TA spoke about quality-of-life issues, mid-lease rent increases, or even Hurricane Sandy, CWCapital perceived it as Brookfield speaking, which was "not helpful." MacArthur also encouraged us to explore a variety of ways to solve our affordable-housing goals, such as limiting our affordability program to only certain sections of the property.

He also suggested that if we were to do a condominium, we might want to do it in Peter Cooper but keep Stuy Town as a rental property. Both were terrible ideas for us, because we could not be perceived as favoring certain sections of the property over others, but MacArthur was offering this as friendly advice in the mode of transparency that I favored. "That's really not possible," I said, perhaps too aggressively. Sheehy jumped in to keep me and MacArthur from turning this friendly conversation into an argument. "Andrew, most importantly, we want you to view the Tenants Association as an ally and as a resource to accomplish what is best for the property." MacArthur looked at me and said, "Just keep an open mind on this stuff."

I watched Doyle, Steinberg, and Marsh's faces as they considered how they would explain to their neighbors that they had let Peter Cooper residents become homeowners while leaving Stuy Town as renters. "Is he kidding? That's never going to happen," I said to the group as we left the restaurant and stood in front of Gramercy Park. "We can't convert only a small part of the property—particularly the part of the community where the local councilman happens to live. They'd string me up in the Oval by my fingernails." There was no disagreement among our small group, but we were very happy that MacArthur was suddenly talking to us, substantively, about the future.

A few hours after our breakfast, however, Bloomberg News reported that the private equity firm Fortress was seeking financing to make a $4.7 billion bid for Stuy Town. It ran directly counter to what MacArthur had said to us only hours earlier. "Just saw this and although not surprised am shell shocked nonetheless," Marsh wrote in an email. While MacArthur had emphasized to us over breakfast that his foreclosure action was just "clean-up," Bagli's *Times* story—which broke, clearly not coincidentally, just hours after our breakfast—explained that a foreclosure would start the process of putting the property up for sale, which "is again likely to attract many buyers." Bagli quoted Richard LeFrak, a billionaire real estate executive who bid for the property in 2006: "I'll definitely take a look at it again. It's still a great asset. It may drive the same feeding frenzy, but it still has all the blemishes it had before." The *Times* story also teed up the importance of Stuy Town for the new mayor, and his goal to make New York a more affordable place to live. "Stuy Town and Peter Cooper Village are critical bulwarks of affordability for middle class families," Deputy Mayor Glen said. "Our housing plan emphasizes preservation, and with so many affordable units at risk in these developments, the stakes are too high to be hands off."[18]

I called James Patchett in the deputy mayor's office that afternoon, shaking with irritation. I told him about our productive breakfast, and now, our sudden fear that we had gotten played by MacArthur. "We need the mayor to call Michael Novogratz at Fortress directly and find a way to slow this down," I said to Patchett, my voice trembling. "This is urgent!" Nine years earlier I had been through a process where MetLife, without the mayor raising a finger, had pursued a quick sale. MacArthur was now saying one thing, with press reports another. I had spent years distrusting MacArthur and did not know whether he was giving us accurate information. Either way, I was terrified that, after years of work, this opportunity was about to slip away again.[19]

Patchett and Glen moved fast. Glen summoned MacArthur and Kane to City Hall on May 29, two weeks before the scheduled foreclosure, to lay out what was really going on. MacArthur started to explain the highly complex situation to her, and CWCapital's role in the resolution. Before he got far, Glen interrupted. "I came from Goldman Sachs, OK? I get it," she said. MacArthur tried to protest, because he knew that even people in the special servicing industry did not really understand the dynamic in Stuy Town, but Glen's message was clear. She wanted CWCapital's explicit commitment that nothing unexpected—like a quick sale to Fortress—would happen at the foreclosure sale. Glen pushed to get CWCapital to enter into a formal agreement with the city, committing them to negotiate the terms of a long-term affordability plan prior to any sale of the property. "You basically have two paths," Glen said. "Let's work together, stay positive, and you save money. Or, this becomes a negative experience, you fight it out with every elected official, and have to spend money on litigation." MacArthur again said that he was pretty sure that Fortress would not bid in the auction on June 13. Glen asked him for a letter confirming this, and CWCapital agreed to provide some documentation. Patchett described the meeting to me as "surprisingly productive."[20]

MacArthur found it less productive. He was not surprised by Glen's activist posture, based on the tenor of the campaign that de Blasio had run.[21] During the primary election, MacArthur had reached out to all the mayoral candidates, except de Blasio—whom he perceived to have little to no chance of winning—to introduce himself and to explain his firm's role in Stuy Town. Comptroller Bill Thompson, whom MacArthur regarded as one of the most level-headed of the group of candidates, was adamant about the need for the city's involvement in whatever path CWCapital chose. "'The city was not involved last time, but it certainly will be this time. I guarantee it,'" Thompson told him.[22] MacArthur's takeaway from these 2013 meetings was that once one of these Democrats stepped in, the city was surely going to be a major factor in the transaction. CWCapital had not moved fast enough to avoid this new political dynamic, and now MacArthur was facing the unpleasant reality of progressive Democrats in City Hall. MacArthur needed to respond to Glen but also wanted a way to push back against her position. The city, after all, did not have any legal rights in this transaction, but as Glen had pointed out, going up against the mayor involved risks. MacArthur resolved that he would not walk back into City Hall without being able to show Glen that he had the power to do whatever he wanted to do without any involvement from her.[23]

But MacArthur had other problems he had to address first. The foreclosure action was generating far more interest than anyone had expected. Centerbridge had notified CWCapital that it was planning to purchase the Government of Singapore's mezzanine position—initially valued at $575 million—in the Stuy Town debt. If Singapore were to sell its position to Centerbridge, Centerbridge could try to take control of the property through the foreclosure process, and might even try to trigger a bankruptcy. The Related Companies, Blackstone, Centerbridge, and others had signed confidentiality agreements, which gave them the right to visit CWCapital's so-called online data room to view the financials of the property. CWCapital was worried that one or more of these real estate tycoons were plotting something to take control of the process away from CWCapital.[24]

Rather than take the risk of opening this process up through a foreclosure sale, MacArthur decided he would cancel the foreclosure altogether. He had another option for taking title, called a "deed in lieu of foreclosure." This mechanism was the equivalent of a typical first mortgage foreclosure. In that case, CWCapital would take over the title to the property and extinguish all of the mezzanine loans.[25] MacArthur decided it was worth it, but he knew he needed to move fast, because if Centerbridge got wind of the fact that CWCapital was about to take this action—and wipe out Centerbridge's interests entirely—they likely would go to court to keep him from making the deed transfer.

In the early morning of June 5, 2014, MacArthur quietly met his personal assistant Janice Duffy, a notary, in the basement of 521 East 20th Street in Peter Cooper. He sat down at a desk, with the official conveyance documents that his lawyers had prepared in front of him. Notably, CWCapital was on both sides of this transaction—as both the "buyer" and the "seller" were CWCapital. The seller's papers (on behalf of the senior mezzanine lenders) were signed by MacArthur, and the buying entities (on behalf of the first mortgage) were signed by CWCapital's president, David Iannarone. With MacArthur's signature, and Duffy's notarization, Stuy Town was officially transferred from Tishman Speyer to CWCapital without anyone else even watching. It was the second time in history that the property was sold, and this time nobody even realized it was happening. "You just sold Stuy Town!" MacArthur said to Duffy. MacArthur had arranged for a member of CWCapital's staff to be standing at the window of the New York City Department of Finance when it opened with a check for $116.6 million, which represented the amount of transfer taxes that were due to the city.[26]

The Department of Finance clerk looked down at the enormous check and looked up at the staffer quizzically. He politely excused himself and disappeared into the back room for an extended period, and eventually came back with a stamped copy acknowledging receipt, making the transfer official. The *Real Deal* later reported that the transfer valued the property at $4.4 billion—Stuyvesant Town at $3.3 billion and Peter Cooper Village at $1.1 billion. All told, CWCapital paid $134 million in transfer taxes, with $116.6 million going to the city and $17.8 million to the state. The June 13 auction, no longer relevant, was canceled. When MacArthur called me to tell me what had happened, I was certain that I did not understand all the implications but was relieved that it seemingly eliminated the possibility of a quick side deal with Fortress—at least for now.[27]

MacArthur now turned back to the issue of City Hall. On June 11, MacArthur wrote a conciliatory letter to Glen and proposed a sixty-day period to explore options that could satisfy the city's policy objectives, while allowing CWCapital to deliver a full recovery to its bondholders. He expressed CWCapital's hope "to remain engaged" with Glen's team toward a "collaborative outcome," and retained a variety of professionals to help with that goal. MacArthur brought on John Kelly and Deborah Van Amerongen of Nixon Peabody, Marty Siroka of Katten Muchin Rosenman, and Jay Neveloff and Paul Selver from Kramer Levin Naftalis & Frankel. Together, they represented some of the city's most talented lawyers on matters of land use, zoning, government regulation of housing, and conversion from rentals to homeownership.[28]

Meanwhile, the Tenants Association and I had already scheduled a rally on the steps of City Hall for June 13, the original date of the foreclosure. Even though the foreclosure was off, we decided to proceed with the event. Marsh had organized neighbors to show up for the rally, which was advertised as a way to "Stop Predators from Stealing Our Community (Again!)." On a day of heavy rain, TA-sponsored school buses left Stuy Town at Marsh's direction, and two hundred of our neighbors came down to City Hall. The mostly older group moved slowly off the buses, with umbrellas drawn. We saw them line up at the security gate, getting drenched, and they kept coming and coming. Once all the tenants made it through security, we gathered on the steps—to call for fairness for Stuy Town tenants. We were joined by Senator Schumer, Congresswoman Maloney, state senator Hoylman, Assemblyman Kavanagh, and newly elected comptroller Scott Stringer. Pointing to the seniors behind me, I called out, "To the sharks in the waters, these are the people that you're looking to push out of their homes. These are the parents, the grandparents, the hardworking New Yorkers of this city. And guess what? They're not afraid of you." I was followed by Senator Schumer and each of the elected officials, making the point that Stuy Town deserved to be free of those predatory practices that had been designed to push rent-stabilized tenants out of their apartments. And speaker after speaker reiterated the point that we were counting on the mayor's support. Hoylman urged government intervention to avoid the loss of more affordable housing. He also pointed out that "the 25,000 resident population of Stuy Town–Peter Cooper is larger than many cities in New York. Imagine the response if, say, Kingston or Glens Falls were being sold off to real estate investors!"[29]

Jen Shykula, our organizer from Berlin Rosen, could barely contain her excitement about what was happening. "Seeing the Stuy Town and Peter Cooper tenants lining up, coming with walkers—it was the face of middle-class New York fighting for their homes. It was huge. This is an extraordinary community, important for the city of New York, and very visible," she recalled. James Patchett, Glen's chief of staff, had stood under the portico of City Hall listening to the speeches. I called him later. "What did you think of the press conference?" I asked. Patchett paused, and circumspectly said he thought it went well. Patchett had an understated style but sounded even more reserved than normal, so I asked him why. Then he added, "You could have been a little nicer to the mayor, I thought." Patchett did not like that we were needling the mayor to do more and laying the entire issue on the doorstep of his administration, when in reality we both knew that there was very little he had the power to do. "It was less 'we can do it together' and more 'we want the mayor to act,'" Patchett said.

"Tell you what," I said. "When the mayor actually does something praiseworthy here, I promise to praise him."[30]

Patchett and I agreed that CWCapital's deed in lieu transfer gave us time to prepare to engage directly with MacArthur. It also, importantly, gave us more of an opportunity to build political support for our case. The mayor's comments in response to our press conference were very helpful. "We're very clear that our job is to ensure affordability at Stuy Town going forward. And that is an area that is one of the biggest concentrations of affordable housing in the city. The city did not play the role it should have in the past decade in terms of defending this affordable housing. We are actively engaged with CWCapital," he said. The city is "in a strong position," but there's "a lot of work to do." Despite the fact that the mayor was posturing (because in reality, we were not in such a strong position), he was now using his bully pulpit in exactly the manner I had hoped for. "This eliminates the circus that could have unfolded at a mezzanine foreclosure sale," I told Bloomberg News for a wrap-up article on the transfer of title. "It is the right step that will give time for a more considered process that can protect not only the bondholders, but also the tenants and the city."[31]

On June 27, a couple of weeks after the canceled foreclosure, Kevin Fullington, who ran the government relations group of the law firm Herrick

Feinstein, called me to tell me that his firm had been retained by "an entity"—the name of which he did not want to share until he met with me—that had bought most of Singapore (GIC's) mezzanine debt. He said that his clients had been hoping to stop the foreclosure and had planned to work with the tenants on a long-term affordability plan. This was interesting to me, but I had also heard that line before from other aspiring owners of Stuy Town. I shared Fullington's comments with Rubin, who speculated that the buyers of GIC's debt likely were Related or Centerbridge. I called my friend Jay Kriegel at Related to ask what they were hearing about Stuy Town. Kriegel said only that they would be interested in putting in a bid at the auction. It wasn't them.

Fullington pulled back the curtain on July 2 and revealed his client to me in my district office, when he showed up with Vivek Melwani, a senior managing director of Centerbridge. I had met Melwani one year earlier at the New York City Half Marathon. I was running with my friend Shai Waisman, who knew Melwani, and when they saw each other, we ended up running about half the race together. He told me, as we ran down the West Side Highway on that March morning in 2013, that he worked at a firm called Centerbridge. At the time, I had very little familiarity with it and did not pay it much mind. Now in my office, in a suit, Melwani explained that Centerbridge had bought the GIC debt and was going to sue CWCapital the next day, just before the July 4 weekend, for breach of the Stuy Town intercreditor agreement. He told me that before CWCapital had canceled the foreclosure, Centerbridge had notified them that it was going to buy the loans in Mezzanine 1–3 from CWCapital on May 29 and that it had also planned to buy Mezzanine 4–9 from GIC. Its goal, he told me, had been to call off the foreclosure sale, engage with tenants and the city, and come up with a workable plan good for all interested parties.

Melwani said that CWCapital was making a deliberate miscalculation of what was owed to the bondholders. In reality, he claimed, Stuy Town was worth over $5 billion—$1.5 billion more than the $3.45 billion that was technically owed on its senior loan. The difference, he said, was properly owed to the other junior lenders, which now included Centerbridge in the shoes of GIC. Had Stuyvesant Town been sold at market value, Centerbridge intended to argue in court, more than $1 billion would have been left over to repay junior investors. Melwani and I resolved to stay in touch as the process unfolded.[32]

Centerbridge sued CWCapital on July 3, claiming that it had been fraudulently cheated out of hundreds of millions of dollars. In response, CWCapital argued that it was well within its rights to conduct the transfer and argued that Centerbridge "does not seek to recoup any alleged loss, but rather to earn more than $1 billion in profit on a highly speculative investment in litigation that it made with eyes wide open." This development was going to muddy the waters, for sure. We had started having productive conversations with MacArthur about the future, and now Centerbridge was creating new complications. Some TA board members viewed this lawsuit as just another obstacle to our ability to wrap this all up. "Centerbridge is going to become the new *Roberts* excuse," Sheehy observed, dejectedly.[33]

Regardless of the new wrinkle, MacArthur continued to surprise us by how open he was being. Over another breakfast on July 9, MacArthur walked us through the current dynamic, from his perspective. He said that he expected to be able to market the property later in 2014, and continued to be willing to do a homeownership plan that included Peter Cooper Village, but not Stuyvesant Town. MacArthur said that he was planning on working out the details of an affordability plan but noted that Glen's team was quietly expressing its preference for a *rental-only* solution, with no opportunity for homeownership. Frustrated, Sheehy started to question why the tenants or CWCapital were even bothering to talk to City Hall if the mayor did not support our conversion plan.

13

THE MAYOR COMES OVER FOR CANNOLI

As encouraged as we were by Mayor de Blasio's public comments about Stuy Town, we continued to hear privately from MacArthur that the de Blasio administration was now actively opposed to our plan of home-ownership. While Patchett had been expressing concern to me, he had not mentioned outright opposition. It was unclear where the truth lay, but it was obvious that we had work to do to persuade the mayor and his team that our plan made the most sense for the city.

In 2006, Mayor Bloomberg had stayed on the sidelines, signaling to MetLife and prospective bidders that this was simply a private transaction with no role for the city to play. For us to be successful in this effort, it was important that de Blasio chart a different course. I called Emma Wolfe, one of the mayor's senior advisers, and explained why it was important to us—and I thought, to him—for the new mayor to do something in support of the tenants in a more public way. De Blasio, after all, wanted to be known for his success in advancing the cause of affordable housing.

While Stuy Town was not explicitly referenced in his affordable-housing plan, I wanted the new mayor to connect his initiative with the plight of Stuy Town, and our fight to save the largest middle-class rental property in America. Wolfe was a veteran strategist who understood the value in showing the tenants that the mayor was on their side. She and I went back and forth about what he could say and when. I suggested that perhaps he just show up in the community and demonstrate his support just by being there. "Maybe he wants to come over to my apartment for a visit?" I asked, partially joking. "You know we could set up a small meeting with tenant leaders, he could be in and out quickly, and his presence would speak volumes." Wolfe laughed. "I actually love that," she said, but needed to "run the traps" to get internal approval. Days later, to my surprise, the mayor had accepted my invitation, and we started the process of hosting our special guest in my Peter Cooper Village apartment.

With only six months under his belt, Mayor de Blasio was already celebrating the financing of 8,700 units of affordable housing. His administration had put $250 million toward the creation of 2,600 new units and the preservation of another 6,140. However, Housing Commissioner Vicki Been was publicly warning that the continuing deregulation of rent-stabilized units, still allowed by state law, would undermine the city's desire to preserve affordable housing. "The tide of deregulation needs to stop," Been told *Crain's*, warning that entire complexes with rent-regulated units, such as Stuy Town and Peter Cooper, could fall out of the system because of mechanisms like vacancy decontrol. To stop the bleeding, she argued, the city needed New York State legislators to pass urgent reform. Commissioner Been had tools, including tax incentives, to preserve existing affordable units like those in Stuy Town, but they couldn't solve all the problems all the time. This was one of the reasons the Tenants Association and I were so energized by a home-ownership plan, which could add another tactic to preserve affordable housing. With little help from the city, we could, on our own, solve a lot of the questions of long-term affordability by giving current residents and future middle-class New Yorkers a chance to become homeowners. Regardless of how it was framed—rental or homeownership—having a long-term affordability plan in Stuy Town fit perfectly into Mayor de

Blasio's housing agenda, and we were going to make that point directly to him while he was sitting in my living room.[1]

James Patchett briefed de Blasio in the SUV as they drove from City Hall up to Peter Cooper. Patchett walked the mayor through the dynamic with CWCapital and its parent, Fortress; Centerbridge's newly filed litigation; as well as the tenants' plan for homeownership with long-term affordability built in. Patchett impressed upon the mayor how little legal leverage the city and the tenants actually had in the transaction. Since the property was not currently subject to a regulatory agreement, and CWCapital was not yet asking for any special tax benefits, Patchett felt that the mayor's ability to influence the outcome was limited to his bully pulpit, and wanted him to use it carefully. "Once we've played that card, we've played it," he said.[2]

Tenant leaders like Marsh, Doyle, Sheehy, Steinberg, Fink, as well as elected officials, milled about my Peter Cooper apartment as we waited for the mayor to arrive at 3 p.m. on July 15. Government staffers and NYPD officers had already cleared the way. We had picked up some cannoli from Veniero's, a beloved neighborhood Italian pastry shop, and put them on the dining room table. Not overly impressed by the scene that was about to unfold in her apartment, Zoe, as she ran off to work that morning, had made me promise only that the place would be clean for our guests. We got a three-minute warning as the mayor was heading upstairs, and I waited at my door for him to come out of the elevator. I watched as de Blasio's long frame moved down the hallway, with Patchett at his side. The mayor gave me an awkward bear hug (he is significantly taller than me) and made his way through the crowded room, shaking hands with the TA leaders. He gave an embrace to the newly elected borough president Gale Brewer, Assemblyman Kavanagh, and Senator Hoylman, who were all present. As was carefully choreographed, he ended up next to me on the couch.

It was highly unusual for a sitting mayor to pay a visit to the home of a member of the city council. It was also less than six months after he had struck a deal to deprive me of the votes to become the council speaker. This dynamic was so sensitive that the mayor's press office strongly objected to any mention of the mayor being in my apartment in his daily press materials. Perhaps they were worried about what any of us might say publicly, or about opening the floodgates to similar invitations from my city council

Figure 13.1. On July 15, 2014, Mayor Bill de Blasio visited my Peter Cooper apartment to meet with Tenants Association leaders and elected officials to talk about how the city could support the tenants' goals for affordable housing. TA board members Soni Fink, Susan Steinberg, and John Marsh listen as the mayor and I discuss the tenants' priorities. Photo credit: William Alatriste.

colleagues. I had assured Emma Wolfe that I would not allow this meeting to go awry on my watch. It was important to all of us that it go well. The optics of a concerned mayor making a personal visit to Stuy Town would surely play well for the "affordable-housing mayor," and it made the point that the center of decision making about the future ran right through the Tenants Association, in my apartment.

After a round of introductions, I took the mayor through the state of play and why we appreciated that he was engaging in a way that his predecessor had not. I said that the tenants stood ready to fight back against any efforts to intimidate and harass rent-stabilized tenants out of their homes, as had been done in the 2006 Tishman Speyer deal. De Blasio nodded earnestly as I spoke. Now that *Roberts* had been settled and CWCapital had taken control, we had not only a plan but a capital partner. What we really needed now was the mayor's direct engagement and support. I turned the meeting over to Marsh, who presented the mayor a signed copy of Charles Bagli's recently published book about the Stuy Town deal, aptly called *Other People's Money*, as a reminder of how far we had come. Marsh made the case for the Tenants Association's partnership with Brookfield and why allowing tenants to own their apartments helped to maximize long-term affordability in our community. Brewer, Hoylman, and Kavanagh reiterated their support for the Tenants Association and its plan.

Mayor de Blasio listened patiently and then responded that he intended to be deeply involved in this transaction and would like to find ways to preserve the housing as affordable for the longest possible term. He gently pushed back, however, against the tenants' condo plan, stating that he had a bias toward rental—rather than homeownership—and was only concerned about the low-rent units in the community. "I will not allow the city to support anything that generates windfall profits," he said.[3] That was mostly good news for us. We were not for windfall profits, either—and we hoped that when the mayor's team dug into it, they would find that homeownership was in fact a viable and positive outcome. Doyle was enthusiastic about the visit. It was truly remarkable that the mayor of New York City was in my living room committing to be deeply involved in the preservation of affordable housing in Stuy Town. "This was a good day," Doyle told me after. I agreed—the mayor's support was critical and gave us real strength.

Crotty saw the news about the mayor's visit and called me up. "Cute, Dan. Cute. Just remember nobody gives two fucks about middle-class white people in Manhattan." His colorful style notwithstanding, he had a point: helping "middle-class white people" in Stuy Town was not necessarily good politics for the mayor. Crotty was right that if we were ultimately going to be successful, we needed to remind everyone that we were part of a coalition that connected Stuy Town to the broader housing movement. Doyle and Marsh were active participants in Tenants PAC, and I had a strong partnership with like-minded elected officials such as my council colleagues Ritchie Torres of the Bronx and Jumaane Williams of Brooklyn, as well as Senator Liz Krueger and Assemblyman Kavanagh, to increase tenant protections citywide. I had authored and passed a bill that, for the first time, gave New York City tenants a right to sue their landlords for harassment, and another to improve transparency of so-called tenant blacklists, which were too often being used to keep honest people from renting apartments.

Now Stuy Town was the poster child for over-leveraged housing, which was affecting tenants citywide, and it was more important than ever to make a connection between the predatory behavior in Stuy Town and similar threats that some of my colleagues were already battling citywide. I asked Torres and Williams if we should consider forming a citywide coalition to push back against predatory acts in housing. Williams formerly had been a tenant advocate and currently chaired the council's housing committee, and Torres was a sharp, newly elected councilman who had seen many units in his own district fall victim to predatory acts by landlords. Both council members had been challenging practices like the ones I had seen in Stuy Town, so together we decided to give more formal structure to our advocacy. Williams, who now is the city's elected public advocate, next in line to the mayoralty, and Torres, now a member of Congress, both embraced the opportunity to expand their reach in defense of tenants. The three of us formed a citywide coalition that we called the Coalition Against Predatory Equity in Housing. Taking a page out of the Stuy Town tenants' book, we organized around four key principles that would protect people from over-leveraged deals.

One core principle was getting the New York City and state pension funds to commit to not doing harm to our city's—or any other city's—affordable-housing stock. The California and Florida pension funds had lost a fortune—along with their credibility in Stuy Town—as their dollars went to support a plan that took aim at middle-class New Yorkers. The pensioners of those two states had invested and lost nearly $1 billion in the Tishman Speyer deal. We also asked that the city take steps to ensure that there would be never be tax breaks or subsidies offered in a deal that would enable or speed up the reduction of affordable housing. And, together, we committed to finding legislative opportunities that would assist tenants in over-leveraged buildings.

Perhaps our most important principle where Stuy Town was concerned was demanding that Fannie Mae and Freddie Mac, the biggest lenders in the 2006 Stuy Town deal, state publicly that they would not lend money in any residential housing deal that put affordable housing at risk. Keeping Fannie and Freddie on the sidelines in Stuy Town would create enormous leverage for us and might prevent a quick sale to Fortress or anyone else without our knowing about it. Congresswoman Maloney and Senator Schumer had each been leading the criticism of Fannie and Freddie for years, arguing that their mission should not include evicting rent-stabilized tenants. In May, Maloney reintroduced legislation that would sharply curtail Fannie and Freddie's ability to invest in transactions that jeopardized affordable housing. Deputy Mayor Glen lent her voice to this point as well, directly calling Mel Watt, the director of the Federal Housing Finance Agency, which supervises Fannie Mae and Freddie Mac, to argue that these agencies simply should not participate in any Stuy Town deal that did not have the support of the city and the tenants.[4]

Over months, we got organized, made demands, and drew others to our cause. Over fifty elected officials and five members of Congress joined our coalition. We followed our activism with a million-dollar initiative in the city budget called Stabilizing NYC, which was designed to support tenants in complexes that had been targeted by predatory equity.[5] Council member Torres and I also introduced—and later passed—legislation that would create a city "watch list" for buildings that had been purchased at a price that was disproportionately high to the buildings' income.

Then, in the summer of 2014, we got a huge boost in our fight. Mel Watt was already aware of the discussions taking place between the tenants, the city, and the potential purchasers of Stuy Town. His agencies had been approached by prospective lenders about refinancing the existing debt. In response to our advocacy, Watt sent a letter to me and Congresswoman Maloney, stating that Fannie and Freddie "would not consider an application for financing until the affordability issues have been resolved to the satisfaction of both the City of New York and the tenants' organization." Watt affirmed that he was closely monitoring any requests regarding Stuy Town and that his staff was going to keep him well briefed.[6]

When I got the letter, I jumped up with excitement. "This is amazing," I hollered to Genevieve Michel as I ran it over to her in our 250 Broadway office. I called Marsh, Steinberg, and Sheehy and circulated the letter to our entire professional team. This was going to help cut off the oxygen from another predatory deal. Someone in Washington had heard our demand, and it was the first point of actual leverage that the tenants had achieved in Stuy Town in ten years. Our persistent protests had yielded a critical bargaining chip: any potential bidder going forward without Fannie and Freddie would face a higher cost of capital, effectively

Figure 13.2. Congresswoman Carolyn Maloney and Senator Chuck Schumer secured Fannie Mae and Freddie Mac's commitment not to lend in any deal that did not have the support of the tenants and the city. They conferred at our City Hall press conference in the pouring rain on June 13, 2014. Photo credit: Daniel Garodnick.

lowering CWCapital's potential sale price.[7] As a result, a deal with the tenants could potentially result in a higher sale price than to anyone else. This was a major turning point for us.

Despite John Sheehy's deep commitment to the Tenants Association and its efforts to deliver a homeownership opportunity for middle-class people, he was himself a person of means. After starting his career as an assistant district attorney, he subsequently earned enough in private practice not only to afford a market-rate three-bedroom unit in Peter Cooper Village, but also to purchase a second home in East Hampton. Sheehy spent a significant time in the Hamptons during the summer but stayed in daily contact with me by email. His next-door neighbor there was a man named A. J. Agarwal, a senior managing director in the real estate division at the Blackstone Group, a private equity and financial services firm based in New York City. Sheehy didn't know Agarwal well but suspected that Blackstone could be of some value to the Tenants Association if our partnership with Brookfield didn't work out. Sheehy had told me that he would try to strike up a conversation with Agarwal if he saw an opportunity during the summer, and I encouraged it. The Sheehy and Agarwal properties were at the end of a cul-de-sac, and their driveways were right next to each other. On Wednesday afternoon, August 20, 2014, Sheehy was out checking his mail when Agarwal and his wife pulled into their driveway. After some brief small talk, Sheehy said to him, optimistically: "By the way, would you guys at Blackstone have any interest in Peter Cooper Stuyvesant Town?"

"Yeah, we would," Agarwal responded. "Why?"[8]

Unknown to Sheehy, Blackstone already had been tracking Stuyvesant Town for over a decade, and it had even considered participating in CWCapital's June 2014 foreclosure, before MacArthur had called it off. In the end, Blackstone had decided against it because it felt that there were too many unresolved issues surrounding the property and was worried about the poisonous political environment that existed for those perceived to be in opposition to the tenants. Internally, Blackstone executives had reasoned that if they were going to come in, they wanted to be welcomed with open arms by the tenants and the city. They did not feel like that was possible in a sixty-day UCC foreclosure time frame. However, noting the strong financial performance of the property, which they believed was largely a function of the fact that it was a great piece of real estate in a very tight market, their interest had been piqued.[9]

Sheehy told Agarwal that he happened to have an apartment in Peter Cooper Village, was a member of the Tenants Association board, and that we had been trying, without success, to work with CWCapital in support of a plan. Agarwal told Sheehy that he had been following the situation. "We definitely would have interest," he said. Sheehy resolved to introduce him to me right after Labor Day, to see if we could explore the idea further. As the Agarwal family proceeded up their driveway, Sheehy smiled. The Tenants Association already had a partner in Brookfield, but they had repeatedly hit a wall with CWCapital. At some point, Sheehy felt that introducing Blackstone to the mix could be exactly the way to shake CWCapital out of its complacency.[10]

The Blackstone Group had already been picking up residential units throughout the country. The firm's money came in significant part from public pension funds, many of whom—as a result of the debacle in Stuy Town—had sworn off investments in ventures that jeopardized affordable housing. Seeing these trends, Blackstone had created a "Core Plus" fund for some of these more sensitive investors. The fund had no fixed end date and enabled Blackstone to acquire properties for investors who wanted to hold them for a long time, with low debt, and a goal of long-term capital appreciation. This was in stark contrast to the short-term, high-return money that Tishman Speyer had used in 2006. The Core Plus strategy was emerging at other firms, too. After the collapse of the housing market—and high-profile defaults like Stuy Town—investors were looking for less flashy investments. "After the credit crisis, capital was taking more boring bets, and had muted expectation returns. People were more cautious," explained Doug Harmon, a real estate broker who had been following Stuy Town since 2006.[11] Blackstone officials like Agarwal felt that Stuy Town could be a perfect asset for that strategy because of how strongly the tenants were pushing for a long-term owner.[12]

On the morning of October 14, 2014, Agarwal came to my district office with his associate, Brian Kim, for a meeting with me, Sheehy, and Marsh. Sheehy set the tone of the meeting and explained that he had hoped we could simply explore some mutual interests. Marsh and I then peppered Agarwal with questions about Blackstone and its priorities. Agarwal was dapper and charming, and told us about Blackstone's investment strategy and its Core Plus fund. Agarwal explained why Blackstone, which had looked at preliminary financial data from CWCapital, was interested in Stuy Town as an investment. In contrast to its traditional higher-yield investments, where it tended to "buy, fix, then sell," this was an opportunity for it to inject stability and to hold it for a long period. Marsh was enthusiastic about Agarwal's presentation. "Patient money is just what we need," he said to me after the meeting. "It takes the target off the backs of tenants."[13]

Sheehy and I told Agarwal and Kim about our unsuccessful efforts to engage CWCapital and noted that while we still had an exclusive partnership with Brookfield, we wanted to have a line of communication open with Blackstone. Agarwal was extremely clear about Blackstone's interest in the property, and it did not include stepping into a political mess: "We only want to be part of this if we are part of the solution. We want to be an institution that would be welcomed by the tenants and by the city," he said. Marsh, Sheehy, and I nodded at each other with satisfaction. Our years of advocacy were affecting the market.[14]

Agarwal reported our conversation in his weekly meeting of Black-stone's property acquisitions team at their Park Avenue headquarters. Jon Gray, the head of the firm's real estate business, listened carefully. To Gray, this represented the most iconic piece of real estate in New York, and he was immediately intrigued. Everyone in the room agreed that this could be an exciting opportunity for Blackstone's Core Plus fund, but only if they could step in with public support. The group did not know exactly when a sale might happen, but they were certain that CWCapital was not going to hold on to the property forever. "We knew the clock was tick-ing, and we wanted to be the best prepared group once that happened," said Nadeem Meghji, senior managing director in the real estate group and head of real estate in the Americas, who was present for the meeting. "If we could wave our magic wand, our objective was to hold property for as long as MetLife did. That would also, we thought, make us a more appealing partner to the city and the community."[15]

Meanwhile, the sixty days that CWCapital had proposed for for-mal discussions with the city came and went without resolution, and MacArthur and Patchett were separately complaining to me about the oth-er's lack of speed and responsiveness. Susan Steinberg emailed me and said that she was getting questions from anxious tenants about why nothing had happened in the sixty-day period. I had no real answer to provide. Because of his frustration with the city—and, I suspected, because of our leverage with Fannie and Freddie—MacArthur was actively working with us. He had suggested to me and Rubin that we start meeting on a weekly basis to devise our own plan and then to try to bring the city along. After many breakfasts, beers, and enough water under the bridge, Rubin and I had finally developed a personal rapport with MacArthur, and we were now feeling like his problem-solving partners. It was also apparent to us based on the frequency of our meetings that we were entering the home stretch. Unfortunately, as happened repeatedly throughout our efforts, we were unable to report anything to our constituents publicly, and they were get-ting impatient. Sheehy continued to email me daily, expressing concern that the tenants' interest in homeownership were getting lost in the shuffle between CWCapital and the city.[16]

Over turkey sandwiches in my district office on September 8, 2014,[17] Rubin proposed to MacArthur that we jointly develop a "stalking horse" proposal whereby CWCapital would strike a deal with us—and the city—on the parameters of an affordability plan, and then we would jointly invite people to make a bid for the property based on that framework. MacArthur claimed to be open to the idea but, as was his custom, did not commit. He reiterated his willingness to do a conversion to homeownership, but for Peter Cooper only. He also shared his own idea of preserving about 2,750 affordable units in Stuy Town and building 750 new ones in a residential development at the Con Ed site across Avenue C, just to the east of Stuy Town. Aware of Stuy Town's unused development rights—and understanding the Tenants Association's strong objection to any new development in Stuy Town itself—MacArthur proposed transferring the air rights to the Con Ed parking lots and building a new residential community there of buildings ranging from thirty to sixty stories. I reminded him that twenty years earlier, the community had shot down the waterfront development known as Riverwalk on the grounds that it would block views, create congestion, and overwhelm Stuy Town and Peter Cooper. I politely explained that this would likely do the same, if not worse—and was likely impractical, because the site was in active use by a public utility. I thought it was a terrible idea but did not want to immediately say no, because I was so encouraged that MacArthur was actually letting down his guard and throwing out ideas. "I think this is likely complicated, but we should give it a look," I told him. He agreed and promised in turn to model out the Tenants Association's homeownership model for the whole property.

On September 29, Senator Schumer asked me to stop by his office to talk about the situation in Stuy Town. I went with my district office chief of staff David Kimball-Stanley and saw New York's senior senator with his feet up on the conference table. I immediately thanked the senator for his advocacy with Mel Watt, the director of FHFA, and for blocking Fannie and Freddie from making loans in Stuy Town without the tenants' and the city's support. That commitment had been a game changer for us, I told him. Schumer acknowledged the good work he had done with Director Watt and said he was pleased with the result. "Listen, we met the CWCapital guys, and we want to be helpful," he told me. He asked what further steps he could take to support the tenants' position. I suggested that he reach out to the top brass at Fortress and ask that they push CWCapital to work with the tenants and to embrace our stalking horse idea. The senator agreed and said he would get to work on it. As I was picking up to leave, Schumer stopped me and said, "By the way, people are telling me that there are pictures of me all over the Stuy Town lobbies? What is that about?" There were in fact flyers in Stuy Town, with images of Governor Cuomo and Speaker Carl Heastie in ten-gallon hats. The Tenants Association had created them to draw attention to the renewal of rent stabilization, saying, "Showdown at the Rent Law Corral. Heastie! Cuomo! Protect Tenants not Big Real Estate." I told Schumer, to his great relief, that people were likely confusing him with Cuomo. I enjoyed knowing that New York's senior senator was not only there every time we needed him for Stuy Town but also as concerned about tenant flyers in lobbies as I would be.

As 2014 came to a close, the Tenants Association needed to decide whether to renew its agreement with Brookfield. Marsh and the TA board were concerned about the feedback that we had all been getting from MacArthur about our partnership and asked me, Rubin, and Kane to advise them on what to do. The principal advantage for the partnership—making a successful preemptive bid for the property—had all but disappeared. Furthermore, MacArthur was telling us repeatedly and clearly that Brookfield was harming his ability to link arms with us. Regardless of why he was saying it, we could not ignore it. I conferred with Rubin and Kane by phone, and they both felt that discontinuing our exclusive agreement with Brookfield would likely foster the freer relationship with CWCapital that we seemed to be developing, enable the Tenants Association to explore partnerships with other capital providers, and allow us more flexibility as we moved on to the next chapter. We were so appreciative of Brookfield's efforts and did not want Barry Blattman to feel like this was a slight. We resolved that I would reach out to Blattman to discuss the sensitive situation and get his reaction. I met Blattman for drinks at the Smith in East Midtown on October 28, 2014, and told him the challenges we were facing, and that we were likely going to recommend that the TA board discontinue our agreement. Blattman concurred with our analysis and was not at all surprised that this was the path we preferred to take. The consummate professional, Blattman generously said that even without an exclusive agreement, Brookfield was always available to the tenants for consultation, and partnership, as the need arose.

I relayed the conversation to Sheehy, who then explained the entire dynamic to the board on a telephone call on November 14. The group debated whether sacrificing our capital partner eliminated any need for

CWCapital to work with us, and whether we would create embarrassing negative publicity for ourselves if our separation became a public matter. Ultimately, the board felt that we would not lose too much by terminating the agreement and that our free agency would allow us to explore alternatives. On the call, the TA board unanimously agreed to terminate the exclusivity agreement, and Marsh formally notified Brookfield of the decision on November 20. On our own once again, we quietly took down the TA/Brookfield website.[18]

As 2014 ended, the conversations between CWCapital and the mayor's office were still moving at a glacial pace. Nobody was happy. They had resolved to work together on a term sheet of the affordability concepts, and draft term sheets were promised, but not delivered. Patchett and MacArthur each continued to blame the other for the delay. I understood from my own conversations with Patchett that Glen's team was focused

Figure 13.3. James Patchett joined the de Blasio administration as chief of staff to Alicia Glen, deputy mayor for economic development. He played an instrumental role on behalf of City Hall in negotiating the affordable-housing deal with Blackstone. Photo credit: Kreg Holt.

on using a tax abatement and means testing apartments at up to 165 percent of the area median income.

On December 6, the Tenants Association assembled a community meeting to give people an opportunity to learn where things stood. We continued to be joined by the elected officials, but gone were the days when we needed an auditorium that accommodated eleven hundred. With the passage of time, interest had waned, and many residents had resigned themselves to the fact that nothing would happen quickly. When I took the stage, I did my best not to rehash everything that had happened prior. Rather, I predicted what might happen next. Either CWCapital would work with us on a prearranged outcome, or it would put the property up for sale. They might even do a conversion to homeownership themselves, I explained. "And if the units are all to be sold at levels that are unaffordable to the people who live here, that is not the outcome we want," I said.[19]

Not only were Rubin and I meeting with MacArthur more regularly, but Rubin and MacArthur discovered that they had daughters in the same class at an independent school on the Upper East Side. Along with our formal get-togethers, MacArthur and Rubin were chatting at school drop-offs about the tenants' conversion plan and the state of the market. MacArthur knew that we had long been targeting sales prices—at maximum—at $500 per square foot for these apartments. Now, in mid-2014, the apartment market was coming back in full swing, and $500 per square foot was beginning to look more like a floor and not a ceiling.

By September 2014, home prices in New York City were 65 percent above the post-crash low they hit in March 2009 and only 11 percent below the record high from May 2006. Sales of condominiums without a doorman in Manhattan—the closest comparable price for a potential Stuy Town condo—were now averaging a whopping $1,797 per square foot. While this was good news for CWCapital and the lenders, it was a disaster for me and the Tenants Association. As property values escalated, the possibility of pricing a condo plan at anywhere near our desired numbers was evaporating. Even assuming a 50 percent discount based on the fact that Stuy Town was far from mass transit or that most of the units were not renovated, the price would still be $900 per square foot—or about $900,000 for a single Stuy Town apartment. What's more, rental real estate was becoming just as valuable as condominiums. In Stuy Town, rents had climbed by 5.9 percent, and the net operating income at Stuyvesant Town Peter Cooper Village had risen to $177.5 million, up 33.6 percent from two years earlier. Analysts expected another big jump in 2014, with net income topping $195 million. Stuy Town also got an appraisal of $3.5 billion, way up from its low of $2.8 billion in 2010.[20]

MacArthur, tracking all these market trends, grabbed Rubin one day at school drop-off and asked if he wanted to have a look at the new upgrades that CWCapital had been making in individual Stuy Town apartments. Rubin had grown up in an unrenovated rent-stabilized apartment in Stuy Town and was eager to see what CWCapital was doing. When MacArthur opened the door to one of the new model apartments, Rubin stopped in his tracks. What Rubin saw was completely different from the apartment that he had grown up in. The kitchen was opened up into the living room, with a bar and seating area. The air conditioners, which traditionally had occupied most of the window space, were dropped down into the wall, bringing in more light and creating less clutter. "It was remarkable," Rubin recalled. "The finishes were not Fifth Avenue extravagant, but they were impressive. Countertops, appliances, lighting. It was a really much more cosmopolitan configuration, unlike anything I had ever seen in that community." MacArthur made the case to Rubin that this space with this finish—even in this location—would command a premium. Rubin did a quick assessment based on his own experience and realized that CWCapital could sell the unit for well over $1,000 a square foot. "And that just struck me," he said. "Either we were not going to be able to do an ownership deal because the tenants were going to get priced out, or CWCapital was settling in for a very long ownership transition period where they are going to massively upgrade the physical plant." Historically the role of special servicers was simply to borrow money to make improvements in order to preserve existing value, but here CWCapital, with the backing of private equity parent company Fortress, was going well beyond that. It was taking major steps to *maximize* the value of the property.[21]

Rubin left MacArthur after his tour and called me in the office to tell me what he had seen. "We are off by an order of magnitude," he said, animatedly. "MacArthur is open to a conversion plan, but he thinks he can get $1.1 million to $1.5 million for an apartment." I sank in my seat. Rubin and I both knew that we couldn't champion a conversion plan of million-dollar apartments. There was no rationale for the city, or the Tenants Association, to embrace prices at that level; no one could call a $1.1 million unit affordable. Between CWCapital's view that it wanted to sell million-dollar apartments and in Peter Cooper only, along with the mayor's skepticism of a conversion plan altogether, I realized that a homeownership option was simply not going to be in the cards for Stuy Town tenants as part of this process. I didn't want to put out a press release making that point, but felt like I needed to find ways to manage some expectations among the TA board and in the community.

The Centerbridge litigation continued to slow down CWCapital, and at the same time, TA board members like John Sheehy and Kevin Farrelly, who had been elected to a newly created position of chairman, were becoming increasingly unhappy with my reports about the dynamic between CWCapital and City Hall. They did not understand why CWCapital would be negotiating a term sheet on affordability directly with the city, rather than working on the homeownership plan with us. They were concerned that there was not an alignment of interests between us and the city—and they were right, if our primary goal was *only* homeownership. Sheehy repeatedly expressed to me his fears that while the city wanted preservation of some amorphous concept of future "affordable housing," existing middle-class tenants' interests were going to get extinguished in the process.[22] On behalf of the conversion committee, Sheehy asked for a meeting with Kane, Rubin, and me, to politely but firmly push us on this point. On the afternoon of January 30, 2015, Dawn Davis, Al Doyle, Kirsten Adahl, John Marsh, Susan Steinberg, and Farrelly all came to my district office. They were unhappy that the mayor did not embrace our homeownership plan—when he was sitting on my couch, or at any point since—and as a result they felt that he was now an obstacle to one of our primary goals. Sheehy and Farrelly were overjoyed that MacArthur was now meeting with us regularly and positively. From their perspective, that meant that we should negotiate our deal with only him—and bring the city along later.

Rubin shared the story about his recent visit to a modern renovated apartment and what it likely meant for apartment prices. He explained that residential property was going up in value and that CWCapital was working to maximize the value of its property. Rubin shared his impression that these modernized apartments would sell for over $1 million and re-minded the group that MacArthur was still pitching a Peter Cooper–only scenario. CWCapital was also seeking to recover much more than what was owed in the $3 billion first mortgage, claiming to be entitled to hundreds of millions of dollars in interest and fees. It was also obvious that the city was uninterested in a homeownership plan and that because of the Centerbridge lawsuit, which could delay the process indefinitely, the conversion plan was no longer realistic. The board members looked despondent. "So the conversion is dead?" Farrelly asked, pointedly. "When precisely were we going to hear about this?"

In a defiant message to me, Kane, and Rubin, the TA conversion committee convened a number of weeks later and unanimously supported a resolution to simply eliminate the city from our discussions and proceed with CWCapital only. From the perspective of some members of the conversion committee, the only affordability that mattered was the opportunity for existing middle-class renters to save money by becoming homeowners. To them, any other discussion of affordability for future tenants was extraneous. "The affordable housing issue gets tossed around in endless meetings going nowhere," Sheehy argued to me. "The time is coming for us to say we are going to try to move ahead with a sale and let the City deal on their issue with the new owner. This isn't a threat, it's just common sense."[23] "I prefer we go back to where we were a year or so ago—with an equity partner and a plan that includes affordability both for owners and renters," Farrelly added. But Sheehy and Farrelly's narrower view of our affordable-housing goals was not the prevailing view of members of the TA board. Steinberg and Marsh were encouraging patience among their colleagues. "The affordable component is absolutely critical to our constituents, whether it slows the process down or not," said Steinberg. "If we engineered a sale without resolution of the affordable component as part of that sale, our constituency will be up in arms. If that happened, we could kiss the TA goodbye. We would have no credibility. Affordability must be baked into a sale."[24]

I called Marsh to confirm the board continued to view *long-term* affordability as a critical goal, despite what the conversion committee was saying directly. Marsh and Steinberg conferred and agreed that this principle was even more important than homeownership and in fact the most important thing that we could do. In contrast to the frustration of the conversion committee, I was feeling rather encouraged that we were now having a direct conversation with both MacArthur and Patchett about the contours of a long-term affordability plan in Stuy Town. Following the directive of the TA president, and not the conversion committee, I proceeded to ask MacArthur and Patchett for a meeting to jointly review how we were going to get to the next step, together. Meetings were scheduled, and canceled, then rescheduled. Finally, on July 8, 2015, Rubin, Kane, and I convened in the Governor's Room of City Hall with MacArthur and Andy Kane from CWCapital, as well as Glen and her team. MacArthur— top two buttons of his shirt unbuttoned, and the *New York Post* in front of him on the table—patiently waited for Glen to kick off the meeting and ask him for an update on where things stood. MacArthur said he was optimistic that CWCapital would win its motion to dismiss the Centerbridge lawsuit, and acknowledged that the delay was "on us." Arguments in that case were scheduled for the fall of 2015, and even if CWCapital won, there likely would be an appeal, and no sale likely could happen until this issue was resolved.[25] He explained that he could not embrace specific plans or partnerships yet because of the litigation. Patchett glanced at me knowingly. We had heard that line before.

14

CLOSING THE DEAL

Doug Harmon, a real estate broker at Eastdil Secured, a financial advisory firm, had earned the reputation of being one of the very best in the business, especially for large and complex assignments. When MetLife had put Stuyvesant Town up for sale in 2006, he lost a beauty contest for brokers—to rival Darcy Stacom of CB Richard Ellis—primarily, he believed, because he raised concerns about the expected value of the property. His views were easily dismissed in the heady days before the credit crisis in 2008. Without regard for the tenants' arguments about preserving middle-class housing, MetLife wanted to shoot the moon for the highest possible price, and Stacom was promising to deliver to them exactly that. Harmon felt that the deal that was being pitched by Stacom was going to have bad consequences for the tenants. "This was middle-class New York, the heartbeat of the city—and I was not comfortable pushing to the last dollar, on the backs of tenants, getting them out of their apartments as fast as you could," he told me later. "I knew on day one that it was going to be a calamity." Harmon had gotten his first big break in New York in the late 1990s when Leona Helmsley, known as the "Queen of Mean," asked him to sell the $5 billion real estate portfolio that she had inherited from her husband, Harry. The portfolio included the Graybar Building, right next to Grand Central, the Starrett-Lehigh Building in Chelsea, and the sprawling 152-acre Villas Parkmerced in southwest San Francisco, another, similarly massive, MetLife development built during World War II. He went on to set the real estate record for the most expensive building sale in New York City history, selling the General Motors Building to Harry Macklowe for $1.4 billion in 2003.[1]

In 2004, when MacArthur worked at Dermot Companies, his firm had hired Harmon to help sell the 239-unit Hudson Crossing development on West 37th Street. Ten years later, MacArthur retained Harmon and his firm to help handle CWCapital's foreclosure sale in Stuy Town, which he had called off at the last minute. Harmon had been following the Stuy Town dynamic closely since he lost out as the broker to Stacom in 2006, and when the foreclosure was ultimately canceled, Harmon started to speak with MacArthur persistently about how he could help solve the complex Stuy Town puzzle.[2]

By the middle of 2015, Harmon was actively urging MacArthur to move toward some sort of a sale. He and his firm were doing record business, and he was seeing a sharp increase in the demand for larger real estate assets. Harmon felt like the market had similar undertones to the time just before the 2008 collapse. He argued to MacArthur that he needed to act, and soon, and to do it in a way that met everyone's interests. Harmon understood that the tenants needed to be satisfied; they had already proved they could depress the sale price through negative publicity and by keeping Fannie and Freddie on the sidelines. "This was not going to be a normal bid situation," Harmon explained to me later. "We needed to perfect the deal and to be able to stand up to any possible public assault." To Harmon, that meant coming up with a plan that would work for all parties and presenting it to them simultaneously—and quickly—to keep it from falling apart. "Think about this like a shoe salesman," Harmon told MacArthur. "The more options the customers have, the more complicated and time consuming the decision will be. In certain selling situations, you have to get in and out, and multiple choices can hamstring the process." In Stuy Town's case, the property had the potential to sell for north of $4 or $5 billion, which meant that there likely wouldn't be too many eligible buyers in any event. To Harmon, the Stuy Town deal required that CWCapital present the right buyer and push for a quick decision. MacArthur charged Harmon with finding a way to establish the market value for the property while keeping it off the front pages of the newspapers. "We had to make a market without awakening the market," Harmon explained to me.[3]

The Centerbridge litigation remained a problem for MacArthur. He could not follow Harmon's advice and sell the property while Centerbridge was arguing that CWCapital had fraudulently taken title. MacArthur was tired of it all and had become increasingly eager to tie up this final loose end. In the early fall, CWCapital and Fortress settled the lawsuit with Centerbridge by giving it the potential for upside recovery in a sale of Stuy Town. The parties had asked the judge for thirty days to finalize the settlement, at which point it would become public as part of the court's records. With Harmon whispering in his ear, MacArthur realized that this thirty-day period gave him a fleeting opportunity to try to propose a solution. When the settlement became public, real estate interests and politicians would be all over him—with both opportunities and demands. MacArthur was most worried about the politicians like me publicly shouting about long-term affordability and further depressing the sale price. Between the Federal Housing Administration's commitment not to lend in a deal that did not have the tenants' explicit support, and Mayor de Blasio's active public engagement, MacArthur had become convinced that the political outcry around a public auction would scare potential bidders away and agreed that the deal needed to be embraced by all the various competing interests.[4]

Harmon, who had, from the sidelines, witnessed the overwhelming greed that characterized the 2006 transaction, was certain that that path could easily be replicated. There surely was an opportunity to sell Stuyvesant Town to someone who didn't care about the politics and who would pay top dollar and seek maximum returns. Such a buyer could conceivably deliver a full recovery to CWCapital but was risky because the tenants and City Hall would be ready to litigate—or even legislate—to stop it. Through years of advocacy, the tenants had created a powerful dynamic whereby the more politically palatable and less risky route was for CWCapital to find a buyer with plenty of cash, patient capital, and an understanding of the complex public concerns. While there were very few buyers who actually fit such a profile, Harmon knew one of them.

Earlier in the year, Harmon had been retained by a partnership group led by the Chetrit family to broker the sale of the Willis Tower, formerly the Sears Tower, in Chicago. Because of the importance of the building to Chicago, Harmon was looking to sell to a firm that could navigate a complex political environment and be a trusted partner to the city. The Blackstone Group had been a bidder for the building, and Harmon had seen firsthand how smoothly its leader, Jon Gray, operated. Gray glided with charm and intellect through meetings with Mayor Rahm Emanuel and others and emerged as the winning bidder. Blackstone had beaten out other players in a complex transaction and also managed to come out looking like a hero. Harmon thought that Gray was extremely impressive. He was reasonable and smart and didn't sweat the small details. He was exactly the sort of leader who Harmon thought would have the sophistication required to solve the Stuy Town multidimensional Rubik's cube.[5]

Jon Gray had joined Blackstone in 1992 right after college, at a time when the firm had only $1 billion under management. By 2015, the year of the Willis Tower deal, it had $335 billion. After 2007, Gray's unit at Blackstone became the biggest real estate investment manager in the entire world and, with a portfolio of fifty thousand rental homes, the largest residential landlord in the US. Gray came to the Willis Tower deal with not only resources but a dose of humility and political savvy that made him particularly successful in his craft. The *Financial Times* described Gray as someone who was poised to be a Master of the Universe but who did not act that way. "I recognize the fragility of success, the Icarus thing," Gray said in a profile. "I don't want my tombstone to just say he had really good internal rates of return."[6] As his former boss, Thomas Saylak, put it, Gray is that guy "you want your daughter to bring home when she's going on dates, somebody you trust with your money, and somebody with steel balls."[7]

In the summer of 2015, with MacArthur's quiet blessing, Harmon had a few early conversations with Gray to assess Blackstone's interest in buying Stuy Town. Gray and his team had been watching Stuy Town since MacArthur's aborted UCC foreclosure in 2014 but were uncertain that Blackstone—or anyone—could ever be welcomed by the tenants and

City Hall. Gray was fully aware that everyone who went near the place, like MetLife, Tishman Speyer, and CWCapital—even investors like the Church of England—tended to get bloodied by the tenants and elected officials. While a year earlier we had enjoyed a positive meeting with Blackstone's A. J. Agarwal, John Sheehy's neighbor, the Tenants Association and I were last seen standing on the steps of City Hall with an assortment of elected officials, including Senator Chuck Schumer, shouting at CWCapital to demand fairness from any new owner. The tenants' strength was at its peak, and Stuy Town had wiped out so much capital, and beat up so many firms, that it carried enormous risk. Nevertheless, Blackstone clearly had the stature to do the deal, and a fund that was suitable for the task. Gray was intrigued by the prospect.[8]

"You are going to be the savior, the white knight," Harmon egged on Gray. "I promise you at the end of this process, the mayor and councilman and the people of the community and the city will be praising you." Gray agreed to put his toe in the water and sign a nondisclosure agreement with CWCapital that would allow his team to review the financials. It was not their first opportunity to do this. Like Harmon, Blackstone already had been through all the details in June 2014, when CWCapital had planned to do a UCC foreclosure. Gray assigned one of his colleagues, Nadeem Meghji, to study this opportunity more closely.[9]

Despite Harmon's promise to Gray that Blackstone would be "the hero," nobody could truly know how the Tenants Association or I would react to the possibility of making a quick deal with Blackstone, a behemoth private equity firm, or anyone else for that matter. It also was brash and surprisingly bold for MacArthur to even allow Harmon to quietly have this conversation with Gray. If the discussions leaked, then other bidders or even the Tenants Association might catch wind of it and try to influence the outcome to their own benefit. And MacArthur worried that if this approach failed and other bidders later heard about it, they might conclude nobody on earth could actually do the deal, which would further depress the market value for CWCapital and its bondholders. MacArthur calculated the risks. He had spent enough time fighting with me and the Tenants Association, and had entertained so many approaches from interested parties over the years. At this point, he just wanted Harmon to try to get it right and present one really solid option to the tenants, the city, Centerbridge, and Fortress. But because of the risks, to be successful any deal had to be done quickly and quietly. Notably, to execute such a strategy, MacArthur would need to put a high level of trust in me and the Tenants Association.[10]

As a backup, Harmon had also quietly sussed out another bidder: a Ruby Schron–led partnership that was prepared to pay full price for the property but without any upfront affordability protections. They were offering a near record-setting amount; such a deal might appear easy but was fraught with conflict and could be challenged at every turn. Harmon believed a Blackstone solution—with real affordability protections—was the right path to pursue. "It would be better politics, and better for the city and for me," Harmon said. "I knew that Jon Gray and Blackstone were going to elevate this transaction," he told me later.[11]

After only two weeks of reviewing the financials and talking to Harmon, both Meghji and Gray concluded that the acquisition of Stuy Town could be a good fit for Blackstone's Core Plus fund. They talked it over with their political and press experts at the firm, all of whom were well aware of the controversy surrounding the property. "You shouldn't touch that with a ten-foot pole," one of them said to Gray. Gray asked if their view would change if they could buy the property with the support of the mayor, the councilman, and the tenants. They looked at each other and shrugged, thinking that that scenario was beyond unlikely, and told him that if he could somehow pull that off, he should go for it.[12]

Gray and his team came to a preliminary agreement with CWCapital on price, but Gray insisted on speaking to the mayor's office, to me, and to the Tenants Association before signing any deal. Gray wanted to be welcomed with open arms, if such a thing were possible. It was good politics, for sure; but also, if the public entities blessed this deal, then Blackstone would be free to borrow funds from Fannie Mae and Freddie Mac, which could lower its costs. "Our transaction was contingent on having those conversations and a feeling that we had strong support from all of those stakeholders," Meghji said.

Harmon thought that engaging the tenants and City Hall was smart, but he was skeptical that any of the parties involved could reliably prove that they had the support of thirty thousand tenants or political officials with divergent views. Was the right approach to have a casual meeting or two? A formal agreement? "They wanted to have a town hall meeting before the deal was even locked!" Harmon told me later, describing Blackstone's approach. MacArthur granted Gray and Meghji ten days to have some personal meetings with me, the Tenants Association, and the city to assess the parties' interest in a deal involving Blackstone. Harmon was particularly nervous about having MacArthur put Blackstone in front of me, because of my influence with the Tenants Association and history of attacking Tishman Speyer and CWCapital for just about everything. MacArthur did not share that worry. Over time, he came to understand that even when I was critical, I could be trusted. MacArthur believed I would have the courage to embrace an opportunity if I believed that it was good for the community. "Don't worry," MacArthur assured Harmon. "Garodnick gets it."[13]

Jon Gray of Blackstone called Deputy Mayor Glen to let her know that Blackstone and CWCapital had a handshake deal with CWCapital to buy Stuy Town, which would include some affordability protections. But, he told her, he had been given only a one-week window to secure the city's blessing and participation. "I know this is not how things usually work," he told her. "But we're not going to ask for a waiver of property taxes forever, and if you're up for this, let's get in a room for a week and figure it out." Glen listened to the details of his pitch, which represented a fleeting opportunity to solve a complicated problem and to ensure that thousands of affordable units would not slip away. The property was already losing 300 to 350 rent-stabilized units every year, and she, Commissioner Been, and the mayor had all publicly stated that they would not allow Stuy Town to become a fully market-rate community. Like me, Glen's team was quite worried about how the city—which had no right to actually dictate the terms of this transaction—was ever going to get this done. Patchett and Meghji spoke the next morning by phone and set up a time to meet in person on the afternoon of Columbus Day, October 12, at City Hall.[14]

Meghji arrived in the Governor's Room on the second floor on Columbus Day with Blackstone's Qahir Madhany, Brian Kim, and Adam Leslie—along with MacArthur. Meghji took in the grandeur of the room and was awed by the gold-framed portraits of US presidents and New York State governors. For most of these Blackstone officials, this was an unusual direct exposure to local government and their first visit to City Hall. "It was the first time on a transaction that we had such direct interaction with the city at the most senior levels, and you felt the magnitude of what you were embarking on when you walked into the room," Meghji said.[15]

Meghji introduced his team to Patchett and expressed Blackstone's desire to have the city's blessing for a deal. He explained that they intended to invest with long-term capital from their new Core Plus fund, and not over-borrow, in contrast to what Tishman Speyer had done. Meghji explained that they hoped to work with Fannie Mae and Freddie Mac to achieve desirable financing and proposed attaching affordability protections to three thousand units in the community as part of the deal. While Patchett quickly waved off that number as too low, he openly shared the various incentives that the city could bring to the table for the right deal, like the waiver of transfer and mortgage recording taxes, which would otherwise be due when the property was sold. After about an hour, everyone parted without any commitments on either side, but resolved to come back together within a couple of days. Patchett then warned Meghji, "But now you need to deal with Dan. He's going to ask who you are, and why you will be better than the last guy." Patchett instructed Meghji to bring me and the tenants into the loop before they came back to City Hall. MacArthur said that he would arrange the meeting, but needed to explain it all to me first.[16]

In the evening of the same day, Zoe, Asher, Devin, and I had just finished having an early family dinner at Don Giovanni's on Tenth Avenue, and we were about to drop Zoe at Penn Station for a work trip to Washington, DC. I looked at my phone to see a text message from MacArthur. "Have time for a beer?" he wrote.

"It's kind of a busy week for me, what night were you thinking?" I responded.

I saw the dots of a quick response on my phone. He followed up: "How about tonight?"

This was obviously not a good night, as Zoe was heading out of town, and I was going to be home alone with a two- and a four-year-old. Nervous about what might be going on, I told him I could do it if he wanted to show up at my apartment at 8:30 p.m., which was after bedtime, with a six-pack in hand. Undeterred by my rather onerous conditions, he agreed.

"What's your address again?" he wrote. "Ha, ha," he added.

"Something's up," I said to Zoe as I kissed her goodbye. I assumed that MacArthur had settled the Centerbridge lawsuit and wanted me to know—but why would this be such an emergency? I texted Patchett to see if he had a minute to chat before my meeting and hurried the kids to bed. I got Patchett on the phone at 8:07 p.m. He told me that he had met with CWCapital earlier in the day and learned that they had in fact settled the Centerbridge lawsuit. MacArthur had presented a buyer who was prepared to put a deal on the table that was in line with what we had been discussing over the prior months—with significant and negotiable amounts of long-term affordability. Patchett believed that CWCapital "had a short fuse" and wanted to wrap this up, presumably because of its Centerbridge settlement. They were willing to commit to keeping Stuy Town and Peter Cooper Village as a unified whole and not building on open spaces. It wasn't a conversion to homeownership—but I knew that had become a long shot—and it sounded like a reasonable opportunity for us. Patchett was encouraged, and based on what I was hearing, I was too.

Twenty-four minutes later, MacArthur walked into my apartment with a six-pack of Kronenbourg. I invited him in, and he took a seat on my couch. With Asher and Devin asleep in the other room, MacArthur and I cracked open two beers. After only a minute of small talk, he said that he had an opportunity that he thought the tenants should consider, and wanted to get my reaction. "I think that I have a way to accomplish many of the goals you have set out to do," he said. At the same time, he explained, his plan would prevent him from holding a bruising public auction that would be like opening Pandora's box. I had already been briefed by Patchett, but in any case listened closely to MacArthur's pitch. He looked unusually nervous as he spoke.

MacArthur told me about his two bidders. One, he said, was interested in a market deal, with no affordability. The other was the Blackstone Group. He explained that Blackstone had a fund with "patient capital," did not want to borrow excessively to do the deal, and did not want to do anything inconsistent with the desires of City Hall or the tenants. "They want to be viewed as another 'MetLife,' which would own the property for thirty to forty years," he told me. The other buyer was unnamed, but MacArthur represented that it had no interest in any deal with us or the city. I opened another two beers—the first ones had gone down surprisingly fast—and handed one to MacArthur. I wasn't sure that the "door number two" scenario was real, but if it was, it would be a repeat of the Tishman Speyer deal.[17]

MacArthur told me that Blackstone was prepared to commit to an affordability plan for three to four thousand units that lasted fifteen years and would make apartments available to middle-class people earning up to 165 percent of the area median income—the same levels we had been discussing with Deputy Mayor Glen. To guarantee it, Blackstone would also subject itself to a regulatory agreement with the city that would protect these units both in Stuy Town and Peter Cooper. I asked—already knowing the answer—if it would include homeownership opportunities for tenants, and MacArthur said that while it would not at the outset, he was certain Blackstone would not rule that out down the line. Regardless, he thought that we should move forward with Blackstone, which he felt addressed our interests and his, while also avoiding a drawn-out transaction with high scrutiny in the public eye.

There was a catch, though. MacArthur shifted in his seat as he explained that he was under a very short time frame for the transaction because he needed to maintain strict confidentiality, a point he impressed on me several times in our conversation. I threw dozens of questions at him. I was concerned how this would impact current rent-stabilized tenants, and asked how we would lock in Blackstone's commitments. Also, because this proposal did not include homeownership, I asked him how we could protect tenants covered by the *Roberts* case, whose rents were set to shoot up in 2020, when the J-51 tax abatement expired. MacArthur knew the answers to most, but not all of my questions, and was open to working out all of the details, including the precise contours of the affordability program. These were all points that we both needed to discuss with Blackstone and the city, he told me.

What MacArthur proposed checked so many boxes for us that I felt both excited and relieved as we continued our conversation and finished our six-pack. A stable owner that was prepared to commit a significant number of rental units to a long-term affordability program was objectively a great outcome. Until that moment, I truly had no idea how we were going to bring this whole decade-long nightmare to an end, and the Tenants Association and I were bracing ourselves for another street-fight public auction. We had fought to be in a position to have this conversation, and half of the time I was fighting with the very person who was sitting in my living room. While fifteen years of affordability, and three thousand units, felt low to me, and I intended to push for more, I told MacArthur that it was certainly worth taking this proposal to the Tenants Association. "Great. Then we need to accelerate conversations with the city, and with the TA leadership," he said. "This will have to get done fast." MacArthur left my apartment, and he told me later that he too exhaled deeply. "I was really hopeful that what I walked in with was going to be perceived as a good thing, and after the meeting I had a feeling of relief."[18]

I briefed Alex Rubin and Meredith Kane by phone the next morning. They were enthusiastic that we now had a path to success, and strongly urged me to pursue the route MacArthur was proposing. Because secrecy was of such importance here, Genevieve Michel, who had become my chief of staff, directed my team to clear the office calendar for the week, without even telling them what exactly was happening. I called John Sheehy and Susan Steinberg—Steinberg had recently taken over from John Marsh as the new TA president—and told them about the meeting. Sheehy, who had introduced me to Blackstone's A. J. Agarwal in my district office the prior year, had hoped that a firm of Blackstone's stature would be interested, and Steinberg sounded relieved. We awaited the first draft of a term sheet from Blackstone that would lay out their proposed affordable-housing plan.

Patchett suggested a meeting at City Hall with me, MacArthur, and Meghji of Blackstone, on Wednesday afternoon, October 14. The agenda would be for us to discuss precisely how many affordable units we could preserve, to whom they would be available, and for how long. It was also my opportunity to meet Meghji and to get a sense of him and Blackstone as a firm. Other than my meeting with Agarwal the prior summer, I had not had any contact with Blackstone. Patchett introduced me to Meghji in the New Amsterdam Conference Room of City Hall, and I greeted MacArthur, who I noted did not have a *New York Post* to show off at this particular meeting. Meghji, originally from Canada, came off as genuine in his approach and explained that his firm was there only because it felt it could solve, rather than cause, problems for us. With MacArthur sitting uncharacteristically quiet by his side, Meghji gave me an overview of Blackstone and its Core Plus fund, and why this was a good fit.

I learned in this meeting that Blackstone intended to partner with a large Canadian pension fund, Ivanhoé Cambridge, and to use their most patient funds, with lower return expectations. Meghji explained that the rents already supported their expected debt payments. In 2006, the deal had been financed with $1 billion in equity and $4.4 billion in debt, with a net operating income of $108 million. Here, Blackstone was proposing for this deal to be financed with $2.7 billion in equity and $2.7 billion in debt, and the net operating income was already $215 million. This difference was a very important point to us after what we had just been through. In contrast to what happened in 2006, Blackstone was looking for lower returns, less debt, less risk, and much longer hold periods. Blackstone and Ivanhoé Cambridge were each planning to put down $1.3 billion in equity, leaving only half of the purchase to be borrowed.[19]

We started to discuss the details of the preservation plan. Naturally, in a preservation deal, there is always a cost to someone, either the owner or the city, for the preservation of every unit of affordable housing. The cheaper the apartment and the greater the number of units, the higher the cost. In order to keep rents down, the city's tools for preserving units included giving a direct subsidy or abating or exempting taxes on the property. We had discussed a variety of options with Glen's team and MacArthur over the prior year, but Meghji had a different thought. Rather than establishing an Article 11 program with an $800 or $900 million subsidy from the city, Blackstone suggested a *onetime* waiver of the transfer and mortgage recording taxes in exchange for a fifteen-year commitment to preserve affordable rental units. Meghji explained that Blackstone did not want continued subsidies because they were concerned that it would make the deal unnecessarily complicated (and perhaps more vulnerable to additional demands from the city later). Regardless of the reason, this framework made the preservation of Stuy Town units rather inexpensive for the city as compared to other deals. This onetime waiver amounted to a little over $200 million in taxes that were otherwise due on the transfer of the property, which meant that the city would get most of the affordability we had been discussing at about 20 percent of the price.[20]

In this meeting, we debated the number of units that would go into the program. In its handshake deal with CWCapital, Blackstone had assumed a fixed cost for affordability, so Meghji was agnostic about whether we achieved that with a larger number of less affordable units or fewer units with deeper affordability protections. I felt very strongly that the top-line number needed to be at or above five thousand units. It was a powerful number because it put nearly half of Stuy Town and Peter Cooper on a track of preservation and invited the possibility of further city and state action down the line. At that volume, the pricing would be aimed at middle class affordability (up to $128,000 for a family of three) and also for a longer term of years. Patchett and I both argued for a term of at least twenty years, as opposed to the ten or fifteen that had initially been floated. I also raised the question of what we were going to do for the *Roberts* tenants, some of whom could see significant rent increases in 2020. Meghji said he would bring those issues back to his colleagues at Blackstone. He reiterated what MacArthur had said in my living room: Blackstone was only in this deal if we wanted them there.

That afternoon, I called John Sheehy and asked him if he could convene the TA's conversion committee and join me and MacArthur at Moelis's office at 399 Park Avenue at two the next afternoon. I told him that we needed to meet CWCapital's prospective buyer as a group, and that it was not only politically sensitive, but it was also time sensitive. As we showed up for the meeting, press reports were already popping up that CWCapital was quietly "shopping" Stuy Town to prospective buyers.[21] Genevieve Michel had wisely changed the location of our meeting from my district office to Moelis's office and had asked Alex Rubin's staff to help us escort Meghji and MacArthur into their offices without attracting too much attention.

Along with Rubin, I huddled with TA board members Sheehy, Adahl, and Newmark for fifteen minutes in advance of the meeting and shared with them exactly what was about to be proposed. They were intrigued but also concerned, particularly for the plight of the *Roberts* tenants, the group that had been most interested in buying their apartments. These people, generally speaking, had more resources than the stabilized tenants with the lowest rents, but with few exceptions they were not rich, and were the most vulnerable to rent increases. These tenants would not be helped at all by a plan that focused exclusively on *future* tenants. I encouraged Adahl and Newmark to raise the issue directly with Meghji and MacArthur when they arrived. Once we were convened in Moelis's corner conference room overlooking Park Avenue, we patched in Meredith Kane and Susan Steinberg by phone. MacArthur opened the meeting and described the events leading to the settlement of the Centerbridge litigation. He explained that two parties had simultaneously approached CWCapital with ideas about the purchase of Stuy Town and Peter Cooper. One was Blackstone, which MacArthur believed was a good fit for us, and the other, the unnamed bogeyman, who was pushing a market deal with no long-term affordability. He said that Meghji was about to describe a plan that likely would have the support of City Hall and could close as early as the following week. MacArthur and I watched the faces of the tenants and saw grimaces all around.

Meghji introduced himself and his firm, saying that Blackstone's fundamental premise was for the deal to work for everyone, and for it to be the owner of the property for the next fifty to one hundred years. His purpose for coming to the TA leadership before the deal was done was to ask for their support. Without it, he again said, Blackstone had no intention of proceeding.

In recognition of the Tenants Association's priorities, Meghji said that there would be absolutely no building on the open spaces and that Peter Cooper and Stuyvesant Town would be kept as a united whole, with the same set of rules. Blackstone proposed that some number of units—Patchett and I had successfully pushed him up to five thousand—remain affordable for a period of time, which was now up to twenty years for middle-class New Yorkers. Under the agreement, those units would burn off over five years beginning in year twenty-one. Sheehy asked about a conversion plan. Meghji responded that it was not currently on the table but that it would not be ruled out for subsequent consideration. MacArthur and I listened as the tenants asked Meghji about how his commitments would be locked in and why we should trust another giant real estate firm. Meghji, unrattled, described how Blackstone's commitments would be firmed up. He patiently answered each question, explaining why this plan was attractive to both Blackstone and tenants, but always coming back to the fact that Blackstone wanted to proceed only if the tenants believed the deal suited their interests.

Newmark and Adahl listened carefully, but they were not at all satisfied. The deal delivered on a number of the Tenants Association's primary goals but did nothing for them as *Roberts* tenants. Because the protections from the *Roberts* lawsuit ended after the J-51 tax abatement expired in 2020, those rents could go way up right away. I had anticipated this reaction, and in earlier conversations with Meghji I had asked him to provide some accommodation for this group. He now mentioned that I had raised the issue with him in a prior meeting and offered to extend protection for *Roberts* tenants from 2020 to 2024, but said that he would need to subject them to 8 percent annual increases during that period to get them to market rate. "There's no way. We can't do that," Newmark said tersely, as Sheehy and Adahl nodded. "An 8 percent increase will mean that I will need to leave the property in 2020," he said. Newmark felt strongly that if Blackstone wanted to earn our support, it would need to do better for *Roberts* tenants. "How about lower increases? How about you give existing residents priority for the new affordable units?" Newmark asked. MacArthur started to sweat. This was going off the rails quickly. "I lost five years of my life in that meeting. I was nervous about people asking for too much. We had momentum, and if we bogged down, it would be a big risk," he recalled. Meghji did not miss a beat and agreed to see if he could find a way to give *Roberts* residents priority for the apartments under the regulatory agreement if they qualified as "middle income."[22]

On October 17, at around noon, Meghji called me and Rubin to say that they had agreed to limit increases for *Roberts* tenants to 5 rather than 8 percent over five years. "Outstanding," said Rubin, "simply outstanding."[23] I reported it back to Sheehy and called Newmark to let him know. He was relieved, and while the compromise was not ideal, he was glad that Blackstone had moved and felt more comfortable supporting the deal. Meghji also asked me to relay to the TA board that, while his firm was open to allowing existing *Roberts* tenants who met the income limitations to have preference for the new affordable units, City Hall was not. The city had been sued for housing discrimination over laws that gave local preferences for housing, and they were not allowing for that in any of their newer housing deals.

Once formalized, the term sheet preserved five thousand units of housing as affordable to the next generation of middle-income tenants for a minimum of twenty years. At the time, about fifty-two hundred units were covered by traditional rent stabilization (in contrast to the rest, which had become rent stabilized because of the *Roberts* litigation), but that number was dwindling at a rate of over three hundred every single year. As those units became vacant, Blackstone would be obligated to rent them to tenants who qualified as middle income. This was defined as earning up to 165 percent of the area median income—or about $128,000 for a family of three for the first 4,500 units, and 80 percent of the area median income—or $62,000 for a family of three for the rest.

The deal also required that Blackstone spread the units in the affordable-housing program across and within all buildings in the development—including in Peter Cooper. The city established a reporting requirement to ensure those conditions were being met and required that the regulations "run with the land," meaning that even if Blackstone sold the property, the rules would continue to exist. After twenty years, if no further legislative or regulatory action were taken, the rents for all these units would be gradually phased up to the market over a five-year period between 2036 and 2041. Blackstone also agreed to put a social worker on premises, generate activities for seniors, designate a point person for the Senior Citizen Rent Increase Exemption, and do wellness checks.

In return for these protections, the city agreed to waive $77 million in mortgage recording taxes and provide Blackstone with a $144 million low-interest forgivable loan through the Housing Development Corporation to cover the cost of the transfer taxes. This was a small fraction of what we anticipated the city would have to spend to preserve affordability. "This package is night-and-day compared with what we had been talking about," Deputy Mayor Alicia Glen later told Bagli at the *Times*. "We're saving taxpayers a lot of money."[24]

The Tenants Association had not yet formally considered or blessed the deal, which was the final—and most important—piece of the puzzle. While a small but influential group was now fully briefed and supportive, the rest of the board needed an opportunity to evaluate what was being proposed, and to cast a vote. They had been engaged, vocal, and committed to this cause for years. Most continued to trust my judgment, but there were still dissenting voices. I worried that this proposed resolution was going to strike some of them as unreasonably fast and, because it did not include homeownership, simply objectionable. Susan Steinberg, as the new board president, asked Kevin Farrelly, the board chair, to call a meeting for Sunday evening, October 18, for the board to evaluate the proposal.

In the intervening two days, I spoke with Emma Wolfe in the mayor's office about how and when to brief the rest of the local elected officials, like Senator Hoylman and Assemblyman Kavanagh, who had been by our side through every phase of this process. Wolfe and I agreed that I would reach out to them first. Zoe and I had planned a weekend away on the East End of Long Island with our friends Andrew Ehrlich, Tania Brief, and their daughters. On a crisp fall day, we brought the kids to Woodside Orchards for cider doughnuts, hay rides, and games. While my kids were climbing on bales of hay, I walked circles around a red barn and spoke to both Senator Hoylman and Assemblyman Kavanagh—who was in Ireland at the time— about the framework of the highly confidential deal that was under way. Periodically, one of my children would bring me an apple cider doughnut as I explained the nature of the preservation plan, the magnitude of the opportunity that was presenting itself, and the need for us to act quickly. Hoylman and Kavanagh each asked questions about the substance—how and why it had come together so fast—and whether the TA was satisfied. Both were pragmatists who understood the complex dynamics, and I felt they were generally supportive of the result. Emma Wolfe followed up my calls with her own to express the mayor's support.

There was a lot of nervous energy at the TA board's Sunday night meeting at John Sheehy's apartment. Several of the TA board members who had been briefed in the intervening days—including Farrelly—were unhappy about the speed with which this proposed plan had taken shape and the fact that they felt they were *reacting to* as opposed to *driving* the conversation. They knew that endorsing this deal would appear to our constituents like a 180-degree turn. For years, the tenants had proposed a conversion to homeownership; now they were suddenly being asked to endorse an all-rental plan, the impacts of which would mostly benefit the next generation of middle-class residents. "Why should we be endorsing a private sale that does not include a conversion?" asked board chair Farrelly in an email in advance of the meeting. "The downside of giving our approval to this private sale is that undoubtedly soon after the closing, the TA will be at loggerheads with the new owner over something. It may be an MCI. It may be a safety issue. It may be Golub notices. It is the nature of the beast that tenants will oppose landlords. How would our members react if we give our blessing to the sale to a particular purchaser when, later, the purchaser does something the tenants don't like? Remember, when a

TA supports a conversion plan, it is essentially endorsing a sale to its own members, not to a new landlord, who may not be the knight in shining armor we think he is."[25]

I braced myself for a difficult meeting. No human being likes to be handed a single option, with pressure to act, particularly when they had been pushing for a different result for nearly ten years. Nearly every member of the board, along with Kane, Rubin, and Genevieve Michel, was present. I had called Marsh, now in retirement from the board, to brief him on the terms and asked him if he would join the meeting to support the deal. He agreed. I sat on a green couch, under floral printed drapes, with the Con Edison power plant outside the window behind me. Farrelly began the meeting, and the room was tense and quiet. Farrelly asked each of the Tenants Association's advisers—Kane, Rubin, and me—to make the case why this was the right deal for the Tenants Association to endorse at this moment.

As the board members listened, with some taking notes, Rubin explained how Manhattan real estate prices had gone way up, and why our proposed conversion plan, even if effectuated, would no longer be accessible to middle-class tenants. He explained that Blackstone intended to use its Core Plus fund to buy the property, which was beneficial to the tenants because it demanded a much smaller return (and created less pressure to raise rents) than the deal Tishman Speyer had struck in 2006. He further explained that Blackstone had partnered with Ivanhoé Cambridge, subsidiary of a Canadian pension fund, and intended to borrow only half the purchase price. Rubin also represented that Blackstone was a conscientious owner, and that we could be certain that it would very much care about not only earning, but keeping, the support of the TA. When he was finished, Farrelly turned to Meredith Kane, who then explained exactly how the preservation of five thousand units would work, and how Blackstone would get locked into its commitment for long-term affordability through a regulatory agreement with the city, which would stay in place even if it sold the property at some point. Finally, Farrelly turned to me. I took a deep breath and acknowledged that many of our neighbors would be disappointed that they would not be able to buy their apartments, but this deal, in my view, was going to be far better for us than letting the property go up for another overheated auction. As a legal matter, we had no leverage over what CWCapital decided to do; the fact that we had any proposal for affordability was the direct result of our outsized advocacy over the years, the support we had from Fannie Mae and Freddie Mac, and MacArthur's understanding of not only our power but also our ability to come to an agreement. I argued that we had in fact driven the conversation, even if the outcome was slightly different from our initial plan.

To me, this was a no-brainer, a moment for the Tenants Association to celebrate the fruits of years of hard work. We were—I hoped—about to endorse a plan that delivered protection for an extraordinary number of units for a considerable period of time. Twenty years was not forever, but the initial MetLife deal with the city had lasted only twenty-five years. Keeping the five thousand units alive for future policy makers to preserve further was critically important. "What elected official is simply going to allow the terms of this deal to expire in 2035?" I asked rhetorically. We were protecting our open spaces from development, we were gaining a long-term owner and keeping the community together as a unified whole. "Don't let this opportunity slip away," I argued. I tried for a moment to ignore the buzzing of my cell phone in my blazer pocket. I pulled it out to silence it and saw that it was Zoe. It was odd, because Zoe knew the sensitive nature of the meeting I was in. I passed the phone to Genevieve Michel as I was midsentence and asked her to pick up and make sure that Zoe was calling me by accident. I saw her face turn grim, as she encouraged me to take the call. I stood up to excuse myself, and Rubin and Kane started to parry questions from the board.

"What's happening?" I asked. I could hear our kids screaming in the background. "Asher has a fish bone stuck in his throat. *It's OK Devin, he'll be OK.* I made fish for dinner. And he's got a bone stuck up in there. *Asher, calm down, sweetie, it's going to be OK, I promise.* I can see it, but I can't get it out, and I think I need to take him to the emergency room," Zoe said. She told me she was going to leave Devin with our neighbors, Samantha and Stephen Shapiro, and head to the hospital with Asher. Both boys were clearly hysterical, Zoe was distraught, and I was only two buildings over. I told her to wait, that I would be right home, and stepped back into the room to quickly explain my urgent and bizarre situation to the group. I gave them a final word of encouragement to endorse this plan and then ran as fast as I could across Peter Cooper. I snatched up Asher in his Batman pajamas and sneakers and took him in a cab to the emergency room of NYU Medical Center. There was nothing else I could do to affect the outcome. My years of work ended with me racing out of the final meeting in a tizzy. Thankfully, Asher was fine. After a series of X-rays, the ER doctors yanked out the fish bone, and we were on our way back home.

While I was in the ER with Asher, the board of the TA discussed the situation. Some felt that Mayor de Blasio had abandoned them because he had not supported a homeownership plan. Others, like Farrelly, questioned why the TA should go out on a limb for this deal at all. "The advisers were ramming it down our throats," Farrelly said. "We were doing exactly what we said we didn't want to do and abandoning our plans for conversion." Some questioned why we weren't preserving more units or finding an affordable-housing developer to be the owner. The overwhelming majority of the group, however, agreed with me that this outcome was the reward for their years of hard work. Marsh, Steinberg, and Doyle all spoke up in support of the deal, observing that it delivered a promise for long-term stability in our community. If MacArthur and Blackstone had not feared the Tenants Association and its elected officials, as well as the political consequences of not doing the right thing, we wouldn't even have been having this conversation. The board gave its approval to the proposed plan, conditioned on Blackstone committing publicly—not just privately—to protecting the open space from development, keeping Stuyvesant Town and Peter Cooper unified, picking up the tab for the years of service that we had gotten from Paul Weiss and Moelis, and ensuring that apartments were marketed to tenants who might be expected to stay for longer periods (and not just students).[26]

The next afternoon, Monday, October 19, I finally met Jon Gray of Blackstone, with Meghji, in the back corner of Le Pain Quotidien on East 44th Street. I had never met Gray before, but his name was repeatedly invoked during our negotiations, and I knew him by reputation. This was an introductory meeting for us and an opportunity to make sure that, through our various surrogates, we had understood each other. I immediately found him to be personally genuine and easy to talk to. Gray reiterated Blackstone's commitment to doing right by the city and the tenants. I was impressed with his sincere approach, and felt that, if tenants had to have a landlord, he was as good as any I could imagine.

I appreciated that Blackstone was true to its word and would not consummate the deal until it was certain it had our blessing—and after the prior night's meeting and vote, I felt that I could give it. I also reminded Gray that the Tenants Association's formal support was contingent on a few factors, all of which Meghji had already agreed to earlier in the day. I welcomed him to the community and told him that I was looking forward to working with him and his team. With my support, and the support of the Tenants Association and the city, Blackstone and Ivanhoé Cambridge felt satisfied that they had what they needed to proceed, and they signed the agreement with CWCapital later that evening.

Bagli, naturally, had the story, and was holding it for the moment that the deal was signed. I had spoken to him earlier in the day and gave him some quotes endorsing the Blackstone deal. I was in a bit of a bind, though. Because of the high level of secrecy that had been necessary to get this deal completed, I had not been able to utter a word to anyone beyond Zoe, the Tenants Association, and Senator Hoylman and Assemblyman Kavanagh. There were advocates, elected officials, and other interested players who deserved to be briefed on this in advance—and would surely be unhappy to read about it in the *New York Times*. I was not going to be responsible for letting this deal fall apart due to premature publicity, but was eager to give them a heads-up as soon as I could. After the meeting with Gray, I headed over to Aretsky's Patroon, a popular East Midtown eatery on 46th Street, where my friend Ken Aretsky had agreed to host a meet-and-greet for me. I had planned to go back to my district office right after the event and make some last-minute calls just before the *Times* story came out.

After mingling for a bit over cocktails, I was formally introduced to the group by Aretsky and began to deliver some remarks about my work as an East Side council member. I spoke for fifteen minutes and took two questions before noticing Genevieve Michel's agitation as she was looking at her iPhone. She was gesturing to me and to her phone, trying to tell me something, which I could not understand as I stood in front of the crowd. Eventually, she walked right up to me in front of the entire room and whispered in my ear: "Bagli's story on the Stuy Town deal just broke." I told the crowd that some exciting news was happening in Stuy Town, a community that had been challenged by the excesses of real estate speculation, which they likely would read about later in the *Times*. Trying not to show the panic that I was feeling, I answered two more questions and then excused myself, thanked Ken Aretsky, and ran back to my district office, three blocks over.

At this point, every moment that went by without my calling to explain myself, I was getting into deeper trouble with various constituents and elected officials. The *Times* headline said it all: "Stuyvesant Town Said to Be Near Sale That Will Preserve Middle-Class Housing." The agreement, the story said, would preserve nearly half the 11,232-unit complex for middle-class families. "This has been a priority for us since Day 1," commented Mayor de Blasio. "We weren't going to lose StuyTown on our watch." In the article, I praised the deal for achieving our core goals of preserving the community as a stable home for New Yorkers today and the future. "This time, the buyer not only has a more patient and stable investment structure, but goes to great lengths to preserve long-term affordability," I said. Once back at the office, I made a round of calls to elected officials, tenants, and anyone I could think of who would need to hear from me.[27]

On the morning of October 20, 2015, the mayoral press team was hard at work. They had set up a podium just off 18th Street and First Avenue, less than two blocks from where in 2006 we had to announce the tenants' first bid in the MetLife auction, and a stone's throw from where we rallied with Senator Schumer in 2010, demanding action from Fannie Mae and Freddie Mac. People had read Bagli's *Times* story, and the news was getting out that there had been a sale of Stuy Town overnight. Curious neighbors and television cameras began to gather, and while most residents did not know that the mayor was coming personally, it was clear that something big was about to happen at that spot. You could feel the quiet tension and hear the uncertain whispers among the people who had assembled to see what was going on.

I put on a crisp blue tie and walked over from my Peter Cooper apartment. I was even more nervous than I had been nine years earlier—the day after my date with Zoe—when I had stood around the corner to announce the long-shot tenant bid. I was now married, a father of two boys, and had nearly a decade of public service under my belt. The first time was aspirational, and we were the scrappy underdog, taking a chance to fight for our community. This was different. After years of trying to explain every move and rationale to our constituents in advance, we had struck a deal, seemingly overnight. It had been the right thing to do but was different from our original goal. This was not the way that I would have preferred to do it, but I had seen enough over the years to know when it was important to say yes to a good option. Before the press conference started, I went over to say hello to a few people I knew from the neighborhood. "What does this mean, Dan?" "What happened to conversion?" "Am I still protected in my rent-stabilized unit?" I stood near the crowd and answered as many questions as I could from nervous neighbors before the event started. Milling around the podium were Blackstone's top executives, including Jon Gray, Nadeem Meghji, and Sheehy's East Hampton neighbor A. J. Agarwal. A huge contingent of mayoral aides, Susan Steinberg, Al Doyle, and much of the Tenants Association board, including John Sheehy, Anne Greenberg, Sherry Kirschenbaum, Soni Fink, and Sandro Sherrod, were also there. Senator Brad Hoylman, Assemblyman Brian Kavanagh, and Borough President Gale Brewer were on hand and had been invited to speak at the event. Mayor de Blasio got out of his SUV on the Stuy Town Loop Road and, together with Deputy Mayor Glen and Housing Commissioner Been, came and joined the group.

I welcomed the crowd and turned the microphone over to Mayor de Blasio, who proudly declared that this was "the mother of all preservation deals," and the largest city-led affordable-housing preservation plan in the history of New York City. "This is a great day for New York City, this is a great victory for tenants everywhere. And this is a great victory for the tenants of Stuyvesant Town and Peter Cooper, and we would not be here but for the fact that you wouldn't give up. You believed in protecting housing for middle class and working people, you believed that that ideal was not dead in New York City and you did something about it." De Blasio lamented that some market-rate units in Stuy Town had gotten to $7,000 or $8,000 a month, "far out of reach of working class and middle-class people," and called this deal a "major part" of his goal to build or preserve two hundred thousand units of housing. He expressed pride in the five thousand units that we preserved, because this deal would give future leaders the opportunity "to come back to this to extend affordability further." Most importantly, he was pleased that he could take the opportunity to "undo the mistake that was made a decade ago."[28]

Assemblyman Kavanagh praised Blackstone, saying that "their announcement here demonstrates that rapacious cold-hearted capitalism that had taken hold in many quarters is not necessary in order to be a responsible steward of investors' money, and also responsible stewards of a community like this." Senator Hoylman called it "a ray of light above Stuy Town after so many years of uncertainty" and cheered the organizing mettle of the Tenants Association. Congresswoman Carolyn Maloney praised the deal, celebrating that—in contrast to what Tishman Speyer had done in 2006—it would not "unleash a new wave of harassment of tenants in affordable apartments."[29]

"We don't typically do press conferences in my line of work," quipped Blackstone's Jon Gray. He described the shared mission and fierce sense of urgency to preserve something special in Stuy Town, and, to applause, he said, "The uncertainty and turmoil that this complex has endured since the financial crisis is definitively over." He explained that Blackstone's patient pool of capital and partnership with Ivanhoé Cambridge would allow it to "own it for a long period of time." I proudly listened as Gray checked off his support of the Tenants Association's principles, which I had sketched out in my living room five years earlier. Susan Steinberg took a stab at explaining to our neighbors why we did not deliver a home-ownership opportunity. Despite our initial idea that homeownership was the only way to retain our community's "stable and middle-class roots," when the value of the property skyrocketed from $1.7 billion to three times that amount, "the idea of ownership became tenuous. But we did not lose sight of the prize. We developed principles which we continued to pursue throughout all of these years—middle-class affordability, keeping our community as a unified whole, and preservation of open spaces. We were insistent that any purchaser would commit to these nonnegotiable principles." Steinberg noted that our doggedness was largely responsible for the outcome, and said, to knowing laughs, that the Tenants Association would continue to advocate for its core interests.[30]

I don't know if I could have predicted the long road we traveled, or the perseverance, strength, and ultimate success of this tenant community. I felt very proud of how far we had come and congratulated my neighbors for this extraordinary outcome, based on years of agitation and hard work. "We all know what typically happens. The deal is done. Tenants are displaced. And money is made," I said. "And that is the story that was probably supposed to happen here, but that is not what is going to happen here today." Because of our advocacy over a decade, "the real

Figure 14.1. We announced our deal with Blackstone on October 20, 2015, in Stuy Town. Jonathan Gray, president and chief operating officer of the Blackstone Group, proclaimed that the "uncertainty and turmoil that this complex has endured since the financial crisis is definitively over." *From left*, Mayor Bill de Blasio, Gray (at lectern), me, Manhattan borough president Gale Brewer, and Tenants Association president Susan Steinberg. Photo credit: Blackstone Group.

estate world had taken notice and our cause became the cause of so many in the tenant movement. We were relentless, and never gave up fighting for our homes." I welcomed Blackstone to our community, recognized the strongest and best tenants association in the entire city, and gave a hearty thanks to Mayor de Blasio, without whose help we would not have been standing there. "We knew right from the start that you would support the tenants' priorities," I said, and thanked him for "setting a tone that made our success almost inevitable."

Not a single speaker mentioned the name Andrew MacArthur or Doug Harmon—both of whom were there to watch the press conference—or CWCapital, Centerbridge, or Fortress. MacArthur, with Harmon at his side, had moved mountains, and balanced several simultaneous sensitive negotiations within a short two-week period—between CWCapital and its parent company Fortress, between CWCapital and Centerbridge, between Blackstone and CWCapital, between Blackstone and the city, and between Blackstone and the tenants—to get this done.[31] Both he and Harmon deserved more recognition than they got.

Harmon smiled as he listened to the speeches. His promise to Gray had come true. Here Gray was, being cheered by the tenants and the mayor of New York City. And at the same time, Harmon would no longer be haunted by the deal that got away from him and then so famously collapsed. He was now the proud adviser of the highest-priced deal ever achieved for any real estate asset of any kind in the world (office, residential, or retail)—at $5.44 billion—all done with long-term affordability protections. "We took an infected property with one of the worst sale histories of all time, with crazy passionate and outspoken tenants, and we flipped every element. We sold it without drama, and everyone could sleep at night. Few deals of such magnitude can have such a fairy tale ending." said Harmon.[32]

Following the press conference, Blackstone immediately released a dynamic video about its investment in Stuy Town, featuring time-lapse sequences, drone shots of the buildings, and images highlighting the beauty of the grounds. "A Middle Class Oasis in New York Is Spared," appeared on the screen, citing the *New York Times* headline. "Middle Class Wins in NYC Housing Deal," and "Middle Class Units Saved," flashed quotes from the *Boston Globe* and *Washington Post.* Jon Gray summarized: "We told the seller that we wanted a comprehensive solution that could end up being a win-win-win. The seller gets a full and fair price, the city maintains affordability, tenants are happy with who takes over and we can make a good investment on behalf of our own investors. And that was the premise of the deal."[33]

The Tenants Association called a community meeting for that following Saturday at Baruch College, billed as an opportunity to meet senior Blackstone officials, like Nadeem Meghji, who would become for this first period the new face of ownership of our community. Meghji stood up in front of a large crowd of tenants and introduced himself and his firm. The *Real Deal* observed that in his remarks Meghji had sprinkled "more appeals to local sentiment than a presidential campaigner in Iowa."[34] He told the group how he used to jog through the complex from his Union Square apartment to the East River and how many Blackstone employees lived in Stuy Town. "We know that we are going to need to earn your trust," he said, answering questions about everything from the community grocery store to the long-term affordability plans. Mayor de Blasio and Senator Schumer both came to the meeting to recognize the work of the Tenants Association and to share in the celebration.

Welcoming the crowd, I took them through the details of the deal that we had struck. I also took a moment to add a little more transparency to the process and say the things that I thought would have actually hurt our chances if I had said them out loud earlier. I reminded my neighbors how little leverage we truly had had in the transaction. Despite our bluster and talk of "demanding a seat at the table," CWCapital had never been required by law to engage with us. It would have been well within its rights to bypass the city entirely or have a public auction. "In fact, they could have simply sold the property to a sovereign wealth fund that could have used vacancy decontrol, Golub notices, and any other tool available, to grind down the rent-stabilized units to zero and use the hundreds of thousands of development rights to build new buildings on the property. Tishman Speyer part two," I said. It was because of the tenants' advocacy and hard work that none of that happened.[35]

As expected, we heard from a small group of tenants who were unhappy with Blackstone, us, and the city. One tenant demanded to know why it was just the Tenants Association and not others who got to be informed of the terms of the deal before it was signed. Steinberg did her best to address the speed at which this all came to be, and how we were not able to consult every resident in real time. Another raised the question of what would happen in twenty years when the affordability component of the agreement was set to expire: "So you'll do in 20 years what Tishman Speyer did in 10," he said, skeptically.[36] We reminded the audience that the original MetLife deal was only for a term of twenty-five years, and that another twenty years provided an additional generation of affordability for families to raise their children within a stable, middle-class community.

Other residents asked us to explain a story from October 22 in the *Wall Street Journal* called "The Stuyvesant Town Deal Sweetener,"[37] which provocatively suggested that the city had quietly granted Blackstone the right to sell and transfer Stuyvesant Town's unused development rights. The reality, however, was very different from what the article claimed. Protecting Stuy Town's open spaces was fundamental to the TA and to me; Blackstone had promised to protect them from development, but in doing so, stranded itself with development rights it could not use. In order to get the deal over the finish line with this important component secured, the city had committed to help Blackstone *explore* transferring the development rights at a date in the future, but that was the extent of the commitment—merely a hand in helping think through options. Any proposed plan would need to go through the city's byzantine land-use approval process and secure the support of two neighboring city council members, as well as a majority of the entire city council, and therefore was far from a given.

No deal makes all people happy all the time. But despite a small minority of dissenting voices, this deal earned widespread support for what it accomplished. The plan had been endorsed by the mayor of New York City, the senior senator from New York, a full assortment of elected leaders, and the Stuyvesant Town Peter Cooper Village Tenants Association. The preservation plan was "widely praised" by the media, even by the anonymous blog *Stuyvesant Town Report*, which said the "winner at this time is affordable housing. At least for twenty years." The *New York Times* editorial board cheered the "impressive deal" we had struck for a relatively "modest price." It also supported the fact that we were standing up for people of middle incomes. "It takes many strata to make a mountain, and New York's affordability crisis weighs heavily on pretty much everybody who is not in the top 1 percent," they wrote.[38] The *Guardian* wrote, "It's a victory beyond numbers—proof that affordable housing can still be a municipal priority on Manhattan island if determined tenants and public officials make it one."[39]

Prominent housing advocates agreed. "Given how few cards the city had to play, they overall did an impressive job of trying to get something good out of a bad situation without getting their pockets picked," explained Benjamin Dulchin, the director of the Association for Neighborhood and Housing Development, an affordable-housing advocacy group. The status quo in Stuyvesant Town and Peter Cooper would have kept the community on track to lose every single one of its affordable units over time. We negotiated a preservation deal of five thousand units, where the alternative—in the absence of any change in state law to strengthen rent stabilization, which we had no reason to believe would happen at the time—was for them to dwindle down to zero. Former housing commissioner Rafael Cestero attributed the deal's success to the advocacy of tenants over the years. "Nobody wanted to go through it all again. The market became smarter and understood that the better outcome was to do it this way," he said. "As for the deal, it was the deal to do."[40]

"Residents Exhale after Stuyvesant Town Is Sold," said a *New York Times* headline the day after the announcement.[41] Nearly ten years, three owners, and many bumps later, our neighbors had set a new model for how a large group of organized tenants could come together and act as viable players in a commercial transaction to advocate and win for their community. While fighting back against bad and illegal acts, managing many discordant views in the community, building coalitions, being challenged by outside investors, and demanding a seat at the table, we always felt that this cause was too important for us to allow for failure. Ultimately, we were able to reach our goal to preserve the middle-class character of the community and extend affordability well into the next generation. But while we had scored a victory, we also knew that the deal was a temporary reprieve. While twenty years covered the next generation of tenants, we all knew that questions about the future of Stuy Town would surface again.

Until then, Stuy Town continues to be a special place to live and raise a family. Both connected to and separate from the excitement of

Figure 14.2. At the end of my city council term on August 15, 2017, NASDAQ invited me to ring the opening bell in celebration of my twelve-year tenure. I spoke about our successes in Stuyvesant Town. Here, I am pictured with Zoe, Asher, and an exuberant Devin. Photo credit: NASDAQ Inc.

the rest of New York, for me and so many other families it has offered community and, most important, stability. As of the writing of this book, I have been a resident for nearly forty-eight years. My dad continues to live in Peter Cooper, in the apartment that we moved into in 1976, and comes over for dinner once a week to visit with his grandsons. My own children play football and baseball on the lawns in front of our building and flit back and forth between the apartments of neighbors, whose kids they met at our local day care.

We talk to our neighbors constantly about schools, safety, and how to manage the extreme cost of living in New York City. Housing expenses are central to those conversations, and the lure of more space, great schools, and a house in the suburbs is simply too irresistible to many. But, as a result of the Tenants Association and its advocacy over a decade, the stability afforded by rent stabilization, a court victory in *Roberts*, and our 2015 agreement, thousands of middle-class New Yorkers don't have to wonder if they will be able to afford the rent when their renewal comes up every two years. The result is a stronger neighborhood and a stronger city.

Epilogue

Loopholes Closed

For its internal communications about Stuy Town, Moelis and Company called its work with the Tenants Association "Project David," because they knew that this was going to be a David-versus-Goliath dynamic.

In situations like this, the little guy normally gets run over by the forces of big banks and real estate. What made our effort different was that our organized tenant group was not only vocal and passionate, we were willing to take a risk by balancing a variety of competing interests and, in a very public way, to try to find solutions. By partnering with professionals who could guide us and capital sources that could give us credibility in the marketplace, we surprised a lot of people and competed on the biggest stage. Above all, it shows that when an organized community steps up with not only passion but also ideas and a practical path to victory, there is a chance for David to prevail.

After the deal closed, there was, for the first time in many years, a feeling of stability in the community. We had been passed from owner to owner for nearly a decade, and with almost every new change came a fresh round of uncertainty and a new battle. Now the property had been sold once more, but this time we had set the terms of our transfer, and our new owner was looking to deliver on our partnership and bring back normalcy and calm to our day-to-day lives.

Blackstone's first move was to install a property manager in the community who could earn the trust of our neighbors, who were still deeply cynical after so many years of problems. Rick Hayduk, the new manager, at first appeared a risky choice for this task. Hayduk was an experienced property manager who had built his reputation managing luxury resorts, hotels, and country clubs. He came directly to us from one of Blackstone's Florida properties called the Boca Raton Resort & Club and was known by the team as the "mayor of Boca." Our middle-class complex was a far cry from the types of high-end resorts Hayduk was used to—in fact, we had deliberately challenged Tishman Speyer's notion of the property as a "luxury enclave"—and I was pretty sure Hayduk had no idea what he was in for. "This guy is going to get eaten alive," I thought.

I remained skeptical of the choice even after I had a chance to interact with him. At our first meeting, Hayduk sat down and genially described his "client-is-never-wrong" strategy that he had employed working with so many retirees in Florida. I looked at him and said, with tongue in cheek, "Are you sure you know what you're getting yourself into here?" There were a lot of clients in Stuy Town, and in my experience, each demanded full attention. Accepting my challenge, he responded with a confident smile, "We are here to serve." I loved his attitude and enjoyed him personally, but thought he was charmingly naive. There was really no comparison between a fancy resort in Boca and the burdens of rent-stabilized tenants in New York City. A handful of tenant leaders had also had a chance to meet him the night before in Farrelly's apartment and largely came to the same conclusion: nice guy, but his luxury hotel management experience seemed a strange fit for Stuy Town.

We were all wrong. Hayduk moved fast, and he earned a reputation for responsive, steady leadership. His first act was to relocate his family into an apartment in Peter Cooper Village, putting himself right in the middle of the community he was there to serve. After his formal appointment in early January, he announced four community events to "meet the new property manager," with coffee and snacks, under a tent in a Stuyvesant Town playground. Hundreds of tenants showed up to meet him; these were the first events of their type in anyone's memory. I went to two of the receptions to say hello to my constituents and also to get a sense of how Hayduk was handling the situation. I watched him work the crowd with ease, give welcoming remarks, with great humility and access, freely handing out his cell phone number to residents. As a line of residents patiently waited for a moment of his time, I politely interrupted, shook his hand, and said gleefully, "Better you than me!"

Within a few months, calls to my office complaining about resident problems dropped off a cliff. What used to be around one hundred calls a week from Stuyvesant Town and Peter Cooper residents complaining about heat, neighbor noise, accounting issues, or many other subjects were now down to a handful. "In a very short time he established a cordial yet firmly-organized approach in running the property. He quickly installed many improvements, ranging from the appearance of the property to its operations," Sheehy said.[1] It was a breath of fresh air. Six months into his tenure, he had gotten the amount of time for certain maintenance requests down from twenty days to three days. He was making personal connections to many residents, who appreciated his earnestness and accessibility. In a moment of candor, Hayduk did admit to me that there were a fair number of people who were giving him a hard time—but he clearly was handling it quite well.

My office liaison to Stuy Town, Howie Levine, came with me to pay Hayduk a visit on July 21, 2016, at the new management office, to see how things were progressing. Hayduk showed us words on the whiteboard in the conference room. They said, "We Create Community in Manhattan. We are good neighbors; we are better today than yesterday; we do the right thing." It concluded, "A little caring goes a long way." He told us that after years of so much conflict with residents, his inherited staff actually felt liberated when their instructions were to help people, as opposed to stonewalling them. When Levine and I left the meeting, we looked at each other, and Levine said, "He is so good." In the final days of 2017, Brick Underground did an analysis to assess the twelve best landlords in Manhattan. Number one on the list was Stuy Town Property Management Services, for its record in addressing maintenance issues.[2]

At the same time, new residents slowly and steadily started occupying the units that were protected by the 2015 deal. Through periodic open lotteries, people whose incomes were below the middle-income thresholds were selected to move into Stuy Town. In earlier times, potential residents had been screened on very different criteria—at first, MetLife looked at their race and denied access to Black residents. They also for years insisted that residents meet a *minimum* income threshold, and met with applicants to assess their "appropriateness." Now, for the first time in the community's history, people were being screened for below-market units based on a *maximum* income threshold. As each year goes by, more and more of these units are being occupied by such income-qualifying residents. And with a deal that removed significant pressure on the landlord to push out existing rent-stabilized tenants, Golub notices became extremely rare, and tenants once again were assured a relatively stable existence.

The middle class in the rest of the city, however, continues to struggle. Even after our success in Stuy Town, New York City's middle class continued to be in full retreat. Sixty-one percent of New Yorkers were ensconced in the middle class in the 1970s, and today, fewer than half are. Middle-class incomes continued to fall faster in New York City than in other major US cities. Of the estimated 175,000 net new private-sector jobs that have been created in New York City since 2017, fewer than 20 percent were paying middle-class salaries, and when you add the costs of housing and other living expenses, middle-class residents continue to get squeezed.[3]

Of course, the hotly debated rent regulation system remains as a firewall against rising housing costs for tenants. From 1974 on, it had been the core mission of the Tenants Association to fight for the renewal and strengthening of rent-stabilization laws in Albany. Those protections ensured that Stuy Town would continue to be affordable to people like Doyle, Steinberg, and Marsh. It was those protections that had created a middle-class community to begin with, which was the baseline for what we were fighting to preserve. Since their inception, those laws had been under attack. Because the New York State Senate had been controlled by Republicans for much of the twentieth century, as a practical matter that meant that tenant-friendly initiatives—like strengthening rent stabilization, ending vacancy decontrol, or reforming the ways tenants paid for major capital improvements—were dead on arrival. At our October 20, 2015, press conference announcing the Stuy Town deal, Senator Hoylman reminded the crowd of this reality: "We won the battle, but not the war. The war is in Albany, folks."[4]

Then, in 2018, everything changed. As part of the blue wave that swept the country that year in the November elections, the Democratic Party took thirty-nine of the sixty-three seats in the New York State Senate. With the Democrats controlling the Senate, the Assembly, and the governor's mansion, they now had complete control over New York State government for the first time in decades.[5] Almost immediately, tenant advocates started developing a strategy to push through some major reforms.

On January 10, 2019, I attended Mayor de Blasio's State of the City speech at Symphony Space as a citizen. I had been term limited from the city council one year earlier, and became the president of the not-for-profit Riverside Park Conservancy. Before the speech started, I ran into my newly inaugurated assemblyman for Stuy Town, Harvey Epstein. I had worked for years with Epstein in his role as a lawyer at the Urban Justice Center and had endorsed him in his race for the New York State Assembly. I knew of the renewed efforts by Democrats to push through stronger rent protections, and asked Epstein what he thought would likely happen. Ending vacancy decontrol, which had done so much harm in Stuy Town, was on the table—as was reforming the MCI rules that so favored landlords, and even the J-51 tax abatement. If enacted, these changes would have significant impact on all rent-stabilized tenants statewide. Additionally, in Stuy Town, we had fourteen hundred tenants whose units had been returned to rent stabilization because of the *Roberts* settlement and who were on the cusp of losing that rent-stabilized status when the J-51 tax abatement expired in 2020. While we had negotiated with Blackstone to slow those units' return to market—capping increases after 2020 to 5 percent a year for five years—those tenants still faced significant rent increases, which for many might be unaffordable. As a group, these *Roberts* tenants had also been the ones most eager to have a homeownership option and had the most reason to be disappointed with the deal we struck.

"I think we will fix all of that, including J-51, Dan, yes," Epstein told me. I was surprised by his confidence only one month into the job. I was so unaccustomed to the notion that the state legislature would ever do anything in favor of tenants. Now Epstein was telling me that not only was the state going to take aim at the traditional loopholes that landlords used to remove apartments from rent stabilization, like vacancy decontrol, but the Democratic-controlled legislature and governor were prepared to go much further and extend protections to a whole new category of units—including the *Roberts* units. "We are changing the rules so that apartments covered by J-51 stay regulated, even after the benefits run out," he told me.

What the legislators actually did, however, defied absolutely all expectations. In June 2019, the New York State Legislature eliminated vacancy decontrol, the most effective tool that landlords had to pull units out of rent stabilization, and which had led to deregulation of more than 155,000 units from the time it was enacted in the 1990s until 2019. The legislators also made rent stabilization *permanent*, which meant that the Tenants Association did not need to fight for its renewal in Albany every few years. Moreover, they repealed the "vacancy bonus," a provision that had allowed landlords to raise rents by up to 20 percent whenever a tenant moved out of a rent-stabilized apartment; and they capped the amount that could be passed on to tenants for major capital improvements. "These reforms give New Yorkers the strongest tenant protections in history," the Senate majority leader, Andrea Stewart-Cousins, and the Assembly speaker, Carl E. Heastie, said in a statement. "For too long, power has been tilted in favor of landlords and these measures finally restore equity and extend protections to tenants across the state."[6]

By making rent stabilization permanent and eliminating vacancy decontrol altogether, the government in Albany had effectively assured that every unit in Stuyvesant Town and Peter Cooper Village became permanently rent stabilized. This included not only the units that had been rent stabilized since 1974 but also the units that had been illegally deregulated and returned to rent stabilization under the *Roberts* case. With a majority vote in both houses of the legislature, and the governor's signature, these officials in Albany had made an even greater impact in Stuy Town than the entire regulatory agreement in Stuyvesant Town that we had fought for a decade to achieve and negotiated so carefully in 2015. With these law changes, Blackstone still retains the obligation to protect five thousand units for middle-class people, but it lost the opportunity to deregulate the *Roberts* units (which it otherwise was allowed to start doing in 2020)—and to recoup most costs of its renovations—dealing it a significant blow.

Despite this profound development, tenant advocates remain on alert. In reality, nothing is ever permanent in New York State law. As vacancy decontrol revealed, these policies can come and go, and then come back again with a vengeance. Blackstone may have assumed the risk of some state law changes when it entered the deal, but it likely did not expect new rules to overturn all its economic assumptions. The Tenants Association became immediately concerned that Blackstone appeared to be taking the position in private conversations that the new state law did not apply to Stuy Town because of the existence of its regulatory agreement with the city. Rather than wait to find out what Blackstone would do, the TA filed a lawsuit seeking a "declaratory judgment" that any deregulation of any Stuy Town unit would be inconsistent with the 2019 state law. Blackstone responded and committed to not raising rents beyond what the new state law allows, until the legal matter is decided. Meanwhile, perhaps inevitably, the real estate community is challenging the validity of the new state law altogether—and rent stabilization generally—calling it an unconstitutional taking of their property. This is a battle that some expect will go all the way to the US Supreme Court.

Through all the twists, I remain optimistic about the future of Stuyvesant Town as a middle-class haven in a city that is increasingly made up of rich people and poor people and little in between. Regardless of what happens with the rent-stabilization laws, we successfully put an asterisk on sixty-four hundred units—five thousand in the regulatory agreement, and fourteen hundred more through the *Roberts* case—as something special, as units that are home to ten to fifteen thousand people and must be treated differently from all the rest, and which future policy makers have an obligation to monitor and protect. And the story of how we got there shows that this community will not let them forget it. There was never a guarantee that there would be a satisfying outcome here. The legacy of the Stuy Town tenants is one of perseverance by passionate neighbors with a cause who fought not only for their own economic safety, but also for that of the generation that would follow them.

ACKNOWLEDGMENTS

First and foremost, I want to thank my neighbors in Peter Cooper Village and Stuyvesant Town, and the board and volunteers of the city's fiercest Tenants Association that simply refused to give up. They were the best possible partners in fighting this most unusual battle, and worked with good humor and steely resolve. Thanks to Al Doyle, for his calm strength, to John Marsh, for his passion and energy, and to Susan Steinberg, for her smarts and humor in difficult times. Longtime resident John Sheehy joined us midway through and helped to bring critical insights and direction to the discussion. Soni Fink passed away before this book was published. Her wit and strength of character kept us focused, and I was grateful for her friendship. And thanks to Steven Sanders, who grew up in Stuy Town, became its assemblyman, and continues to always be a thoughtful and devoted supporter of our community. Each of them not only was a leader in this journey but also was very helpful in making sure that I told this story accurately.

My friends Julie Ehrlich and Steven Newmark agreed to join the Tenants Association board at my urging and threw themselves wholeheartedly into the cause, devoting countless hours and significant brainpower over many years. And, of course, colorful and passionate longtime resident John Crotty put lots of big ideas in my head—and then gave me the critical tools to execute them.

I was fortunate to have a very talented city council staff over twelve years. I am endlessly grateful to them for their devotion to our constituents and for keeping me sane throughout. Many of them were involved in the Stuy Town saga, including Justine Almada, who literally walked three miles in the snow for her job interview, and was my first liaison to Stuy Town; Andrew Sullivan, my city council campaign manager and first chief of staff; Marianna Vaidman Stone, who showed up to help me on every single difficult land-use project that I encountered over twelve years; Dan Pasquini, who headed our early communications team; David Kimball-Stanley, who was my district chief of staff; and Ilona Kramer, who started as an intern and returned to become my chief of staff. Thanks as well to Gretchen Kruesi, Grace Phillipp, Anicka Kolarik, Priom Ahmed, Shayla Mars, Emma Lowe, Matt Scanlan, Lily Mandlin, Tim Laughlin, Elena Aarons, and Howie Levine, all of whom fielded hundreds of calls from Stuy Town residents with every complaint you could imagine. And to Ellen Gustafson, who for years smoothly helped me to move through my day and made it look easy.

Special recognition to my chief of staff and friend Genevieve Michel, the brass-knuckled Californian who for five years was my chief adviser and partner in all matters, including the race to be city council speaker (though it's still too bad she doesn't know how to drive). She was, and is, an important sounding board for me, and was also gracious enough to be one of the early readers of this book.

Thank you to Sabina Mollot and Chris Hagedorn of *Town & Village* newspaper, for allowing me to bury myself in the archives of the paper's headquarters in New Rochelle for research. And extra thanks to Sabina for going through her own finicky computer to identify useful photos.

I want to express my appreciation to William Kelly and the late Marie Beirne, who spent considerable time interviewing Stuy Town residents on video and allowed me to view the rough footage. Thank you to Sherry

Glied, dean of NYU Wagner School, for hosting me as a Visiting Scholar and giving me the space to focus, and to my Hunter College Grove Scholars Juan Cambeiro, Isidora Echeverria, Florimond Le Goupil-Maier, and Nicole Retsepter, who helped with some early research.

Meredith Kane, Alex Kornberg, and Brian Hermann of Paul Weiss, and Alex Rubin and Bill Derrough of Moelis & Company were instrumental in our efforts. They took enormous risks, personal and professional, to support the Stuy Town tenants, and never wavered in their commitment to the cause. I'd also like to thank Paul Weiss in particular, for giving me great training as a lawyer and then supporting every professional effort that I have ever undertaken. That of course includes my friend Andrew Ehrlich, who served as my campaign treasurer, best man at my wedding, and who has been with me every step of this journey.

Thank you to everyone I interviewed for this book, whose names and quotes appear throughout. I enjoyed reliving the events with you. Thanks also to Janette Sadik-Khan, Paul Elie, and Harold Holzer for helping me to develop my initial proposal and get it off the ground, and to Rohit Aggarwala for his early guidance. With much appreciation to Peter McGuigan, my agent at Ultra Literary, who knew just the right moment to break out the tequila; to my editor Michael McGandy for recognizing the importance of this story; and to the team at Cornell University Press, including Clare Kirkpatrick Jones, Ashley Julia Britts, Karen Hwa, and Brock Edward Schnoke.

I am very lucky to have some wonderful friends who were willing to jump in as turbo proofreaders at the eleventh hour, when my bleary eyes could no longer see words. Jesse Johnston, Tania Brief, Marianna Vaidman Stone, Sigal Mandelker, Jean Weinberg, Michael Woloz, and Jeff Wald— you went above and beyond, and for that, I am incredibly grateful. You are the best.

Thank you to my friend Jean Manas, for giving me so much unsolicited guidance over the years—including encouraging me to write a book. I was bound to take your advice at some point.

To my mom and dad, Barbara and David Garodnick, who gave me everything I needed for success in life. They filled me with strength and confidence, and always worked to find ways to reduce my stress. They were just about the best parents that anyone could hope for. I miss my mom very much, and suspect that she would have loved that her son actually wrote a book. My dad continues to be by my side, cheering me on and firmly believing that I would be the winner in any political office for which I might ever run, at any level.

I am incredibly grateful for my two dynamic sons, Asher, who is empathetic and wise beyond his years, and Devin, who is filled with creativity and determination. These boys bring me life's greatest joy, and their presence reminds me every day about what really matters.

And for my incredibly talented, smart, thoughtful wife, Zoe, who read this book more times than she reasonably had time to do, gave me brutally honest feedback, and is my very best friend and editor: I love you very much. This would not have happened without you.

NOTES

Prologue

1. Jon Gray, chief operating officer, Blackstone Group, public statement, October 20, 2015, https://www1.nyc.gov/office-of-the-mayor/news/736-15/mayor-local-elected-officials-tenant-leaders-20-year-agreement-blackstone-and#/0.

2. New York City Department of Housing Preservation and Development, https://www1.nyc.gov/site/hpd/renters/affordable-housing.page; Andy A. Beveridge, "Stuyvesant Town and Peter Cooper Village, Then and Now," Gotham Gazette, September 14, 2006, https://www.gothamgazette.com/demographics/3362-stuyvesant-town-and-peter-cooper-village-then-and-now.

3. Janny Scott, "Cities Shed Middle Class, and Are Richer and Poorer for It," *New York Times*, July 23, 2006, https://www.nytimes.com/2006/07/23/weekinreview/23scott.html.

4. David Madland, "The Middle Class Grows the Economy, Not the Rich," Center for American Progress, December 7, 2011, https://www.americanprogress.org/issues/economy/news/2011/12/07/10773/the-middle-class-grows-the-economy-not-the-rich-2/.

1. Activism from the Start

1. Joseph A. Spencer, "New York City Tenant Organizations and the Post–World War I Housing Crisis," in *The Tenant Movement in New York City, 1904–1984*, ed. Ronald Lawson (Rutgers University Press, 1986), accessed July 15, 2019, http://www.tenant.net/Community/history/hist02a.html; New York City Rent Guidelines Board, *2018 Housing Supply Report*, May 24, 2018.

2. Charles V. Bagli, *Other People's Money: Inside the Housing Crisis and the Demise of the Greatest Real Estate Deal Ever Made* (New York: Dutton, 2013), 10.

3. Mark Naison, "From Eviction Resistance to Rent Control—Tenant Activism in the Great Depression," in Lawson, *Tenant Movement*, chap. 3; Arthur Simon, *Stuyvesant Town USA: Pattern for Two Americas* (New York: NYU Press, 1970), 21; "Metropolitan Life Makes Housing Pay," *Fortune*, April 1946.

4. "Act to Aid Housing Here," *New York Times*, February 20, 1943, 16; Warren Moscow, "Dewey Signs Bill Cutting Income Tax," *New York Times*, February 19, 1943, 26; Simon, *Stuyvesant Town USA*, 20–22; Bagli, *Other People's Money*, 14–15.

5. "East Side Suburb in City to House 30,000 after War," *New York Times*, April 19, 1943, 1.

6. "East Side Suburb," *New York Times*, April 19, 1943, 1; Simon, *Stuyvesant Town USA*, 22; Moscow, "Dewey Signs Bill."

7. Simon, *Stuyvesant Town USA*, 25; Loula Lasker, "Housing Plans Disapproved," Letters to the Editor, *New York Times*, May 28, 1943, 22; Robert Moses, "Stuyvesant Town Defended," Letters to the Editor, *New York Times*, June 3, 1943, 20.

8. Simon, *Stuyvesant Town USA*, 49.

9. "New Housing Unit Is Approved, 5 to 1," *New York Times*, May 21, 1943, 8; "Stuyvesant Town Approved by Board," *New York Times*, June 4, 1943, 23.

10. "Stuyvesant Town Approved," 23; Simon, *Stuyvesant Town USA*, 33.

11. Simon, *Stuyvesant Town USA*, 35; "Housing Projects to Increase Rents," *New York Times*, June 12, 1947, 25.

12. "Sues Stuyvesant Town," *New York Times*, June 8, 1943; Vera Penavic, "Vintage NYC Photos: The Gas House District That Became Stuy Town," Untapped New York, https://untappedcities.com/2016/04/18/vintage-nyc-photos-the-gas-house-district-that-became-stuy-town/; "Uprooted Thousands Starting Trek from Site for Stuyvesant Town," *New York Times*, March 3, 1945, 13.

13. "Uprooted Thousands."

14. "Uprooted Thousands."

15. "Last Tenant Vacated in Stuyvesant Town," *New York Times*, May 5, 1946.

16. "7,000 Rush Pleas for Housing in '47," *New York Times*, June 6, 1946, 29; "Stuyvesant Town to Get Its First Tenants Today," *New York Times*, August 1, 1947, 19.

17. Housing Projects to Increase Rents, *New York Times*, June 12, 1947, 25; "Increase in Rent for Stuyvesant Town and Riverton Houses Is Asked of City," *New York Times*, April 25, 1947, 12.

18. Woldoff, Morrison, and Glass, *Priced Out*, 20.

19. "Stuyvesant Town Upheld on Appeal," *New York Times*, December 21, 1948, 27; "Stuyvesant Town Answers Protest," *New York Times*, November 19, 1949, 9.

20. "Stuyvesant Town Negro Ban Upheld by Court of Appeals," *New York Times*, July 20, 1949, 1.

21. "Tenants Protest Bias," *New York Times*, April 6, 1949, 58.

22. "Negro Couple Guests in Stuyvesant Town, First of Their Race Admitted to Project," *New York Times*, August 12, 1949, 19.

23. Amy Fox, "Battle in Black and White," *New York Times*, March 26, 2006, https://www.nytimes.com/2006/03/26/nyregion/thecity/battle-in-black-and-white.html.

24. "Negro 'House Guests' in Stuyvesant Town 'Introduced' at Party for A.L.P. Aspirant," *New York Times*, October 31, 1949, 27.

25. "Council Passes Bill Barring Bias in All City-Aided Private Housing," *New York Times*, February 17, 1951, 1; "Mayor Stays Silent on Stuyvesant Town," *New York Times*, August 26, 1950, 11; "Housing Unit Hints End of Negro Ban," *New York Times*, August 9, 1950, 30.

26. Simon, *Stuyvesant Town USA*, 91; "Council Passes Bill Barring Bias in All City-Aided Private Housing"; Martha Biondi, *To Stand and Fight: The Struggle for Civil Rights in Postwar New York City* (Cambridge, MA: Harvard University Press, 2003), 135.

27. Simon, *Stuyvesant Town USA*, 91; Fox, "Battle in Black and White."

28. Simon, *Stuyvesant Town USA*, 98; Fox, "Battle in Black and White."

29. "Stuyvesant Town Drops Evictions as Halley Intervenes as Mediator," *New York Times*, January 21, 1952, 1; Fox, "Battle in Black and White"; Simon, *Stuyvesant Town USA*, 99.

30. Biondi, *To Stand and Fight*, 135.

31. Alvin Doyle Jr., interview with the author, New York, May 13, 2017; Steven Sanders, phone interview with the author, September 28, 2017.

32. Doyle interview.

33. Doyle interview.

34. Sanders interview.

35. Sanders interview.

36. Woldoff, Morrison, and Glass, *Priced Out*, 28; Sanders interview; Mike Arsham, interview with William Kelly, provided to the author.

2. Time for a Tenants Association

1. Gabe Pressman, "Stuy Town & Middle Class Renters Battling for Survival," NBC New York, January 27, 2010, http://www.nbcnewyork.com/news/local/The-Battle-of-Middle-Class-Renters-to-Survive--82727457.html.

2. Corinne Demas, *Eleven Stories High: Growing Up in Stuyvesant Town, 1948–1968* (Albany: SUNY Press, 2000), 3.

3. Steven Sanders, phone interview with the author, July 22, 2019.

4. Sanders interview.

5. Timothy Collins, *An Introduction to the NYC Rent Guidelines Board and the Rent Stabilization System*, NYC Rent Guidelines Board, updated and revised February 2018, https://www1.nyc.gov/assets/rentguidelinesboard/pdf/history/historyoftheboard.pdf; Michael Greenberg, "Tenants under Siege: Inside New York City's Housing Crisis," *New York Review of Books*, August 17, 2017, https://www.nybooks.com/articles/2017/08/17/tenants-under-siege-inside-new-york-city-housing-crisis/.

6. William E. Farrell, "Governor Signs Measure to Decontrol Empty Flats," *New York Times*, June 3, 1971, 31.

7. G. Martin Gansberg, "City Rent Chief to Help Tenants Bar Harassment," *New York Times*, June 30, 1971, 1.

8. Farrell, "Governor Signs Measure"; Gansberg, "City Rent Chief to Help."

9. Gansberg, "City Rent Chief to Help"; William E. Farrell, "Decontrolled Apartments Show Sharp Rise in Rents," *New York Times*, August 8, 1971, 1.

10. Farrell, "Decontrolled Apartments Show Sharp Rise"; Peter Kihiss, "City Will Publicize Names of Landlords Who Harass," *New York Times*, March 5, 1973, 33.

11. Elizabeth Kolbert, "A Name from the Past on Rent Fights," *New York Times*, May 5, 1997, http://www.nytimes.com/1997/05/05/nyregion/a-name-from-the-past-on-rent-fights.html; Joseph P. Fried, "Rockefeller Urges Rent-Increase Study for Vacated Units," *New York Times*, October 3, 1973, 37.

12. Kolbert, "Name from the Past."

13. Wendy Schuman, "Stuyvesant Town, with Tax Reprieve, Enters New Era," *New York Times*, June 16, 1974, 1.

14. Schuman, "'Enters New Era," 1.

15. "Nelson Rockefeller," *Encyclopedia Britannica*, https://www.britannica.com/biography/Nelson-Rockefeller; Sanders interview.

16. Al Doyle, testimony to the New York City Council, September 25, 2006.

17. Schuman, "Enters New Era," 1.

18. Al Doyle, interview with the author, New York, May 13, 2017.

19. Steven Sanders, interviews with the author, September 28, 2017, and July 22, 2019; Doyle interview.

20. Doyle interview; Marcelo Rochabrun and Cezary Podkul, "The Fateful Vote That Made New York City Rents So High," ProPublica, December 15, 2016, https://www.propublica.org/article/the-vote-that-made-new-york-city-rents-so-high.

21. Rochabrun and Podkul, "Fateful Vote"; Steven Wishnia, "Push for Stronger NY Rent Laws Goes up against Powerful Landlord Lobby," Gothamist, March 21, 2019, https://gothamist.com/2019/03/21/rent_reform_tenant_protections.php.

22. Dennis Hevesi, "Residential Real Estate; Manhattan Rents Go Ever Upward," *New York Times*, November 10, 2000, 42; Stuytown (Stuyvesant Town website), accessed July 22, 2019, https://www.stuytown.com/nyc-apartments-for-rent/2-bedrooms/3-page.

23. Joseph B. Treaster, "MetLife Issues Nearly 500 Million Shares to Policyholders," *New York Times*, April 6, 2000, 7.

24. Soni Fink, interview with the author, New York, January 18, 2018.

25. Fink interview; John Marsh, interview with the author, New York, May 13, 2017.

26. Marsh interview.

27. Marsh interview; Susan Steinberg, interview with the author, New York, January 10, 2018.

28. Marsh interview; Doyle testimony to Rent Guidelines Board, June 19, 2007; Thomas Lueck, "Met Life Tenants Win $4 Million in Suit over Botched Windows," *New York Times*, March 14, 1997, 5.

29. Marsh interview.

30. Marsh interview; Tina Kelley, "Peter Cooper Village Owner Accused of Fraud on Wiring," *New York Times*, August 23, 2000, 3.

31. Marsh interview.

32. Marsh interview; Fink interview.

33. Marsh interview.

34. Kelley, "Peter Cooper Village Owner Accused of Fraud."

35. Marsh interview; Sanders interview, September 28, 2017; Doyle interview.

36. Konrad Putzier, "How Stuy Town Was Won," Real Deal, October 29, 2015, https://therealdeal.com/2015/10/29/how-stuy-town-was-won/; Sanders interview, September 28, 2017.

37. American Civil Liberties Union, "Surveillance under the Patriot Act," https://www.aclu.org/issues/national-security/privacy-and-surveillance/surveillance-under-patriot-act.

38. Adam Rose, phone interview with the author, June 5, 2019; Thomas J. Lueck, "East Side Tenants Oppose Electronic Entry System," *New York Times*, March 16, 2005, https://www.nytimes.com/2005/03/16/nyregion/east-side-tenants-oppose-electronic-entry-system.html.

3. An Unexpected Challenge

1. Adam Rose, phone interview with the author, June 5, 2019; John Marsh, interview with the author, New York, May 13, 2017.

2. Rose interview.

3. Marsh interview.

4. Susan Steinberg, interview with the author, New York, January 10, 2018.

5. MetLife press release, July 18, 2006.

6. John Crotty, interview with the author, New York, January 12, 2018.

7. Crotty interview.

8. Crotty interview; Daniel L. Doctoroff, *Greater Than Ever: New York's Big Comeback* (New York: Public Affairs 2017), 83.

9. Crotty interview.

10. Steinberg interview.

11. Al Doyle, email to Tenants Association Board of Directors, July 26, 2006.

12. Crotty interview.

13. Leonard Grunstein, phone interview with the author, September 15, 2017.

14. Josh Barbanel, "The Evolution of Reluctant Capitalists," *New York Times*, May 15, 2005, https://www.nytimes.com/2005/05/15/realestate/the-evolution-of-reluctant-capitalists.html.

15. Clarissa-Jan Lim, "Renters Hoping to Remain at the West Village Houses," AM New York, August 1, 2013, https://www.amny.com/news/renters-hoping-to-remain-at-the-west-village-houses-2/; Josh Barbanel, "The Evolution of Reluctant Capitalists," *New York Times*, May 15, 2005.

16. Ben Smith, "Curious Case of Cuomo and the Cut-Price Apartments," *New York Daily News*, May 29, 2006, https://www.nydailynews.com/archives/news/curious-case-cuomo-cut-price-apartments-article-1.593495.

17. Grunstein interview.

18. Marsh interview; Grunstein interview.

19. Charles V. Bagli and Janny Scott, "110-Building Site in N.Y. Is Put Up for Sale," *New York Times*, August 30, 2006, https://www.nytimes.com/2006/08/30/nyregion/30stuyvesant.html; Marianna Vaidman Stone, email to the author, August 26, 2006.

20. Email from constituent to author, August 21, 2006; Michael McKee, "How the Landlords Weakened Our Rent Laws," Tenants Political Action Committee, May 1, 2008; Grunstein interview.

21. Marsh interview.

22. Steven Sanders, email to the author, August 23, 2006.

4. Making a Bid

1. Charles V. Bagli and Janny Scott, "110-Building Site in N.Y. Is Put Up for Sale," *New York Times*, August 30, 2006, https://www.nytimes.com/2006/08/30/nyregion/30stuyvesant.html.

2. Susan Steinberg, email to the author, August 30, 2006; Bagli and Scott, "Up for Sale."

3. Susan Steinberg, interview with the author, New York, January 10, 2018.

4. Janny Scott, "Official Sees Way to Buy 2 Developments," *New York Times*, September 5, 2006, http://www.nytimes.com/2006/09/05/nyregion/05stuyvesant.html?pagewanted=print.

5. Alan Berube, "The Middle Class Is Missing (New York)," Brookings Institution, July 8, 2006, https://www.brookings.edu/opinions/the-middle-class-is-missing-new-york/.

6. Janny Scott, "Cities Shed Middle Class, and Are Richer and Poorer for It," *New York Times*, July 23, 2006, https://www.nytimes.com/2006/07/23/weekinreview/23scott.html; State of New York City's Housing and Neighborhoods in 2006, Furman Center for Real Estate and Urban Policy, New York University, https://furmancenter.org/research/sonychan/2006-report; Elizabeth Hayes, "N.Y.C. So Costly You Need to Earn Six Figures to Make Middle Class," *New York Daily News*, February 6, 2009, https://www.nydailynews.com/news/money/n-y-costly-earn-figures-middle-class-article-1.389003; Berube, "Middle Class Is Missing"; Amy O'Leary, "What Is Middle Class in Manhattan?," *New York Times*, January 18, 2013, https://www.nytimes.com/2013/01/20/realestate/what-is-middle-class-in-manhattan.html.

7. Jen Chung, "Tenants Want to Bid on Stuyvesant Town–Peter Cooper Village," Gothamist, September 5, 2006, http://gothamist.com/2006/09/05/tenants_want_to.php; Observer staff, "The Morning Read," *New York Observer*, September 5, 2006, http://observer.com/2006/09/the-morning-read-september-5-2006/; Steinberg interview.

8. David Lombino, "Schumer Backs Federal Funds to Aid Stuyvesant Sale," *New York Sun*, September 6, 2006.

9. NYC press release (website of the City of New York), "Mayor Bloomberg Details Nation's Largest Municipal Housing Plan to Build and Preserve 165,000 Units of Affordable Housing," February 23, 2006, https://www1.nyc.gov/office-of-the-mayor/news/059-06/mayor-bloomberg-details-nations-largest-municipal-housing-plan-build-pre serve-165-000-units#/0.

10. Rafael Cestero, phone interview with the author, June 12, 2019.

11. Charles V. Bagli, "Council Tries to Buy Time for Stuyvesant Town Tenants," *New York Times*, October 12, 2006, https://www.nytimes.com/2006/10/12/nyregion/12stuyvesant.html.

12. Steve Cuozzo, "A False Panic—No Rent Threat to Stuytown," *New York Post*, September 6, 2006, https://nypost.com/2006/09/05/a-false-panic-no-rent-threat-to-stuytown/.

13. Scott, "Cities Shed Middle Class."

14. Sam Schaeffer, email to Maura Keaney, September 7, 2006.

15. John Crotty, interview with the author, New York, January 12, 2018.

16. Crotty interview; Daniel L. Doctoroff, *Greater Than Ever: New York's Big Comeback* (New York: Public Affairs, 2017), 82–83.

17. CB Richard Ellis, Offering Memorandum / Stuyvesant Town Peter Cooper Village, https://therealdeal.com/wp-content/uploads/2015/11/Stuy-Town-offering-book.pdf; Andrew MacArthur, interview with the author, New York, February 15, 2018.

18. David M. Levitt, "Big New York Complex to Draw Heated Bidding," *Chicago Tribune*, August 31, 2006, https://www.chicagotribune.com/news/ct-xpm-2006-09-10-0609 100093-story.html.

19. Maura Keaney, interview with the author, New York, January 31, 2018.

20. Keaney interview.

21. Steinberg interview.

22. Maura Keaney, email to the author, September 25, 2006; Steinberg interview.

23. Justine Almada, interview with the author, New York, January 15, 2019; Michael McKee, post on the Stuyvesant Town Peter Cooper Village Tenants Association Forum regarding market-rate tenants, September 19, 2006.

24. Al Doyle, testimony before the New York City Council, September 25, 2006; Joy Garland, testimony before the New York City Council, September 25, 2006.

25. Leonard Grunstein, email to the author, January 2, 2020.

26. CB Richard Ellis, Offering Memorandum.

27. Grunstein email, January 2, 2020.

28. John Marsh, interview with the author, New York, May 13, 2017.

29. Letter from executive board of Central Labor Council to Mayor Michael Bloomberg, September 29, 2006.

5. Regrouping after the Loss

1. Charles V. Bagli, "Tenants' Bid among a Dozen for Complexes," *New York Times*, October 6, 2006, https://www.nytimes.com/2006/10/06/nyregion/06stuyvesant.html.

2. Daniel J. Slatz, email to the author, October 6, 2006; Al Doyle, email to the author, October 7, 2006; Maura Keaney, email to the author, October 6, 2006.

3. Soni Fink, email to the TA board of directors, October 8, 2006.

4. CB Richard Ellis, Offering Memorandum / Stuyvesant Town Peter Cooper Village, 2006, https://therealdeal.com/wp-content/uploads/2015/11/Stuy-Town-offering-book.pdf.

5. Steven Sanders, email to the author, August 23, 2006.

6. "City Council Introduces Bill to Study the Impact of the Sale of Major Rental Housing Developments That Will Drastically Reduce the Supply of Affordable Units," council press release, October 11, 2006; Bagli, "Tenants' Bid"; Juan Gonzalez, "Little Bid That Could," *New York Daily News*, October 13, 2006.

7. Charles V. Bagli, "MetLife Completes Sale of Stuyvesant Town," *New York Times*, November 17, 2006, https://www.nytimes.com/2006/11/17/nyregion/17cnd-stuy.html; David Lombino, "MetLife: Sale of East Side Buildings Will Not Alter Character of Properties," *New York Sun*, September 26, 2006, https://www.nysun.com/new-york/metlife-sale-of-east-side-buildings-will-not/40366/.

8. Gonzalez, "Little Bid."

9. Bill Egbert, "'Where's Mike?' Ask Stuy Town Protesters," *New York Daily News*, October 16, 2006.

10. Gonzalez, "Little Bid."

11. Dan Pasquini, email to the author, October 17, 2006.

12. Charles V. Bagli, "$5.4 Billion Wins Two Complexes in New York Deal," *New York Times*, October 18, 2006, https://www.nytimes.com/2006/10/18/nyregion/18stuyvesant.html; Leonard Grunstein, phone interview with the author, September 15, 2017.

13. Maura Keaney, interview with the author, New York, January 31, 2018.

14. Keaney interview.

15. "$5.4 B!," *New York Daily News*, October 18, 2016; Grunstein interview.

16. Al Doyle, John Marsh, and Susan Steinberg, letter to PCV/ST community, October 17, 2006.

17. Charles V. Bagli, "$5.4 Billion Wins Two Complexes in New York Deal," *New York Times*, October 18, 2006, https://www.nytimes.com/2006/10/18/nyregion/18stuyvesant.html; Grunstein interview.

18. New York City Housing Development Corporation, "Mayor Bloomberg's New Housing Marketplace Plan," https://www.housingonline.com/Documents/Marc%20Jahr.pdf; Keaney interview.

19. Damien Cave, "City Plans Middle-Income Project on Queens Waterfront," *New York Times*, October 20, 2006, https://www.nytimes.com/2006/10/20/nyregion/20queens.html.

20. Cave, "City Plans"; Amy Westfeldt, "Historic Apartment Complex Sold to Developer for $5.4 Billion," Associated Press, October 18, 2006.

21. Andrew Sullivan, email to the author, October 20, 2006.

22. Daniel R. Garodnick, email to Christine Quinn, October 20, 2006.

23. Robert Speyer, letter to PCV/ST community, October 2006.

24. CB Richard Ellis, Offering Memorandum / Stuyvesant Town Peter Cooper Village, https://therealdeal.com/wp-content/uploads/2015/11/Stuy-Town-offering-book.pdf; Association for Neighborhood and Housing Development, "Predatory Equity, the Evolution of a Crisis," November 2009, https://anhd.org/wp-content/uploads/2016/01/Predatory_Equity-Evolution_of_a_Crisis_Report.pdf.

25. Charles V. Bagli, *Other People's Money: Inside the Housing Crisis and the Demise of the Greatest Real Estate Deal Ever Made* (New York: Dutton, 2013), 227; Adam Rose, phone interview with the author, June 5, 2019.

26. Randy Kennedy, "Rent Deregulation Has Risen Sharply under 1997 Law," *New York Times*, August 8, 1998, 1, http://www.nytimes.com/1998/08/08/nyregion/rent-deregulation-has-risen-sharply-under-1997-law.html; Michael Greenberg, "Tenants under Siege: Inside

New York City's Housing Crisis," *New York Review of Books*, August 17, 2017, https://www.nybooks.com/articles/2017/08/17/tenants-under-siege-inside-new-york-city-housing-crisis/.

27. Association for Neighborhood and Housing Development, "Predatory Equity."

28. Laura Gottesdiener, "How Wall Street Screwed Over Tenants in New York City," *Mother Jones*, April 8, 2014, https://www.motherjones.com/politics/2014/04/predatory-equity-wall-street-screwed-over-renters-new-york-city/; Association for Neighborhood and Housing Development, "Predatory Equity"; Adam Pincus, "Harbor Group Takes Control of $31M Distressed Vantage Portfolio," *Real Deal*, August 3, 2011, https://therealdeal.com/2011/08/03/harbor-group-takes-control-of-31m-distressed-vantage-portfolio/.

29. Association for Neighborhood and Housing Development, "Predatory Equity"; Gottesdiener, "How Wall Street."

30. Terry Pristin, "Fear of Defaults after a Flurry of Apartment House Sales," *New York Times*, August 26, 2008, https://www.nytimes.com/2008/08/27/business/27default.html.

31. John Crotty, interview with the author, New York, January 12, 2017.

32. Susan Steinberg, interview with the author, New York, January 10, 2018.

33. Jim Roth, interview with the author, New York, December 17, 2017; Steinberg interview.

34. Darryl Seavey, letter to Sherwin Belkin, January 16, 1996.

35. Seavey letter to Belkin, January 16, 1996.

36. Sophia Hollander, "Behind an Outsize Court Case, Two Everyday Tenants," *New York Times*, March 13, 2009, http://www.nytimes.com/2009/03/15/nyregion/thecity/15stuy.html.

6. Pushing Back against a New Owner

1. John Marsh, interview with the author, New York, May 13, 2017.

2. Gabriel Sherman, "Clash of the Utopias," *New York Magazine*, February 1, 2009, http://nymag.com/realestate/features/53797/.

3. Marsh interview.

4. Sam Himmelstein, phone interview with the author, November 2, 2017.

5. Himmelstein interview.

6. Alan Finder, "Fred Knapp, Private Eye, Scourge of Illegal Tenants," *New York Times*, May 9, 1988, B1.

7. Adam Rose, phone interview with the author, June 5, 2019.

8. Marsh interview; Himmelstein interview.

9. James Fishman, phone interview with the author, November 12, 2017.

10. Charles V. Bagli, "Stuyvesant Town Revenues Have Fallen, Report Says," *New York Times*, July 23, 2008, https://www.nytimes.com/2008/07/23/nyregion/23stuyvesant.html.

11. Fishman interview.

12. Sherwin Belkin, email to the author, January 22, 2008.

13. Bagli, "Stuyvesant Town Revenues."

14. Charles V. Bagli, *Other People's Money: Inside the Housing Crisis and the Demise of the Greatest Real Estate Deal Ever Made* (New York: Dutton, 2013), 312–13.

15. Roberts v. Tishman Speyer, 874 N.Y.S.2d 97 (N.Y. App. Div. 1st Dep't 2009).

16. Alex Schmidt, phone interview with the author, September 19, 2017.

17. Schmidt interview; Alex Schmidt, email to the author, August 8, 2019.

18. Alex Schmidt, email to the author, January 3, 2020; "Legal Superstar: Skadden Arps Slate Meagher & Flom's Jay Kasner," Law360, May 15, 2006, https://www.law360.com/articles/6574/legal-superstar-skadden-arps-slate-meagher-flom-s-jay-kasner.

19. Schmidt interview.

20. Eric Rachway, "The 2008 Crash: What Happened to All That Money," History, September 14, 2018, https://www.history.com/news/2008-financial-crisis-causes; "Lehman

Brothers Collapse Stuns Global Markets," CNN.com, September 15, 2008, http://edition.cnn.com/2008/BUSINESS/09/15/lehman.merrill.stocks.turmoil/index.html; Matt Egan, "Lehman Brothers: When the Financial Crisis Spun out of Control," CNN Business, September 14, 2008, https://www.cnn.com/2018/09/30/investing/lehman-brothers-2008-crisis/index.html.

21. Egan, "Lehman Brothers."

22. Kimberly Amadeo, "AIG Bailout, Cost, Timeline, Bonuses, Causes, Effects," Balance, March 15, 2019, https://www.thebalance.com/aig-bailout-cost-timeline-bonuses-causes-effects-3305693.

23. Sophia Hollander, "Behind an Outsize Court Case, Two Everyday Tenants," *New York Times*, March 13, 2009, https://www.nytimes.com/2009/03/15/nyregion/thecity/15stuy.html.

24. John Marsh, instant message to the author, March 5, 2009.

25. Schmidt interview.

26. Susan Steinberg, interview with the author, New York, January 10, 2018.

27. Charles V. Bagli, "Big Landlord Found to Have Wrongly Raised Rents," *New York Times*, March 5, 2009, https://www.nytimes.com/2009/03/06/nyregion/06stuy.html.

28. Schmidt interview.

29. Schmidt interview.

30. Schmidt interview.

31. Schmidt interview.

32. Alex Schmidt, email to the author, January 3, 2020.

33. Charles V. Bagli, "Court Deals Blow to Owners of Apartment Complex," *New York Times*, October 22, 2009, https://www.nytimes.com/2009/10/23/nyregion/23stuytown.html?_r=1&hp.

34. Bagli, "Court"; Lingling Wei and Craig Karmin, "An Apartment Complex Teeters," *Wall Street Journal*, October 15, 2009, https://www.wsj.com/articles/SB125547827547583747.

35. Sabina Mollot, "Tenants Celebrate Ruling but Still Have Concerns," *Town & Village*, October 29, 2009; Steinberg interview.

36. Alex Schmidt, email to the author, October 22, 2009.

37. Statement from Wolf Haldenstein Adler Freeman & Herz LLP and Bernstein Liebhard LLP, November 23, 2009; Joint Statement from Tishman Speyer, Wolf Haldenstein Adler Freeman & Herz, and Bernstein Liebhard, December 14, 2009.

7. Preparing for an Uncertain Future

1. Lingling Wei and Craig Karmin, "An Apartment Complex Teeters," *Wall Street Journal*, October 15, 2009, https://www.wsj.com/articles/SB125547827547583747.

2. Thomas A. Corfman, "Tishman Speyer Defaults on Big Chicago Loan," *Crain's New York Business*, December 4, 2009, https://www.crainsnewyork.com/article/20091205/FREE/912059998/tishman-speyer-defaults-on-big-chicago-loan.

3. Josh Barbanel, "Sharp Price Drops in Manhattan Apartments," *New York Times*, July 2, 2009; Corfman, "Tishman Speyer Defaults."

4. Stuyvesant Town Peter Cooper Village Tenants Association, "Statement of Principles for Engagement with Stuyvesant Town and Peter Cooper Village Tenants," November 8, 2009.

5. Stuyvesant Town Peter Cooper Village Tenants Association, "Statement of Principles for Engagement with Stuyvesant Town and Peter Cooper Village Tenants," November 8, 2009.

6. Author email to Justine Almada, November 13, 2009; Kaja Whitehouse, "StuyTown Tenants Set List of Demands," *New York Post*, December 9, 2009, https://nypost.com/2009/12/09/stuytown-tenants-set-list-of-demands/.

7. Richard Parkus and Harris Trifon, "Special Report: Outlook for Stuy Town & J-51 Participating Properties," Deutsche Bank, November 30, 2009.

8. Charles V. Bagli, *Other People's Money: Inside the Housing Crisis and the Demise of the Greatest Real Estate Deal Ever Made* (New York: Dutton, 2013), 316.

9. Eliot Brown, "Fitch: Stuy Town Loans Transferred to Special Servicer," *New York Observer*, November 7, 2009; Adam Rose, phone interview with the author, June 5, 2019.

10. Charles V. Bagli and Christine Haughney, "Wide Fallout in Failed Deal for Stuyvesant Town," *New York Times*, January 25, 2010, https://www.nytimes.com/2010/01/26/nyregion/26stuy.html?dbk.

11. Charles V. Bagli, "Partners Near Default on Stuyvesant Town," *New York Times*, January 7, 2010, https://www.nytimes.com/2010/01/08/nyregion/08stuy.html; Al Doyle, email to the author, January 8, 2010.

12. Jerry Ascierto, "CWCapital Sold to Fortress Investment Group," MultiFamily Executive, January 1, 2010, https://www.multifamilyexecutive.com/business-finance/debt-equity/cwcapital-sold-to-fortress-investment-group_o.

13. CWCapital website, https://www.cwcapital.com/cwcapital/; Charles Spetka, email to author, January 14, 2010; Al Doyle, email to the author, January 14, 2010.

14. Charles Spetka, letter to the author, January 22, 2010, https://www.scribd.com/doc/25873223/CW-Capital-1-22-2010.

15. Eliot Brown, "Stuy Town Servicer Wants 'Fair and Just' Outcome, Praises Garodnick," *New York Observer*, January 26, 2010, https://observer.com/2010/01/stuy-town-servicer-wants-fair-and-just-outcome-praises-garodnick/.

16. Bagli, *Other People's Money*, 318, 320.

17. Letter from New York elected officials to Michael J. Williams and Charles Haldeman Jr., October 26, 2009; David Ellis, "U.S. Seizes Fannie and Freddie," CNN Money, September 7, 2008, https://money.cnn.com/2008/09/07/news/companies/fannie_freddie/.

18. "Mayor Bloomberg, Senator Schumer, Congressman Serrano, Speaker Quinn and Fannie Mae Announce Housing Developer Led by Mo Vaughn Will Purchase Troubled South Bronx Housing Portfolio," official website of the City of New York, December 2, 2009, https://www1.nyc.gov/office-of-the-mayor/news/517-09/mayor-bloomberg-senator-schumer-congressman-serrano-speaker-quinn-fannie-mae-announce; Michael McLaughlin, "Sen. Schumer Calls Collapse of Stuyvesant Town / Peter Cooper Village Deal 'an Opportunity,'" *New York Daily News*, January 31, 2010, https://www.nydailynews.com/life-style/real-estate/sen-schumer-calls-collapse-stuyvesant-town-peter-cooper-village-deal-opportunity-article-1.459266.

19. Stuyvesant Town Peter Cooper Village Tenants Association, press release, January 31, 2010; Emily Heil, "Chuck Schumer and That 'Most Dangerous Place' Joke," *Washington Post*, April 1, 2015, https://www.washingtonpost.com/news/reliable-source/wp/2015/04/01/chuck-schumer-and-that-most-dangerous-place-joke/?utm_term=.7dcd627378a6.

20. Author remarks, January 30, 2010.

21. Office of US Senator Chuck Schumer, "Schumer to Fannie and Freddie, Largest Debt Holders of Stuy Town: Use Leverage to Ensure Maintenance Kept Up in Short Term and Properties Only Sold to Owners Who Will Keep It as Middle Class," press release, January 26, 2010.

22. Rose interview.

23. Meredith Kane, interview with the author, New York, January 30, 2018.

24. Kane interview.

25. Kane interview.

26. Sam Lovett, email to the author, February 18, 2010; Kane interview.

27. Alex Rubin, interview with the author, New York, March 5, 2018.

28. Kane interview.

29. Susan Steinberg, interview with the author, New York, January 10, 2018.

30. Rubin interview.

31. Susan Steinberg, email to the author, November 25, 2019.

32. Rubin interview.

33. Lingling Wei, "Tenants Flex Muscles," *Wall Street Journal*, April 13, 2010; Eliot Brown, "Man Who Would Rule Stuy Town," *New York Observer*, April 21, 2010, https://commercialobserver.com/2010/04/the-man-who-would-rule-stuy-town/.

34. Rafael Cestero, phone interview with the author, June 12, 2019.

35. Rose interview.

36. Kane interview.

37. John Sheehy, interview with the author, New York, January 22, 2018.

38. Soni Fink, email to the author, January 26, 2018.

39. Resident, email to Al Doyle, September 29, 2010.

40. Author, email to Julie Ehrlich and Steven Newmark, June 11, 2010.

41. Stuyvesant Town Peter Cooper Village Tenants Association, Merriman River Group, STPCV TA Results.

42. "Appaloosa Bid to Join Stuyvesant Town Foreclosure Suit Is Denied," *New York Post*, April 30, 2010, https://nypost.com/2010/04/30/appaloosa-bid-to-join-stuyvesant-town-foreclosure-suit-is-denied/; author notes, July 9, 2010.

43. Author notes, May 19, 2010; Cestero interview.

44. Lingling Wei and Nick Timiraos, "Control of Stuyvesant Takes Center Stage," *Wall Street Journal*, January 26, 2010, https://www.wsj.com/articles/SB1000142405274870 4762904575025621634376554; "Billionaire Eyes Stuyvesant Town Swoop," *Property Week*, January 26, 2010, https://www.propertyweek.com/news/billionaire-eyes-stuyvesant-town-swoop/3156919.article; Lois Weiss, "Trump Says He'll Jump at StuyTown Takeover," *New York Post*, January 29, 2010, https://nypost.com/2010/01/29/trump-says-hell-jump-at-stuytown-takeover/.

45. David Indiviglio, "After an Ugly 2010, the Housing Market Won't Look Much Better in 2011," *Atlantic*, January 6, 2011, https://www.theatlantic.com/business/archive/2011/01/after-an-ugly-2010-the-housing-market-wont-look-much-better-in-2011/69009/.

46. Andrew MacArthur, interview with the author, New York, February 15, 2018.

8. Suddenly the "Prettiest Girl at the Dance"

1. Doug Harmon, phone interview with the author, February 6, 2019; Charles V. Bagli, "Hedge Fund Moves on Stuyvesant Town and Peter Cooper Village," *New York Times*, February 24, 2010, https://www.nytimes.com/2010/02/25/nyregion/25stuytown.html.

2. Lingling Wei and Nick Timiraos, "Control of Stuyvesant Takes Center Stage," *Wall Street Journal*, January 26, 2010, https://www.wsj.com/articles/SB10001424052748704762904575025621634376554; "In Stuyvesant Town, Fannie Mae, Freddie Mac Staring at Another Lehman Brothers Loser," Shadow Proof, January 27, 2010, https://shadowproof.com/2010/01/27/in-stuyvesant-town-fannie-mae-freddie-mac-staring-at-another-lehman-brothers-loser/.

3. Wei and Timiraos, "Center Stage."

4. Wei and Timiraos, "Center Stage."

5. Wei and Timiraos, "Center Stage"; Joey Arak, "Even God Losing Money on Stuy Town," Curbed New York, October 14, 2009, https://ny.curbed.com/2009/10/14/10530592/even-god-losing-money-on-stuy-town.

6. Lingling Wei and Craig Karmin, "An Apartment Complex Teeters," *Wall Street Journal*, October 15, 2009, https://www.wsj.com/articles/SB125547827547583747; Charles V. Bagli and Christine Haughney, "Wide Fallout in Failed Deal for Stuyvesant Town," *New York Times*, January 25, 2010, https://www.nytimes.com/2010/01/26/nyregion/26stuy.html?dbk;

Gabe Pressman, "Stuy Town and Middle Class Renters Battling for Survival," 4 New York, January 27, 2010, http://www.nbcnewyork.com/news/local/The-Battle-of-Middle-Class-Renters-to-Survive--82727457.html.

7. Alison Gregor, "Ranking New York's Top Legal Wranglers," *Real Deal*, April 1, 2010, https://therealdeal.com/issues_articles/ranking-new-yorks-top-legal-wranglers/; Michael Powell, "Stuyvesant Town, Former Middle-Class Bastion, Awaits Mayoral Help," *New York Times*, June 9, 2014, https://www.nytimes.com/2014/06/10/nyregion/stuyvesant-town-former-middle-class-bastion-awaits-mayoral-help.html?_r=0; Daniel L. Doctoroff, *Greater Than Ever: New York's Big Comeback* (New York: Public Affairs, 2017), 83; Henry Grabar, "The Saving of Stuy Town: Has Corporate Greed in New York Been Dealt a Blow?," *Guardian*, October 29, 2015, https://www.theguardian.com/cities/2015/oct/29/stuyvesant-town-corporate-greed-affordable-housing-new-york.

8. Alex Rubin, email to Andrew MacArthur, July 1, 2010.

9. Larry Kwon, email to the author, July 30, 2010.

10. Author notes, August 7, 2017; "The Logic behind Bill Ackman's Purchase of General Growth Properties," Seeking Alpha, January 14, 2009, https://seekingalpha.com/article/114750-the-logic-behind-bill-ackmans-purchase-of-general-growth-properties; General Growth Properties, Macrotrends, https://www.macrotrends.net/stocks/charts/GGP//stock-price-history; Zaw Thiha Tun, "Bill Ackman's Greatest Hits and Misses," Investopedia, June 25, 2019, https://www.investopedia.com/articles/investing/032216/bill-ackmans-greatest-hits-and-misses.asp.

11. Author notes, August 7, 2010.

12. Eliot Brown, "Enter Ackman," *New York Observer*, August 10, 2010.

13. Charles V. Bagli, *Other People's Money: Inside the Housing Crisis and the Demise of the Greatest Real Estate Deal Ever Made* (New York: Dutton, 2013), 306, 317.

14. Author notes, January 12, 2010.

15. Author notes, January 12, 2010.

16. Amanda Fung, "Upstart Roils Stuy Town Battle," *Crain's New York Business*, August 15, 2010.

17. "Winthrop Joins with Pershing Square to Acquire Senior Mezzanine Debt on New York's Largest Residential Property," CNN Money, August 9, 2010, https://money.cnn.com/news/newsfeeds/articles/globenewswire/198847.htm.

18. Pershing Square & Winthrop, press release, "Winthrop Joins with Pershing Square to Acquire Senior Mezzanine Debt on New York's Largest Residential Property," August 9, 2010; Cyrus Sanati, "Ackman Lays Out His Plan for Stuyvesant Town," *New York Times*, August 13, 2010, https://dealbook.nytimes.com/2010/08/13/ackman-lays-out-his-plan-for-stuyvesant-town/; Adam Piore, "Ackman Looks for a Magic Trick," *Real Deal*, October 1, 2010, https://therealdeal.com/issues_articles/ackman-looks-for-a-magic-trick/; Author email to Alex Rubin and Meredith Kane, August 9, 2010.

19. Author notes, August 11, 2011.

20. Sanati, "Plan for Stuyvesant Town."

21. Amanda Fung, "Partnership Eyes New Future for Stuy Town," *Crain's New York Business*, August 9, 2010, https://www.crainsnewyork.com/article/20100809/REAL_ESTATE/100809845/partnership-eyes-new-future-for-stuy-town; Lingling Wei, "Mortgage Trustees Sue to Block Stuyvesant Town Foreclosure," *Wall Street Journal*, August 19, 2010, https://www.wsj.com/articles/SB10001424052748703649004575437911766797600; Dealbook, "The Battle for Stuyvesant Town: First Shots Fired," *New York Times*, August 19, 2010, https://dealbook.nytimes.com/2010/08/19/the-battle-for-stuy-town-first-shots-fired/; Ilaina Jonas and Jonathan Stempel, "Iconic NYC Housing Complex's Foreclosure Halted," Reuters, August 19, 2010, https://uk.reuters.com/article/us-stuyvesanttown-ackman-law

suit/iconic-nyc-housing-complexs-foreclosure-halted-idUKTRE67H5CH20100819; Amanda Fung, "Court Suspends Stuy Town Foreclosure," *Crain's New York Business*, August 19, 2010, https://www.crainsnewyork.com/article/20100819/REAL_ESTATE/100819771/court-suspends-stuy-town-foreclosure; Eliot Brown, "Ackman's Stuy Town Foreclosure Halted—for Now," *Commercial Observer*, August 19, 2010, https://commercialobserver.com/2010/08/ackmans-stuy-town-foreclosure-haltedfor-now/; Kaja Whitehouse, "StuyTown Skirmish," *New York Post*, August 19, 2010, https://nypost.com/2010/08/19/stuytown-skirmish/.

22. John Marsh, email to John Sheehy, August 19, 2010; author statement, August 18, 2010; Andrew MacArthur, letter to Alex Rubin, August 25, 2010.

23. Author notes, August 26, 2010.

24. Alex Rubin, email to the author, August 11, 2010.

25. Author notes, August 18, 2010.

26. Meredith Kane, interview with the author, January 30, 2018.

27. John Sheehy, email to the Tenants Association board, September 2, 2010; John Sheehy, interview with the author, New York, January 22, 2018.

28. Author notes, September 2, 2010; author email to Charles Bagli, September 2, 2010.

29. Author notes, September 2, 2010.

30. Author notes, September 2, 2010.

31. Charles V. Bagli, "In Latest Battle for Control of Stuyvesant Town, the Tenants Are Wooed," *New York Times*, September 2, 2010, https://www.nytimes.com/2010/09/03/nyregion/03stuytown.html.

32. Bagli, "Tenants Are Wooed"; Michael Ashner, email to Bill Ackman, Meredith Kane, and Alex Rubin, September 14, 2010.

33. Author notes, September 3, 2010.

34. William Ackman, email to the author, September 4, 2010.

35. TA board email exchange, September 6, 2010; author notes, September 6, 2010.

36. Rafael Cestero, phone interview with the author, June 12, 2019.

37. Pershing Square & Winthrop, Stuyvesant Town Peter Cooper Village Tenants Association board meeting discussion materials, September 7, 2010.

38. Board meeting discussion materials, September 7, 2010.

39. Soni Fink, email to Susan Steinberg et al., September 7, 2010; James Roth, email to the TA board, September 7, 2010.

40. James Roth, email to the TA board, September 7, 2010.

41. Bill Ackman and Michael Ashner, letter to Stuyvesant Town Peter Cooper Village Tenants Association, September 9, 2010; author notes, September 13, 2010.

42. Author notes, September 13, 2010.

43. Matthew Feldman, email to Alex Rubin, Daniel Garodnick, et al., September 22, 2010; Kane interview.

44. Andrew MacArthur, email to Alex Rubin, September 28, 2010.

45. Bill Ackman, email to Alex Rubin, September 28, 2010; author email to Alex Rubin and Meredith Kane, September 28, 2010.

46. Matt Chaban, "Ackman Breaks Even on Stuy Town, Still Wants to Own the Place," *Observer*, October 27, 2010, https://observer.com/2010/10/ackman-breaks-even-on-stuy-town-still-wants-to-own-the-place/.

9. Finding a Partner

1. Andrew MacArthur, interview with the author, New York, February 15, 2018.

2. Rose Associates, Peter Cooper Village Stuyvesant Town Community update, February 7, 2011.

3. Paul Bubny, "CWCapital, Ackman Settle Stuy-Town Dispute," GlobeSt., October 27, 2010.

4. Al Doyle, email to the author, November 8, 2010; Al Doyle statement, November 8, 2010; Al Doyle, email to Andrew MacArthur, December 14, 2010.

5. Author notes, September 29, 2010.

6. Charles V. Bagli, "Stuyvesant Town Foreclosure Sale Is Approved," *New York Times*, September 28, 2010, https://cityroom.blogs.nytimes.com/2010/09/28/foreclosure-sale-approved-for-stuy-town-peter-cooper-village/.

7. Email from TA board member to the author, September 28, 2010.

8. John Marsh, email to the TA board, October 4, 2010.

9. John Sheehy, email to Julie Ehrlich and Al Doyle, October 18, 2010.

10. Moelis & Company, presentation to the Board of Directors of the Stuyvesant Town Peter Cooper Village Tenants Association, October 26, 2010.

11. Meredith Kane, interview with the author, New York, January 30, 2018.

12. John Dillon, telephone message to Stuyvesant Town Peter Cooper Village Tenants Association, October 5, 2010.

13. Julie Ehrlich, email to the author, December 21, 2010.

14. Adam Rose, phone interview with the author, June 5, 2019.

15. Rose interview; John Marsh, interview with the author, New York, May 13, 2017.

16. Steven Moore, email to the author, March 15, 2011.

17. Steven Moore, email to the author, March 3, 2011; CUNY survey, attached to Susan Steinberg email to Meredith Kane, March 17, 2011.

18. Alex Rubin, interview with the author, New York, March 5, 2018; Barry Blattman, interview with the author, April 17, 2018.

19. Rubin interview.

20. Blattman interview; author email to Alex Rubin and Meredith Kane, April, 13, 2011.

21. Blattman interview.

22. Letter from Barry Blattman to Moelis & Company, Paul, Weiss, Rifkind, Wharton & Garrison LLP, and author, May 11, 2011.

23. Rubin interview; Al Doyle email to the author, May 26, 2011; Moelis & Company, Stuyvesant Town Peter Cooper Village Tenants Association updated Process Timeline, October 2011.

24. Jimmy Vielkind, "This Is a Revolution? Jeff Klein's Independent Democrats Rise Up, Then Settle Down," Politico, June 2, 2011, https://www.politico.com/states/new-york/city-hall/story/2011/06/this-is-a-revolution-jeff-kleins-independent-democrats-rise-up-then-settle-down-000000.

25. David Jones, "Court Rules That Stuy Town and Peter Cooper Rent-Stabilization Decision Applies Retroactively," *Real Deal*, August 19, 2011, https://therealdeal.com/2011/08/19/court-of-appeals-rules-that-stuy-town-rent-stabilized-decision-applies-retroactively-in-roberts-vs-tishman-speyer/.

26. Alex Rubin, email to the author, June 29, 2011; Michael Ashner, email to Meredith Kane, June 23, 2011; Meredith Kane, email to Alex Rubin and the author, June 23, 2011.

27. Brookfield Asset Management, status update to the Stuyvesant Town Peter Cooper Village Tenants Association Board of Directors, August 11, 2011.

28. Barry Blattman, email to Alex Rubin et al., September 12, 2011; author notes, September 23, 2011.

29. Drew Grant, "City Council Members' Letter to Bloomberg regarding Zuccotti Park 'Eviction,'" Observer, October 13, 2011, https://observer.com/2011/10/city-council-members-letter-to-bloomberg-regarding-zuccotti-park-eviction/; Alex Rubin, email to the author, October 14, 2011.

30. Lowell Baron, email to Andrew MacArthur, November 9, 2011.

31. James Barron and Colin Moynihan, "City Reopens Park after Protesters Are Evicted," *New York Times*, November 15, 2011, https://www.nytimes.com/2011/11/16/nyregion/po lice-begin-clearing-zuccotti-park-of-protesters.html; Andrew MacArthur, email to Lowell Baron, November 9, 2011.

32. Charles V. Bagli, "Tenants Trying Again to Buy Stuyvesant Town and Peter Cooper Village," *New York Times*, November 29, 2011, https://www.nytimes.com/2011/11/30/nyre gion/stuyvesant-town-and-peter-cooper-tenants-hope-to-buy-apartments.html.

33. Stuyvesant Town Peter Cooper Village Tenants Association, "Tenants Association and Brookfield Have Partnered to Bid for Ownership," email to community, November 30, 2011.

10. Challenged from the Outside

1. Letter from Gerald Guterman to Peter Cooper Village Stuyvesant Town Tenants Association, September 20, 2010; author notes, May 21, 2010; Elliman Report, "Manhattan Decade 2002–2011, Miller Samuel Inc., https://www.millersamuel.com/files/2012/02/Manhattan_10YR_2011.pdf.

2. Soni Fink, email to the TA board, September 21, 2010.

3. Alan Oser, "Managing Those 'Occupied' Apartments," *New York Times*, April 7, 1985, 7; "A Memorable Launching," *New York Times*, September 21, 1986, 9; Georgia Dullea, "Coming of Age on the Ocean: A Bar Mitzvah aboard the QE2," *New York Times*, September 16, 1986, B1.

4. Dullea, "Coming of Age"; Andree Brooks, "Guterman's Troubles Jolt Client Co-ops," *New York Times*, April 17, 1988, 9.

5. Sandra Salmans, "New Yorkers & Co.; His Pitch Lures 'Instant Insiders,'" *New York Times*, November 28, 1985, 3.

6. Theresa Agovino, "Old Stuy Town Suitor Pops Back In," *Crain's New York Business*, December 2, 2011; John Marsh, interview with the author, New York, January 29, 2018; Kaja Whitehouse, "StuyTown Tenants Wooed," *New York Post*, December 2, 2011, https://nypost.com/2011/12/03/stuytown-tenants-wooed/.

7. John Marsh, undated notes, via email to the author, June 3, 2016; David Levitt, "Brookfield Intends to Give CWCapital an Offer for Stuyvesant Town by April," Bloomberg, December 3, 2011, https://www.bloomberg.com/news/articles/2011-12-04/brookfield-intends-to-give-cwcapital-an-offer-for-stuyvesant-town-by-april.

8. Stuyvesant Town Peter Cooper Village Tenants Association, community email, December 9, 2011.

9. Author remarks, Stuyvesant Town Peter Cooper Tenants Association, December 2, 2011.

10. Various long-term residents, letter to David Iannarone, October 8, 2010.

11. Joe Lisanti, "Guterman Deal Too Good to Be True," letter to the editor, *Town & Village*, December 15, 2011; Bruno Guarino, "Good-Buy, Stuy We Know," letter to the editor, *Town & Village*, December 15, 2011.

12. Jen Shykula, phone interview with the author, April 11, 2018.

13. Sara Polsky, "Curbed Awards '11 Real Estate: Shitshows, Shockers & More!," Curbed, December 27, 2011, https://ny.curbed.com/2011/12/27/10413266/curbed-awards-11-real-estate-shitshows-shockers-more; website, www.STPCVFacts.Org, announced January 26, 2012; author email to Alex Rubin, January 27, 2012.

14. Matt Tepper, email to the author, December 19, 2011.

15. *Stuyvesant Town Report* (blog), December 19, 2011.

16. Author notes, January 24, 2012.

17. Stuyvesant Town Peter Cooper Village Tenants Association, minutes, January 25, 2012; tenant email to Tenants Association board and author, January 24, 2012.

18. Shykula interview.

19. Shykula interview.

20. Brookfield Asset Management, "Conforming Offer," April 30, 2012.

21. Author notes, January 24, 2012; Adam Rose, email to John Marsh, February 7, 2012; author notes, January 24, 2012.

22. Susan Steinberg, interview with the author, New York, January 10, 2018.

23. Lowell Baron, email to Alex Rubin, May 14, 2012; author notes, June 28, 2012; Darrell Wheeler, "CMBS Strategy," Amherst Securities Group LP, March 22, 2012.

24. Author notes, June 28, 2012.

25. Author notes, August 14, 2012.

26. Eliot Brown, "Stuyvesant Town Strategy," *Wall Street Journal*, April 21, 2013, https://www.wsj.com/articles/SB10001424127887323551004578436862450162392.

27. Author notes, May 10, 2013; John Sheehy, email to Tenants Association board of directors, August 29, 2012.

28. Lauren Young, email to the author, September 21, 2012.

29. John Marsh, letter to Chuck Spetka, October 16, 2012.

30. Author letter to Charles Spetka, October 15, 2012.

31. Stuyvesant Town Peter Cooper Village Tenants Association, email to community, October 16, 2012.

32. Sara Polsky, "Tenants Would Just Like Stuy Town to Be Sold Already," Curbed, October 16, 2012, https://ny.curbed.com/platform/amp/2012/10/16/10317346/tenants-would-just-like-stuy-town-to-be-sold-already; Mary Johnson, "Stuy Town Tenants Cut Out Middleman in Bid to Buy Complex," DNA Info, October 16, 2012, https://www.dnainfo.com/new-york/20121016/stuy-town/stuy-town-tenants-cut-out-middleman-bid-buy-complex/; "Improved Outlook for Stuy Town Loan," Structured Credit Investor (SCI), October 24, 2012, http://www.structuredcreditinvestor.com/article_loggedOut.asp?subtype=notloggedon&Status=8&SID=35013&ISS=22632.

33. Ilona Kramer notes, October 26, 2012.

11. Under Water, Actual Water

1. Pete Donohue, "Partial New York Subway Service Restored on Some Lines after Hurricane Sandy Flooded System," *New York Daily News*, November 1, 2012, https://www.nydailynews.com/new-york/subways-rolling-new-york-article-1.1195359.

2. Andrew MacArthur, email to the author, November 7, 2012.

3. Charles V. Bagli, "$68.7 Million Settlement on Stuyvesant Town Rents," *New York Times*, November 29, 2012, https://www.nytimes.com/2012/11/30/nyregion/68-7-million-settlement-on-stuyvesant-town-rents.html; Andrew MacArthur, interview with the author, New York, February 15, 2018.

4. Oshrat Carmiel, "Stuyvesant Town Settlement Clears Path to Sale of Complex," Bloomberg, November 30, 2012, https://www.bloomberg.com/news/articles/2012-11-30/stuyvesant-town-settlement-clears-path-to-sale-of-complex.

5. Bagli, "$68.7 Million Settlement."

6. Author notes, February 12, 2013.

7. Author notes, February 12, 2013.

8. Alex Rubin, email to the author, February 12, 2013.

9. John Sheehy, email to Meredith Kane, May 30, 2013; Kim Velsey, "Tenants in Sandy-Damaged Buildings Protest Landlord-Friendly Rent Reduction Policy," *Observer*, March 22, 2013, https://observer.com/2013/03/tenants-in-sandy-damaged-buildings-protest-landlord-friendly-rent-reduction-policy/.

10. Letter from elected officials to Andrew MacArthur, May 28, 2013.

11. MacArthur interview.

12. Stuyvesant Town Peter Cooper Village Tenants Association, statement, May 15, 2013; Daniel Geiger, "Stuy Town Rent Hikes Infuriate Tenants," *Crain's New York Business*, May 15, 2013, https://www.crainsnewyork.com/article/20130515/REAL_ESTATE/130519931/stuy-town-rent-hikes-infuriate-tenants.

13. Letter from Andrew MacArthur to the author, June 4, 2013.

14. MacArthur interview; letter from Andrew MacArthur to the author, June 4, 2013; email from CWCapital representative to resident.

15. Author email to Charles Bagli, May 29, 2013.

16. Micah Lasher, phone interview with the author, October 14, 2019; Sabina Mollot, "Mid-lease Increases to Be Reversed in Cases of Misrepresentation," *Town & Village*, June 17, 2013, https://town-village.com/2013/06/17/mid-lease-increases-to-be-reversed-in-cases-of-misrepresentation/.

17. Mollot, "Mid-lease Increases to Be Reversed."

18. CWCapital, statement, June 15, 2013.

19. Stuyvesant Town Peter Cooper Village Tenants Association email to community, June 15, 2013.

12. A New Start

1. John Sheehy, interview with the author, New York, January 22, 2018.

2. Nick Powell, "Exclusive: Big 3 County Leaders Appear to Have Votes to Make Garodnick Speaker," *City & State*, December 17, 2013.

3. James Patchett, interview with the author, New York, March 27, 2018.

4. Patchett interview.

5. Housing New York, a Five-Borough, Ten-Year Plan, https://www1.nyc.gov/assets/housing/downloads/pdf/housing_plan.pdf.

6. DataUsa, https://datausa.io/profile/geo/new-york-ny/; author notes, March 31, 2014.

7. Author notes, March 31, 2014.

8. Brookfield Asset Management Inc. Stuyvesant Town Peter Cooper Village Tenants Association Presentation to Deputy Mayor Glen, May 2014.

9. Brookfield Asset Management Inc. Stuyvesant Town Peter Cooper Village Tenants Association Presentation to Deputy Mayor Glen, May 2014.

10. Brookfield Asset Management Inc. Stuyvesant Town Peter Cooper Village Tenants Association Presentation to Deputy Mayor Glen, May 2014.

11. Brookfield Asset Management Inc. Stuyvesant Town Peter Cooper Village Tenants Association Presentation to Deputy Mayor Glen, May 2014.

12. Brookfield Asset Management Inc. Stuyvesant Town Peter Cooper Village Tenants Association Presentation to Deputy Mayor Glen, May 2014.

13. Author notes, May 22, 2014.

14. John Sheehy, email to Kane, Rubin, and the author, May 2, 2014.

15. Mitchell L. Berg and Harris B. Freidus, "UCC Foreclosure," New York Law Journal, January 14, 2009, https://www.law.com/newyorklawjournal/almID/1202427423329/?slreturn=20191112131819.

16. Joy Wiltermuth, "Stuytown Bid Set for Controversy," Reuters, May 17, 2014, https://www.reuters.com/article/stuytown-cmbs/stuytown-bid-set-for-controversy-idUSL 6N0O23CB20140516.

17. Wiltermuth, "Stuytown Bid."

18. Ilona Kramer, notes, May 13, 2014; Charles V. Bagli, "Stuyvesant Town, Bastion of Affordable Housing, Is on Way Back to Auction," New York Times, May 13, 2014, https:// www.nytimes.com/2014/05/14/nyregion/stuyvesant-town-lender-prepares-to-foreclose-on-a-loan-for-the-complex.html.

19. Sarah Mulholland, "Fortress Said to Be Preparing Bid to Buy Stuyvesant Town," Bloomberg News, May 14, 2014, https://www.bloomberg.com/news/articles/2014-05-13/fortress-said-to-be-preparing-bid-to-buy-stuyvesant-town; John Marsh, email to the author, May 13, 2014.

20. Andrew MacArthur, interview with the author, New York, February 15, 2018; Ilona Kramer, notes, June 2, 2014.

21. Ilona Kramer notes, June 2, 2014.

22. MacArthur interview.

23. Ilona Kramer, notes, June 2, 2014; MacArthur interview.

24. Author notes.

25. MacArthur interview.

26. MacArthur interview; Adam Pincus, "Stuy Town Deed Transfer Values Complex at $4.4B," Real Deal, June 5, 2014, https://therealdeal.com/2014/06/05/stuy-town-deed-values-development-at-4-4b.

27. MacArthur interview; Pincus, "Stuy Town Deed Transfer."

28. Andrew MacArthur, letter to Alicia Glen, June 10, 2014.

29. Jessica Daley, "CWCapital Is Officially Stuy Town's Owner, But for How Long?," Curbed, June 6, 2014, https://ny.curbed.com/2014/6/6/10090842/cwcapital-is-officially-stuy-towns-owner-but-for-how-long.

30. Jen Shykula, phone interview with the author, April 11, 2018; Patchett interview.

31. Sally Goldenberg, "Capital Real Estate Roundup," Politico, June 18, 2014; Jennifer Henderson, "Auction for Stuy Town Canceled, CWCapital Takes Property via Deed in Lieu of Foreclosure," Commercial Observer, June 6, 2014, https://commercialobserver.com/2014/06/ auction-for-stuy-town-canceled-as-cwcapital-grabs-deed-in-lieu-of-foreclosure/.

32. Linda Chiem, "CWCapital Fires Back at Junior Lenders' Stuy Town Title Suit," Law360, August 19, 2014; "Stuy Town Lenders Sue CWCapital over Alleged $1B 'Windfall,'" Real Deal, July 3, 2014.

33. David M. Levitt, Sarah Mulholland, and Christie Smythe, "CWCapital Sued by Stuyvesant Town Lenders Over Takeover," July 3, 2014, Bloomberg News, https://www.bloom berg.com/news/articles/2014-07-03/cwcapital-sued-by-stuyvesant-town-lenders-over-takeover; Chiem, "CWCapital Fires Back"; John Sheehy, email to the author, July 12, 2015.

13. The Mayor Comes Over for Cannoli

1. "De Blasio Makes Strides toward Affordable Housing Goals," Real Deal, July 10, 2014, https://therealdeal.com/2014/07/10/de-blasio-administration-makes-strides-toward-affordable-housing-g.

2. James Patchett, interview with the author, New York, March 27, 2018.

3. Author notes, July 17, 2014.

4. Congresswoman Carolyn Maloney, press release, May 14, 2014; Patchett interview.

5. Abigail Savitch-Lew and Amelia Spittal, "Boom and Bust Have Gone, but 'Predatory Equity' Remains a Housing Threat, Say Advocates," City Limits, July 6, 2017, https://citylimits.org/2017/07/06/boom-and-bust-have-gone-but-predatory-equity-remains-a-housing-threat-say-advocates/.

6. Letter from Melvin Watt to Daniel Garodnick and Carolyn Maloney, June 26, 2014.

7. Charles V. Bagli, "Lenders Enlisted in Effort to Preserve Stuyvesant Town for the Middle Class," *New York Times*, June 11, 2014, https://www.nytimes.com/2014/06/12/nyre gion/lenders-enlisted-in-effort-to-preserve-stuyvesant-town-for-the-middle-class.html.

8. John Sheehy, interview with the author, New York, January 22, 2018.

9. Nadeem Meghji, interview with the author, New York, March 28, 2018.

10. Sheehy interview.

11. Doug Harmon, phone interview with the author, February 6, 2019.

12. Meghji interview; Rebecca Burns, "Public Pensions Invest Big in Blackstone's Controversial Rental Properties," Al Jazeera, October 16, 2015, http://america.aljazeera.com/articles/2015/10/16/public-pensions-invest-big-in-blackstones-controversial-rental-proper ties.html; Charles V. Bagli and Christine Haughney, "Wide Fallout in Failed Deal for Stuyvesant Town," *New York Times*, January 25, 2010, https://www.nytimes.com/2010/01/26/nyregion/26stuy.html?dbk.

13. John Marsh, note to the author, December 31, 2019.

14. Author notes.

15. Jon Gray, phone interview with the author, January 7, 2020; Meghji interview.

16. Susan Steinberg, email to the author, August 7, 2014; John Sheehy, email to the author, August 12, 2014.

17. Alex Rubin, email to Andrew MacArthur and the author, September 8, 2014.

18. Author email to Meredith Kane and Alex Rubin, December 1, 2014.

19. Author email to TA board leaders, December 5, 2014.

20. Peter Grant, "Investor Group Gets behind Parkmerced Development," *Wall Street Journal*, November 25, 2014, https://www.wsj.com/articles/investor-group-gets-behind-parkmerced-development-1416955502; "Analysis of 200 Luxury Condo Sales in Manhattan," *Wall Street Journal*, November 14, 2014; Commercial Real Estate Direct Staff Report, "StuyTown/Cooper Village Generated $178Mln of NOI Last Year," Commercial Real Estate Direct, May 8, 2014, https://www.crenews.com/top_stories_-_free/stuytown-cooper-village-generated-$178mln-of-noi-last-year.html; Charles V. Bagli, "Stuyvesant Town, Bastion of Affordable Housing, Is on Way Back to Auction," *New York Times*, May 13, 2014, https://www.nytimes.com/2014/05/14/nyregion/stuyvesant-town-lender-prepares-to-foreclose-on-a-loan-for-the-complex.html; "No Near Term Sale Seen for Stuy Town," Real Estate Finance Intelligence, October 17, 2014.

21. Alex Rubin, interview with the author, New York, March 5, 2018.

22. John Sheehy, email to the author, August 8, 2014.

23. John Sheehy, email to the author, June 26, 2015.

24. John Sheehy, email to the author, June 26, 2015; Kevin Farrelly, email to Susan Steinberg, July 1, 2015; Susan Steinberg, email to John Sheehy and Kevin Farrelly, July 1, 2015.

25. John Sheehy notes, July 9, 2015.

14. Closing the Deal

1. Doug Harmon, phone interview with the author, February 6, 2019.

2. Harmon interview.

3. Harmon interview.

4. Andrew MacArthur, phone interview with the author, December 18, 2019; Harmon interview.

5. Harmon interview.

6. Henry Sender, "Investment Strategy: The New Property Barons," *Financial Times*, April 3, 2016, https://www.ft.com/content/e2e00d74-e76e-11e5-bc31-138df2ae9ee6.

7. Sender, "Investment Strategy"; "Inside Jon Gray's Ascent at Blackstone," *Real Deal*, March 18, 2018, https://therealdeal.com/2018/03/18/inside-jon-grays-ascent-at-blackstone/.

8. Harmon interview; Jon Gray, phone interview with the author, January 7, 2020.

9. Harmon interview; Nadeem Meghji, interview with the author, New York, March 28, 2018.

10. Harmon interview.

11. Harmon interview.

12. Gray interview.

13. Meghji interview; Harmon interview; Gray interview; MacArthur interview.

14. Gray interview; Konrad Putzier, "How Stuy Town Was Won," *Real Deal*, October 29, 2015, https://therealdeal.com/2016/08/16/how-blackstone-won-stuy-town/; James Patchett, interview with the author, New York, March 27, 2018; Meghji interview.

15. Meghji interview.

16. Patchett interview.

17. Author notes, October 12, 2015.

18. Author notes, October 12, 2015; Andrew MacArthur, interview with the author, New York, February 15, 2018.

19. John Sheehy, email to the author et al., October 16, 2015; Putzier, "How Stuy Town Was Won."

20. MacArthur interview, February 15, 2018.

21. Danielle Kane, "CWCapital Shopping Massive Peter Cooper–Stuyvesant Apartment Complex," Real Estate Finance and Investment, October 16, 2015.

22. MacArthur interview, February 15, 2018.

23. Alex Rubin, email to the author, October 17, 2015.

24. Charles V. Bagli, "Stuyvesant Town Said to Be Near Sale That Will Preserve Middle-Class Housing," *New York Times*, October 19, 2015, https://www.nytimes.com/2015/10/20/nyregion/stuyvesant-town-said-to-be-near-sale-that-will-preserve-middle-class-housing.html.

25. Kevin Farrelly, email to John Sheehy et al., October 16, 2015.

26. Kevin Farrelly, interview with the author, New York, March 13, 2018; John Sheehy, interview with the author, New York, January 22, 2018.

27. Bagli, "Stuyvesant Town Said to Be Near Sale."

28. Mayor Bill de Blasio, public statement, October 20, 2015, https://www1.nyc.gov/office-of-the-mayor/news/736-15/mayor-local-elected-officials-tenant-leaders-20-year-agreement-blackstone-and#/0.

29. Assemblyman Brian Kavanagh, public statement, October 20, 2015, https://www1.nyc.gov/office-of-the-mayor/news/736-15/mayor-local-elected-officials-tenant-leaders-20-year-agreement-blackstone-and#/0; Senator Brad Hoylman, public statement, October 20, 2015, https://www1.nyc.gov/office-of-the-mayor/news/736-15/mayor-local-elected-officials-tenant-leaders-20-year-agreement-blackstone-and#/0; Mayor Bill de Blasio, press release, October 20, 2015.

30. Jon Gray, public statement, October 20, 2015, https://www1.nyc.gov/office-of-the-mayor/news/736-15/mayor-local-elected-officials-tenant-leaders-20-year-agreement-black stone-and#/0.

31. Harmon interview.

32. Harmon interview.

33. Blackstone video, "Blackstone and Ivanhoé Cambridge Agree to Acquire Stuyvesant Town and Peter Cooper Village," November 5, 2015, https://www.youtube.com/watch?v=V3u_etdPpJU.

34. Putzier, "How Stuy Town Was Won."

35. Author notes, October 24, 2015.

36. Sabina Mollot, "Blackstone Addresses Tenants' Concerns," *Town & Village*, October 29, 2015, https://town-village.com/2015/10/29/blackstone-addresses-tenants-concerns/.

37. Eliot Brown and Laura Kusisto, "The Stuyvesant Town Deal Sweetener," *Wall Street Journal*, October 22, 2015.

38. Editorial board, "A Middle-Class Oasis in New York Is Spared," *New York Times*, October 21, 2015, https://www.nytimes.com/2015/10/21/opinion/a-middle-class-oasis-in-new-york-is-spared.html.

39. Brown and Kusisto, "Stuyvesant Town Deal Sweetener"; Henry Grabar, "The Saving of Stuy Town: Has Corporate Greed in New York Been Dealt a Blow?," *Guardian*, October 29, 2015, https://www.theguardian.com/cities/2015/oct/29/stuyvesant-town-corporate-greed-affordable-housing-new-york.

40. Kevin Sweeting, "How Stuy Town Got a Tourniquet While Blackstone Gets Billions," Gothamist, March 31, 2016, http://gothamist.com/2016/03/31/stuy_town_affordable_housing.php; Rafael Cestero, phone interview with the author, June 12, 2019.

41. Sarah Maslin Nir, "Residents Exhale after Stuyvesant Town Is Sold," *New York Times*, October 21, 2015, https://www.nytimes.com/2015/10/22/nyregion/residents-exhale-after-stuyvesant-town-is-sold.html.

Epilogue

1. John Sheehy, interview with the author, New York, January 22, 2018.

2. "The 12 Best Landlords in Manhattan: A Brick Underground Guide," Brick Underground, December 27, 2017, https://www.brickunderground.com/rent/best-manhattan-landlords.

3. John Aidan Byrne, "The Exodus of New York City's Endangered Middle Class," *New York Post*, December 22, 2018; "Three Big Reasons Why Middle Class Is Leaving New York City," USA Really, December 24, 2018.

4. Jesse McKinley and Shane Goldmacher, "Democrats Finally Control the Power in Albany. What Will They Do with It?," *New York Times*, November 7, 2018, https://www.nytimes.com/2018/11/07/nyregion/democrats-ny-albany-cuomo-senate.html; Brad Hoylman, public statement, October 20, 2015, https://www1.nyc.gov/office-of-the-mayor/news/736-15/mayor-local-elected-officials-tenant-leaders-20-year-agreement-blackstone-and#/0.

5. McKinley and Goldmacher, "Democrats Finally Control."

6. Luis Ferré-Sadurní, Jesse McKinley, and Vivian Wang, "Landmark Deal Reached on Rent Protections for Tenants in N.Y.," *New York Times*, June 11, 2019, https://www.nytimes.com/2019/06/11/nyregion/rent-protection-regulation.html.

Index